Brand Name
LIGHT &
NATURAL

COOKBOOK

*Healthy, Additive-Free
Recipes for the Good Life*

Edited by Hedi Levine

Published by DS-MAX Canada, Inc.
250 Granton Drive
Richmond Hill, Ontario L4B 1H7, Canada

Copyright © 1996 The Triangle Group, Ltd.

All photographs copyright © 1996 George G. Wieser, except for Stonyfield Yogurt photographs copyright © Becky-Luigart Stayner, and photographs courtesy of Coleman Beef, The Birkett Mill and The National Honey Board.

Produced by The Triangle Group, Ltd.
227 Park Avenue
Hoboken, NJ 07030

Editorial Director: Hedi Levine
Design Director: Tony Meisel
Composition: Diane Specioso
Origination: Creative Edge Graphic Design

Manufactured in the United States of America

ISBN 1-55185-900-9

CONTRIBUTORS

AKC Commodoties, Albert's Organics, Andy Boy, Arrowhead Mills, The Birkett Mills/Wolff's Kasha, California Olive Oil Corp., Cheshire Garden Herbal Vinegars, Coleman Natural Meats, Community Mill and Bean/Old Savannah, Delftree Farm Shiitake Mushrooms, Devansoy/Devansweet, East Wind Nut Butters, Fantastic Foods, Fish Brothers, Frieda's, The Green House Fine Herbs, Green Leaf Produce, Health Sea Inc., Horizon Organic Dairy (Yogurt). Imagine Foods /Rice Dream Indian Rock Produce. International Resources, Knox Mountain Farm, R.W. Knudson, Lundberg Family Farms, Maple Acres, Mercantile Food Company/Rapunzel Organic Chocolate and American Prairie brands, Mill Valley Organic and Natural Foods, Montana Flour and Grain/Kamut and Amberwaves brands, Mori-Nu Tofu, Muir Glen Organic Tomato Products, Nasoya Foods Inc. (Tofu), National Honey Board, Omega Nutrition, Once Again Nut Butter, Organically Grown/ Ladybug Produce, Pavich Family Farms, Purity Foods – Vita Spelt, Putney Pasta ,Quong Hop & Co /The Soy Deli, Red Star Yeast, Roman Meal, Sea Run, Shelton's Poultry, Stonyfield Yogurt, Spectrum Naturals, Surata Foods, Texmatic Rice, Tofutti, Uncle Dave's Kitchen, US Mills/ Erewhon, Walnut Acres Organic, Westbrae Natural Foods/Little Bear/Westsoy White Wave, Workstead Industries, Zumbro IFP/ Jerusalem Artichoke Flour.

Stonyfield Farm recipes included with the permission of Stonyfield Farm, reprinted from The Stonyfield Farms Cookbook, copyright © 1991.

The publisher would also like to thank Fishes Eddie and store manager Paul Ewinghouse, 889 Broadway, New York, NY 10003, Tel. 212-420-9020 for dishes, glassware, silverware and other props.

CONTENTS

The Natural Foods Industry in the United States represents more than 7.5 billion dollars of sales yearly. That translates into a healthy amount of grain, bean and tofu nourishment for ourselves and our families. When we shop for natural foods our choices are driven by a desire to feel good now and to remain healthy longer; to help prevent diseases – like heart disease, a variety of cancers, obesity and high blood pressure – that often relate directly to diet; and to protect the earth with sustainable farming practices.

These goals are mirrored by the food manufacturers who grow and process the natural foods we buy. Their priorities are reflected in products that are processed without synthetic additives, artificial colors, flavors, sweeteners and hydrogenated or solvent extracted oils. Many of the manufacturers who contributed recipes to *The Light & Natural Cookbook* grow their foods without using pesticides, herbicides and fungicides in soil that has been free of chemicals for at least three years. These products can be labeled *certified organic* if the farms are evaluated by an outside organization.

All of our contributors have established reputations for providing good food for good health.

Walnut Acres Organic Farms has been an organic farm for five decades. Since 1946 founder Paul Keene and his family have been farming against the grain of conventional American agriculture. When he started, organic was considered old-fashioned, but like many of the trends of the natural foods industry, his techniques have assumed cutting edge status. Now Walnut Acres is a demonstration farm for sustainable techniques and a model for the Department of Agriculture in Pennsylvania.

Keene's commitment to organic grew out of a deep moral conviction; but organic farming makes good business sense as well. Muir Glen Organic Tomato products continue the tradition. In 1988 a small group of investors made the decision to commit significant resources to developing a commercially viable venture in producing organic tomato products. They named the company after John Muir, a great environmentalist, and they hired Craig Weakley, a leading Integrated Pest Management specialist from the University of California at Davis. Less than a decade later they've achieved their goal of bringing organic tomatoes to the commercial market. But that's not all. Through their work from their base in Sierra, California, they've reduced the use of certain fungicides and pesticides in their extended agricultural community.

Muir Glen tomatoes taste great. They are packed in enamel-lined recyclable cans and their labels are printed on recycled paper. Muir Glen donates 10 percent of their profits to organizations that work to protect the environment.

Americans have always been encouraged to vote with their pocketbooks, so it is not surprising to discover that a generation of natural food companies took root during a heightened period of political activism during the sixties. Despite inevitable swings in the pendulums of politics and free love, the counterculture diet continues to find its way into the American mainstream.

Erewhon Natural Foods has been around for 30 years. Its name refers to novelist Samuel Butler's utopia where it was a crime to be sick and everyone was responsible for their own health. Erewhon's whole grain naturally-sweetened cereals represent their commitment to this ideal. The sixties also spawned R.W. Knudsen (which now owns the organic producer Santa Cruz Natural and Heinke Juices), a family-owned business based in Chico, California.

In 1960 a Texas wheat farmer wanted to do more with his wheat than sell it to national flour companies who processed it elsewhere and mixed it with inferior grain, only to ship it back to his local market. So he began stone grinding the wheat he grew without pesticides or fertilizer or irrigation and selling it locally. The company grew into Arrowhead Mills. Natural foods customers embraced his product for what it had – the wheat germ and the bran and vitamins – and for what it didn't have – pesticide and fungicide residues. With more than 200 products, Arrowhead Mills has evolved into one of the largest organic growers of whole grain foods, beans and seeds. They have literally helped write the standards for organic agriculture in Texas and for the nation.

Healthy eating means different things to different people. Always has. Is there a politically correct way to eat? Would everyone agree what it is? Is there a consensus about anything concerning our diets and a diet for a healthy planet? Certain concepts stand out like bullets: low fat (anywhere from 30 percent of calories consumed to the more moderate 20 percent); low sodium; high complex carbohydrates; and high fiber. Experts agree that diets designed to cure health ills or prevent them converge on a common principle: eat a wide variety of unprocessed high-carbohydrate foods in moderate amounts.

In other words, eat your starch, eat your vegetables, and eat a lot of different kinds. Frieda's, Inc. has done a lot to make that possible by making a huge variety of fruits and vegetables available to the public. In 1962 Frieda Caplan renamed the Chinese Gooseberry; today's Kiwi is readily available, high in vitamin C and very tasty. We can thank her for the profusion of elephant garlic, passion fruit and alfalfa sprouts and for mass marketing quinoa, Jerusalem artichokes (Frieda's Sunchokes) and fresh black-eyed peas.

To maintain a dietary ideal of variety and moderation does not require that you eliminate any one food group from your diet. Since animal foods are higher in fat, especially saturated fats, it is important to balance their place in your diet with ample plant sources for protein as well. But in any case, look for meat, chicken and fish that has been healthfully raised. Coleman Beef raises cattle on pesticide- and antibiotic-free feed. They graze their cattle in an environmentally conscious rotation. Sea Run, raises steelhead salmon in tide-swept Maine waters without antibiotics and chemicals. Some individuals, some families, perhaps some populations are at a higher risk for high blood pressure caused by high-sodium diets. But a low-sodium diet hurts no one. About a 1,000 milligrams a day are recommended. Processed foods contain lots of secret salt. Read labels. And when cooking, minimize salt by heightening flavors in other ways. Fresh herbs are a wonderful antidote to the tendency to salt food beyond what's necessary for flavor or recommended for health.

Once again, a grower's consciousness meets a market demand, this one perhaps unique to the nineties. Paul Friedman, the founding farmer of Green House Fine Herbs, grows, packages and sells between $10 and $20 million in fresh herbs each year from his Oceanside, California herb farm. His herbs and other green products (lettuces, edible flowers) are grown largely according to organic standards, and are often delivered to retail markets within 24 hours after harvest.

Regardless of who grows and processes my food, I'm responsible for putting together meals that are a balance of the starches, vegetables and protein I need to maintain my health. The recipes collected in *The Light & Natural Cookbook* have not been adapted to meet any particular dietary standard and have been altered only when necessary to clarify the manufacturer's intended meaning. The manufacturers have developed and tested them so that you can easily assemble healthful meals from the ingredients you have easy access to in the stores. But when you cook from the recipes in this book – or any cookbook, for that matter – always apply your dietary needs, and the balance of any given meal, to the recipe's mix.

For example, soy sauce is sodium. You can reduce a recipe's sodium content by cutting the salt or soy sauce in half or substituting low-sodium soy sauce. Cut fat calories by using minimal oil and sauté in nonstick skillets. Substitute low-fat or nonfat soy milk for regular soy milk or whole dairy milk. Above all, enjoy the universe of foods we have available to us. I, for one, am grateful.

In the summer months I'm grateful for the local produce I can buy in my farmer's market; in the fall, I'm grateful for the potatoes and squash and chard that I can get there. In the dead of winter I'm grateful for the huge white Albert's Organics truck I see unloading at my favorite natural foods store. When I shop there I see my priorities reflected on the shelves. And when I take the food home and prepare it, I see my own best intentions fulfilled.

Hedi Levine

FLAX EGG REPLACER

1 tbs (15 ml) NUTRI-FLAX
3 tbs (45 ml) water

Put Nutri-Flax in small bowl. Add water; mix. Let sit for 2-3 minutes. Ready when thick. Use as an egg replacer in baking. Replaces 1 egg.

Approximate nutritional analysis per egg replacer:
Calories 38, Protein 3 g, Carbohydrates 3 g, Fat 2 g, Cholesterol 0 mg, Sodium 6 mg

PANCAKES

½ cup (120 ml) whole wheat pastry flour
½ cup (120 ml) unbleached white flour
1 cup (240 ml) plus 2 tbs (30 ml) Original RICE DREAM
2 tbs (30 ml) canola oil
1 tsp (5 ml) egg replacer powder
1½ tsp (8 ml) baking powder
¼ tsp (1 ml) sea salt

VARIATION:
1 egg, lightly beaten
1 tbs (15 ml) canola oil
2 tsp (10 ml) baking powder

Gently mix all ingredients. Let batter stand for 2 minutes. Mix in 2 tbs more of Rice Dream. Lightly oil pan or griddle; heat over medium-high heat. Use ¼ cup of batter for each pancake. Cook about 1½ minutes on each side. Enjoy with your favorite pancake toppings. Serves 3.

Variation: To make this recipe using an egg, eliminate egg replacer powder and add an egg and change the quantities of the oil and baking powder.

Approximate nutritional analysis per serving:
Calories 273, Protein 6 g, Carbohydrates 40 g, Fat 11 g, Cholesterol 10 mg, Sodium 224 mg

Approximate nutritional analysis per serving variation:
Calories 248, Protein 7 g, Carbohydrates 40 g, Fat 7 g, Cholesterol 62 mg, Sodium 230 mg

PAT'S SUNDAY MORNING CRÊPES

¾ cup (180 ml) unbleached flour
1 tsp (5 ml) baking powder
½ tsp (3 ml) sea salt
2 eggs
1 cup (240 ml) Original RICE DREAM
¼ tsp (1 ml) vanilla
fruit juice-sweetened jam, conserves or your own fruit fillings

Mix together wet and dry ingredients with a few swift strokes to avoid excessive bubbles. Crêpes can be made any size, as desired. Cook on lightly oiled pan or griddle, about a minute on each side. Spread on filling of your choice. Roll up or fold over to serve, or enjoy a regular stack, like pancakes. Serves 4.

Approximate nutritional analysis per serving:
Calories 149, Protein 5 g, Carbohydrates 25 g, Fat 3 g, Cholesterol 94 mg, Sodium 439 mg

WHOLE WHEAT-BUTTERMILK PANCAKES

1 cup (240 ml) AMBERWAVES
  BRAND Organic Whole Wheat
  Flour
1 tsp (5 ml) baking soda
½ tsp (3 ml) baking powder
1 tbs (15 ml) sugar
1 cup (240 ml) buttermilk
2 tbs (30 ml) oil
2 eggs

Mix together dry ingredients. Beat together last three ingredients. Add to dry ingredients and mix well. Bake on slightly oiled hot griddle. Serves 4.

Approximate nutritional analysis per serving:
Calories 231, Protein 9 g, Carbohydrates 28 g, Fat 10 g, Cholesterol 96 mg, Sodium 735 mg

HONEY-WHEAT HOTCAKES

1¼ cups (295 ml) AMBERWAVES
  BRAND Organic Whole Wheat
  Flour
3 tsp (15 ml) baking powder
1 tsp (5 ml) honey
½ tsp (3 ml) salt
1¼ cups (295 ml) milk
3 tbs (45 ml) oil
1-2 slightly beaten eggs

Mix together all ingredients. Bake on hot griddle. Yields 12 hotcakes, serves 4.

Approximate nutritional analysis per serving:
Calories 272, Protein 9 g, Carbohydrates 33 g, Fat 13 g, Cholesterol 55 mg, Sodium 570 mg

GLUTEN-FREE PANCAKES

1 cup (240 ml) ARROWHEAD MILLS
  Rice or Millet Flour
½ cup (120 ml) ARROWHEAD
  MILLS Soy Flour
½ cup (120 ml) ARROWHEAD
  MILLS Corn Meal
1 tbs (15 ml) non-alum
  baking powder
¼ tsp (1 ml) sea salt, optional
1 egg, beaten
1½ cups (355 ml) water
2 tbs (30 ml) ARROWHEAD MILLS
  Unrefined Vegetable Oil

Combine all dry ingredients. Stir together all liquids; add to dry ingredients. Bake on preheated 350°F-375°F (180°C-190°C) griddle. Turn only once. Yields 12 pancakes, serves 4.

Approximate nutritional analysis per serving:
Calories 332, Protein 9 g, Carbohydrates 50 g, Fat 11 g, Cholesterol 47 mg, Sodium 382 mg

WHOLE WHEAT-BUTTERMILK PANCAKES

WHOLE WHEAT PANCAKE MIX FOR AN ARMY

MIX:
5 cups (1.2 l) AMBERWAVES BRAND
   Organic Whole Wheat Flour
4 tbs (60 ml) baking powder
⅓ cup (80 ml) sugar
1 tbs (15 ml) salt
1⅔ cups (400 ml) instant nonfat
   dry milk

1 cup (240 ml) water
1 egg
2 tbs (30 ml) oil
1⅓ cups (320 ml) Mix

Combine Mix ingredients and store in airtight container. When ready to cook, mix a scant 1½ cups of the dry ingredients with the already combined next four ingredients. If cooking the total recipe, mix:

5 cups (1.2 l) water
5 eggs
¼ cup (60 ml) oil

and combine with entire Mix recipe.
   Cook on hot griddle. Yields 5 dozen pancakes, serves 20.

Approximate nutritional analysis per serving:
Calories 136, Protein 6 g, Carbohydrates 29 g, Fat 6 g, Cholesterol 1 mg, Sodium 645 mg

KAMUT BANANA GRIDDLE CAKES

2 cups (480 ml) KAMUT BRAND
   Flour or rice or oat flour
3 tbs (45 ml) date sugar or honey
¼ tsp (1 ml) cream of tartar
½ tsp (3 ml) salt, or orsa salt
¼ cup (60 ml) oat bran, optional
¼ cup (60 ml) chopped walnuts
1 cup (240 ml) mashed bananas
2 eggs, separated
1-2 cups (240-480 ml) soy or
   goat milk

Mix together all ingredients except egg whites. Add enough milk to make light batter. Whip egg whites until stiff. Fold gently into batter. Pour onto moderately hot griddle. Use a little oil or butter on griddle. Serves 4.
   Note: Cast iron is an excellent nonstick cooking medium. Perfect heat dissipation, no aluminum and inexpensive.

Approximate nutritional analysis per serving:
Calories 308, Protein 7 g, Carbohydrates 33 g, Fat 18 g, Cholesterol 94 mg, Sodium 303 mg

KAMUT BANANA GRIDDLE CAKES

SOUR CREAM-APPLE PANCAKES

¾ cup (180 ml) ARROWHEAD
   MILLS Whole Wheat Flour
1 tsp (5 ml) non-alum
   baking powder
½ tsp (3 ml) sea salt, optional
¼ tsp (1 ml) cinnamon
1 tbs (15 ml) honey
1 medium apple, grated
1 egg, beaten or egg replacer
1 tsp (5 ml) pure vanilla
½ cup (120 ml) sour cream
1 cup (240 ml) water or buttermilk

In large bowl combine dry ingredients. Combine remaining ingredients, mixing well; add to dry ingredients and stir until just blended. Cook on preheated griddle 350°F (180°C) for 3-5 minutes, turning only once. Serve hot. Yields 12 pancakes, serves 4.

Approximate nutritional analysis per serving:
Calories 194, Protein 5 g, Carbohydrates 28 g, Fat 8 g, Cholesterol 60 mg, Sodium 153 mg

BLUE BUCK CAKES

1 cup (240 ml) ARROWHEAD MILLS
   Blue Cornmeal
1 cup (240 ml) ARROWHEAD MILLS
   Buckwheat Flour
¾ tsp (4 ml) sea salt, optional
1½ tbs (25 ml) non-alum
   baking powder
2 cups (480 ml) milk or soy milk
1½ tsp (8 ml) ARROWHEAD MILLS
   Unrefined Vegetable Oil
½ cup (120 ml) blueberries

Mix dry ingredients and liquids separately. Stir mixtures together just until lumps disappear. Pour batter onto hot oiled griddle, turning once. Serve hot. Serves 4.

Approximate nutritional analysis per serving:
Calories 287, Protein 10 g, Carbohydrates 54 g, Fat 4 g, Cholesterol 5 mg, Sodium 615 mg

BLUE BUCK CAKES

POTATO PANCAKES

2 cups (480 ml) ARROWHEAD
   MILLS Potato Flakes
¼ cup (60 ml) ARROWHEAD MILLS
   Gluten-Free Pancake Mix
2½ cups (590 ml) water
1 egg, beaten
1 small onion, diced
½ tsp (3 ml) onion powder, garlic
   powder, or lemon pepper,
   optional

Mix first 2 ingredients. Stir in water and onion. Stir in egg. For spicier cakes add to dry mixture onion or garlic powder or lemon pepper. Salt and pepper to taste. Let stand 1-2 minutes. Bake on well oiled, preheated griddle until golden brown. Turn once. Serves 4.

Approximate nutritional analysis per serving:
Calories 128, Protein 4 g, Carbohydrates 25 g, Fat 2 g, Cholesterol 47 mg, Sodium 84 mg

WOW! WAFFLES

3 eggs, separated
2¼ cups (540 ml) STONYFIELD
   FARM Nonfat Plain Yogurt
2 tbs (30 ml) nonfat dry milk
½ tsp (3 ml) baking soda
1 tbs (15 ml) honey
⅓ cup (80 ml) quick-cooking oats
⅓ cup (80 ml) cornmeal
⅓ cup (80 ml) margarine or butter,
   melted
1 cup (240 ml) unbleached
   all-purpose flour
1 tbs (15 ml) baking powder
pinch salt, optional
1-2 tbs (15-30 ml) milk, optional

Combine the egg yolks, yogurt, dry milk, soda and honey in a large bowl. Beat with a wire whisk. Stir in the oats and cornmeal, then add the margarine and stir again. Sift in the flour, baking powder, and optional salt. Beat well, then cover the bowl and let the mixture sit for 15 minutes. Beat the egg whites until stiff, then fold them into the mixture. If the batter is too thick, add 1-2 tbs milk.

Preheat a waffle iron to the high setting, oil it, and cook the batter. Serve the waffles on warm plates. Yields 8 waffles.

As accompaniments, you might offer warm maple syrup; fresh, sliced fruit or berries; and yogurt.

To freeze the waffles, cool them on a rack, then place the rack of waffles in the freezer. Store the frozen waffles in tightly sealed plastic bags. To reheat, pop them in the toaster.

Approximate nutritional analysis per waffle:
Calories 234, Protein 9 g, Carbohydrates 27 g, Fat 10 g, Cholesterol 92 mg, Sodium 497 mg

WOW! WAFFLES

WHOLE GRAIN WAFFLES

⅔ cup (160 ml) whole wheat flour
⅔ cup (160 ml) brown rice flour
⅔ cup (160 ml) low fat soy flour
1 tsp (5 ml) baking soda
1 tsp (5 ml) baking powder
½ tsp (3 ml) salt
2 tbs (30 ml) wheat germ
1½ cups (355 ml) skim milk
1 cup (240 ml) STONYFIELD FARM
    Nonfat Plain Yogurt
3 tbs (45 ml) butter, melted
3 eggs, separated

Whisk together the flours, soda, baking powder, salt and wheat germ in a large bowl. In a smaller bowl, mix together the milk, yogurt, cooled butter, and egg yolks. Add the milk mixture to the dry ingredients and stir until everything is thoroughly blended. In a separate bowl, whip the egg whites until stiff peaks form. Fold the egg whites into the batter. Cook on a hot, oiled waffle iron. Yields 10 waffles.

Approximate nutritional analysis per waffle:
Calories 168, Protein 9 g, Carbohydrates 21 g, Fat 2 g, Cholesterol 67 mg, Sodium 373 mg

WAFFLES-N-FRUIT

1 cup (240 ml) WESTSOY
3 tbs (45 ml) canola oil
2 eggs
2 tsp (10 ml) honey, optional
1½ cups (355 ml) flour
1 tbs (15 ml) non-alum
    baking powder
½ tsp (3 ml) salt, optional
½ cup (120 ml) fruit, cut into
    small pieces

In medium bowl, combine soy milk, canola oil, eggs and honey. Beat well with electric mixer. In a separate bowl sift together flour, baking powder and salt. Add liquid ingredients to dry and beat well. Add more soy milk if necessary to obtain a batter the consistency of heavy cream. (Thin batter makes tender waffles.) Add fruit to batter. Cook in preheated waffle iron. Yields 10 waffles.

Approximate nutritional analysis per waffle:
Calories 140, Protein 4 g, Carbohydrates 20 g, Fat 5 g, Cholesterol 35 mg, Sodium 140 mg

WAFFLES-N-FRUIT

CRUNCHY WAFFLES

1½ cup (355 ml) ARROWHEAD
    MILLS Whole Wheat Flour
2 tsp (10 ml) non-alum
    baking powder
½ tsp (3 ml) ground ginger
2 eggs
1½ cups (355 ml) buttermilk
    or 1 cup (240 ml) buttermilk plus
    ½ cup (120 ml) water
¼ cup (60 ml) maple syrup or honey
¼ cup (60 ml) ARROWHEAD MILLS
    Unrefined Vegetable Oil
½ cup (120 ml) chopped pecans
plain yogurt

STRAWBERRY-BANANA SAUCE:
1½ cups (355 ml) maple syrup
1 cup (240 ml) sliced bananas
2 cups (480 ml) strawberries, hulled
and halved

Combine dry ingredients; stir well. Beat eggs until thick and lemon colored. Add flour mix, buttermilk, syrup and oil. Beat until smooth. Cook on hot, lightly oiled waffle iron, sprinkling the top with chopped pecans before cooking. Serve with Strawberry-Banana Sauce and plain yogurt. Yields 4 waffles.

    Strawberry-Banana Sauce: Combine all ingredients in a heavy saucepan. Cook over medium-high heat 10 minutes, stirring occasionally, serve hot. Yields 3½ cups, serves 7.

Approximate nutritional analysis per waffle:
Calories 496, Protein 13 g, Carbohydrates 54 g, Fat 28 g, Cholesterol 97 mg, Sodium 372 mg

Approximate nutritional analysis per ½ cup serving sauce:
Calories 223, Protein .6 g, Carbohydrates 57 g, Fat .5 g, Cholesterol 0 mg, Sodium 7 mg

ANYTIME WAFFLES

2¼ cups (540 ml) all-purpose flour,
    sifted
4 tsp (20 ml) baking powder
½ tsp (3 ml) salt
1½ tbs (25 ml) ZUMBRO Jerusalem
    Artichoke Flour
2 eggs, beaten
2¼ cups (540 ml) milk
¾ cup (180 ml) canola oil

Sift together dry ingredients. Combine remaining ingredients; add liquid ingredients to dry just before baking, beating only until moistened (batter will be thin). Bake in preheated baker. Yields 11 waffles.

Approximate nutritional analysis per serving:
Calories 708, Protein 14 g, Carbohydrates 62 g, Fat 45 g, Cholesterol 99 mg, Sodium 853 mg

CRUNCHY WAFFLE

PEANUT BUTTER WAFFLES

1 cup (240 ml) flour
½ tsp (3 ml) salt
2 tsp (10 ml) baking powder
2 eggs, beaten
¼ cup (60 ml) honey
1 tsp (5 ml) vanilla
½ cup (120 ml) EAST WIND
    Peanut Butter
1½ cups (355 ml) milk

Stir together the flour, salt, and baking powder. In a separate bowl, beat the eggs, honey, vanilla, and peanut butter. Then mix in the milk. Add the liquid mixture to the dry and stir until the ingredients are smooth. Bake on a hot, oiled waffle iron. Yields 4 waffles.

Peanut Butter Pancakes: Use the same recipe as above, but use only ¾ cup (180 ml) milk and cook in a frying pan or on a griddle.

Approximate nutritional analysis per waffle:
Calories 463, Protein 14 g, Carbohydrates 57 g, Fat 20 g, Cholesterol 97 mg, Sodium 611 mg

CREAMY PEACH MELBA BREAKFAST BREAD

3 eggs
½ cup (120 ml) light cream or
    half-and-half
1 cup (240 ml) STONYFIELD FARM
    Low Fat Peach Yogurt
1 cup (240 ml) STONYFIELD FARM
    Low Fat Raspberry Yogurt
1 tsp (5 ml) vanilla
1 loaf Italian, French or challah
    bread, thickly sliced
1 tbs (15 ml) butter or margarine
1 tbs (15 ml) oil
fresh peaches or raspberries,
    for garnish
STONYFIELD FARM Low Fat Peach
    or Raspberry Yogurt, for garnish

Beat the eggs and combine with the cream, yogurts, and vanilla. Mix well. Pour into 1-2 shallow rectangular pans. Place the bread in the egg mixture, cover, and let stand overnight, turning once or twice during the standing period to make sure the mixture soaks through the slices.

The next morning, prepare a hot nonstick griddle or frying pan with a combination of vegetable oil and butter or margarine. Lightly brown each side of the bread slices, cooking slowly over low heat to firm the custard. Serve immediately with a garnish of fresh peach slices or raspberries and a dollop of peach or raspberry yogurt. Serves 5.

Approximate nutritional analysis per serving:
Calories 475, Protein 17 g, Carbohydrates 68 g, Fat 15 g, Cholesterol 131 mg, Sodium 684 mg

CREAMY PEACH MELBA BREAKFAST BREAD

BOBBIE'S BALANCED BREAKFAST

1 large unpeeled apple, cored
   and diced
¾ cup (180 ml) rolled oats
¼ cup (60 ml) maple syrup
½ cup (120 ml) chopped walnuts
1 cup (240 ml) STONYFIELD FARM
   Nonfat Plain Yogurt
2 tbs (30 ml) wheat germ
ground cinnamon, optional
ground nutmeg, optional

Stir the apple, oats, maple syrup and walnuts into the yogurt. Sprinkle with wheat germ. Top with cinnamon and nutmeg if desired. Serves 2.

Approximate nutritional analysis per serving:
Calories 543, Protein 21 g, Carbohydrates 74 g, Fat 21 g, Cholesterol 2 mg, Sodium 99 mg

BARLEY-AMARANTH WAFFLES

¾ cup (180 ml) ARROWHEAD
   MILLS Amaranth Flour
1 cup (240 ml) ARROWHEAD MILLS
   Barley Flour
1 tbs (15 ml) non-alum
   baking powder
¼ tsp (1 ml) sea salt, optional
1½ cups (355 ml) skim milk,
   soy milk or water
3 tbs (45 ml) ARROWHEAD MILLS
   Unrefined Vegetable Oil

Combine liquids and dry ingredients separately, then mix liquid ingredients into dry with a hand mixer. Pour onto hot, nonstick-surface griddle. Thin batter with additional water if needed. May be used for pancakes also. Yields 4 waffles.

Approximate nutritional analysis per waffle:
Calories 423, Protein 14 g, Carbohydrates 63 g, Fat 14 g, Cholesterol 2 mg, Sodium 426 mg

BOBBIE'S BALANCED BREAKFAST

YOGURT WAFFLES

1 cup (240 ml) STONYFIELD FARM
   Nonfat Plain Yogurt
3 eggs
½ cup (120 ml) whole wheat flour
⅓ cup (80 ml) oat bran
pinch salt
¼ cup (60 ml) vegetable oil
½ cup (120 ml) milk
1½ tsp (8 ml) vanilla
1½ tsp (8 ml) ground cinnamon
½ cup (120 ml) chopped nuts,
   optional

Combine all the ingredients in a blender or stir them together until they are well mixed. Cook the waffles on a hot, oiled waffle iron. Serve them hot, topped with more yogurt, fresh or preserved fruit, maple syrup, honey, or peanut butter. Yields 4 waffles.

Approximate nutritional analysis per waffle w/o topping:
Calories 284, Protein 12 g, Carbohydrates 23 g, Fat 18 g, Cholesterol 142 mg, Sodium 172 mg

RICE DREAM FRENCH TOAST

1½ cups (355 ml) Original
   RICE DREAM
1 tsp (5 ml) cinnamon powder
3 tbs (45 ml) arrowroot powder
   or 2 eggs
6 slices whole wheat bread
3-4 tbs (45-60 ml) oleic safflower oil
   or butter

In a wide bowl, whisk together Rice Dream, cinnamon, and eggs or arrowroot. Cut bread into triangles; soak bread in the Rice Dream mixture until softened, 1-3 minutes. Heat portions of the oil or butter in a frying pan or griddle, over medium-high heat. Add several pieces of the soaked bread; do not overcrowd the pan. Cook evenly on both sides for 2-3 minutes or until each is browned. Serve immediately with your favorite fruits, jam or maple syrup. Serves 3.

Approximate nutritional analysis per serving:
Calories 328, Protein 5 g, Carbohydrates 42 g, Fat 17 g, Cholesterol 0 mg, Sodium 291 mg

WILD RICE & DRIED FRUIT CEREAL

2 cups (480 ml) cooked FRIEDA'S
   Wild Rice
1¾ cups (415 ml) water
1 cup (240 ml) oats
⅔ cup (160 ml) raisins, or chopped
   dried apricots, dates, or other
   dried fruit
¼ tsp (1 ml) ground cinnamon
brown sugar or honey

In a medium saucepan combine cooked rice with water, oats, fruit and cinnamon. Bring mixture to boiling; reduce heat. Cook, stirring frequently, about 5 minutes, or until oats are done. Serve as hot cereal with brown sugar or honey. Serves 4.

Approximate nutritional analysis per 1 cup serving:
Calories 244, Protein 7 g, Carbohydrates 53 g, Fat 2 g, Cholesterol 0 mg, Sodium 7 mg

WILD RICE & DRIED FRUIT CEREAL

GRANOLA

4 cups (960 ml) rolled oats
2 tbs (30 ml) ZUMBRO Jerusalem
    Artichoke Flour
¾ cup (180 ml) raw sunflower seeds
¾ cup (180 ml) unsweetened
    coconut
½ cup (120 ml) unbleached
    sesame seeds
¾ cup (180 ml) slivered almonds
1 tbs (15 ml) cinnamon
⅔ cup (160 ml) pure maple syrup
    or honey
⅓ cup (80 ml) oil

Combine ingredients in large heavy skillet. You don't want to fill the skillet too full; if it isn't big enough, heat the granola in batches. Cook over medium heat, 300°F (150°C) in electric fry pan, stirring constantly to cook evenly and prevent burning. Cooks in about 10 minutes. Watch granola carefully, it scorches easily! Yields 6 cups, serves 12.

Approximate nutritional analysis per ½ cup serving:
Calories 351, Protein 10 g, Carbohydrates 36 g, Fat 20 g, Cholesterol 0 mg, Sodium 7 mg

JIM'S GRANOLA

1 cup (240 ml) ARROWHEAD MILLS
    Popcorn
4 cups (960 ml) ARROWHEAD
    MILLS Oat Flakes
1 cup (240 ml) ARROWHEAD MILLS
    Wheat Flakes
1 cup (240 ml) ARROWHEAD MILLS
    Barley Flakes
2 cups (480 ml) ARROWHEAD
    MILLS 7 Grain Cereal or
    Cracked Wheat
2 cups (480 ml) coconut, optional
1 cup (240 ml) ARROWHEAD MILLS
    Sunflower Seeds
1 cup (240 ml) peanuts
1 cup (240 ml) ARROWHEAD MILLS
    Mechanically Hulled Sesame
    Seeds
1-2 cups (240-480 ml) honey or
    other sweetener
½ cup (120 ml) ARROWHEAD
    MILLS Unrefined Vegetable Oil
1 tbs (15 ml) mapleine, vanilla,
    or other flavor

OPTIONAL INGREDIENTS:
1 cup (240 ml) raisins
1 cup (240 ml) dates, chopped
1 cup (240 ml) dried apricots,
    chopped
½ cup (120 ml) dried pineapple,
    chopped
½ cup (120 ml) dried papaya,
    chopped
1 cup (240 ml) almonds, chopped
1 cup (240 ml) pecans, chopped
1 pkg banana chips

Pop popcorn. Combine all dry ingredients. Combine honey, oil, and flavoring in a separate bowl. Stir honey mixture into dry ingredients. Bake in non-preheated oven at 350°F (180°C) for 45 minutes, stirring every 15 minutes. Remove from oven; stir in fruit. Cool. Yields 12 cups, serves 24.

Approximate nutritional analysis per ½ cup serving w/o fruit:
Calories 295, Protein 9 g, Carbohydrates 36 g, Fat 15 g, Cholesterol 0 mg, Sodium 77 mg

JIM'S GRANOLA

ROMAN MEAL GRANOLA

6 cups (1.4 l) regular rolled oats
3 cups (720 ml) ROMAN MEAL
   Cereal
1½ cups (355 ml) sunflower kernels
1 cup (240 ml) chopped almonds
1 cup (240 ml) nonfat dry milk
1½ cups (355 ml) packed brown
   sugar
⅔ cup (160 ml) honey
½ cup (120 ml) vegetable oil
½ tsp (3 ml) vanilla

In 6-quart bowl or larger, thoroughly mix oats, cereal, sunflower kernels, almonds, dry milk and brown sugar. In small saucepan, blend honey and oil; warm over medium heat until heated through. Remove from heat and add vanilla; pour over first mixture and mix thoroughly. Spread in 15x10x1-inch pan. Bake at 250°F (121°C) for about 30 minutes, stirring once. Turn out onto brown paper (supermarket bags work fine) to cool thoroughly. Store in airtight containers. Yields 14 cups, serves 28.

Approximate nutritional analysis per ½ cup serving:
Calories 282, Protein 8 g, Carbohydrates 41 g, Fat 11 g, Cholesterol .4 mg, Sodium 19 mg

WHEAT BERRY PORRIDGE

1 cup (240 ml) uncooked wheat
   berries
2 cups (480 ml) water
1 cup (240 ml) STONYFIELD FARM
   Nonfat Plain Yogurt
¼ cup (60 ml) fresh lemon juice
1 unpeeled apple, cored and grated
2 bananas, sliced
2 peaches, peeled, pitted and sliced
1-2 cups (240-480 ml) grapes, halved
¼ tsp (1 ml) ground ginger
½ tsp (3 ml) ground cinnamon
dash of ground nutmeg

Cook the wheat berries in water over low heat for 4-6 hours or until the water is absorbed. (A crockpot is especially useful for this step.) Remove from heat and allow the berries to cool, then mix in the remaining ingredients and chill. Let stand for ½ hour at room temperature before serving. Yields 1½-2 quarts, serves 4.

Approximate nutritional analysis per serving:
Calories 175, Protein 6 g, Carbohydrates 40 g, Fat .9 g, Cholesterol 1 mg, Sodium 48 mg

WHEAT BERRY PORRIDGE

CREAMY GOLDEN BREAKFAST CEREAL

¼ cup (60 ml) **ARROWHEAD MILLS Amaranth Flour**
¼ cup (60 ml) **ARROWHEAD MILLS Millet Flour**
¼ cup (60 ml) yellow corn flour
pinch of salt
¼ cup (60 ml) **ARROWHEAD MILLS Sesame Tahini or Ground Sesame Seeds**
3 cups (720 ml) water

Mix flours, salt and tahini together. Add water and stir. Simmer over low heat until thick and creamy, stirring constantly with a wire whisk to prevent lumping or burning. Once thick, serve hot with milk or soy milk and favorite sweetener. Serves 6.

Approximate nutritional analysis per serving:
Calories 127, Protein 4 g, Carbohydrates 15 g, Fat 7 g, Cholesterol 0 mg, Sodium 24 mg

WHOLE WHEAT COUSCOUS BREAKFAST CEREAL

¼ cup (60 ml) raisins or currants
2 cups (480 ml) apple juice
1 cup (240 ml) **FANTASTIC FOODS Whole Wheat Couscous**

In a saucepan, add raisins to apple juice and bring to a boil. Add couscous, lower heat, cover and cook for 5 minutes. Serve with your favorite toppings such as fresh fruit, yogurt or chopped walnuts. Serves 6.

Approximate nutritional analysis per ½ cup serving:
Calories 243, Protein 7 g, Carbohydrates 53 g, Fat .4 g, Cholesterol 0 mg, Sodium 12 mg

WHOLE WHEAT COUSCOUS BREAKFAST CEREAL

CREAMY HEARTY OATMEAL

2 cups (480 ml) Original
    RICE DREAM
1 cup (240 ml) old-fashioned
    rolled oats
¼ cup (60 ml) raisins or
    chopped dates
pinch of sea salt
¼ tsp (1 ml) cinnamon, optional
sprinkle of roasted nuts or seeds,
    and fresh fruit

Place first five ingredients in saucepan. Bring to a boil. Cover, leaving lid ajar to prevent boiling over, reduce heat to very low and simmer for 10 minutes. Stir often. Serve topped with roasted nuts or seeds and fresh fruit of your choice. Serves 3.

Approximate nutritional analysis per 1 cup serving:
Calories 225, Protein 5 g, Carbohydrates 46 g, Fat 3 g, Cholesterol 0 mg, Sodium 63 mg

CREAMY HEARTY OATMEAL

GARLIC AND CHEESE GRITS

2 cups (480 ml) cold water
½ cup (120 ml) ARROWHEAD
    MILLS Yellow or White Corn
    Grits
1 tsp (5 ml) sea salt, optional
½ lb (230 g) sharp cheddar cheese,
    grated
2 tbs (30 ml) butter
1 egg, beaten or egg replacer
¼ tsp (1 ml) cayenne or Tabasco
¼ tsp (1 ml) paprika
1 clove garlic, crushed
    or ¼ tsp (1 ml) garlic powder

In large saucepan, mix well the water, grits and salt. Bring to simmer and cook until grits are very thick; remove from heat. Oil 13x9-inch baking dish. Stir together in saucepan the grits and remaining ingredients; pour into prepared dish and spread evenly. Sprinkle top with additional paprika. Bake for 30-35 minutes at 350°F (180°C). Serves 4.

Approximate nutritional analysis per serving:
Calories 370, Protein 17 g, Carbohydrates 17 g, Fat 26 g, Cholesterol 122 mg, Sodium 425 mg

GARLIC AND CHEESE GRITS

SWISS-STYLE OATS

3 cups (720 ml) water
1 cup (240 ml) mixed dried fruit,
 chopped
1 tsp (5 ml) sea salt, optional
2 tbs (30 ml) honey
1⅓ cups (320 ml) ARROWHEAD
 MILLS Oat Flakes (rolled oats)
2 tbs (30 ml) ARROWHEAD MILLS
 Wheat Germ
¼ cup (60 ml) slivered almonds,
 toasted

Bring water to a boil; stir in fruit, salt and honey. Bring to boil again. Add oats; stir; lower heat to simmer. Cover and simmer 15 minutes. Stir before serving. Sprinkle each serving with 1½ tsp wheat germ and 1 tbs almonds. Serve with milk. Serves 4.

Approximate nutritional analysis per serving:
Calories 264, Protein 7 g, Carbohydrates 51 g, Fat 5 g, Cholesterol 0 mg, Sodium 9 mg

FISH BROTHERS OMELET OR SCRAMBLED EGGS

2-3 eggs
1 tbs (5 ml) milk
1 tbs (15 ml) grated cheddar cheese
3 oz (90 g) FISH BROTHERS
 Smoked Salmon or Smoked
 Albacore
2 tbs (10 ml) low-calorie sour cream

Mix eggs and milk. Add cheese and smoked fish. Remove from heat when done and add sour cream. Serves 1.

Approximate nutritional analysis per serving:
Calories 323, Protein 31 g, Carbohydrates 3 g, Fat 20 g, Cholesterol 463 mg, Sodium 856 mg

EGGS ELEGANTE WITH MUSHROOM SAUCE

SAUCE:
2 oz (60 ml) FRIEDA'S Fresh
 Mushrooms (such as fresh
 Oyster, Chanterelles, Shiitake
 or Japanese Honey Mushrooms),
 chopped
2 tbs (60 ml) butter
2 tbs (60 ml) flour
½ cup (120 ml) chicken broth
pepper, to taste
½ cup (120 ml) dairy sour cream
¼ tsp (1 ml) Worcestershire sauce
dash hot pepper sauce

3-4 English muffins, split and
 toasted
6-8 poached eggs
FRIEDA'S Watercress Sprigs,
 for garnish

For Sauce, sauté mushrooms in melted butter for 3 minutes or until tender. Stir in flour. Add chicken broth; cook and stir until mixture thickens. Stir in sour cream, pepper, Worcestershire and pepper sauce. Cook and stir 2 minutes more or until mixture is heated through.

To serve, place a split English muffin, cut sides up, on each dinner plate. Place a poached egg on each muffin half. Spoon sauce over; garnish with watercress sprigs. Serve immediately. Serves 3.

Approximate nutritional analysis per serving:
Calories 473, Protein 20 g, Carbohydrates 34 g, Fat 27 g, Cholesterol 460 mg, Sodium 808 mg

EGGS ELEGANTE WITH MUSHROOM SAUCE

BANANA-TOFU FRENCH TOAST

1 cup (240 ml) water
1 ½ cups (355 ml) medium-soft tofu
¼ tsp (1 ml) nutmeg, optional
3 ½ tbs (55 ml) maple syrup
¼ cup (60 ml) SOLAIT
1 tsp (5 ml) cinnamon
½ tsp (3 ml) salt
1 large ripe banana
8 slices whole wheat bread

Blend all ingredients in blender or food processor, except bread, until smooth. Pour into shallow dish. Preheat griddle. Dip bread slices and place on hot, oiled griddle. Brown both sides. Serve with applesauce (or other fruit sauce), peanut butter, maple syrup, orange juice. Serves 4.

Approximate nutritional analysis per serving w/o accompaniments:
Calories 374, Protein 17 g, Carbohydrates 61 g, Fat 9 g, Cholesterol 0 mg, Sodium 695 mg

BREAKFAST BANANAS FOR TWO

2 ripe bananas
1 ½ cups (355 ml) STONYFIELD
    FARM Nonfat Plain Yogurt
½-1 cup (120-240 ml) raisins,
    to taste
1 oz cube (30 g) cheddar cheese,
    medium sharp or sharp
2 tbs (30 ml) maple syrup,
    or to taste

Slice the bananas like thick coins into a medium-large bowl. Add the yogurt and stir, then add the raisins and stir again. Cut the cheese into small cubes the size of raisins and add to the mixture. Add the maple syrup. Mix it all up. Serves 2.

Approximate nutritional analysis per serving:
Calories 317, Protein 15 g, Carbohydrates 54 g, Fat 6 g, Cholesterol 18 mg, Sodium 231 mg

BREAKFAST BANANAS FOR TWO

SURPRISE BREAKFAST PUFFERS

4 tbs (60 ml) orange marmalade
1 tsp (5 ml) grated orange rind
¼ tsp (1 ml) cinnamon
¼ tsp (1 ml) nutmeg
¼ cup (60 ml) butter
¼ cup (60 ml) honey
2 eggs
2 cups (480 ml) ARROWHEAD
    MILLS Whole Wheat Flour
2 tsp (10 ml) non-alum
    baking powder
½ tsp (3 ml) sea salt, optional
1 cup (240 ml) buttermilk

Combine first four ingredients; set aside. In a mixing bowl, cream butter and honey; add eggs, one at a time, until well blended. Gradually stir in next three ingredients; mix well. Slowly add buttermilk. Spoon 2 tbs batter into oiled muffin cups; add 1 tsp orange filling and fill ⅔ full with batter. Bake in preheated oven at 400°F (205°C) for 20-25 minutes. Yields 12.

Approximate nutritional analysis per puffer:
Calories 162, Protein 5 g, Carbohydrates 26 g, Fat 5 g, Cholesterol 46 mg, Sodium 128 mg

BULGUR WHEAT "SAUSAGE" PATTIES

2 cups (480 ml) ARROWHEAD
    MILLS Bulgur Wheat, cooked
    (1 cup [240 ml] raw)
1 tbs (15 ml) crushed basil leaves
1 egg
¾ tsp (4 ml) sage
¾ tsp (4 ml) poultry seasoning
sea salt to taste, optional
¼ cup (60 ml) ARROWHEAD MILLS
    Whole Wheat Flour
¾ cup (180 ml) grated cheddar
    cheese, optional
oil or nonstick spray

Mix the bulgur wheat, egg, basil, sage, poultry seasoning, salt and optional cheese together. Chill slightly. Form into patties and dip in whole wheat flour. Fry in a small amount of oil until lightly browned. These may be wrapped in individual packages and reheated. Cook like hamburger meat or add to casseroles in place of meat. Yields 8 medium patties or 30 sausage balls.

Variation: Form into cocktail-size balls and serve with sweet and sour sauce.

Approximate nutritional analysis per patty w/o cheese:
Calories 61, Protein 3 g, Carbohydrates 12 g, Fat .8 g, Cholesterol 0 mg, Sodium 9 mg

Approximate nutritional analysis per patty w/cheese:
Calories 103, Protein 5 g, Carbohydrates 12 g, Fat 4 g, Cholesterol 11 mg, Sodium 75 mg

Approximate nutritional analysis per sausage ball w/o cheese:
Calories 16, Protein .7 g, Carbohydrates 3 g, Fat .2 g, Cholesterol 0 mg, Sodium 2 mg

Approximate nutritional analysis per sausage ball w/ cheese:
Calories 28, Protein 1 g, Carbohydrates 3 g, Fat 1 g, Cholesterol 3 mg, Sodium 20 mg

BREAKFAST HASH

1-2 tbs (15-30 ml) olive oil
1 cup (240 ml) KNOX MOUNTAIN
  FARM Not-So-Sausage, prepared
  and chopped
1 large potato, boiled, peeled and
  cut into small slices
1 large onion, chopped
1 clove garlic, diced or pureed
⅛ tsp (.5 ml) black pepper
¼ tsp (1 ml) salt

Heat oil in skillet, add all ingredients, cover and sauté until crisp and brown, then turn over and sauté other side. Serves 8.

Approximate nutritional analysis per serving:
Calories 188, Protein 18 g, Carbohydrates 18 g, Fat 2 g, Cholesterol 0 mg, Sodium 218 mg

INDIAN ROCK'S APPLE DUMPLINGS

2 cups (480 ml) flour
¼ tsp (1 ml) salt
3 tbs (45 ml) sugar
1 tbs (15 ml) baking powder
¾ cup (180 ml) unsalted butter
½ cup (120 ml) skim milk or
  buttermilk
3 apples, peeled, cored
  and quartered

Combine flour, salt, 2 tbs sugar and baking powder and mix in cold butter with fingers. Add the skim milk. Work into dough. Roll out dough into 12 circles. Place 1 apple quarter in each piece of dough. Pinch dough closed. Sprinkle remaining sugar over dumplings. Place on greased cookie sheet and bake 35-40 minutes in a preheated 350°F (180°C) oven until golden brown. Yields 12 dumplings.

Approximate nutritional analysis per dumpling:
Calories 215, Protein 3 g, Carbohydrates 25 g, Fat 12 g, Cholesterol 31 mg, Sodium 135 mg

SOUTHWEST TOFU SCRAMBLER

1½ medium potatoes
  or 1 large potato
10½-oz pkg (315 g) MORI-NU
  Silken Lite Tofu, firm, crumbled
2 tsp (10 ml) margarine
2 dashes turmeric
¼ cup (60 ml) green onion, chopped
¾ cup (180 ml) red pepper,
  in julienne strips
1 cup (240 ml) mushrooms, sliced
3 tbs (45 ml) picante sauce

Microwave potatoes for 5-6 minutes on high or use baked potatoes. Cool and slice thin. Add crumbled tofu to melted margarine in Teflon skillet. Add 2 dashes of turmeric and cook on high for 5 minutes. Add vegetables and potato and cook 5 minutes or until vegetables are tender crisp. Stir in picante sauce and serve. Serves 2.

Approximate nutritional analysis per 1⅓ cup serving:
Calories 231, Protein 14 g, Carbohydrates 33 g, Fat 6 g, Cholesterol 0 mg, Sodium 354 mg

INDIAN ROCK'S APPLE DUMPLINGS

Overleaf: SOUTHWEST TOFU SCRAMBLER

BREADS & MUFFINS

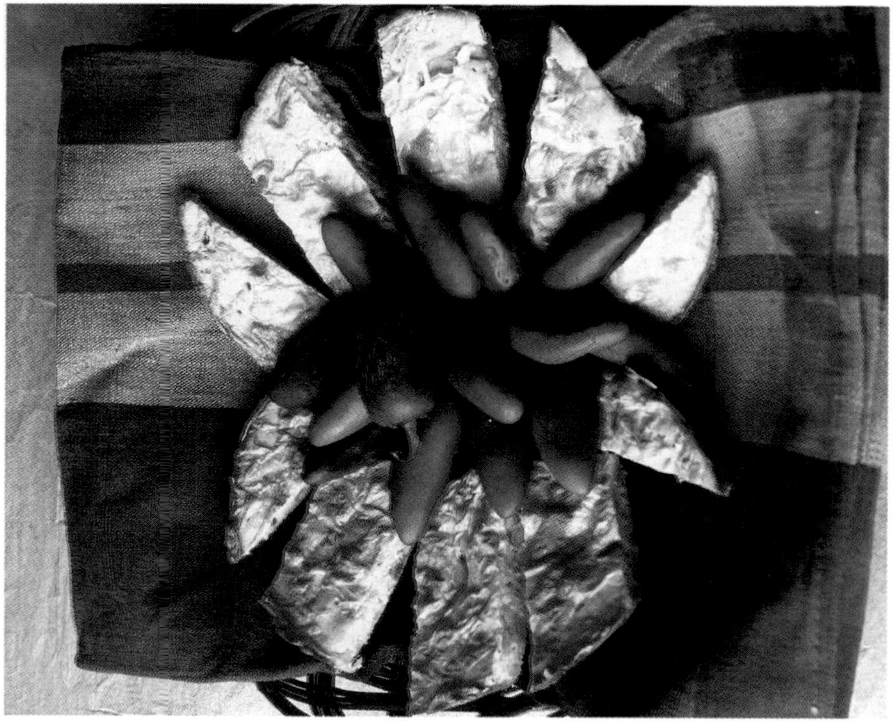

FLAX EGG REPLACER

1 tbs (15 ml) NUTRI-FLAX
3 tbs (45 ml) water

Put Nutri-Flax in small bowl. Add water; mix. Let sit for 2-3 minutes. Ready when thick. Use an egg replacer in baking. Replaces 1 egg.

Approximate nutritional analysis per egg replacer:
Calories 38, Protein 3 g, Carbohydrates 3 g, Fat 2 g, Cholesterol 0 mg, Sodium 6 mg

HONEY WHEAT SODA BREAD

2 cups (480 ml) whole wheat flour
½ tsp (3 ml) salt
1 tsp (5 ml) baking soda
2 tbs (30 ml) honey
1 cup (240 ml) buttermilk
1 egg, slightly beaten

In large mixing bowl, combine flour, salt and soda. Make well in center. Add honey, buttermilk and egg. Stir just until moistened. Batter will be soft. Place in greased 1-quart casserole. Bake at 375°F (190°C) for 20-25 minutes. Cool completely before slicing. Serves 12.

Approximate nutritional analysis per serving:
Calories 92, Protein 4 g, Carbohydrates 19 g, Fat 1 g, Cholesterol 16 mg, Sodium 168 mg

Courtesy of The National Honey Board.

SPICY BROWN BREAD

¾ cup (180 ml) ARROWHEAD
MILLS Blue Cornmeal
¾ cup (180 ml) ARROWHEAD
MILLS Whole Wheat Pastry Flour
2 tsp (10 ml) non-alum
baking powder
¼ tsp (1 ml sea salt, optional
2 tsp (10 ml) carob powder
½ tsp (3 ml) cinnamon
½ tsp (3 ml) ginger
½ tsp (3 ml) nutmeg
¾ cup (180 ml) milk or soy milk
½ cup (120 ml) unsulphured
molasses
1 tsp (5 ml) lemon extract

Combine dry and liquid ingredients in separate bowls, then stir together until smooth. Batter seems thin but it will thicken. Pour batter into oiled pan. Bake at 350°F (180°C) for 20 minutes or until knife test proves done. Yields 6 cupcakes or 1 8-inch-square pan.

Approximate nutritional analysis per serving:
Calories 197, Protein 5 g, Carbohydrates 44 g, Fat 1 g, Cholesterol 1 mg, Sodium 196 mg

SPICY BROWN BREAD

Opposite: HONEY WHEAT SODA BREAD

POPPY SEED & WALNUT BREAD

1¾ cups (415 ml) all-purpose flour
1¼ cups (295 ml) THE BIRKETT
    MILLS Light or
    Whole Buckwheat Flour
2 cups (480 ml) granulated sugar
1½ tsp (8 ml) baking soda
½ tsp (3 ml) salt
1½ cups (355 ml) vegetable oil
4 eggs, lightly beaten
1½ cups (355 ml) milk
1 tsp (5 ml) vanilla extract
10-oz jar (300 g) prepared poppy
    seed filling
2 cups (480 ml) finely chopped
    apples
1 cup (240 ml) chopped walnuts

POPPY SEED & WALNUT BREAD

Preheat oven to 350°F (180°C). Sift first 5 ingredients into large mixing bowl. Beat in oil, eggs, milk and vanilla. Stir in poppy seed filling, apples and walnuts. Divide batter evenly among 2 5x9-inch pans. Bake until toothpick inserted in center comes out clean, about 50 minutes. Cool in pans about 5 minutes, then remove. Delicious warm or at room temperature. Yields 2 large loaves, 8 slices per loaf.

Approximate nutritional analysis per slice:
Calories 522, Protein 8 g, Carbohydrates 61 g, Fat 29 g, Cholesterol 48 mg, Sodium 231 mg

ZUCCHINI BREAD

3 eggs, slightly beaten
¾ cup (180 ml) oil
1 cup (240 ml) maple syrup
2½ cups (590 ml) zucchini, grated
1 tbs (15 ml) vanilla
3 cups (720 ml) whole wheat
    pastry flour
2½ tbs (40 ml) ZUMBRO Jerusalem
    Artichoke Flour
1 tsp (5 ml) salt
1 tsp (5 ml) baking soda
¼ tsp (1 ml) baking powder
1 tsp (15 ml) cinnamon
½ cup (120 ml) nuts, chopped

Combine eggs, oil, syrup, zucchini and vanilla. Sift flours, salt, soda, baking powder and cinnamon. Add nuts to dry ingredients. Then add liquid ingredients. Divide batter into two. Bake in greased, floured loaf pans at 300°F (150°C) for 75 minutes. Yields 2 loaves, 8 slices per loaf.

Approximate nutritional analysis per slice:
Calories 244, Protein 5 g, Carbohydrates 33 g, Fat 12 g, Cholesterol 35 mg, Sodium 234 mg

ZUCCHINI BREAD

WHOLE WHEAT BANANA BREAD

1 cup (240 ml) brown sugar
   or ¾ cup (180 ml) honey
½ cup (120 ml) butter or margarine
2 eggs, beaten
2 ripe bananas, mashed
2 cups (480 ml) AMBERWAVES
   BRAND Organic Whole Wheat
   Flour
½ tsp (3 ml) salt
1 tsp (5 ml) baking powder
½ tsp (3 ml) baking soda
1 cup (240 ml) oatmeal
½ cup (120 ml) chopped walnuts
   or sunflower seeds

Cream together sugar, butter and eggs. Add bananas. In separate bowl mix flour, salt, baking powder and soda. Add to banana mixture. Add oatmeal and nuts and mix well. Pour into 2 greased and floured 8-inch bread pans. Bake at 350°F (180°C) for 50-60 minutes. This recipe can be doubled. Yields 2 loaves, 8 slices per loaf.

Approximate nutritional analysis per slice:
Calories 200, Protein 8 g, Carbohydrates 27 g, Fat 9 g, Cholesterol 39 mg, Sodium 207 mg

WHOLE WHEAT BANANA BREAD

FRUIT 'N' WHEAT BANANA BREAD

2 cups (480 ml) EREWHON Fruit 'n'
   Wheat Cereal
½ cup (120 ml) currants
2 cups (480 ml) whole wheat
   pastry flour
1 tsp (5 ml) cinnamon
¼ tsp (1 ml) salt
¾ tsp (4 ml) baking soda
1¼ cups (295 ml) mashed banana
grated rind of 1 lemon
juice of 1 lemon
½ cup (120 ml) maple syrup
¼ cup (60 ml) canola oil

Preheat oven to 350°F (180°C). Combine cereal and currants in a large mixing bowl. Sift together flour, cinnamon, salt and baking soda. Add to mixing bowl. Place mashed bananas in a small bowl. Add rind and lemon juice, maple syrup and canola oil. Whisk together. Add wet ingredients to dry ingredients, stirring to combine gently. Pour batter into oiled 9-inch loaf pan and bake for 40-50 minutes or until toothpick comes out clean. Yields 1 loaf, 8 slices per loaf.

Approximate nutritional analysis per slice:
Calories 332, Protein 7 g, Carbohydrates 64 g, Fat 8 g, Cholesterol 0 mg, Sodium 224 mg

FRUIT 'N' WHEAT BANANA BREAD

VIRTUALLY ALLERGY-FREE BANANA BREAD

3 very ripe bananas
juice of 1 lemon
½ cup (120 ml) soy margarine
½ cup (120 ml) honey
1¾ cups (415 ml) VITA-SPELT Flour
¼ cup (60 ml) rice bran
½ tsp (3 ml) salt
½ tsp (3 ml) cardamom
1 tsp (5 ml) cinnamon
½ tsp (3 ml) baking powder
½ tsp (3 ml) baking soda
½-1 cup (120-240 ml) walnuts,
    chopped

Preheat oven to 375°F (190°C). Mash bananas. Add lemon juice and mix until smooth. In another bowl, cream margarine and honey until creamy. Add banana mix to butter mix, cream well. In a separate bowl mix all dry ingredients together. Add to banana mix, stir just until moistened. Fold in nuts. Scrape into a greased loaf pan. Bake for approximately 30-45 minutes. Let cool slightly before removing from pan to a rack. Yields 1 loaf, 8 slices per loaf.

Approximate nutritional analysis per slice:
Calories 184, Protein 4 g, Carbohydrates 35 g, Fat 5 g, Cholesterol 0 mg, Sodium 244 mg

ROMAN MEAL BANANA-NUT BREAD

1⅓ cups (320 ml) all-purpose flour
¾ cup (180 ml) granulated sugar
2 tsp (10 ml) baking powder
½ tsp (3 ml) salt
⅔ cup (160 ml) ROMAN MEAL
    Cereal
½ cup (120 ml) chopped nuts
1 cup (240 ml) mashed bananas
½ cup (120 ml) skim milk
⅓ cup (80 ml) vegetable oil
3 egg whites
    or 2 whole eggs
1 tbs (15 ml) lemon juice

In large bowl mix flour, sugar, baking powder, salt, cereal and nuts. In small bowl, combine remaining ingredients; beat with fork to mix. Add to dry ingredients and stir just until blended. Bake in greased 9x5x3-inch loaf pan at 350°F (180°C) for about 50 minutes or until pick inserted in center comes out clean. Cool 5 minutes. Remove from pan. Cool completely on rack. Yields 1 loaf, 8 slices per loaf.

Approximate nutritional analysis per slice:
Calories 339, Protein 7 g, Carbohydrates 49 g, Fat 14 g, Cholesterol .3 mg, Sodium 285 mg

VIRTUALLY ALLERGY-FREE BANANA BREAD

CRANBERRY BREAD

2 cups (480 ml) ARROWHEAD
   MILLS Whole Wheat Flour
1½ tsp (8 ml) non-alum
   baking powder
1 tsp (5 ml) sea salt, optional
¼ cup (60 ml) nonfat instant
   milk powder, optional
juice of 1 orange
2 tbs (30 ml) ARROWHEAD MILLS
   Unrefined Safflower Oil
enough hot water to bring liquid
   ingredients to ¾ cup (180 ml)
¾ cup (180 ml) raw honey
1 egg, beaten or egg replacer
1 cup (240 ml) chopped walnuts
1 tbs (15 ml) grated orange rind,
   optional
1 cup (240 ml) whole raw
   cranberries

Mix the flour, baking powder, salt and milk powder. Mix the orange juice, oil and water. Add the honey and egg to the liquid. Stir the liquid ingredients into the dry mixture. Add the nuts, optional orange rind and berries and fold together. Pour into an oiled loaf pan. Bake at 325°F (165°C) for 50 minutes to 1 hour. Cool on rack. Serve plain or lightly buttered. Yields 1 loaf, 8 slices per loaf.

Approximate nutritional analysis per slice:
Calories 341, Protein 9 g, Carbohydrates 52 g, Fat 13 g, Cholesterol 23 mg, Sodium 102 mg

CRANBERRY BREAD

CRANBERRY-OAT BREAD

¾ cup (180 ml) honey
⅓ cup (80 ml) vegetable oil
2 eggs
½ cup (120 ml) skim milk
2½ cups (590 ml) all-purpose flour
1 cup (240 ml) quick-cooking
   rolled oats
1 tsp (5 ml) baking soda
1 tsp (5 ml) baking powder
½ tsp (3 ml) salt
½ tsp (3 ml) ground cinnamon
2 cups (480 ml) fresh or frozen
   cranberries
1 cup (240 ml) chopped nuts

Combine the honey, oil, eggs and milk in large bowl; mix well. Combine flour, oats, baking soda, baking powder, salt and cinnamon in medium bowl; mix well. Stir liquid ingredients into dry mixture. Fold in cranberries and nuts. Spoon into two 8½x4½x2½-inch greased and floured loaf pans.

Bake in preheated 350°F (180°C) oven for 40-45 minutes or until wooden toothpick inserted near center comes out clean. Cool in pans on wire racks 15 minutes. Remove from pans; cool completely on wire racks. Yields 2 loaves, 8 slices per loaf.

Approximate nutritional analysis per slice:
Calories 256, Protein 7 g, Carbohydrates 36 g, Fat 10 g, Cholesterol 25 mg, Sodium 203 mg

Courtesy of The National Honey Board.

PINEAPPLE-COCONUT-MACADAMIA NUT BREAD

4 eggs
¼ cup (60 ml) oil
1 cup (240 ml) R. W. KNUDSEN FAMILY Pineapple Coconut Juice
½ cup (120 ml) chopped fresh pineapple
3 cups (720 ml) flour
1 tbs (15 ml) baking powder
½ cup (120 ml) chopped macadamia nuts

Preheat oven to 350°F (180°C). Combine eggs, oil, juice and pineapple; stir thoroughly. Sift flour and baking powder together; add to egg mixture. Mix well; fold in nuts. Pour onto greased 9x5-inch bread pan. Bake for 50 minutes. Yields 1 loaf, 8 slices per loaf.

Approximate nutritional analysis per slice:
Calories 344, Protein 8 g, Carbohydrates 43 g, Fat 16 g, Cholesterol 94 mg, Sodium 218 mg

PINEAPPLE-COCONUT-MACADAMIA NUT BREAD

BERRY BREAKFAST CAKE

1½ cups (355 ml) ARROWHEAD MILLS Blue Cornmeal
½ cup (120 ml) ARROWHEAD MILLS Unbleached White flour
1 tbs (15 ml) non-alum baking powder
2 egg whites
½ cup (120 ml) blueberry or boysenberry syrup
1 tbs (15 ml) ARROWHEAD MILLS Unrefined Vegetable Oil
1½ cups (355 ml) skim milk or soy milk
1 cup (240 ml) blueberries or boysenberries

Combine first three ingredients. Beat egg whites until fluffy. Beat together berry syrup, oil and skim milk, and gently fold in egg whites. Stir in dry ingredients, pour batter into an oiled cake pan, sprinkle with berries, and place on a baking sheet. Bake at 425°F (220°C) for 30 minutes until golden. Serve hot with butter or your favorite syrup. Yields 1 loaf, 8 slices per loaf.

Approximate nutritional analysis per slice:
Calories 220, Protein 6 g, Carbohydrates 44 g, Fat 2 g, Cholesterol < 1 mg, Sodium 83 mg

BERRY BREAKFAST CAKE

WHOLE WHEAT-CORN BREAD

1 cup (240 ml) cornmeal
1 cup (240 ml) AMBERWAVES
   BRAND Organic Whole Wheat
   Flour
1 tbs (15 ml) baking powder
1 tsp (5 ml) salt
¼ cup (60 ml) honey
½ cup (120 ml) oil
1 cup (240 ml) skim milk
2 eggs

Heat oven to 450°F (230°C). Mix together first 4 dry ingredients. Add rest of ingredients. Mix. Beat vigorously for 2 minutes. Pour into greased 8-inch square pan. Bake 25-30 minutes. Serve warm with honey, molasses or chili. Yields 1 bread, 16 squares per bread.

Approximate nutritional analysis per square:
Calories 148, Protein 3 g, Carbohydrates 18 g, Fat 8 g, Cholesterol 24 mg, Sodium 240 mg

WHOLE WHEAT-CORN BREAD

BLUE CORN BREAD

1 cup (240 ml) ARROWHEAD MILLS
   Blue Cornmeal
½ cup (120 ml) ARROWHEAD
   MILLS Barley Flour or any
   ARROWHEAD MILLS flour
1½ tsp (8 ml) non-alum
   baking powder
¼ tsp (1 ml) sea salt, optional
1 tbs (15 ml) honey or maple syrup
1 egg, beaten or egg replacer
1 cup water or milk

Combine liquids and slowly add to combined dry ingredients. Oil bread or muffin pan. Bake at 425°F (220°C) for 15-20 minutes, until top and sides become golden brown. Yields 1 8-inch bread or 6 muffins.

Approximate nutritional analysis per muffin:
Calories 134, Protein 4 g, Carbohydrates 27 g, Fat 2 g, Cholesterol 31 mg, Sodium 139 mg

BLUE CORN BREAD

CORN BREAD WITH CHILES

1 cup (240 ml) blue or yellow
    cornmeal
1 tbs (15 ml) baking powder
¼ cup (60 ml) Parmesan cheese
½ cup (120 ml) OMEGA
    Sunflower Oil
2 free-range eggs, beaten
1 cup (240 ml) buttermilk,
    sour cream or yogurt
2 cups (480 ml) corn kernels
3½ oz (105 g) reduced-fat
    mozzarella cheese, grated
2-4 green chiles, chopped, optional

Preheat oven to 375°F (190°C). Mix dry ingredients. Add sunflower oil, eggs and buttermilk. Fold in corn. Pour ⅓ batter into greased 8x8-inch pan. Cover with cheese and chiles. Top with remaining batter. Bake for 30-40 minutes or until lightly brown. Yields 1 bread, 4 squares per bread.

Approximate nutritional analysis per square:
Calories 690, Protein 20 g, Carbohydrates 47 g, Fat 50 g, Cholesterol 137 mg, Sodium 784 mg

CORN BREAD WITH CHILES

MAPLE SYRUP-CORN BREAD

1 cup (240 ml) cornmeal
1¼ cups (295 ml) whole wheat flour
3 tsp (15 ml) baking powder
½ tsp (3 ml) salt
1 egg, well beaten
½ cup (120 ml) maple syrup
¾ cup (180 ml) skim milk
3 tbs (45 ml) oil

Mix dry ingredients together. Add remaining ingredients and stir until well blended. Pour into well-greased 9x9-inch pan. Bake for 20 minutes at 400°F (205°C). Cut into squares and serve hot with butter. Yields 1 bread, 9 squares.

Approximate nutritional analysis per square:
Calories 216, Protein 5 g, Carbohydrates 37 g, Fat 6 g, Cholesterol 22 mg, Sodium 300 mg

Courtesy of Michigan Maple Syrup Association and Cooperative Extension Services Michigan State University.

MAPLE SYRUP-CORN BREAD

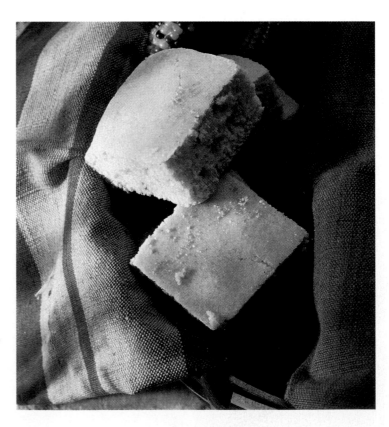

SAVORY BARLEY-CORN BREAD

1 cup (240 ml) ARROWHEAD MILLS
   Blue or Yellow Cornmeal
½ cup (120 ml) precooked
   ARROWHEAD MILLS
   Bits-O-Barley
1 tsp (5 ml) baking soda
½ tsp (3 ml) sea salt, optional
1 egg, lightly beaten
2 tbs (30 ml) ARROWHEAD MILLS
   Unrefined Vegetable Oil
1 cup (240 ml) buttermilk
2 tbs (30 ml) honey
⅓ cup (80 ml) finely chopped onion
½ cup (120 ml) canned whole
   kernel corn

Preheat oven to 350°F (180°C). Mix the cornmeal, Bits-O-Barley, baking soda and sea salt. Add the egg, oil, buttermilk, honey, onion and corn and mix only until the dry ingredients are moistened. Turn into well-oiled and heated large iron skillet. Bake 30-35 minutes or until well browned. Cut in wedges and serve hot. Yields 1 bread, 8 slices per bread.

Approximate nutritional analysis per slice:
Calories 144, Protein 19 g, Carbohydrates 25 g, Fat 5 g, Cholesterol 24 mg, Sodium 230 mg

SIMPLE SPELT CORN BREAD

1 cup (240 ml) VITA-SPELT Flour
½ cup (120 ml) sugar
½ tsp (3 ml) salt
1 tsp (5 ml) baking soda
2 tsp (10 ml) baking powder
1 cup (240 ml) yellow cornmeal
1 cup (240 ml) milk
2 eggs
2 tbs (30 ml) canola oil

Preheat oven to 425°F (220°C). Combine and mix dry ingredients. Add milk, eggs and canola oil. Pour into greased 8- or 9-inch cast-iron skillet or greased muffin pan. Bake approximately 20-30 minutes or until golden. Yields 1 loaf, 8 slices per loaf.

Approximate nutritional analysis per slice:
Calories 182, Protein 4 g, Carbohydrates 30 g, Fat 5 g, Cholesterol 47 mg, Sodium 354 mg

SAVORY BARLEY-CORN BREAD

7-GRAIN OATMEAL CAKE

1 cup (240 ml) ARROWHEAD MILLS
   Canola Oil
2 cups (480 ml) maple syrup
1½ tsp (8 ml) vanilla
2 cups (480 ml) ARROWHEAD
   MILLS Unbleached White Flour
⅜ cup (90 ml) ARROWHEAD MILLS
   Low Fat Soy Flour
½ cup (120 ml) cold water
½ cup (120 ml) soy milk
1½ tsp (8 ml) grated lemon rind
1½ tsp (8 ml) sea salt, optional
3 egg whites
2 tsp (10 ml) cinnamon
2 tsp (10 ml) non-alum
   baking powder
1 cup (240 ml) cooked ARROWHEAD
   MILLS 7 Grain Cereal
5 cups (1.2 l) ARROWHEAD MILLS
   Rolled Oats
½ cup (120 ml) raisins, optional
½ cup (120 ml) chopped walnuts,
   or nuts of choice

Cream together oil, syrup and vanilla. In a separate bowl, mix the 2 flours, water, milk, rind, sea salt, egg whites, cinnamon and baking powder until smooth. Then mix the two mixtures together and add cereal, oats, raisins and nuts. Mix well and fill oiled 9x13-inch cake pan ¾ full. Bake 350°F (180°C) until light golden brown. This is not a very sweet cake. May be served with apple butter, honey, etc. Serves 20.

Approximate nutritional analysis per serving:
Calories 356, Protein 8 g, Carbohydrates 50 g, Fat 15 g, Cholesterol 0 mg, Sodium 62 mg

BANANA-NUT KAMUT BREAD

2 eggs, separated
½ cup (120 ml) oil
¼ cup (60 ml) honey
1⅓ cups (320 ml) mashed bananas
½ tsp (3 ml) cream of tartar
½ tsp (3 ml) baking soda, optional
2½ cups (590 ml) KAMUT BRAND
   Flour
⅓ cup (80 ml) chopped walnuts

Mix together in bowl, egg yolks, oil, honey and bananas. Add cream of tartar, soda and flour. This should be a thick batter. Add nuts. Mix ⅓ of egg whites with batter; gently fold in remaining egg whites. Pour batter into lightly greased 8x8-inch or loaf pan. Bake at 350°F (180°C) for about 50 minutes until toothpick inserted in center comes out clean. Serves 16.

Approximate nutritional analysis per serving:
Calories 186, Protein 4 g, Carbohydrates 25 g, Fat 9 g, Cholesterol 23 mg, Sodium 7 mg

7-GRAIN OATMEAL CAKE

AMARANTH BAKING POWDER BREAD

1 cup (240 ml) ARROWHEAD MILLS
   Amaranth Flour
1½ cups (355 ml) ARROWHEAD
   MILLS Brown Rice or
   Whole Wheat Flour
1 tbs (15 ml) non-alum
   baking powder
1 tsp (5 ml) sea salt, optional
1 cup (240 ml) milk, soy milk
   or water
3 tbs (45 ml) honey
2 tbs (30 ml) ARROWHEAD MILLS
   Unrefined Vegetable Oil
2 egg whites, beaten, if using
   rice flour

Mix dry and liquid ingredients separately; beat egg whites, then combine all ingredients. Pour batter into well-oiled 8x4-inch pan and bake at 350°F (180°C) about 45 minutes. Cool 10 minutes before removing loaf to rack. Serves 8.

Approximate nutritional analysis per serving:
Calories 268, Protein 8 g, Carbohydrates 47 g, Fat 6 g, Cholesterol 1 mg, Sodium 220 mg

AMARANTH BAKING POWDER BREAD

RAISIN-WALNUT KAMUT MUFFINS

TOPPING:
½ cup (120 ml) KAMUT BRAND
   Flour
⅓ cup (80 ml) chopped walnuts
¼ cup (60 ml) sugar
¼ cup (60 ml) melted margarine

1½ cups (355 ml) KAMUT BRAND
   Flour
2 tbs (30 ml) baking powder
1 tsp (5 ml) salt
1 tsp (5 ml) cinnamon
1 cup (240 ml) raisins
½ cup (120 ml) oil
2 eggs, beaten
½ cup (120 ml) honey
¾ cup (180 ml) buttermilk

In small bowl mix together Topping ingredients. Set aside.
   In large mixing bowl combine dry ingredients. Stir in raisins. In small bowl combine oil, eggs, honey and buttermilk. Stir well into dry ingredients. Line muffin tins with baking cups or grease well. Fill ⅔ full with batter. Sprinkle 1 heaping tbs of topping on each muffin. Bake at 350°F (180°C) for 15-18 minutes. Muffins are done when toothpick inserted in center comes out clean. Do not overcook. Yields 18 muffins.

Approximate nutritional analysis per muffin:
Calories 215, Protein 4 g, Carbohydrates 30 g, Fat 11 g, Cholesterol 21 mg, Sodium 324 mg

RAISIN-WALNUT KAMUT MUFFINS

ALMA STREET CAFE MUFFINS

4½ cups (1 l) unbleached white flour
1¾ cup (415 ml) OMEGA Hazelnut
  Flour
1 tbs (15 ml) sea salt
4 tbs (60 ml) baking powder
2½ cups (590 ml) unsalted butter,
  melted
3 cups (720 ml) sugar, fructose
  or sucanat
10 free-range eggs, beaten
2 cups (480 ml) buttermilk

Mix flour, hazelnut flour, salt and baking powder. Combine butter and sugar, mix well, then add eggs and buttermilk. Combine dry ingredients with buttermilk mixture. Bake at 375°F (190°C) for approximately 30 minutes until golden brown. Yields 24 muffins.

Approximate nutritional analysis per muffin:
Calories 339, Protein 7 g, Carbohydrates 30 g, Fat 23 g, Cholesterol 130 mg, Sodium 558 mg

OATMEAL-RAISIN MUFFINS

1 cup (240 ml) buttermilk
1 cup (240 ml) quick oats
1 cup (240 ml) AMBERWAVES
  BRAND Organic Whole
  Wheat Flour
1 tsp (5 ml) baking powder
½ tsp (3 ml) baking soda
½ tsp (3 ml) salt
2 tsp (10 ml) cinnamon
⅓ cup (80 ml) softened butter
  or margarine
¼ cup (60 ml) firmly packed
  brown sugar
1 tbs (15 ml) honey
1 egg
½ cup (120 ml) raisins or dried
  apples, chopped

Boil and stir buttermilk and oats for 2 minutes. Let cool. Preheat oven to 400°F (205°C). Mix flour, baking powder, soda, salt and cinnamon in medium bowl. In large bowl cream together butter, brown sugar, honey and egg. Mix in cooled oat mixture. Add raisins. Add dry ingredients and mix with spoon only until dry ingredients are moistened. Fill greased muffin tins ⅔ full. Bake 25-30 minutes. Yields 12 muffins.

Approximate nutritional analysis per muffin:
Calories 157, Protein 4 g, Carbohydrates 23 g, Fat 6 g, Cholesterol 30 mg, Sodium 263 mg

ALMA STREET CAFE MUFFINS

HEARTY MUFFINS

2 cups (480 ml) boiling water
2 cups (480 ml) natural bran
2 cups (480 ml) buttermilk
½ cup (120 ml) honey, melted
2 eggs, beaten
2¼ cups (540 ml) stone-ground
    whole wheat flour
⅓ cup (80 ml) ZUMBRO Jerusalem
    Artichoke Flour
1 cup (240 ml) ground flaxseed
    or oatmeal
2½ tsp (13 ml) baking soda
1½ tsp (8 ml) salt
1¼ cups (295 ml) raisins, optional

Pour boiling water over bran. To this add buttermilk, honey and eggs. Mix well. Mix together flours, flaxseed, soda and salt. Add liquid ingredients to dry and mix until blended. Batter should not be too stiff. Stir in raisins. Bake at 350°F (180°C) for 20-30 minutes. Yields 12 large muffins.

Approximate nutritional analysis per muffin:
Calories 216, Protein 8 g, Carbohydrates 46 g, Fat 2 g, Cholesterol 33 mg, Sodium 583 mg

ORGANIC YOGURT MUFFINS

2 cups (480 ml) cake flour,
    preferably organic
    or 1¾ cups (415 ml) all-purpose
    flour, preferably organic
½ tsp (3 ml) salt
2 tsp (10 ml) baking soda
1 cup (240 ml) HORIZON Organic
    Yogurt, any flavor
1 beaten egg

All ingredients should be at room temperature, about 75°F (24°C). Preheat oven to 400°F (205°C).

Sift together flour, salt and baking soda. Set aside. Combine yogurt and egg. Add these to the dry ingredients with a few swift strokes. Pour the batter into a muffin pan and bake at once for 20-25 minutes. Yields 12 muffins.

Approximate nutritional analysis per muffin:
Calories 77, Protein 3 g, Carbohydrates 15 g, Fat .5 g, Cholesterol 16 mg, Sodium 317 mg

ORGANIC YOGURT MUFFINS

BUSY BEE
BRAN MUFFINS

3 eggs
½ cup (120 ml) salad oil
½ cup (120 ml) honey
3½ cups (840 ml) 100% bran cereal
1½ cups (355 ml) skim milk
2¼ cups (600 ml) flour
1 tsp (5 ml) cinnamon
4 tsp (20 ml) baking soda
½ cup (120 ml) seedless raisins or
    chopped dried fruit, optional

In small bowl, blend together eggs, oil and honey. In large mixing bowl, combine bran with milk and let stand 5 minutes. Add egg mixture to cereal and blend lightly. Mix in flour, cinnamon and soda. Add raisins, if desired. Spoon into paper-lined or greased muffin pan cups. Bake at 350°F (180°C) 25-30 minutes. Yields 16 muffins.

Approximate nutritional analysis per muffin:
Calories 215, Protein 5 g, Carbohydrates 34 g, Fat 9 g, Cholesterol 36 mg, Sodium 437 mg

Courtesy of The National Honey Board.

RAISIN-BRAN
MUFFINS

15-oz box (450 g) EREWHON
    Raisin Bran
5 cups (1.2 l) whole wheat flour
5 tsp (25 ml) baking soda
2 tsp (10 ml) sea salt
1 cup (240 ml) nonfat yogurt
1¼ cups (295 ml) molasses
3¼ cups (780 ml) nonfat buttermilk
3 egg whites

Mix together cereal, flour, soda and sea salt. Add yogurt, molasses and buttermilk. Mix well. Beat egg whites until stiff and fold into batter. Fill paper-lined muffin tins half full and bake in 375°F (190°C) oven for 20-25 minutes. Refrigerate extra batter in tightly covered container for up to 6 weeks, using as desired. Yields 3½ dozen.

Approximate nutritional analysis per muffin:
Calories 119, Protein 5 g, Carbohydrates 26 g, Fat 1 g, Cholesterol 1 mg, Sodium 312 mg

BUSY BEE BRAN MUFFINS

THE ROMAN MEAL MUFFIN

THE BASIC MUFFIN:
1 cup (240 ml) ROMAN MEAL
   Cereal
1½ cups (355 ml) all-purpose flour
1 tbs (15 ml) baking powder
⅓-½ cup (80-120 ml) sugar
½ tsp (3 ml) salt, optional
1 egg, slightly beaten
1 cup (240 ml) skim milk
⅓ cup (80 ml) vegetable oil

BLUEBERRY VARIATION:
1 cup (240 ml) blueberries, fresh
   or drained frozen or canned

**CINNAMON & DRIED FRUIT
VARIATION:**
1 cup (240 ml) dried fruit, chopped
   (raisins, dates, apricots, apples,
   figs or prunes)
1 tsp (5 ml) ground cinnamon

Heat oven to 400°F (205°C). In large bowl stir together dry ingredients. In a medium bowl mix egg, milk and oil. Stir egg mixture into the dry ingredients, mixing just enough to moisten, batter will be lumpy. Spoon evenly into 12 greased or paper-lined 2½-inch muffin cups. Bake about 20-25 minutes or until golden brown. Yields 12 muffins.

Blueberry Muffins: Add blueberries along with the dry ingredients.

Cinnamon & Dried Fruit Muffins: Add dried fruit and cinnamon along with the dry ingredients.

Approximate nutritional analysis per basic muffin:
Calories 168, Protein 3 g, Carbohydrates 23 g, Fat 7 g, Cholesterol 16 mg, Sodium 153 mg

Approximate nutritional analysis per blueberry muffin:
Calories 173, Protein 3 g, Carbohydrates 25 g, Fat 7 g, Cholesterol 16 mg, Sodium 153 mg

Approximate nutritional analysis per cinnamon and raisin muffin:
Calories 194, Protein 4 g, Carbohydrates 32 g, Fat 6 g, Cholesterol 16 mg, Sodium 161 mg

Approximate nutritional analysis per cinnamon and date muffin:
Calories 232, Protein 5 g, Carbohydrates 42 g, Fat 6 g, Cholesterol 16 mg, Sodium 159 mg

Approximate nutritional analysis per cinnamon and apricot muffin:
Calories 187, Protein 4 g, Carbohydrates 30 g, Fat 6 g, Cholesterol 16 mg, Sodium 161 mg

Approximate nutritional analysis per cinnamon and apple muffin:
Calories 166, Protein 4 g, Carbohydrates 24 g, Fat 6 g, Cholesterol 16 mg, Sodium 158 mg

Approximate nutritional analysis per cinnamon and fig muffin:
Calories 177, Protein 4 g, Carbohydrates 27 g, Fat 6 g, Cholesterol 16 mg, Sodium 159 mg

Approximate nutritional analysis per cinnamon and prune muffin:
Calories 213, Protein 5 g, Carbohydrates 37 g, Fat 6 g, Cholesterol 16 mg, Sodium 159 mg

BLUEBERRY-OAT BRAN MUFFINS

1 cup (240 ml flour
4 tsp (20 ml) non-alum
   baking powder
½ tsp (3 ml) salt
1 cup (240 ml) oat bran
1 cup (240 ml) blueberries, rinsed
1 cup (240 ml) WESTSOY
¼ cup (60 ml) unsweetened fruit
   juice concentrate (apple, white
   grape, pineapple, etc.)
¼ cup (60 ml) melted margarine
2 egg whites, beaten until frothy

Preheat oven to 400°F (205°C). Sift flour, baking powder and salt together into a large bowl. Stir in oat bran, then blueberries. Mix together soy milk, fruit juice concentrate, margarine and egg whites. Combine the two mixtures and stir just enough to moisten ingredients, 12-15 strokes. Grease muffin cups or spray with no-stick cooking spray and fill ⅔ with batter. Bake 20-25 minutes or until well browned. Yields 12 muffins.

Approximate nutritional analysis per muffin:
Calories 120, Protein 4 g, Carbohydrates 18 g, Fat 5 g, Cholesterol 0 mg, Sodium 300 mg

GRANNY SMITH BUCKWHEAT MUFFINS

4 cups (960 ml) Granny Smith
   apples, peeled and diced into
   ¼-inch cubes
1 cup (240 ml) sugar
2 large eggs, beaten lightly
½ cup (120 ml) oil
2 tsp (10 ml) vanilla extract
1 cup (240 ml) THE BIRKETT
   MILLS Light or Whole
   Buckwheat Flour
1 cup (240 ml) whole wheat flour
2 tsp (10 ml) baking soda
2 tsp (10 ml) cinnamon
1 tsp (5 ml) salt
1 cup (240 ml) raisins
1 cup (240 ml) walnuts,
   coarsely chopped

Toss together apples and sugar in large bowl. Whisk or beat together eggs, oil and vanilla. Stir together well buckwheat flour, whole wheat flour, baking soda, cinnamon and salt. Stir egg mixture into apple mixture. Add flour mixture and stir just enough to combine, batter will be stiff. Stir in raisins and walnuts. Divide batter among 18 well-greased muffin cups. Bake in middle of 350°F (180°C) oven for 25-30 minutes. Serve warm or cold. Yields 18 muffins.

Approximate nutritional analysis per muffin:
Calories 241, Protein 5 g, Carbohydrates 34 g, Fat 11 g, Cholesterol 31 mg, Sodium 270 mg

**GRANNY SMITH
BUCKWHEAT MUFFINS**

GLUTEN-FREE ORANGE MUFFINS

1½ cups (355 ml) ARROWHEAD
   MILLS Millet or Rice Flour
½ cup (120 ml) ARROWHEAD
   MILLS Soy Flour
1 tbs (15 ml) non-alum
   baking powder
½ tsp (3 ml) sea salt, optional
¼ tsp (1 ml) orange flavoring
1 cup (240 ml) water or orange juice
¼ cup (60 ml) ARROWHEAD MILLS
   Unrefined Vegetable Oil
¼ cup (60 ml) rice syrup

Combine all dry ingredients. Mix all liquids; add to dry ingredients. For muffins, fill cups full, bake at 375°F (190°C) for 15-20 minutes. Yields 12 muffins.

Approximate nutritional analysis per muffin:
Calories 199, Protein 5 g, Carbohydrates 35 g, Fat 6 g, Cholesterol 0 mg, Sodium 123 mg

GLUTEN-FREE ORANGE MUFFINS

BANANA MUFFINS

1 cup (240 ml) OMEGA Hazelnut
   Flour
1¼ cups (295 ml) whole wheat flour
2 tsp (10 ml) baking soda
1 tsp (10 ml) cinnamon
½ tsp (3 ml) nutmeg
¼ tsp (1 ml) sea salt
2 free-range eggs
½ cup (120 ml) maple syrup
¼ cup (60 ml) OMEGA Safflower Oil
1 tsp (5 ml) vanilla
1⅓ cups (320 ml) banana, mashed
¼ cup (60 ml) nonfat yogurt
1 tsp (5 ml) lemon zest

Preheat oven to 375°F (190°C). Combine hazelnut flour, whole wheat flour, baking soda, cinnamon, nutmeg and salt. Separately, beat together eggs, maple syrup, safflower oil and vanilla. Stir in banana, yogurt and lemon zest. Add this mixture to dry ingredients and stir until moistened. Fill oiled muffin tins with batter. Bake for 20 minutes. Yields 12 muffins.

Approximate nutritional analysis per muffin:
Calories 196, Protein 8 g, Carbohydrates 28 g, Fat 8 g, Cholesterol 31 mg, Sodium 269 mg

ORANGE-HAZELNUT MUFFINS

¾ cup (180 ml) hot water
1 cup (240 ml) raisins or currants
1 tbs (15 ml) orange zest, chopped
1¾ cups (415 ml) whole wheat flour
1⅓ cups (320 ml) OMEGA Hazelnut
   Flour
1 tbs (15 ml) baking powder
1 tsp (5 ml) sea salt
½ cup (120 ml) unsalted butter
2 free-range eggs, beaten
1 cup (240 ml) orange juice
   concentrate
½ cup (120 ml) maple syrup

Soak raisins in hot water and orange zest overnight; reserve water. Preheat oven to 375°F (188°C). Mix dry ingredients. Cut in butter. Combine eggs, orange juice concentrate and syrup, then add to dry ingredients. Mix in raisins, zest and any remaining soaking water. Do not overmix. Place in oiled muffin tins. Bake at 375°F (190°C) for 20-25 minutes. Yields 12 muffins.

Approximate nutritional analysis per muffin:
Calories 306, Protein 10 g, Carbohydrates 47 g, Fat 11 g, Cholesterol 52 mg, Sodium 314 mg

ORANGE-HAZELNUT MUFFINS

APPLESAUCE MUFFINS

¾ cup (180 ml) **ROMAN MEAL Cereal**
1½ cups (355 ml) **all-purpose flour**
1 tbs (15 ml) **baking powder**
⅓ cup (80 ml) **sugar**
½-1 tsp (3-5 ml) **cinnamon**
½ tsp (3 ml) **salt, optional**
½ cup (120 ml) **raisins, chopped dates, dried apricots or dried apples, optional**
1 egg, **slightly beaten**
¾ cup (180 ml) **skim milk**
¼ cup (60 ml) **vegetable oil**
1 cup (240 ml) **applesauce**

Heat oven to 400°F (205°C). In a large bowl stir together dry ingredients and raisins. In a medium bowl mix egg, milk, oil and applesauce. Stir egg mixture into the dry ingredients, mixing just to moisten, batter will be lumpy. Spoon evenly into 12 greased or paper-lined 2½-inch muffin cups. Bake about 20-25 minutes or until golden brown. Serve warm with chunks of jalapeño, jack or cheddar cheese and some fresh fruit. Yields 12 muffins.

Approximate nutritional analysis per muffin:
Calories 173, Protein 3 g, Carbohydrates 29 g, Fat 5 g, Cholesterol 16 mg, Sodium 152 mg

CARAWAY-RYE MUFFINS

¾ cup (180 ml) **ROMAN MEAL Cereal**
¾ cup (180 ml) **all-purpose flour**
¾ cup (180 ml) **rye flour**
1 tbs (15 ml) **baking powder**
3 tbs (45 ml) **brown sugar**
2 tsp (10 ml) **caraway seeds**
1 tsp (5 ml) **grated orange peel**
½ tsp (3 ml) **salt, optional**
1 egg, **slightly beaten**
1 cup (240 ml) **skim milk**
⅓ cup (80 ml) **vegetable oil**

Heat oven to 400°C (205°C). In a large bowl stir together dry ingredients and seasonings. In a medium bowl mix egg, milk and oil. Stir egg mixture into the dry ingredients, mixing just enough to moisten, batter will be lumpy. Spoon evenly into 12 greased or paper-lined 2½-inch muffin cups. Bake about 20-25 minutes or until golden brown. Yields 12 muffins.

Approximate nutritional analysis per muffin:
Calories 143, Protein 3 g, Carbohydrates 17 g, Fat 7 g, Cholesterol 16 mg, Sodium 154 mg

CARAWAY-RYE MUFFINS

VITA-SPELT CARBO-MUFFINS

1¾ cups (415 ml) VITA-SPELT Flour
¼ tsp (1 ml) salt
¼ tsp (1 ml) baking soda
1 tsp (5 ml) baking powder
½ tsp (3 ml) cinnamon
⅓ cup (80 ml) raisins
⅓ cup (80 ml) walnuts, chopped
1 cup (240 ml) carrots, grated
½ cup (120 ml) apple, finely diced
¾ cup (180 ml) apple juice
1 egg, slightly beaten
3 tbs (45 ml) canola oil
1 tsp (5 ml) vanilla extract

Preheat oven to 400°F (205 C) and prepare muffin cups. Combine all dry ingredients in one bowl and mix well. Combine all wet and other ingredients in another bowl and mix well. Add the liquid ingredients to the dry. Mix together until just moistened. Fill muffin cups and bake for approximately 20 minutes, or until done. Allow muffins to cool on wire rack a few minutes before removing. Continue cooling muffins on wire rack. Yields 12 muffins.

Approximate nutritional analysis per muffin:
Calories 104, Protein 2 g, Carbohydrates 12 g, Fat 6 g, Cholesterol 16 mg, Sodium 120 mg

MEXICAN CORN MUFFINS

⅔ cup (160 ml) ROMAN MEAL Cereal
1⅓ cups (320 ml) all-purpose flour
1 tbs (15 ml) baking powder
3 tbs (45 ml) sugar
½ tsp (3 ml) salt, optional
½-1 tsp (3-5 ml) chili powder
1 egg, slightly beaten
1 cup (240 ml skim milk
¼ cup (60 ml) vegetable oil
½-¾ cup (120-180 ml) corn, cooked and drained

Heat oven to 400°F (205°C). In a large bowl stir together dry ingredients. In a medium bowl mix egg, milk, oil and corn. Stir egg mixture into the dry ingredients, mixing just enough to moisten, batter will be lumpy. Spoon evenly into 12 greased or paper-lined 2½-inch muffin cups. Bake about 20-25 minutes or until golden brown. Yields 12 muffins.

Approximate nutritional analysis per muffin:
Calories 137, Protein 3 g, Carbohydrates 19 g, Fat 6 g, Cholesterol 16 mg, Sodium 155 mg

LINDA'S OATMEAL MUFFINS

2 packets EREWHON Instant Oatmeal, any variety
1 cup (240 ml) skim milk or soy milk
1 egg, slightly beaten
¼ cup (60 ml) canola oil
½ cup (120 ml) EREWHON Oat Bran with Toasted Wheat Germ
½ cup (120 ml) whole wheat flour
2 tbs (30 ml) baking powder
½ tsp (3 ml) salt
½ tsp (3 ml) baking soda

Preheat oven to 400°F (205°C). Line muffin pan with paper muffin liners. Soak instant oatmeal in milk for 10 minutes. Add egg and oil to oatmeal mixture; mix well. Add dry ingredients to wet, mix only enough to moisten. Bake 12-15 minutes. Yields 12 muffins.

Approximate nutritional analysis per muffin:
Calories 102, Protein 3 g, Carbohydrates 12 g, Fat 6 g, Cholesterol 16 mg, Sodium 407 mg

BLUE CORN-BLUEBERRY MUFFINS

1 cup (240 ml) ARROWHEAD MILLS
   Blue Cornmeal
1 cup (240 ml) ARROWHEAD MILLS
   Unbleached White Flour
2 tsp (10 ml) non-alum
   baking powder
½ tsp (3 ml) sea salt, optional
1½ cups (355 ml) water
2-4 tsp (10-20 ml) honey
¼ cup (60 ml) ARROWHEAD MILLS
   Unrefined Vegetable Oil
1 tsp (5 ml) vanilla
1 cup (240 ml) fresh or frozen
   blueberries

Stir dry ingredients together. Combine liquid ingredients. Mix liquid and dry ingredients and stir until just mixed. Gently stir in blueberries. Fill oiled muffin tins ⅔ full. Bake in preheated oven at 400°F (205°C) for 20 minutes or until done. Yields 12 muffins.

Approximate nutritional analysis per muffin:
Calories 133, Protein 2 g, Carbohydrates 19 g, Fat 5 g, Cholesterol 0 mg, Sodium 82 mg

7-GRAIN CORN MUFFINS

2 cups (480 ml) ARROWHEAD
   MILLS 7 Grain Cereal, cooked
2 cups (480 l) water
2 tbs (30 ml) maple syrup
2 tbs (30 ml) ARROWHEAD MILLS
   Unrefined Vegetable Oil
2 tsp (10 ml) sea salt, optional
¼ cup (60 ml) ARROWHEAD MILLS
   Original Instant Oatmeal
2 cups (480 ml) ARROWHEAD
   MILLS Yellow Cornmeal

Mix first 6 ingredients in blender until very smooth. Mix cornmeal in with a spoon. Fill oiled muffin cups ½ full. Bake at 375°F (190°C) for 35-45 minutes. Yields 16 muffins.

Approximate nutritional analysis per muffin:
Calories 139, Protein 4 g, Carbohydrates 25 g, Fat 3 g, Cholesterol 0 mg, Sodium 5 mg

GRAPE JUICE-SWEETENED CORN MUFFINS

1 cup (240 ml) ARROWHEAD MILLS
Blue Cornmeal
1 cup (240 ml) ARROWHEAD MILLS
Whole Wheat Pastry Flour
2 tsp (10 ml) non-alum
baking powder
¼ tsp (1 ml) sea salt, optional
¼ tsp (1 ml) nutmeg
½ cup (120 ml) chopped nuts
1 egg, beaten or egg replacer
1 tbs (15 ml) ARROWHEAD MILLS
Unrefined Vegetable Oil
3 tbs (45 ml) sugar or natural
sweetener
¼ cup (60 ml) plain nonfat yogurt
1¼ cups (280 ml) grape juice
1 tsp (5 ml) lemon extract

Combine dry ingredients, and mix in nuts. In a separate bowl, mix liquids together, then combine with dry ingredients. Batter will seem thin but it will thicken. Pour batter into oiled muffin tins, ⅔ full. Bake at 425°F (220°C) for 15 minutes. Cool before serving. This recipe can also be used to make pancakes. Yields 12 muffins.

Approximate nutritional analysis per muffin:
Calories 155, Protein 5 g, Carbohydrates 25 g, Fat 5 g, Cholesterol 16 mg, Sodium 92 mg

COLUSA CORN MUFFINS

⅔ cup (160 ml) skim milk
⅓ cup (80 ml) melted butter or
margarine
½ cup (120 ml) honey
2 eggs
1½ cups (355 ml) whole wheat flour
⅔ cup (160 ml) cornmeal
2½ tsp (13 ml) baking powder
¼ tsp (1 ml) salt

VARIATION:
1 large pear or apple, pared,
cored and diced

In small bowl, beat together milk, butter, honey and eggs. Set aside. In large bowl, stir together dry ingredients. Add honey mixture. Stir just enough to barely moisten flour. Do not overmix. Spoon batter into paper-lined or greased muffin pan cups. Bake at 350°F (180°C) for 20-25 minutes. Serve warm. Yields 18 muffins.
    Variation: Add pear or apple to flour mixture.

Approximate nutritional analysis per muffin:
Calories 122, Protein 3 g, Carbohydrates 20 g, Fat 4 g, Cholesterol 30 mg, Sodium 144 mg

Courtesy of The National Honey Board.

COLUSA CORN MUFFINS

KAMUT BISCUITS

1 cup (240 ml) KAMUT BRAND
  Flour
1 cup (240 ml) white flour
½ cup (120 ml) dry instant
  powdered milk
1 tsp (5 ml) salt
2 tbs (30 ml) baking powder
¾ cup (180 ml) water
⅓ cup (80 ml) vegetable oil

Stir together dry ingredients, add water and oil. Stir until well mixed. Knead in bowl 10-15 times. Roll out to ¾-inch thickness and cut into 2-inch squares or diamonds or cut with biscuit cutter. Place 2 inches apart on baking sheet. Bake at 450°F (230°C) for 8-10 minutes or until golden on top. Yields 12 biscuits.

Approximate nutritional analysis per biscuit:
Calories 139, Protein 3 g, Carbohydrates 18 g, Fat 6 g, Cholesterol .5 mg, Sodium 437 mg

OLD-FASHIONED BAKING POWDER BISCUITS

2 cups (480 ml) flour
3 tsp (15 ml) non-alum
  baking powder
½ tsp (3 ml) salt
6 tbs (90 ml) cold margarine
1 cup (240 ml) Unsweetened
  WESTSOY

Preheat oven to 450°F (230°C). Mix dry ingredients together and cut margarine until mixture is the consistency of coarse cornmeal. Add soy milk and stir just until dough comes free from sides of the bowl. Turn the dough onto a floured board, shape into a ball, and gently knead 10 times. Roll out ½-inch thick and cut with a 2-inch biscuit cutter dipped into flour. Brush tops of biscuits lightly with a little soy milk. Place biscuits on an ungreased baking sheet. Bake until lightly browned, 14-16 minutes. Yields 12 biscuits.

Approximate nutritional analysis per biscuit:
Calories 130, Protein 3 g, Carbohydrates 17 g, Fat 6 g, Cholesterol 0 mg, Sodium 280 mg

SPICY PUMPKIN MUFFINS

⅔ cup (160 ml) ROMAN MEAL
  Cereal
1⅓ cup (320 ml) all-purpose flour
1 tbs (15 ml) baking powder
⅓ cup (80 ml) brown sugar,
  firmly packed
½ tsp (3 ml) salt
½ tsp (3 ml) ground cinnamon
¼ tsp (1 ml) ground nutmeg
¼ tsp (1 ml) ground ginger
¼ tsp (1 ml) ground cloves
1 egg, slightly beaten
1 cup (240 ml) skim milk
⅓ cup (80 ml) vegetable oil
¾ cup (180 ml) canned or cooked,
  mashed pumpkin, sweet
  potatoes, yams or winter squash

Heat oven to 400°F (205°C). In a large bowl stir together dry ingredients and spices. In a medium bowl mix egg, milk, oil and pumpkin. Stir egg mixture into the dry ingredients, mixing just enough to moisten, batter will be lumpy. Spoon evenly into 12 greased or paper-lined 2½-inch muffin cups. Bake about 20-25 minutes or until edges of muffins start to pull from sides. Yields 12 muffins.

Approximate nutritional analysis per muffin:
Calories 217, Protein 3 g, Carbohydrates 19 g, Fat 7 g, Cholesterol 16 mg, Sodium 228 mg

OLD-FASHIONED BAKING POWDER BISCUITS

HONEYED SWEET POTATO BISCUITS

2 cups (480 ml) unbleached flour
1 tbs (15 ml) baking powder
½ tsp (3 ml) salt
¼ cup (60 ml) shortening
1 tbs (15 ml) grated orange peel
1 tbs (15 ml) grated lemon peel
¾ cup (180 ml) sweet potatoes,
   baked until tender, peeled
   and mashed
⅓ cup (80 ml) honey
½ cup (120 ml) approximately,
   skim milk

In large bowl, mix flour, baking powder and salt. Cut in shortening until mixture resembles peas. Add orange and lemon peels, sweet potatoes and honey and mix well. Add enough milk to make a soft, but not sticky, dough. Turn out onto floured board and knead 3-4 times. Pat to 1-inch thickness and cut out 2¼-inch rounds. Place on ungreased cookie sheet and bake at 400°F (205°C) for 15-18 minutes or until lightly browned. Yields 10 biscuits.

Approximate nutritional analysis per biscuit:
Calories 194, Protein 3 g, Carbohydrates 34 g, Fat 5 g, Cholesterol .2 mg, Sodium 270 mg

Courtesy of The National Honey Board.

MARY'S BISCOTTI DI ZIPPY WINE BISCUITS

MARY'S BISCOTTI DI ZIPPY WINE BISCUITS

2½ cups (600 ml) flour
6 tbs (90 ml) UNCLE DAVE'S
   Bloody Mary Fixin's*
1½ tbs (25 ml) baking powder
½ cup (120 ml) red wine
½ cup (120 ml) olive oil

Preheat oven to 325°F (107°C). Mix everything in a food processor until just combined. Don't overprocess. Remove and divide into 4 equal parts. Roll each into a log and slice ¼-inch thick. Place on ungreased baking sheets and bake 20-30 minutes until biscuits are lightly brown on bottom. Yields 20 biscuits.
   For extra zip, sprinkle more Blood Mary Fixin's on biscuits before baking.

*Not included in nutritional analysis due to unavailability of nutrient data.

Approximate nutritional analysis per biscuit:
Calories 124, Protein 2 g, Carbohydrates 16 g, Fat 6 g, Cholesterol 0 mg, Sodium 37 mg

SAVORY BREAKFAST BRAN MUFFINS

1¼ cups (295 ml) water
1 tbs (15 ml) ARROWHEAD MILLS
    Unrefined Vegetable Oil
1 egg or egg replacer
½ cup (120 ml) cheese, grated
½ cup (120 ml) onion, chopped
¼ cup (60 ml) green chiles,
    chopped
2 cups (480 ml) ARROWHEAD
    MILLS Bran Muffin Mix
½-1 tsp (3-5 ml) salt, optional

Preheat oven to 350°F (180°C). Mix water, oil and egg together in large bowl. Add cheese, onions and chiles. Add muffin mix and salt; stir briefly. Fill oiled muffin cups ⅔ full and bake for 30-35 minutes, or until toothpick comes out clean. Yields 12 muffins.

Approximate nutritional analysis per muffin:
Calories 126, Protein 6 g, Carbohydrates 16 g, Fat 4 g, Cholesterol 21 mg, Sodium 128 mg

SAVORY WILD RICE DINNER MUFFINS

2 cups (480 ml) ARROWHEAD
    MILLS Wild Rice Pancake &
    Waffle Mix
¼ cup (60 ml) Parmesan cheese
1 tsp (5 ml) Italian seasoning
½ tsp (3 ml) garlic powder
½ tsp (3 ml) salt, optional
1 egg or egg replacer
2 tbs (30 ml) ARROWHEAD MILLS
    Canola Oil
1½ cups (355 ml) skim milk or
    milk substitute

Preheat oven to 400°F (205°C).
    Stir dry ingredients together. Beat liquids together in separate bowl. Add dry mixture to liquids and stir well. Divide into 12 muffin cups and bake for 20 minutes, or until done. Yields 12 muffins.

Approximate nutritional analysis per muffin:
Calories 130, Protein 4 g, Carbohydrates 19 g, Fat 4 g, Cholesterol 18 mg, Sodium 96 mg

MRS. PAVICH'S ORGANIC RAISIN SCONES

2 cups (480 ml) unbleached flour
2 tsp (10 ml) baking powder
2 tbs (30 ml) granulated raw sugar,
    turbinado
½ tsp (3 ml) salt
6 tbs (90 ml) low fat margarine or
    butter, cut into small bits
1 cup (240 ml) PAVICH Organic
    Select Thompson Seedless
    Raisins
½ rind of a lemon, grated
2 large eggs, well beaten
½ cup (120 ml) plus 1 tbs (15 ml)
    skim milk

Preheat oven to 425°F (220°C). Sift flour, baking powder, 1 tbs sugar and salt into a mixing bowl. Add margarine and gently work into flour mixture with hands until coarse crumbs form. Add raisins and lemon rind. Make a well in the dough; add eggs and ½ cup milk. Mix with spoon until dough clumps together. Knead for just 30 seconds then turn onto a lightly floured surface. Cut dough in half and form each half into a ball. Flatten to form 2 circles about ¾-inch thick, 5 inches in diameter. Cut each into 8 pie-shaped wedges. Place 1 inch apart on lightly greased baking sheet. Brush with 1 tbs milk and dust with remaining sugar. Bake in center of oven for 12-15 minutes or until lightly browned. Yields 16 scones.

Approximate nutritional analysis per scone:
Calories 116, Protein 2 g, Carbohydrates 22 g, Fat 2 g, Cholesterol .3 mg, Sodium .5 mg

AMBERWAVES WHOLE WHEAT BREAD

2 tbs (30 ml) active dry yeast
1 cup (240 ml) warm water
1 cup (240 ml) skim milk, scalded and cooled
500 mg vitamin C, crushed
⅓ cup (80 ml) honey
¼ cup (60 ml) oil
2 tsp (10 ml) salt
2 eggs, beaten
5½ cups (1.3 l) AMBERWAVES BRAND Organic Whole Wheat Flour

Dissolve yeast in water. Add milk, vitamin C, honey, oil, salt, eggs and 2½ cups flour. Mix with electric hand beater for 3-4 minutes. Cover and let rise until doubled. It will be sticky and spongy. Mix in 3 cups flour and knead by hand until smooth. Cover and let rise until doubled. Punch down and shape into 2 loaves.

Place in greased, warm 7½x3½x2½-inch pans and let rise until loaves are 5¾ inches high. Bake at 375°F (190°C) for 40 minutes. Bread is done when it sounds hollow when tapped. Remove from pans immediately and cool on racks. Yields 2 loaves, 16 slices per loaf.

Approximate nutritional analysis per slice:
Calories 104, Protein 4 g, Carbohydrates 18 g, Fat 2 g, Cholesterol 12 mg, Sodium 142 mg

JERUSALEM ARTICHOKE-WHOLE WHEAT BREAD

1 pkg yeast
½ cup (120 ml) warm water
2½ cups (590 ml) hot water
2 tbs (30 ml) oil
3 tbs (45 ml) honey
1 tsp (5 ml) salt
5-6 cups (1.2-1.4 l) whole wheat flour
½ cup (120 ml) ZUMBRO Jerusalem Artichoke Flour

Dissolve yeast in warm water and let stand a few minutes. Combine hot water, oil, honey and salt in mixing bowl (hot water readily dissolves the salt, liquefies the honey and makes a warm place for the yeast). Before adding the yeast mixture, make sure the water is just warm to the touch; if it is too warm, add a little flour to cool it down. Gradually add the rest of the flour, using just enough so the dough is not sticky. Knead on floured surface for 10 minutes. Turn into oiled bowl, cover with wet cloth and let rise in warm place for 90 minutes. After raising, knead dough a few seconds and divide and shape into loaves or buns.

Place in baking pans that have been sprayed with a nonstick coating and let rise 30 minutes. Bake in 350°F (180°C) oven for 35-45 minutes. Bread is done when it sounds hollow when tapped. For a soft crust, brush bread tops with margarine. Yields 2 loaves, 16 slices per loaf.

Approximate nutritional analysis per slice:
Calories 90, Protein 3 g, Carbohydrates 18 g, Fat 1 g, Cholesterol 0 mg, Sodium 68 mg

AMBERWAVES WHOLE WHEAT BREAD

CARROT-BANANA-HONEY WHEAT BREAD

2 pkgs active dry yeast
2¼ cups (540 ml) warm water
    (105-115°F [41-46°C]), divided
3 cups (720 ml) whole wheat flour
1 cup (240 ml) carrots,
    finely shredded
1 cup (240 ml) ripe bananas,
    mashed
½ cup (120 ml) butter or margarine,
    softened
⅓ cup (80 ml) honey
1 tbs (15 ml) salt
½ tsp (3 ml) ground cinnamon
4-6 cups (960-1440 ml) all-purpose
    flour
2 tbs (30 ml) butter or margarine,
    melted

Dissolve yeast in ½ cup warm water in large bowl. Stir in whole wheat flour, remaining 1¾ cups warm water, carrots, bananas, softened butter, honey, salt and cinnamon; beat until smooth using an electric mixer. Mix enough all-purpose flour to make a soft dough.

Knead dough on lightly floured surface about 10 minutes or until smooth and elastic. Shape dough into a ball. Place in greased large bowl; turn to grease all sides. Cover bowl and set in warm place to rise about 1 hour until doubled in bulk.

Punch down dough; divide into two equal pieces. Roll each piece on lightly floured surface into 18x9-inch rectangle. Overlap the sides, folding into thirds to form 6x9-inch rectangle. Roll each piece tightly from 6-inch side, jelly-roll style. Pinch ends and seams to seal; place in greased 9x5x3-inch loaf pan. Brush tops with 2 tbs melted butter. Cover and set in warm place to rise about 1 hour or until doubled in bulk.

Bake in preheated 375°F (190°C) oven 40-45 minutes or until loaves sound hollow when tapped and crust is brown. Remove from pans and cool on wire racks. Yields 2 loaves, 16 slices per loaf.

Approximate nutritional analysis per slice:
Calories 136, Protein 4 g, Carbohydrates 22 g, Fat 4 g, Cholesterol 10 mg, Sodium 239 mg

Courtesy of The National Honey Board.

ROMAN MEAL HOMEMADE BREAD

2 cups (480 ml) ROMAN MEAL
    Cereal
⅔ cup (160 ml) nonfat dry milk
1 tbs (15 ml) salt
2 pkgs active dry yeast
5½ cups (1.3 l) all-purpose flour
⅓ cup (80 ml) honey
¼ cup (60 ml) vegetable oil
1 tbs (15 ml) molasses
2½ cups (590 ml) very warm water
    (115-120°F [46-49°C])

In large bowl blend cereal, dry milk, salt, yeast and 3 cups flour. Add honey, oil, molasses and water. Stir to mix; beat 60 strokes. Blend in remaining 2½ cups flour. On lightly floured board, knead dough until it feels springy, about 5 minutes, adding just enough flour to hands and board to prevent sticking. Grease bowl; return dough to bowl, turning once to grease top. Cover and let rise in a warm place until doubled, about 1 hour. Punch down and turn dough over. Cover and let rise 30 minutes.

Form into 2 loaves and place in well greased 9x5x3-inch loaf pans. Grease tops of loaves; cover and let rise until doubled, about 45 minutes. Bake at 400°F (205°C) for about 40 minutes. Bread is done when it sounds hollow when tapped. Remove from pans and cool on racks. Yields 2 loaves, 16 slices per loaf.

Approximate nutritional analysis per slice:
Calories 131, Protein 4 g, Carbohydrates 25 g, Fat 2 g, Cholesterol .3 mg, Sodium 209 mg

CARROT-BANANA-HONEY WHEAT BREAD

NEW EASY 7-GRAIN BREAD

1½ cups (355 ml) boiling water
1 cup (240 ml) ARROWHEAD MILLS
    7 Grain Cereal
2 pkgs dry yeast
½ cup (120 ml) warm water
6 tbs (90 ml) ARROWHEAD MILLS
    Canola Oil
½ cup (120 ml) egg replacer
    or 2 eggs, beaten
5½ cups (1.3 l) ARROWHEAD
    MILLS Whole Wheat Flour
½ cup (120 ml) honey
2 tsp (10 ml) sea salt, optional

Pour boiling water over cereal in large mixing bowl. Dissolve yeast in warm water. When cereal is lukewarm, add yeast and all remaining ingredients except 3 cups flour. Beat vigorously for 2 minutes. Work in remaining flour. Divide dough in half and spread into bottoms of two oiled loaf pans. Let rise until doubled and bake at 375°F (190°C) for 35-45 minutes. Yields 2 loaves, 16 slices per loaf.

Approximate nutritional analysis per slice:
Calories 124, Protein 4 g, Carbohydrates 22 g, Fat 3 g, Cholesterol 0 mg, Sodium 3 mg

NEW EASY 7-GRAIN BREAD

MOLASSES-WALNUT WHEAT BREAD

3-3½ cups (720-840 ml) whole
    wheat flour
1½ tsp (8 ml) salt
1½ tsp (8 ml) cinnamon
1 pkg RED STAR Active Dry Yeast
    or QUICK RISE Yeast
¾ cup (180 ml) water
3 tbs (45 ml) oil
3 tbs (45 ml) molasses
1½ tsp (8 ml) lemon juice
¼ cup (60 ml) egg whites
½ cup (120 ml) raisins
½ cup (120 ml) walnuts, chopped

In large mixing bowl, combine 1 cup flour, salt, cinnamon and yeast. Heat water, oil, molasses and lemon juice to 120-130°F (49-54°C). Add to flour mixture; beat with electric mixer 3 minutes on medium speed. Add egg whites, raisins and walnuts; beat 1 minute. By hand, stir in remaining flour to make a stiff dough. Turn out onto floured surface, knead until smooth and elastic, about 5-7 minutes. Place in greased bowl, turning to grease top. Cover; let rise in warm place about 1 hour (30 minutes for Quick Rise Yeast).

Punch down dough. On lightly floured surface, form dough into a round loaf. Place on greased cookie sheet. Cover; let rise until doubled, about 1 hour (30 minutes for Quick Rise Yeast). Bake in preheated 375°F (190°C) 35-40 minutes or until loaf sounds hollow when tapped. Remove from cookie sheet; let cool. Yields 1 loaf, 16 slices per loaf.

Approximate nutritional analysis per slice:
Calories 152, Protein 5 g, Carbohydrates 24 g, Fat 5 g, Cholesterol 0 mg, Sodium 210 mg

MOLASSES-WALNUT WHEAT BREAD

ZUCCHINI BREAD
(Bread Machine)

½ cup (120 ml) buttermilk
1 tbs (15 ml) oil
½ cup (120 ml) zucchini, grated
2 tbs (30 ml) green onion, chopped
¼ cup (60 ml) red pepper, chopped
2 tbs (30 ml) Romano cheese, grated
2 tbs (30 ml) sugar
1 tsp (5 ml) salt
½ tsp (3 ml) lemon pepper
½ cup (120 ml) oatmeal
2½ cups (590 ml) bread flour
1½ tsp (8 ml) RED STAR Active Dry
    Yeast or QUICK RISE Yeast

Select the yeast that is appropriate for your automatic bread machine. All ingredients should be at room temperature. Place ingredients in pan in the order suggested by the machine's manual. Yields 1 loaf, 16 slices per loaf.

Approximate nutritional analysis per slice:
Calories 103, Protein 3 g, Carbohydrates 19 g, Fat 2 g, Cholesterol 1 mg, Sodium 152 mg

ZUCCHINI BREAD

BEAN AND CHILI BREAD

3-3½ cups (720-840 ml) all-purpose
    flour
½ cup (120 ml) cornmeal
2 tsp (10 ml) chili powder
1 tbs (15 ml) dried onion flakes
3 tbs (45 ml) sugar
1 tsp (5 ml) salt
1 pkg RED STAR Active Dry Yeast or
    QUICK RISE Yeast
2 tbs (30 ml) canola oil
1 cup (240 ml) fat-free refried beans
¾ cup (180 ml) water
1 egg white
1 tbs (15 ml) water

In large mixing bowl, combine 1 cup flour, cornmeal, chili powder, onion flakes, sugar, salt and yeast. Heat oil, refried beans and water to 120-130°F (49-54°C). Add to flour mixture; beat with electric mixer 3 minutes on medium speed. By hand, stir in remaining flour to make a firm dough. Turn out onto a floured surface; knead until smooth and elastic about 5-7 minutes. Place in greased bowl, turning to grease top. Cover; let rise in warm place about 1 hour (30 minutes for Quick Rise Yeast).

Punch down dough. On lightly floured surface, roll dough into a 7x15-inch rectangle. Starting with shorter side, roll up tightly, pressing dough into roll with each turn. Pinch edges and ends to seal. Place in greased 9x5-inch loaf pans. Cover; let rise until double, about 45 minutes (30 minutes for Quick Rise Yeast). Brush top of loaf with mixture of egg white and water. Sprinkle generously with dried onion flakes. Bake in preheated 375°F (190°C) oven for 20-25 minutes or until loaf sounds hollow when tapped. Remove from pan and cool. Yields 1 loaf, 16 slices per loaf.

Approximate nutritional analysis per slice:
Calories 162, Protein 5 g, Carbohydrates 30 g, Fat 2 g, Cholesterol 0 mg, Sodium 271 mg

TOMATO-OLIVE BREAD

4-4½ cups (960-1080 ml) all-purpose flour
4 tbs (60 ml) sugar
2 tsp (10 ml) salt
4 tsp (20 ml) Italian seasoning or a mixture of dried oregano, basil, marjoram and parsley
1 pkg RED STAR Active Dry Yeast or QUICK RISE Yeast
1¼ cups (295 ml) water
3 tbs (45 ml) olive oil
6 sun-dried tomato halves, rehydrated
20 extra large pitted ripe olives, chopped
cornmeal

In large mixing bowl, combine 2 cups flour, sugar, salt, Italian seasoning and yeast. Heat water and oil to 120-130°F (49-54°C). Add to flour mixture. Beat with electric mixer 3 minutes on medium speed. Add tomato halves and olives; beat 1 additional minute. By hand, stir in remaining flour to make a stiff dough. Turn out onto floured surface, knead until smooth and elastic about 5-7 minutes. Place in greased bowl, turning to grease top. Cover; let rise in warm place about 1 hour (30 minutes for Quick Rise Yeast).

Punch down dough. On lightly floured surface, roll dough into a 7x15-inch rectangle. Starting with shorter side, roll up tightly, pressing dough into roll with each turn. Pinch edges and taper ends to seal. Place on greased cookie sheet sprinkled with cornmeal. Cover; let rise until doubled, about 45 minutes (30 minutes for Quick Rise Yeast). With very sharp knife, make 2-3 diagonal slashes across top of loaf. Bake in preheated 425°F (220°C) oven for 25-30 minutes or until loaf sounds hollow when tapped. Remove from cookie sheet; cool. Yields 1 loaf, 16 slices per loaf.

Approximate nutritional analysis per slice:
Calories 160, Protein 4 g, Carbohydrates 28 g, Fat 4 g, Cholesterol 0 mg, Sodium 343 mg

DUTCH DOUBLE DILL BREAD

1 pkg active dry yeast
2 cups (480 ml) water, 105-115°F (41-46°C)
2 tbs (30 ml) salad oil
3 tbs (45 ml) honey
1 cup (240 ml) plain yogurt, or dairy sour cream
2 tsp (10 ml) salt
1 tbs (15 ml) dill weed
1 tbs (15 ml) dill seeds
5 cups (1.2 l) whole wheat flour
3 cups (720 ml) rye flour

In small bowl, combine yeast and ½ cup warm water. Set aside for 5-10 minutes. Combine remaining water, salad oil, honey, yogurt, salt, dill and dill seeds in large bowl. Add yeast mixture, then whole wheat flour, a cup at a time, stirring well after each addition. Add rye flour until mixture becomes too difficult to stir. Begin kneading, adding additional flour to keep the dough from becoming too sticky. Knead for at least 10 minutes. Shape into ball. Lightly grease clean mixing bowl. Place dough in bowl, turning to grease the top. Cover. Let rise in warm, draft-free place until doubled in size.

Punch down. Turn dough out onto lightly floured board. Knead 1 minute. Shape into round loaves or place in greased 9x5x3-inch loaf pans. Cover. Let rise in warm, draft-free place until loaves are double in size, about 30 minutes. Bake at 425°F (220°C) for 15 minutes. Reduce heat to 350°F (180°C). Bake another 25-30 minutes or until bread sounds hollow when tapped. Yields 2 large loaves, 16 slices per loaf.

Approximate nutritional analysis per slice:
Calories 117, Protein 4 g, Carbohydrates 23 g, Fat 2 g, Cholesterol 1 mg, Sodium 138 mg

Courtesy of The National Honey Board.

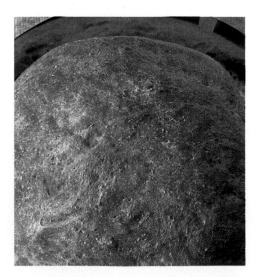

DUTCH DOUBLE DILL BREAD

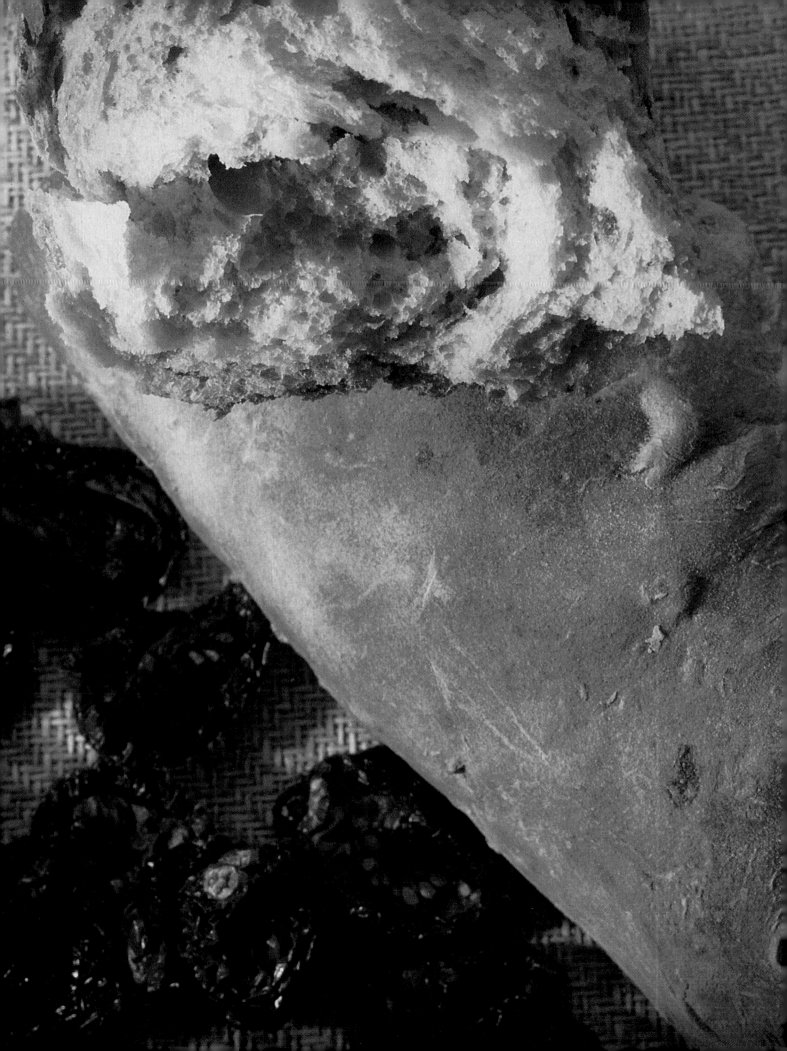

RAISED MULTIGRAIN CORN BREAD

½ cup (120 ml) yellow cornmeal
½ cup (120 ml) rolled oats
½ cup (120 ml) 100% bran cereal
¼ cup (60 ml) wheat germ
2 cups (480 ml) boiling water
2 pkgs active dry yeast
½ cup (120 ml) warm water,
    115-120°F (46-49°C)
⅓ cup (80 ml) honey
2 tbs (30 ml) butter or margarine,
    melted
1 tsp (5 ml) salt
2 cups (480 ml) whole wheat flour
3 cups (720 ml) unbleached flour

NO-NEED-TO-KNEAD PUMPERNICKEL BREAD

3 tbs (45 ml) dry yeast
⅔ cup (160 ml) warm water
2 tsp (10 ml) honey
3½ cups (840 ml) VITA-SPELT Flour
1½ cups (355 ml) rye flour
2 tbs (30 ml) molasses
⅔ cup (160 ml) warm water
1 tsp (5 ml) or less, sea salt
⅓ cup (80 ml) oat bran
1⅓ cup (320 ml) water, warm
½ tbs (8 ml) butter
1 tbs (15 ml) sesame seeds, unhulled

In a 1-quart glass measuring cup or bowl, combine cornmeal, oats, bran and wheat germ. Pour in boiling water. Stir thoroughly. Set aside to cool. Place yeast in large mixing bowl. Add warm water. Stir to dissolve yeast. Add honey, butter and salt. Mix thoroughly. Add cooled cornmeal mixture. Stir until smooth. Stir in whole wheat flour. Gradually add unbleached flour, one cup at a time, until mixture is stiff enough to knead, about 2½ cups. Sprinkle remaining flour on board. Knead dough for 10-12 minutes until smooth. Add additional flour as necessary. Shape dough into ball. Lightly grease a clean mixing bowl. Place dough in warm draft-free place until doubled in size, about 1½ hours.

Punch dough down to remove air bubbles. Turn out onto lightly floured board. Divide dough in half. Shape each half into a round loaf. Place loaves on a large lightly greased cookie sheet or 2 pie plates. Cover. Place in warm, draft-free place until doubled in size, about 1 hour. Bake in preheated oven at 350°F (180°C) for 40-50 minutes or until bread sounds hollow when tapped. Remove loaves from cookie sheet. Cool on wire racks. Yields 2 loaves, 16 slices per loaf.

Approximate nutritional analysis per slice:
Calories 105, Protein 3 g, Carbohydrates 21 g, Fat 1 g, Cholesterol 2 mg, Sodium 82 mg

Courtesy of The National Honey Board.

NO-NEED-TO-KNEAD PUMPERNICKEL BREAD

Sprinkle yeast over ⅔ cup warm water. Add honey and stir. Warm flours by placing in a 250°F (121°C) oven for 20 minutes. Combine molasses with the next ⅔ cup warm water. Combine the yeast mixture with the molasses mixture. Stir into warmed flour. Add salt, oat bran and the remaining 1⅓ cup water. Butter a loaf pan; turn in dough. Sprinkle with sesame seeds. Let rise to top of pan. Bake at 400°F (205°C) for approximately 35 minutes or until tested done. Let cool on a rack for at least 10 minutes before removing. Yields 1 loaf, 16 slices per loaf.

Approximate nutritional analysis per slice:
Calories 141, Protein 5 g, Carbohydrates 29 g, Fat 1 g, Cholesterol 1 mg, Sodium 139 mg

HARVEST SPELT BREAD

2 pkgs active dry yeast
½ cup (120 ml) warm water,
   110-115°F (43-46°C)
1 cup (240 ml) warm milk,
   110-115°F (43-46°C)
2 tbs (30 ml) butter, melted
½ cup (120 ml) maple syrup
1 egg, beaten
3 cup (720 ml) Whole Grain
   VITA-SPELT Flour
1 tsp (5 ml) cinnamon
1 tsp (5 ml) allspice
½ tsp (3 ml) salt
1 16-oz can (480 g) pumpkin
3 cups (720 ml) White
   VITA-SPELT Flour

Dissolve yeast in the warm water. Separately, combine warm milk, melted butter, maple syrup, and egg. Combine whole grain spelt flour, spices and salt. Add milk mixture and spelt mixture to the dissolved yeast. Add pumpkin and mix thoroughly. Add the white spelt flour, as needed, to form a dough. Turn onto a lightly floured surface and knead until slightly elastic, 3-5 minutes. Cover and let rise until doubled.

Punch down and divide in half. Shape into 2 loaves, round or oblong. Cover again and allow to rise until doubled. Bake in a 350°F (180°C) oven for approximately 45 minutes or until loaves sound hollow when tapped. Yields 2 loaves, 16 slices per loaf.

Approximate nutritional analysis per slice:
Calories 110, Protein 4 g, Carbohydrates 22 g, Fat 2 g, Cholesterol 8 mg, Sodium 48 mg

SWEDISH RYE BREAD

2 cups (480 ml) milk, scalded
   and cooled
2 tsp (10 ml) salt
1-2 tbs (15-30 ml) caraway seeds
¼ cup (60 ml) maple syrup
2 tbs (30 ml) mild molasses
1 pkg active dry yeast dissolved in
   ¼ cup (60 ml) warm water
2 cups (480 ml) rye flour
3 tbs (45 ml) oil or melted
   shortening
3-4 cups (720-960 ml) white flour

Combine milk, salt, caraway, maple syrup and molasses in mixing bowl. Add yeast (dissolved in water) and the rye flour. Beat until smooth, about 75 strokes. Cover, let stand until bubbly and foamy, 1-2 hours or overnight. Stir down; add oil. Gradually work in white flour until a stiff dough is formed. Knead thoroughly until smooth. Let rise until doubled in bulk. Punch down, let rise again until doubled. Bake at 375°F (190°C) about 35-40 minutes, until loaf sounds hollow when tapped. Remove from pans and cool on rack. Yields 2 medium loaves, 16 slices per loaf.

Approximate nutritional analysis per slice:
Calories 94, Protein 2 g, Carbohydrates 17 g, Fat 2 g, Cholesterol 1 mg, Sodium 142 mg

Courtesy of the Michigan Maple Syrup Association and Cooperative Extension Services Michigan State University.

MILLET BREAD

1 cup (240 ml) buttermilk or
   plain yogurt
¼ cup (60 ml) butter
1 tbs (15 ml) honey
1 pkg active dry yeast
¼ cup (60 ml) warm water
2 eggs
2 cups (480 ml) ARROWHEAD
   MILLS Millet Flour
½ cup (120 ml) ARROWHEAD
   MILLS Low Fat Soy Flour

Combine yogurt and butter in saucepan, heating slowly to melt butter. Dissolve yeast and honey in the warm water; add yogurt mixture and blend. Beat in eggs; add flours and beat well. Pour into well-oiled 4x8-inch loaf pan and let rise for 45 minutes. Bake at 375°F (190°C) for 40-45 minutes or until loaf sounds hollow when tapped. Cool before cutting. Yields 1 loaf, 16 slices per loaf.

Approximate nutritional analysis per slice:
Calories 110, Protein 5 g, Carbohydrates 16 g, Fat 4 g, Cholesterol 32 mg, Sodium 53 mg

KAMUT BREAD I

Unlike common wheat bread, Kamut Brand Flour doesn't invite the addition of seeds or other coarse-grained foods which could inhibit the gluten's ability to rise. Making Kamut Bread is like making any bread, however, its dough is a little slower in absorbing water and it requires a few extra minutes of kneading time. Also, because the gluten from Kamut Brand wheat is more compact, it forms a better bread when baked in smaller loaves. To bake in a large loaf pan, form the dough into 2 small loaves, place them end-to-end in the pan and bake as normal.

2 tsp (10 ml) active dry yeast
2½ cups (590 ml) warm water
2 tbs (30 ml) olive oil, optional
2 tsp (10 ml) salt
6½ cups (1.6 l) KAMUT BRAND
    Flour, plus extra for kneading

VARIATION:
1½ tbs (25 ml) dried mustard
    powder
1 tbs (15 ml) ground cumin
¼ tsp (1 ml) turmeric

Place the yeast and warm water in a large mixing bowl and let stand until the yeast softens, about 5 minutes. Whisk in the oil, salt and 2 cups of the flour. Mix until uniform. Continue to incorporate the flour, a cup or two at a time, into the yeast mixture. Beat with a wooden spoon until smooth. Knead on a floured surface for 20 minutes, occasionally slam the dough down vigorously to develop the gluten.

Place the dough in a large bowl, cover tightly with plastic wrap and let rise until doubled, about 1½ hours. The dough will have spring but be more dense than a conventional wheat loaf.

Punch the dough down, divide into 2 loaves and allow to rest for 5 minutes. Knead it briefly, shape into 2 rounded loaves and place in well-oiled bread pans, 5½x4 inches, or form 2 small loaves in one oversize 9x5-inch pan. Allow to rise for 30-45 minutes or until it arches over the top of the pans. Bake in a preheated oven at 425°F (220°C) for 10 minutes. Reduce heat and bake for about an hour or until the crust is golden, the loaf comes easily out of the pan and sounds hollow when thumped on the bottom. Cool on a rack. Yields 2 loaves, 16 slices per loaf.

Variation: To enhance this bread's golden color, and to give it an intriguing flavor, mix in the dried mustard powder, ground cumin and turmeric with the initial 2 cups of flour before adding it to the yeast and water.

Approximate nutritional analysis per slice:
Calories 97, Protein 3 g, Carbohydrates 20 g, Fat 1 g, Cholesterol 0 mg, Sodium 133 mg

KAMUT BREAD II (no yeast! no eggs!)

4 cups (960 ml) KAMUT BRAND
    Flour
2 cups (480 ml) water
1 pinch vitamin C crystals,
    or crush a tablet
3 tbs (45 ml) honey
¾ cup (180 ml) oil
½ tsp (3 ml) cream of tartar

Whisk 2 cups flour, water, vitamin C, honey and oil together for about 15 minutes. Cover the bowl with damp cloth overnight or 10 hours. Mix 1 cup flour into mixture until mix is elastic, and knead for about 20 minutes, then leave for one hour. Then mix rest of ingredients and again knead until gluten is developed, as much as 30 minutes. Put in loaf tin, cover and leave rise for ½ day. Bake 40 minutes at 350°F (180°C). Use toothpick to test.
Yields 1 large loaf, 16 slices per loaf.

Approximate nutritional analysis per slice:
Calories 212, Protein 4 g, Carbohydrates 28 g, Fat 11 g, Cholesterol 0 mg, Sodium 0 mg

QUICK BUNS

1¾ cups (415 ml) warm water
½ cup (120 ml) oil
¼ cup (60 ml), heaping, sugar
3 tbs (45 ml) yeast
1½ tsp (8 ml) salt
2 eggs
5¼ cups (1.3 l) AMBERWAVES
    BRAND Organic Whole Wheat
    Flour

Mix together water, oil, sugar and yeast and let stand 15 minutes. Add salt, eggs and flour. Mix well and shape into buns. Let stand 15 minutes. Bake at 425°F (220°C) for 10 minutes.
Yields 2 dozen buns.

Approximate nutritional analysis per bun:
Calories 145, Protein 4 g, Carbohydrates 22 g, Fat 5 g, Cholesterol 16 mg, Sodium 140 mg

WHOLE WHEAT CRESCENT ROLLS

½ cup (120 ml) honey
½ cup (120 ml) hot water
2 tbs (30 ml) yeast
½ cup (120 ml) dry potato flakes
1½ cups (355 ml) warm water
1 tsp (5 ml) salt
3 tbs (45 ml) shortening
⅔ cup (160 ml) dry instant milk
5-5½ cups (1.2-1.3 l) AMBERWAVES BRAND Organic Whole Wheat Flour
½ cup (120 ml) softened butter or margarine

In small bowl dissolve honey in ½ cup hot water. Stir in yeast. Let stand 15 minutes. Mix together potato flakes, remaining water, salt, shortening and dry milk. Mix in 2 cups of the flour. Beat 5 minutes. Add yeast mixture and beat 1 minute longer. Add remaining flour. Knead until smooth and elastic.

Divide dough in half. On lightly floured surface roll each half into a 12-inch circle. Spread ¼ cup margarine on each circle. Cut each circle into 12 wedges. Roll each wedge, starting with wide edge and rolling towards point. Place point down on greased baking sheet about 2 inches apart. Let sit for 20 minutes. Bake at 350°F (180°C) for 12-15 minutes. Yields 24 rolls.

Approximate nutritional analysis per roll:
Calories 166, Protein 4 g, Carbohydrates 26 g, Fat 6 g, Cholesterol 11 mg, Sodium 141 mg

WHOLE WHEAT CRESCENT ROLLS

HOLIDAY DINNER ROLLS

2 tbs (30 ml) dry yeast
¾ cup (180 ml) warm water
¼ cup (60 ml) honey
¼ tsp (1 ml) sea salt, optional
¼ cup (60 ml) vegetable oil plus enough water to make ⅓ cup (80 ml) liquid
1 egg
   or ¼ cup (60 ml) egg replacer
½ cup (120 ml) prepared ARROWHEAD MILLS Potato Flakes
1½ cups (355 ml) ARROWHEAD MILLS Whole Wheat Flour
2 cups (480 ml) unbleached white flour

Dissolve yeast in warm water in large bowl. Leave until bubbly, about 10 minutes. Add honey, salt, oil, egg, potatoes and half of flours. Beat thoroughly. Add enough flour to make manageable dough. Turn out onto lightly floured board and knead for 10 minutes until dough is smooth and elastic. Place in lightly oiled bowl, turning once to coat. Set in warm place and let rise for 1 hour.

Punch down, turn onto floured board and shape into desired shape of roll. Place rolls on greased cookie sheet. Cover lightly with plastic or cotton towel and place in warm place to rise until light, about 20-30 minutes. Bake at 375°F (190°C) for 15-20 minutes. Yields 2 dozen rolls.

Approximate nutritional analysis per roll:
Calories 101, Protein 3 g, Carbohydrates 17 g, Fat 3 g, Cholesterol 8 mg, Sodium 4 mg

HOLIDAY DINNER ROLLS

TOASTED AMARANTH ROLLS

1½ cups (355 ml) lukewarm water
1½ tbs (25 ml) ARROWHEAD
    MILLS Unrefined Vegetable Oil
3 tbs (45 ml) honey or maple syrup
1½ tsp (8 ml) sea salt, optional
1½ tsp (8 ml) active dry yeast
1 cup (240 ml) ARROWHEAD MILLS
    Amaranth Flour
2¼ cups (540 ml) ARROWHEAD
    MILLS Whole Wheat Flour
soft butter, optional
honey, optional
cinnamon, optional
chopped nuts, optional
raisins, optional
dried lemon peel, optional
toasted amaranth seeds, optional

Mix first 5 ingredients together, then stir in flours. Roll dough onto a lightly floured surface, about ¼-inch thick. Brush with butter and sprinkle with remaining ingredients, except amaranth seeds. Toast seeds in a dry skillet until lightly browned. Roll up dough and slice 2 inches thick. Place on sides, close together in an oiled pan. Sprinkle with amaranth seeds and bake at 350°F (180°C) for 30-40 minutes. Yields 24 rolls.

Approximate nutritional analysis per roll:
Calories 85, Protein 3 g, Carbohydrates 16 g, Fat 2 g, Cholesterol 0 mg, Sodium 3 mg

AMARANTH RYE STICKS

1 pkg active dry yeast
1½ cups (355 ml) warm water
1 tbs (15 ml) nonfat dry milk
1 tbs (15 ml) molasses
½ tsp (3 ml) sea salt, optional
3¼ cups (780 ml) ARROWHEAD
    MILLS Rye Flour
½ cup (120 ml) ARROWHEAD
    MILLS Amaranth Flour
1 tsp (5 ml) caraway seeds
ARROWHEAD MILLS Sesame
    Seeds, optional

Dissolve yeast in warm water; stir in milk, molasses and salt. Add all flours. Stir in caraway seeds. Knead dough about 5 minutes. Cut into 36 pieces and roll into sticks approximately 5 inches long. Roll in sesame seeds. Place on an oiled baking sheet, spray with water, then bake at 425°F (220°C) for 18-20 minutes or until lightly browned. Yields 36 sticks.

Approximate nutritional analysis per stick:
Calories 45, Protein 1 g, Carbohydrates 9 g, Fat .4 g, Cholesterol 0 mg, Sodium 2 mg

AMARANTH RYE STICKS

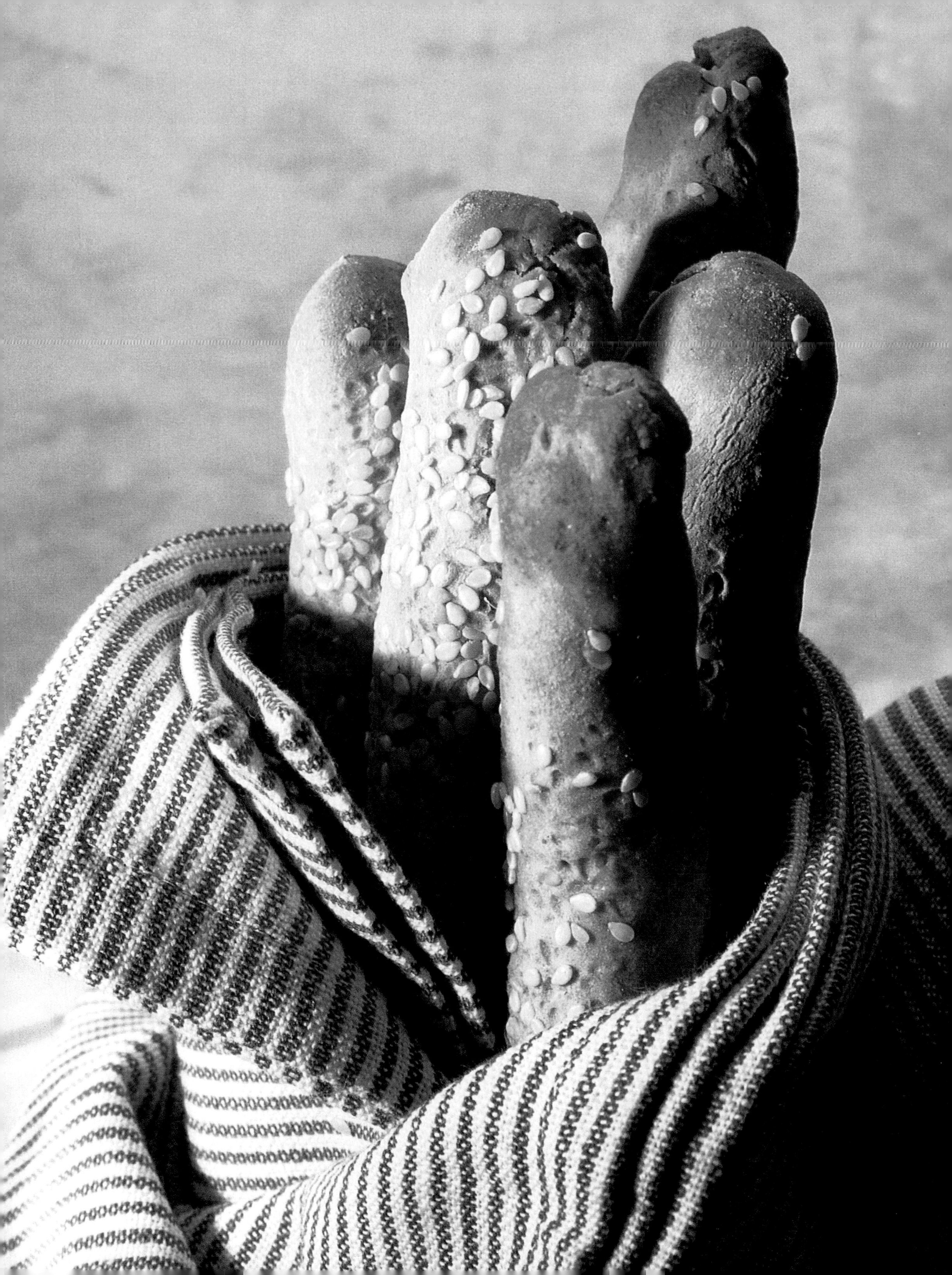

KAMUT SICILIAN-STYLE PIZZA

1 tbs (15 ml) active dry yeast
2½ cups (590 ml) warm water
2 tsp (10 ml) salt
2 tbs (30 ml) olive oil
2 lbs (910 g) KAMUT BRAND Flour

WHOLE WHEAT PIZZA CRUST

1 tbs (15 ml) yeast
1½ cups (355 ml) warm water
3 cups (720 ml) AMBERWAVES
    BRAND Organic Whole Wheat
    Flour
1½ tsp (8 ml) salt
1 tsp (5 ml) honey
cornmeal, optional

Place the yeast in warm water in a large mixing bowl and let stand for 10 minutes or until foam develops.

Mix in the salt, oil and 1 cup of flour at a time into the yeast mixture. Beat vigorously with a wooden spoon until smooth. Knead on a floured surface for 15 minutes or for 600 strokes. To help the gluten develop, vigorously punch the dough a few times with your fist or slam the dough on the board.

Place the dough in a lightly oiled bowl, cover tightly with plastic wrap and let rise until doubled, about 1½ hours. The dough should be springy and soft.

Divide the dough in half. Roll the dough, or stretch with your fingers, to cover 2 14x11-inch or 15-inch diameter, greased baking pans. Cover the dough with your choice of pizza toppings. Bake in a 450°F (230°C) oven for 20-30 minutes. Yields 2 15-inch diameter crusts or 2 14x11-inch crusts, 8 slices per crust.

Variations: Use this recipe to make small loaves of bread or dinner rolls. The unique gluten found in Kamut Brand Grain performs best in flat breads or in small loaves which do not contain chunky ingredients, such as dried fruits, nuts, seeds or whole grains.

Approximate nutritional analysis per slice w/o topping:
Calories 223, Protein 8 g, Carbohydrates 47 g, Fat 3 g, Cholesterol 0 mg, Sodium 267 mg

WHOLE WHEAT PIZZA CRUST

Dissolve yeast in water. Mix together all ingredients, except cornmeal. Beat vigorously with fork until smooth. Let rise until double. Shape into 2 greased pizza, or 11x14½-inch, pans. Lightly oil dough before putting on sauce to prevent dough from becoming soggy. Bake topped pizza at 425°F (220°C) for 20 minutes. Yields 2 crusts, 8 slices per crust.

For crispier crust, sprinkle cornmeal on greased pan before laying down the dough.

Approximate nutritional analysis per slice w/o topping:
Calories 79, Protein 3 g, Carbohydrates 17 g, Fat .4 g, Cholesterol 0 mg, Sodium 201 mg

KAMUT SICILIAN-STYLE PIZZA

SECRET SOURDOUGH BISCUITS

SOURDOUGH STARTER MIX:
3 cups (720 ml) milk, scalded
2 tbs (30 ml) plain yogurt
1 cup (240 ml) flour

BISCUITS:
6 cups (1.4 l) OLD SAVANNAH Whole Wheat or Unbleached White Flour
3 tbs (45 ml) sugar
1 tbs (15 ml) baking powder
1 tbs (15 ml) salt
1 tbs (15 ml) dry yeast
½ cup (120 ml) warm water
pinch sugar
1 cup (240 ml) Crisco
1½ cups (35 ml) Sourdough Starter Mix
1½ cups (355 ml) buttermilk

Sourdough Starter Mix: Cool 2 cups scalded milk to 80-90°F (27-32°C) and add yogurt. Let mixture sit in a warm place for two days until it appears to be like runny yogurt. Then add 1 cup cooled scalded milk and flour. Let mixture sit for a couple of days. Continue to replenish weekly with equal parts of scalded milk and flour to keep starter going. Yields 4 cups.

Biscuits: Sift together flour, sugar, baking powder and salt. In a separate container add dry yeast to warm water and sugar; cut in Crisco to "pea" size. Mix in Sourdough Starter with buttermilk. Add the yeast to this and stir. Mix liquids into the flour mixture. It should be sticky but not too moist. Flour hands and remove about half of dough to a floured surface. Pat out to ¾-inch thickness. Cut biscuits and place on a greased baking sheet. Let rise for a few minutes. Bake in 400°F (205°C) oven for about 17 minutes. These biscuits freeze very well. Yields 4 dozen biscuits.

Approximate nutritional analysis per biscuit:
Calories 101, Protein 3 g, Carbohydrates 13 g, Fat 5 g, Cholesterol .4 mg, Sodium 176 mg

SECRET SOURDOUGH BISCUITS

KAMUT FLATBREAD

2 cups (480 ml) KAMUT BRAND Flour
½ tsp (3 ml) sea salt
1 tbs (15 ml) sugar or sucanat
2 tsp (10 ml) baking powder
1 cup (240 ml) plain nonfat yogurt
2 tbs (30 ml) canola oil

Preheat oven to 450°F (230°C). Mix in flour, sea salt, sugar or sucanat and baking powder in a medium bowl. Add yogurt and oil. Stir until the flour is moistened and a smooth stiff dough forms. Turn the dough onto a greased baking sheet. Form the dough into a round loaf 8 inches in diameter and ½-inch thick. Prick the top with a fork. Bake for 10-15 minutes until loaf is browned. Cut into wedges and serve warm. Yields 1 round loaf, 8 servings per loaf.

Approximate nutritional analysis per serving:
Calories 164, Protein 6 g, Carbohydrates 29 g, Fat 4 g, Cholesterol .6 mg, Sodium 279 mg

KAMUT FLATBREAD

KAMUT INDIAN FRY BREAD

2 cups (480 ml) KAMUT BRAND
    Flour
3 tbs (45 ml) honey
    or 2 tbs (45 ml) date sugar
1 tsp (3 ml) baking powder, optional
1 tsp (5 ml) orsa salt
water
canola, safflower or vegetable oil
    for frying

Combine first 4 ingredients and add enough water until it forms a stiff dough ball. Pinch off approximately 2 tbs of dough. Pat out to make a round flat patty. Poke a hole in the middle with a fork. Be sure to keep fingers, counter and dough ball well floured or it will get sticky. Fry in about 1 inch of oil until golden, turning only once. Drain on napkin, repeat for rest of dough. Delicious with meat or veggies or great hot with honey. Also with sprouts as a sandwich. Yields 16 fry breads.

Approximate nutritional analysis per serving:
Calories 67, Protein 2 g, Carbohydrates 16 g, Fat 3 g, Cholesterol 0 mg, Sodium 133 mg

RHUBARB PATCH MUFFINS

¾ cup (180 ml) ROMAN MEAL
    Cereal
1½ cups (355 ml) all-purpose flour
1 tbs (15 ml) baking powder
¼ cup (60 ml) sugar
1 tsp (5 ml) cinnamon, optional
½ tsp (3 ml) salt, optional
1 egg, slightly beaten
¾ cup (180 ml) apple juice
¼ cup (60 ml) vegetable oil
1 cup (240 ml) Rhubarb Sauce

RHUBARB SAUCE:
1 qt (960 ml) fresh rhubarb,
    chopped
¾ cup (180 ml) sugar

Heat oven to 400°F (205°C). In a large bowl stir together dry ingredients. In a medium bowl mix egg, apple juice, oil and Rhubarb Sauce. Stir egg mixture into dry ingredients, mixing just enough to moisten, batter will be lumpy. Spoon evenly into 12 greased or paper-lined 2½-inch muffin cups. Bake 20-25 minutes or until golden brown. Yields 12 muffins.

Rhubarb Sauce: In medium saucepan combine rhubarb and sugar. Cover and cook over medium heat until sugar is dissolved and fruit is tender, about 5 minutes. Stir until smooth. Cool.

Approximate nutritional analysis per muffin:
Calories 231, Protein 3 g, Carbohydrates 45 g, Fat 5 g, Cholesterol 16 mg, Sodium 209 mg

SMOKED TOFU CANAPÉS

12 garlic cloves, unpeeled
1 tbs (15 ml) olive oil
6 oz (180 g) SOY DELI Hickory
    Smoke Flavored Baked Tofu
3 slices bread
1 cup (240 ml) small mushrooms
¼ tsp salt

Sprinkle unpeeled garlic cloves with olive oil and wrap in aluminum foil. Bake in a moderate oven until tender, about 20-30 minutes. Slice tofu into 12 thin slices, 1 for each canapé. Cut out bread circles large enough to fit the tofu slices. Sauté the bread on one side in olive oil over low heat in a skillet until golden brown. Sauté small mushrooms in olive oil over medium-high heat until tender and brown. Season with salt. Layer canapés by squeezing out the garlic "meat" from each clove onto a bread circle, spreading with a knife. Top each circle with a slice of tofu and a mushroom. Place on a cookie sheet and bake for 3-4 minutes at 400°F (205°C). Serve while hot. Yields 12 canapés.

Approximate nutritional analysis per canapé:
Calories 57, Protein 4 g, Carbohydrates .3 g, Fat 2 g, Cholesterol .2 mg,
Sodium 81 mg

EXOTIC DRIED FRUIT MIX

1 3-oz pkg (90 g) FRIEDA'S Coconut
    Shreds
½ cup (120 ml) FRIEDA'S Dried
    Jackfruit, slivered or whole
½ cup (120 ml) FRIEDA'S Dried
    Bing Cherries
¼ cup (60 ml) FRIEDA'S Dried
    Starfruit
2 tbs (30 ml) FRIEDA'S Crystallized
    Ginger, chopped
1 tbs (15 ml) FRIEDA'S Dried
    Blueberries
1 tbs (15 ml) FRIEDA'S Dried
    Cranberries

Mix all ingredients together. Store in an airtight container. Yields 3 cups, serves 6.

Approximate nutritional analysis per ½ cup serving:
Calories 100, Protein .9 g, Carbohydrates 14 g, Fat 5 g, Cholesterol 0 mg,
Sodium 38 mg

ASIAN PARTY MIX

1 4-oz pkg (120 g) FRIEDA'S Crispy
    Noodles
1 cup (240 ml) unsalted dry-roasted
    peanut halves
1 cup (240 ml) FRIEDA'S Dried
    Persimmons, Crystallized Pine
    apple or Crystallized Ginger,
    or a combination of all
1 cup (240 ml) dried apricots,
    chopped
½ cup (120 ml) shredded coconut
3 tbs (45 ml) melted butter or
    margarine
1 tbs (15 ml) sesame seeds

In a large bowl stir together the noodles, peanuts, dried fruit and coconut. Drizzle melted butter over; toss to coat. Sprinkle sesame seeds over mixture; toss again. Spread mixture out on an ungreased 15x10-inch jelly roll pan. Toast at 350°F (180°C) for 10-15 minutes or until hot; stirring occasionally. Turn mixture out onto paper towels to cool. Yields 5 cups, serves 10.

Approximate nutritional analysis per ½ cup serving:
Calories 273, Protein 6 g, Carbohydrates 31 g, Fat 16 g, Cholesterol 9 mg,
Sodium 128 mg

SPICY OVEN-TOASTED ALMONDS WITH TAMARI

4 tsp (20 ml) SPECTRUM WORLD EATS Asian Oil
2 tsp (10 ml) tamari soy sauce
4 oz (120 g) raw almonds

Preheat oven to 450°F (230°C). Combine oil and tamari in a small bowl. Add the almonds, stir to coat thoroughly. Let stand for 10 minutes. Place the nuts on a baking sheet then place in a preheated oven for 5 minutes. Remove and serve warm or room temperature. Serves 4.

Approximate nutritional analysis per serving:
Calories 208, Protein 6 g, Carbohydrates 592 g, Fat 19 g, Cholesterol 0 mg, Sodium 138 mg

ROSEMARY VEGETABLE FOCCACIA BREAD

1 lb (455 g) frozen bread dough, thawed
olive oil spray
1 tbs (15 ml) GREEN HOUSE Fresh Rosemary, finely chopped
½ onion, minced
½ cup (120 ml) prepared pasta sauce
2 zucchini thinly sliced
½ lb (230 g) mushrooms, sliced
½ cup (120 ml) red bell pepper, chopped
½ cup (120 ml) green pepper, chopped
3 tomatoes, thinly sliced
¼ cup (60 ml) Parmesan cheese, grated

Place bread dough on lightly floured surface. Flatten slightly and spray with olive oil spray. Sprinkle with fresh rosemary and onion and knead well to mix thoroughly. Roll out dough to a 9x6-inch rectangle. Place on 12x9-inch baking sheet. Press dough out until it fills pan. Spray pan with olive oil spray. Bake at 400°F (205°C) for 10 minutes. Remove bread from oven. Top with sauce then layer zucchini, mushrooms and peppers. Top with tomatoes and cheese. Return to oven and bake 10-15 minutes. Serves 12.

Approximate nutritional analysis per serving:
Calories 136, Protein 5 g, Carbohydrates 24 g, Fat 2 g, Cholesterol 3 mg, Sodium 295 mg

OUTSTANDING POPCORN

1 cup (240 ml) popcorn
1 tsp (5 ml) CALIFORNIA CLASSICS Sesame Oil, Garlic Oil or Fra Diavalo Oil
salt, to taste, optional

Drizzle or pop hot popcorn with oil. Season with salt. Serves 1.

Approximate nutritional analysis per serving:
Calories 70, Protein 1 g, Carbohydrates 6 g, Fat 5 g, Cholesterol 0 mg, Sodium .3 mg

ROSEMARY VEGETABLE FOCCACIA BREAD

UNCLE'S DAVE'S EASY NUTS

3 tbs (45 ml) UNCLE DAVE'S Honey
3 tbs (45 ml) UNCLE DAVE'S
    Bloody Mary Fixin's*
1-2 tbs (15-30 ml) warm water
2 cups (480 ml) shelled almonds

Preheat oven to 375°F (190°C). Mix honey and fixin's to form a paste. Add just enough water to make paste spreadable. Add almonds and toss to coat well. Spread on an ungreased cookie sheet and bake 10 minutes. After 5 minutes check and loosen with a spatula. When done, allow to cool slightly before removing from sheet. If they stick, put back in warm oven for a minute. Store in airtight container. Yields 2 cups, serves 8.

Not included in the nutritional anlaysis due to unavailabilty of nutrient data.

Approximate nutritional analysis per serving w/o Bloody Mary Fixin's.
Calories 233, Protein 7 g, Carbohydrates 14 g, Fat 19 g, Cholesterol 0 mg, Sodium 4 mg

FLAVOR CRUMBLES SNACK MIX

3 cups (720 ml) ARROWHEAD
    MILLS Nature Os, Puffed Rice,
    Puffed Wheat, Puffed Millet
    and popped Popcorn in any
    combination
1½ cups (355 ml) peanuts,
    sunflower seeds, pumpkin seeds
    or sesame seeds or any
    combination
6 tbs (90 ml) ARROWHEAD MILLS
    Fresh! Oil

SEASONING:
2 tsp (10 ml) garlic powder
1 tsp (5 ml) dried oregano
1 tsp (5 ml) dried basil
    or a combination of: onion
    powder, soy sauce, chili powder,
    Italian seasoning, grated
Parmesan cheese

Mix cereals and seeds together. Stir desired seasoning into oil and combine with dry mix. Spread mixture onto an ungreased baking sheet and bake at 250°F (121°C) for 20 minutes. Serve as snacks or as a garnish on soups, salads or pasta. Yields 4½ cups, serves 18.

Approximate nutritional analysis per ¼ cup serving:
Calories 122, Protein 3 g, Carbohydrates 5 g, Fat 11 g, Cholesterol 0 mg, Sodium 1 mg

BUCKWHEAT PRETZELS

BUCKWHEAT PRETZELS

3½ cups (840 ml) all-purpose flour
⅔ cup (160 ml) THE BIRKETT
    MILLS Light or Whole
    Buckwheat Flour
2 tsp (10 ml) salt
2 eggs
1 cup (240 ml) milk
1 egg white, slightly beaten
sesame seeds, poppy seeds
    and/or coarse salt

In large bowl, mix two flours and salt. Add eggs and milk, blend to form a medium-soft dough. Knead dough on a floured board for a few minutes. Place dough into a sealed container or zipper-top plastic bag; let rest for about 20 minutes. Cut dough into 12-16 pieces, depending upon pretzel size you prefer. Roll each piece into a rope and twist into desired shape. Place pretzels on a lightly oiled baking sheet, brush with egg white. Sprinkle with salt, sesame or poppy seeds. Bake at 425°F (220°C) for 15-20 minutes. Serve warm. Yields 14 pretzels.

Approximate nutritional analysis per pretzel:
Calories 146, Protein 5 g, Carbohydrates 28 g, Fat 1 g, Cholesterol 27 mg, Sodium 326 mg

SPICY INDIAN SNACK

½ cup (120 ml) small red lentils
1½ cups (355 ml) water
1 tbs (15 ml) canola oil
1½ tsp (8 ml) curry powder
½ cup (120 ml) raw cashew pieces
¼ cup (60 ml) shelled unsalted
   pistachios
¼ tsp (1 ml) sea salt
2 cups (480 ml) EREWHON KAMUT
   Flakes
1 cup (240 ml) EREWHON Crispy
   Brown Rice Cereal

Rinse the red lentils and place in a medium size bowl. Add the water and allow to soak for 1-2 hours or until beans have swollen and absorbed some water.

Drain lentils well. Heat a 9-inch or 10-inch skillet. Add the oil and heat briefly over medium-high heat. Add the curry powder and cook for 15 seconds. Add the drained lentils, stirring to coat with oil and spices. Cook, stirring constantly, for 3 minutes. Add the cashew pieces and continue to cook for another 5 minutes. Reduce heat if necessary to prevent burning of lentils and nuts.

Stir in pistachios, salt and flakes. Cook another 5 minutes. The flakes will get slightly toasted. Add the cereal and cook for 2 minutes more. Remove snack from skillet to a large tray, plate or pizza pan. Let cool completely before storing in an airtight container. Serves 12.

This spicy concoction can be eaten simply as a snack or can be a crunchy addition to an Indian meal.

Approximate nutritional analysis per serving:
Calories 123, Protein 5 g, Carbohydrates 16 g, Fat 5 g, Cholesterol 0 mg, Sodium 80 mg

SHRIMP WONTONS

3 tbs (45 ml) oil
1 clove garlic, minced
1 medium onion, minced
1 egg, beaten
¼ cup (60 ml) bread crumbs
½ lb (230 g) shrimp or chicken,
   diced
3 tbs (45 ml) soy sauce
12-oz pkg (360 g) NASOYA Won Ton
   Wrappers (40 wrappers)

Heat oil in skillet to medium heat. Sauté onion and garlic until transparent. Add tofu and shrimp or chicken. Sauté for 3 minutes. Take mixture out of skillet. Place in bowl with bread crumbs; add soy sauce and beaten egg and mix together. Place a teaspoon of mixture into each won ton wrapper and deep fry until golden brown; or drop into soup and simmer for 5 minutes.
Yields 40 wontons.

Approximate nutritional analysis per wonton:
Calories 50, Protein 3 g, Carbohydrates 6 g, Fat 2 g, Cholesterol 17 mg, Sodium 146 mg

SHRIMP WONTONS

Opposite: SPICY INDIAN SNACK

STUFFED SPINACH WONTONS

1 tbs (15 ml) oil
1 small clove garlic, minced
2 carrots, finely chopped
1 medium onion, minced
2 cups (480 ml) chopped spinach
3 tbs (45 ml) sesame seeds
1 egg
½ cup (120 ml) bread crumbs
½ tsp (3 ml) fresh ground ginger, optional
1 tbs (15 ml) sherry
3 tbs (45 ml) soy sauce
12-oz pkg (360 g) NASOYA Won Ton Wrappers (40 wrappers)

Combine first six ingredients and sauté at medium heat for 5 minutes. Combine in a bowl with next six ingredients. Fill wonton wrappers and deep fry until brown. Yields 40 wontons.

Approximate nutritional analysis per wonton:
Calories 43, Protein 2 g, Carbohydrates 7 g, Fat 1 g, Cholesterol 5 mg, Sodium 142 mg

MUSHROOM STUFFED MUSHROOMS

22-24 whole regular mushrooms, about 1-1½ inches wide, cleaned and stems removed
2 tbs (30 ml) butter
1 clove garlic, minced
4 oz (120 g) FRIEDA'S Fresh or Dried Mushrooms, such as fresh Japanese Honey Mushrooms, Oyster, Pom Pom, Shiitake or Wood Ear, or reconstituted dried Cepes, Morels, Shiitake, Wood Ear, Oyster or Porcini, finely chopped
2 tbs (30 ml) chopped green onion
1 tbs (15 ml) flour
¼ cup (60 ml) light cream
1 tbs (15 ml) FRIEDA'S Fresh Basil, chopped
    or 1 tsp (5 ml) crushed dried basil
1 tbs (15 ml) chopped parsley
¼ tsp (1 ml) pepper
slivered almonds or pine nuts for garnish

Set aside whole regular mushrooms; chop stems and reserve. In skillet, melt butter. Sauté reserved stems with garlic, chopped mushrooms and onion about 3 minutes, or until tender. Sauté 3-5 minutes more over low heat, or until nearly all liquid is absorbed. Sprinkle mixture with flour; add cream. Cook and stir 1 minute more. Add basil, parsley and pepper; stir to blend well. Remove from heat. Place whole mushroom caps stem side up on a lightly greased baking sheet. Spoon mushroom mixture into caps, mounding slightly. Sprinkle a few almonds or pine nuts over each mushroom. Bake in a 375°F (190°C) oven for 10 minutes. Run under broiler 2 minutes just to brown. Serve hot. Yields 18 mushrooms.

Approximate nutritional analysis per mushroom:
Calories 29, Protein .4 g, Carbohydrates 2 g, Fat 2 g, Cholesterol 7 mg, Sodium 15 mg

MUSHROOM STUFFED MUSHROOMS

DOLMAS
Stuffed Grape Leaves

¼ lb (115 g) lean ground lamb
1 cup (240 ml) chopped onion
2 cloves garlic, minced
2 tbs (30 ml) olive oil
1 cup (240 ml) WOLFF'S Kasha,
    medium granulation
1 egg, slightly beaten
¼ cup (60 ml) minced fresh parsley
1 tsp (5 ml) dried dillweed
1 tsp (5 ml) crushed dried mint
    leaves
½ tsp (3 ml) ground coriander
¼ tsp (1 ml) cinnamon
2½ cups (590 ml) hot seasoned
    chicken broth
½ cup (120 ml) fresh lemon juice
1-lb jar (455 g) grape leaves in brine

In large skillet, sauté lamb, onions and garlic in oil just until meat loses its pinkness. Combine kasha with egg, then add to skillet along with herbs and spices, 1 cup of the broth and ¼ cup of the lemon juice. Simmer, covered, 5 minutes; remove from heat and cool. Plunge grape leaves briefly into hot water to separate them, then drain. On clean, flat surface, place leaf shiny side down, trim and discard stem. Spoon 2-4 tbs filling at the stem end, fold sides of leaves over filling and roll up. Arrange dolmas, touching each other, in an oiled 7x11-inch baking dish, forming two layers. Pour remaining broth and ¼ cup lemon juice over dolmas, cover dish with foil, weight the top with a heat-proof pan or dish to keep the dolmas from unwinding.

Bake at 325°F (165°C) for 60 minutes. Turn heat off but leave dolmas in oven 30 minutes more. Remove from cooking liquid before serving warm or chilled. Yields 50 dolmas.

Note: Stuffed unbaked dolmas can be frozen up to 3 months.

Approximate nutritional analysis per stuffed grape leaf:
Calories 22, Protein 1 g, Carbohydrates 2 g, Fat 1 g, Cholesterol 6 mg, Sodium 44 mg

TABOULI DOLMAS
Stuffed Grape Leaves

1 pkg FANTASTIC FOODS
    Tabouli Salad Mix
⅓ cup (80 ml) olive oil
1¼ cups (295 ml) cold water
⅔ cup (160 ml) tomato sauce
1 jar grape leaves, rinsed (30 leaves)
1 clove garlic, chopped
1 (240ml) cup water

Place tabouli in a bowl and add oil and cold water. Mix together and let stand for about 1 hour until liquids are absorbed. Then mix in tomato sauce. Place grape leaf on a flat surface with stem end facing up, clip stem if long. Put 1-2 tbs of tabouli in the center, fold the side of the leaf in then roll up tightly starting at stem end. Place stuffed leaves in a shallow stovetop pan in a single layer with the folded side down. Cover with a single layer of flat grape leaves. Sprinkle chopped garlic over leaves. Add 1 cup of water, cover pan and simmer for 45 minutes checking occasionally on water level. Serve cold. Yields 30 grape leaves.

Approximate nutritional analysis per stuffed grape leaf:
Calories 57, Protein 2 g, Carbohydrates 7 g, Fat 4 g, Cholesterol 0 mg, Sodium 126 mg

STUFFED SHIITAKE MUSHROOMS

2 cups (480 ml) FANTASTIC FOODS
    Brown Jasmine Rice
4 cups (960 ml) water
2 lbs (910 g) fresh shiitake
    or regular mushrooms
2 tsp (10 ml) olive oil
1 tbs (15 ml) butter
¾ cup (180 ml) red onion,
    finely chopped
1 cup (240 ml) green pepper, cored,
    seeded and finely chopped
2 tsp (10 ml) dried basil
5 tbs (75 ml) nonfat cream cheese
salt and pepper to taste
fresh parsley, optional

Cook rice in water as directed. Set aside. Clean the mushrooms; discard the stems if using shiitake mushrooms. In large skillet, sauté the mushrooms in olive oil and butter until golden brown on both sides; set aside. Sauté onion, green pepper and basil until the onion is golden. Stir in rice, cream cheese, salt and pepper. Preheat oven to 350°F (180°C). Arrange mushrooms, rib side up, on a rimmed cookie sheet. Divide the rice mixture among the mushrooms. Bake just until the mushrooms are reheated, about 10 minutes. Top each with a parsley sprig, if desired. Serves 11.

Approximate nutritional analysis per serving:
Calories 205, Protein 6 g, Carbohydrates 40 g, Fat 3 g, Cholesterol 5 mg, Sodium 94 mg

VEGETARIAN SAUSAGE & VEGETABLE LUMPIA ROLLS

1⅓ cups (320 ml) boiling water
1 pkg FANTASTIC Nature Sausage
¼ cup (60 ml) vegetable oil, plus additional oil for deep-frying
½ cup (120 ml) minced green onion
1 cup (240 ml) fine diced bean sprouts
1½ cups (355 ml) fine diced mushrooms
1 cup (240 ml) fine diced blanched carrots
1 cup (240 ml) fine diced boiled potatoes
1 cup (240 ml) blanched peas
¼ cup (60 ml) soy sauce
1 clove minced garlic
2 packages (50 wrappers) Filipino lumpia wrappers

TANGY SOY SAUCE:
1 cup (240 ml) soy sauce
1 cup (240 ml) rice wine vinegar
¼ tsp (1 ml) minced garlic
strip ginger root

Add boiling water to sausage. Mix well and let stand for 20 minutes minimum. Add ¼ cup vegetable oil to a large, deep, nonstick skillet. Turn on medium heat, add sausage mixture, spreading evenly over the surface of the skillet. Brown small chunks of sausage mixture. Reduce heat to low and add green onions, bean sprouts, mushrooms, carrots and potatoes. Heat mixture thoroughly then fold in green peas. Add soy sauce and minced garlic and stir again. Turn off heat and let mixture cool.

In the meantime, thaw the lumpia wrappers, separate them and place them in the folds of a damp cloth. To fold a roll, place the lumpia wrapper flat on the counter in a diamond position. Place one heaping teaspoon of the mixture in the center. Fold the bottom point over the mixture then fold both sides of the wrapper into the center and finish rolling almost to the end of the top point. Dampen the top point with water and fold over the roll. Place the completed lumpia rolls under a damp towel until ready to cook. Deep-fry the rolls until golden brown or bake for 10 minutes at 400°F (205°C). Yields 50 rolls.

Tangy Soy Sauce: For a quick snappy dip, combine soy sauce and rice vinegar. Add minced garlic and strip of ginger root. Yields 2 cups.

Approximate nutritional analysis per roll w/o sauce:
Calories 77, Protein 2 g, Carbohydrates 4 g, Fat 6 g, Cholesterol .2 mg, Sodium 110 mg

Approximate nutritional analysis per 1 tbs serving sauce:
Calories 6, Protein 1 g, Carbohydrates 1 g, Fat 0 g, Cholesterol 0 mg, Sodium 514 mg

BLUE CABBAGE ROLLS

12 large steamed cabbage leaves
1 cup (240 ml) ARROWHEAD MILLS Blue Cornmeal
½ cup (120 ml) chopped green onions
½ cup (120 ml) corn
¼ tsp (1 ml) powdered garlic
¼ tsp (1 ml) dried thyme
¼ tsp (1 ml) dried oregano
1 cup (240 ml) unseasoned tomato sauce
2 cups (480 ml) water
1 cup (240 ml) grated cheese

While steaming cabbage leaves, mix remaining ingredients except cheese in saucepan and stir with a wire whisk over medium heat until mixture is very thick. Be cautious to keep mixture stirred thoroughly. Roll 1 tbs mixture into each cabbage leaf. Place in baking dish and cover with cheese. Bake for 10 minutes at 300°F (150°C). Serves 6.

Approximate nutritional analysis per serving:
Calories 191, Protein 11 g, Carbohydrates 25 g, Fat 6 g, Cholesterol 13 mg, Sodium 564 mg

BLINI
Russian Appetizer Pancakes

2 cups (480 ml) milk
1 tbs (15 ml) sugar
1 pkg active dry yeast
2 cups (480 ml) all-purpose flour
2 tbs (30 ml) melted butter
    or margarine
3 eggs, separated
¾ tsp (4 ml) salt
½ cup (120 ml) THE BIRKETT
    MILLS Buckwheat Flour
caviar
smoked salmon
minced onion
sour cream or yogurt cheese

Scald milk, pour into a large bowl. When lukewarm, add sugar and yeast, mixing well to dissolve yeast. Stir in 1 cup of the all-purpose flour; cover bowl and set in warm place until "sponge" doubles in volume, about 1½ hours. Combine butter, egg yolks and salt. Stir down the sponge and add butter-egg mixture, along with buckwheat flour and remaining 1 cup all-purpose flour. Beat egg whites until stiff but not dry, then gently fold into batter. Cook batter, 1 tablespoon per blini, on a hot buttered griddle or skillet. Flip blini to brown second side after batter appears set on top. Cover blini with a towel and hold in 200°F (93°C) oven until serving. Accompany blini with caviar, smoked salmon, minced onion, sour cream or yogurt. Yields 40 blini.

Approximate nutritional analysis per blini w/o accompaniments:
Calories 44, Protein 2 g, Carbohydrates 7 g, Fat 1 g, Cholesterol 16 mg, Sodium 57 mg

GARBANZO-POTATO PANCAKES

1 cup (240 ml) ARROWHEAD MILLS
    Garbanzo Flour
1 cup (240 ml) ARROWHEAD MILLS
    Potato Flakes
½ cup (120 ml) onion,
    finely chopped
1 medium zucchini squash
    or cucumber, grated
½ tsp (3 ml) sea salt, optional
2 tsp (10 ml) non-alum
    baking powder
2 cups (480 ml) water

VARIATION:
½ cup (120 ml) ARROWHEAD
    MILLS Whole Wheat Flour
1 tbs (15 ml) oil
2 tsp (10 ml) of tamari soy sauce
garlic

Mix the dry ingredients and the vegetables together. Add the water and stir well. Cook like pancakes on an oiled skillet or griddle. Yields 12 pancakes.

Variations: For lighter, extra tasty pancakes, substitute the whole wheat flour for ½ cup of the potato flakes. Add oil, tamari soy sauce and a little garlic to the water and stir into the dry mixture. Cook as directed.

Approximate nutritional analysis per pancake:
Calories 60, Protein 3 g, Carbohydrates 11 g, Fat .9 g, Cholesterol 0 mg, Sodium 90 mg

Approximate nutritional analysis per pancake variation:
Calories 81, Protein 3 g, Carbohydrates 14 g, Fat 2 g, Cholesterol 0 mg, Sodium 146 mg

BLINI

PEANUT BUTTER SPECIALTY SANDWICHES

½ cup (120 ml) EAST WIND
    Peanut Butter
2 tbs (30 ml) lemon juice
1 tbs (15 ml) raisins or dates
1 small apple, diced
12 slices whole wheat bread

Stir together peanut butter with lemon juice, raisins and apple. Spread on lightly toasted bread of your choice. Yields ¾ cup peanut butter for 6 sandwiches.

Approximate nutritional analysis per sandwich:
Calories 332, Protein 10 g, Carbohydrates 44 g, Fat 14 g, Cholesterol 0 mg, Sodium 385 mg

PEPPER TOFU STEAK SANDWICH

FILLING:
6-oz pkg (180 g) WHITE WAVE
    Baked Tofu Italian Style
½ medium green pepper, julienned
½ medium roasted red pepper,
    julienned
½ small onion, julienned
2 tbs (30 ml) olive oil
1 tsp (5 ml) Worcestershire sauce
2 6-inch French rolls

RELISH:
1 large dill pickle, chopped
½ small tomato, chopped
¼ small onion, chopped
salt, to taste
¼ tsp (1 ml) dried oregano
¼ tsp (1 ml) dried thyme
black pepper, fresh ground, to taste
salt, to taste

Sauté tofu, peppers and onion in oil over medium-high heat until onions are lightly browned. Add Worcestershire sauce and sauté a minute more. Cut the bread in half horizontally and remove some of the bread from the insides of each half. Set bread aside.

    Relish: While tofu and veggies are browning, make a relish of pickle, tomato and onion. Add a little salt and set aside.

    Drizzle both sides of the bread with a little oil. Place tofu mixture in rolls. Add relish on top. Drizzle with more oil. Rubbing between thumb and fingers, sprinkle oregano and thyme. Salt and pepper. Yields 2 sandwiches.

Approximate nutritional analysis per sandwich:
Calories 542, Protein 27 g, Carbohydrates 51 g, Fat 26 g, Cholesterol 0 mg, Sodium 861 mg

PEPPER TOFU STEAK SANDWICH

TEMPEH REUBEN

8-oz pkg (240 g) WHITE WAVE
    Original Soy Tempeh,
    cut into quarters
2 tbs (30 ml) olive oil
pinch onion powder
pinch garlic powder
1-2 tbs (15-30 ml) tamari soy sauce

RUSSIAN DRESSING:
½ cup (120 ml) mayonnaise
    or soy mayo
¼ cup (60 ml) ketchup
1 tsp (5 ml) horseradish sauce
1 tsp (5 ml) onion, chopped
½ tsp (3 ml) Worcestershire sauce

4 slices rye bread
3 tbs (45 ml) butter, softened,
    optional
¾ cup (180 ml) sauerkraut, warmed
3 oz (90 g) Swiss cheese, sliced

Cut tempeh in half, then slice to half its thickness. Pour oil into skillet and coat both sides of tempeh. Sprinkle with a dash of both garlic and onion powder and sauté over medium-low heat until golden. Add soy sauce and cook a minute more.

Russian Dressing: Mix together mayonnaise, ketchup, horseradish, onion and Worcestershire sauce.

Butter one side of the bread or toast bread. Build sandwiches, butter side out, as follows: 1 tbs dressing, tempeh, sauerkraut then cheese. Sauté sandwiches until bread is golden brown. Yields 2 sandwiches.

Approximate nutritional analysis per sandwich:
Calories 708, Protein 39 g, Carbohydrates 47 g, Fat 42 g, Cholesterol 38 mg, Sodium 2222 mg

SMOKY SALMON SANDWICH

8 slices ROMAN MEAL Honey and
    Oat Bran Bread
3 tbs (45 ml) diet margarine,
    optional
7½-oz can (225 g) salmon,
    drained and flaked
1½ tbs (25 ml) low-calorie
    mayonnaise
½ cup (120 ml) chopped celery
1 tbs (15 ml) finely chopped onion
1 tsp (5 ml) lemon juice
2 drops liquid hickory smoke
    seasoning
1 thinly sliced tomato
lettuce or romaine leaves

Spread each bread slice with 1 tsp margarine. In medium bowl, combine salmon, mayonnaise, celery, onion and seasonings. Divide salmon mixture between 4 bread slices and spread to edges. Add tomato slices and lettuce. Close with remaining bread slices. Yields 4 sandwiches.

Approximate nutritional analysis per sandwich:
Calories 222, Protein 15 g, Carbohydrates 25 g, Fat 8 g, Cholesterol 16 mg, Sodium 553 mg

SMOKY SALMON SANDWICH

GUACAMOLE

2 very ripe medium avocados
1½ tbs (35 ml) lemon juice
2 tbs (30 ml) red onion,
    finely chopped
hot red pepper sauce, to taste
¼ tsp (1 ml) ground cumin
2 cloves garlic, pressed or minced
1 tsp (5 ml) salt
2 medium tomatoes, peeled, seeded,
    coarsely chopped
2 tbs (30 ml) cilantro, finely chopped
4 MILL VALLEY Tostada Organic
    Blue Bowls

GUACAMOLE

In medium bowl, mash avocado with fork until soft and puréed. Add lemon juice, onion, hot red pepper sauce, cumin, garlic and salt and mix to combine. Gently mix in tomatoes and cilantro.

Preheat tostada bowls for 3-5 minutes in a 350°F (180°C) oven, fill with guacamole and serve. Yields 4 tostadas.

Approximate nutritional analysis per tostada:
Calories 281, Protein 4 g, Carbohydrates 26 g, Fat 21 g, Cholesterol 0 mg, Sodium 554 mg

BLENDER SALMON MOUSSE WITH TANGY YOGURT-DILL SAUCE

MOUSSE:
15-oz can (450 g) plus 7½-oz can
    (225 g) salmon
1 small onion, sliced
juice of 1½ large lemons
1 envelope plus 1 tbs (15 ml)
    unflavored gelatin
½ cup (120 ml) boiling water
¾ cup (180 ml) STONYFIELD FARM
    Plain Low Fat Yogurt
¾ cup (180 ml) mayonnaise
1½ tsp (8 ml) paprika
5 tbs (75 ml) minced fresh dill
    or 2 tsp (10 ml) dried dill

SAUCE:
¾ cup (180 ml) STONYFIELD FARM
    Plain Low Fat Yogurt
¼ cup (60 ml) mayonnaise
½ tsp (3 ml) prepared mustard
2 tbs (30 ml) minced fresh dill

Mousse: Drain and reserve the liquid from the canned salmon into 1½-quart fish-shaped mold; coat the mold thoroughly with the liquid to oil it, then discard the liquid.

Place in a blender or food processor the sliced onion and the lemon juice, and sprinkle the dry gelatin over this. Add ¼ cup boiling water slowly while running the blender at purée speed. Stop the blender and add the yogurt, mayonnaise and paprika; purée for 15-20 seconds more.

Break the salmon into small chunks and combine with the yogurt mixture in the blender; blend on the purée setting for 1½ minutes or a little more, if necessary, until all ingredients are thoroughly blended. Add the dill and blend briefly until mixed. Pour the mixture into the fish mild and refrigerate until firm, 2-3 hours or overnight.

Sauce: Thoroughly mix all the ingredients by hand; refrigerate for at least 1 hour.

Half an hour before serving, remove the Mousse and Sauce from the refrigerator. Spread the sauce on a large serving platter.

Loosen the mousse from the mold by running the point of a sharp knife all around the edge of the mousse. Invert the mold on top of the sauce and allow the mousse to slide naturally out of the mold. Serve with crackers or cut-up raw vegetables. Serves 6-8 as an appetizer.

Approximate nutritional analysis per serving:
Calories 233, Protein 13 g, Carbohydrates 3 g, Fat 19 g, Cholesterol 36 mg, Sodium 441 mg

BLENDER SALMON MOUSSE
WITH TANGY YOGURT-DILL SAUCE

FLEX YOUR TEX-MEX QUESADILLAS

2 16-oz cans (960 g) kidney or black
   beans, undrained
4 large flour tortillas
8-oz jar (240 ml) UNCLE DAVE'S
   Tex Mex Pasta Sauce
1 cup (240 ml) cheddar or
   mozzarella cheese, shredded
sour cream, optional

Empty beans into skillet. Over medium-high heat, mash beans all over bottom until thick and mushy. Take 2 tortillas and on each, layer beans, pasta sauce and cheese. Top with remaining 2 tortillas. Microwave at high for 1-1½ minutes or brown in a nonstick pan 2 minutes on each side. Cut each quesadilla in pie wedges and top with a dollop of sour cream. Serves 8 as an appetizer.

Approximate nutritional analysis per serving:
Calories 292, Protein 13 g, Carbohydrates 37 g, Fat 10 g, Cholesterol 15 mg, Sodium 717 mg

ENCHILADAS MADE WITH TOFU

28-oz can (840 ml) tomato sauce
1½ tbs (25 ml) garlic powder
1 medium onion, chopped
2 oz (60 g) green chiles, diced
4 tsp (20 ml) chili powder
¼ tsp (1 ml) basil
16 oz (480 g) WHITE WAVE Tofu
½ cup (120 ml) WHITE WAVE Soy A
   Melt, cheddar flavor
¾ cup (120 ml) WHITE WAVE Soy A
   Melt, mozzarella flavor
9-12 small corn tortillas
2 tbs (30 ml) soy oil
1-2 dry oz (30-60 g) black olives,
   sliced

Mix tomato sauce, garlic, onion, chiles, chili powder and basil together in a sauce pan and simmer for 15 minutes to create sauce. Preheat oven to 350°F (180°C).

Drain tofu and crumble. Grate Soy A Melt (all of the cheddar and ½ cup of the mozzarella) or dairy cheese. Mix tofu and Soy A Melt together in a bowl to create filling.

Heat 1½ tbs oil in frying pan; heat tortillas individually in pan until soft. Use remaining oil to grease 9x13-inch baking dish. Place filling in tortilla, roll and place in baking dish seam side down. Cover with sauce. Grate remaining Soy A Melt or dairy cheese and sprinkle on tortillas with sliced olives. Bake covered for 15-20 minutes. Serves 6.

Approximate nutritional analysis per serving:
Calories 373, Protein 21 g, Carbohydrates 39 g, Fat 18 g, Cholesterol 0 mg, Sodium 1267 mg

SLOPPY JOES

1 medium onion, chopped
1 medium green pepper, chopped
2 cloves garlic, chopped
2 tbs (30 ml) olive oil
3 6.1-oz pkgs (550 g) SOY DELI
   Barbecue Style Tofu Burgers
2 cups (480 ml) tomato sauce
1 tbs (15 ml) chili powder
½ tsp (3 ml) cumin powder
5 burger buns

Sauté onion, green pepper and garlic in oil until tender. Crumble and add tofu burgers. Continue cooking until hot and add tomato sauce, chili powder and cumin powder. Serve over toasted burger buns. Yields 5 sandwiches.

Approximate nutritional analysis per sandwich:
Calories 485, Protein 24 g, Carbohydrates 45 g, Fat 19 g, Cholesterol 0 mg, Sodium 1106 mg

VEGETARIAN TOSTADA & AVOCADO DRESSING

4 8-inch tortillas
2 cups (480 ml) grated cheddar
   cheese
4 cups (960 ml) shredded lettuce
16-oz jar (480 ml) 3-bean salad,
   drained
2 cups (480 ml) alfalfa sprouts
14½-oz can (435 g) MUIR GLEN
   Organic Diced Tomatoes,
   drained
¼ cup (60 ml) green onion, chopped

AVOCADO DRESSING:
3 large avocados, peeled, pitted
   and coarsely mashed
1 tbs (15 ml) lemon juice
½ cup (120 ml) nonfat plain yogurt
   or sour cream
2 cloves garlic, minced
⅓ cup (809 ml) green onion,
   chopped
¼ tsp (1 ml) salt
dash Tabasco

SALSA
2 14½-oz cans (870 g) MUIR GLEN Organic Diced
   Tomatoes, undrained
¾ cup (180 ml) red onion, chopped
1 green onion, chopped
½ jalapeño chile, seeded and minced
2 tbs (30 ml) fresh cilantro, chopped
2 cloves garlic, minced
4 tsp (20 ml) lime juice
¼ tsp (1 ml) salt

Heat oven to 450°F (230°C). Sprinkle tortillas lightly with water and bake 4-5 minutes, until crisp, turning once during baking. In layers, top each tortilla with ⅓ cup Avocado Dressing, ¼ cup cheese, 1 cup lettuce, ⅓ cup bean salad, ½ cup sprouts, ⅓ cup tomatoes, 1 tbs green onion and another ¼ cup cheese. Garnish with Salsa and Avocado Dressing. Serves 4.

Avocado Dressing: Combine in order given, stirring well after each addition. Yields 2 cups.

Salsa: In large bowl, combine ingredients; blend well. Cover and chill 3-4 hours before serving. Note: For a hotter salsa, increase red onion to 1½ cups and use whole chili. Yields 4½ cups.

Approximate nutritional analysis per serving tostada w/o salsa:
Calories 659, Protein 26 g, Carbohydrates 46 g, Fat 43 g, Cholesterol 60 mg, Sodium 1186 mg

Approximate nutritional analysis per ⅓ cup serving avocado dressing:
Calories 177, Protein 3 g, Carbohydrates 10 g, Fat 16 g, Cholesterol .4 mg, Sodium 117 mg

Approximate nutritional analysis per ½ cup serving salsa:
Calories 26, Protein 1 g, Carbohydrates 5 g, Fat 0 g, Cholesterol 0 mg, Sodium 211 mg

BA BA GANOUJ

2 medium eggplants
1½ tbs (40 ml) lemon juice
½ cup (120 ml) EAST WIND Tahini
3 cloves garlic, minced
½ cup (120 ml) parsley, chopped
1 tsp (5 ml) salt, or to taste
¼ cup (60 ml) scallions, minced
black pepper to taste
1 tbs (15 ml) olive oil

VARIATION:
onions, chopped
mushrooms, chopped
or 1 cup (240 ml) plain
   nonfat yogurt
½ tsp (3 ml) cumin
dash of cayenne

To prepare the eggplant, cut the stems off, prick the skin all over, place on a well-oiled baking sheet and bake at 325°F (165°C) for an hour or until eggplants are wrinkled and soft.

After the eggplants have cooled down, scoop out the insides and mash them with all the other ingredients except for the olive oil. Chill this mixture then drizzle the oil over the top. Serve Ba Ba Ganouj as a side dish with Mediterranean entrees. Serves 6 as a side dish.

Variation: Try adding sautéed onions and mushrooms or yogurt, cumin and cayenne.

Approximate nutritional analysis per serving:
Calories 198, Protein 5 g, Carbohydrates 17 g, Fat 14 g, Cholesterol 0 mg, Sodium 365 mg

FALAFEL

Falafel is a deep-fried chick-pea patty, a traditional Mediterranean dish. Serve Falafel in warm pita bread with chopped fresh vegetables, Hummus and Tahini-Lemon Sauce. Serve with a side of eggplant Ba Ba Ganouj, a cold rice salad and garnish with parsley.

4 cups (960 ml) cooked chick-peas
3 cloves garlic, minced
½ cup (120 ml) scallions, minced
3 tbs (45 ml) EAST WIND Tahini
2 eggs, beaten
  or ¾ cup (180 ml) soy milk
3 tbs (45 ml) flour
½ tsp (3 ml) cumin
½ tsp (3 ml) turmeric
¼ tsp (1 ml) cayenne
1½ tsp (8 ml) salt
dash black pepper
oil for frying

TAHINI LEMON SAUCE:
1 cup (240 ml) EAST WIND Tahini
2 tbs (30 ml) lemon juice
2 tsp (10 ml) honey
1½ cups (355 ml) warm water
2 tbs (30 ml) parsley
2 cloves garlic, minced
  or 1 tsp (5 ml) powdered garlic
2 tsp (10 ml) cumin
1 tsp (5 ml) black pepper
1 tsp (5 ml) paprika
1 tsp (5 ml) coriander
½ tsp (3 ml) salt
1 tbs (15 ml) olive oil
1½ cups (355 ml) yogurt, optional,
  for creamier sauce

Mash chick-peas in a food processor or heavy-duty blender. Stir in the remaining ingredients except oil and chill. When batter is cold, with well-floured hands, roll mixture into 1-inch balls. Lightly flour and flatten into patties for frying.

In a heavy skillet, heat about 1 inch of oil. When hot, deep-fry falafel until light brown, turning once. Drain on a paper bag. Serve hot, wrapped in warm pita bread with shredded lettuce, diced tomato and cucumber, Hummus and Tahini-Lemon Sauce. Yields 24 patties.

Tahini-Lemon Sauce: In a blender or food processor, combine all ingredients until smooth and creamy. Alter the amount of water to reach desired consistency. Serve at room temperature over steamed vegetables or with Falafel. Yields 1½ cups.

For a creamier sauce, add 1½ cups yogurt to the sauce and perhaps a little more of the spices. Alter the amount of water to reach your desired consistency. Yields 3 cups.

Approximate nutritional analysis per falafel:
Calories 67, Protein 3 g, Carbohydrates 9 g, Fat 2 g, Cholesterol 16 mg, Sodium 142 mg

Approximate nutritional analysis per 2 tbs serving sauce:
Calories 137, Protein 4 g, Carbohydrates 5 g, Fat 12 g, Cholesterol 0 mg, Sodium 90 mg

Approximate nutritional analysis per 2 tbs serving sauce variation:
Calories 77, Protein 3 g, Carbohydrates 4 g, Fat 6 g, Cholesterol .3 mg, Sodium 57 mg

FALAFEL

HUMMUS

3 cups (720 ml) chick-peas, cooked
1 cup (240 ml) water, including
  the liquid drained from the
  chick-peas
½ cup (120 ml) EAST WIND Tahini
¼ cup (60 ml) lemon juice
2 tbs (30 ml) tamari or soy sauce
6 garlic cloves, minced
1-2 tsp (5-10 ml) paprika, for color,
  optional

Mash chick-peas in a food processor or heavy-duty blender. Add the remaining ingredients, stirring until well combined. Serve chilled as a dip with celery and carrot sticks and pita wedges. Hummus is also served as a falafel (chick-pea patty) topping. Serves 6.

Approximate nutritional analysis per ½ cup serving:
Calories 266, Protein 12 g, Carbohydrates 28 g, Fat 13 g, Cholesterol 0 mg, Sodium 276 mg

INSTANT FALAFEL

1½ cups (355 ml) **ARROWHEAD MILLS Garbanzo Flour**
1 cup (240 ml) cold water
1 medium onion
2 cloves garlic
½ bunch fresh parsley
hot green pepper, to taste, minced
½ tsp (3 ml) cumin
salt, to taste
pepper, to taste
¼ tsp (1 ml) non-alum baking powder
pinch baking soda

Mix all ingredients, except soda, together in a food processor or blender. Mix thoroughly.* When ready to fry, mix in the soda. Shape into small patties, 1½ inches in diameter and ½-inch thick. Fry in deep, hot oil until lightly browned and crisp. Serve hot with tomatoes in pita bread. Add cucumber pickles if desired. Serves 4.

*Note: Falafel may be frozen at this stage. Thaw completely before adding soda and cooking.

Approximate nutritional analysis per serving:
Calories 326, Protein 10 g, Fat 18 g, Carbohydrates 36 g, Cholesterol 0 mg, Sodium 103mg

GARBANZO DIP WITHOUT TAHINI

1 cup (240 ml) **ARROWHEAD MILLS Garbanzo Flour**
1½ cups (355 ml) water
1 cup (240 ml) tofu
¼ cup (60 ml) lemon juice
¼ cup (60 ml) water
1 tbs (15 ml) honey
¾ tsp (4 ml) sea salt, optional
¼ tsp (1 ml) or more garlic powder

Mix the garbanzo flour and water in saucepan. Bring to a simmering boil, stirring constantly. Remove from heat. Mix the remaining ingredients in blender and blend until smooth. Stir into the cooked garbanzo paste. As the dip sits, it will become thicker. If necessary, add a little water to reach the desired consistency. Chill before serving. Yields 3 cups, serves 6.

Approximate nutritional analysis per ½ cup serving:
Calories 129, Protein 8 g, Carbohydrates 19 g, Fat 4 g, Cholesterol 0 mg, Sodium 12 mg

WHITE BEAN PURÉE

14-oz can (420 g) **AMERICAN PRAIRIE Organic Great Northern Beans, rinsed and drained**
2 tbs (30 ml) onion, chopped
1 tsp (5 ml) garlic, finely chopped
¼ tsp (1 ml) sea salt
1 tbs (15 ml) lemon juice
2 tsp (10 ml) olive oil
hot pepper sauce, optional

In food processor or blender combine first 6 ingredients and blend until smooth, 60-90 seconds. If desired, add hot pepper sauce to taste. Transfer to serving bowl, cover and refrigerate 2 hours. Serve with toasted pita bread or other crispy bread. Yields 1 cup.

Approximate nutritional analysis per 2 tbs serving:
Calories 70, Protein 4 g, Carbohydrates 11 g, Fat 1 g, Cholesterol 0 mg, Sodium 68 mg

WHITE BEAN PURÉE

ANASAZI BEAN SPREAD

1 cup (240 ml) ARROWHEAD MILLS Anasazi Beans
½ medium onion
1 stalk celery
¼ cup (60 ml) tofu, drained
1 tbs (15 ml) ARROWHEAD MILLS Unrefined Olive Oil
½ tsp (3 ml) vege-sal or similar seasoning
½ tsp (3 ml) chili powder
½ tsp (3 ml) oregano
½ tsp (3 ml) basil
¼ tsp (1 ml) garlic powder

Blend together in blender or food processor until smooth. Great for dips or sandwich spread. Serves 8.

Approximate nutritional analysis per serving:
Calories 50, Protein 2 g, Carbohydrates 6 g, Fat 2 g, Cholesterol 0 mg, Sodium 132 mg

BLACK BEAN DIP WITH MARJORAM

2 15-oz cans (900 g) low-sodium black beans, drained
1 cup (240 ml) diced white onion
1 tbs (15 ml) garlic, chopped
1 tbs (15 ml) chili powder
¼ tsp (1 ml) white pepper
1 tbs (15 ml) cumin
water
2 cups (480 ml) nonfat yogurt, plain
4 tbs (60 ml) GREEN HOUSE Fresh Marjoram, chopped
3 cups (720 ml) jicama sticks
2½ cups (590 ml) celery sticks
2½ cups (590 ml) carrot sticks

Place beans, onion, garlic, chili powder, white pepper and cumin into a food processor and process until smooth, adding water until desired consistency is reached. Remove to a bowl and fold in the yogurt and marjoram. Serve with jicama, celery and carrot sticks. Serves 8.

Approximate nutritional analysis per serving:
Calories 236, Protein 13 g, Carbohydrates 41 g, Fat 3 g, Cholesterol 1 mg, Sodium 109 mg

BLACK-EYED PEA HABAÑERO DIP

11-oz pkg (330 g) FRIEDA'S Black-eyed Peas, cooked and drained
⅓ cup (80 ml) rehydrated FRIEDA'S Dried Tomatoes, chopped
⅓ cup (80 ml) red or green bell pepper, chopped
¼ cup (60 ml) red onion, minced
1 clove FRIEDA'S Elephant Garlic, peeled and chopped
2 tbs (30 ml) fresh FRIEDA'S Cilantro Leaves, minced
1 FRIEDA'S Dried Habañero Chile, reconstituted, seeded and finely chopped
fresh cilantro, chopped tomato or red onion, garnish

In blender container or food processor bowl, place all ingredients. Cover and process until smooth. Garnish as desired. Serve with tortillas chips, Frieda's Jicama Sticks or other fresh vegetables. Yields 2½ cups.

Approximate nutritional analysis per ½ cup serving:
Calories 232, Protein 16 g, Carbohydrates 42 g, Fat .9 g, Cholesterol 0 mg, Sodium 86 mg

BLACK BEAN DIP WITH MARJORAM

CUBAN BLACK BEAN DIP

11-oz pkg (330 g) FRIEDA'S Black Beans, cooked according to package directions and cooled
⅓ cup (80 ml) tomato, chopped
⅓ cup (80 ml) green or red bell pepper, chopped
¼ cup (60 ml) red onion, minced
1 clove FRIEDA'S Elephant Garlic, peeled and chopped
2 tbs (30 ml) fresh cilantro leaves, minced
1 FRIEDA'S Habañero Chile, reconstituted, seeded and finely chopped
fresh cilantro, chopped tomato or red onion for garnish

In blender coontainer or food processor bowl, place all ingredients. Cover and process until smooth. Garnish as desired. Serve with tortilla chips, jicama sticks or other fresh vegetables. Yields 2½ cups.

Approximate nutritional analysis per ½ cup serving:
Calories 223, Protein 15 g, Carbohydrates 41 g, Fat .8 g, Cholesterol 0 mg, Sodium 11 mg

MINTED VEGGIE DIP

1¼ cups (295 ml) plain nonfat yogurt
¾ cup (180 ml) light sour cream
3 cloves garlic, minced
1 cucumber, peeled, seeded and chopped
1 tbs (15 ml) GREEN HOUSE Fresh Mint, chopped
salt to taste
pepper to taste
8 cups (1.9 l) assorted raw veggies, jicama or yambean, celery, broccoli, carrots, etc., cut into sticks or florets

Put all ingredients into food processor or blender and process until very well combined. Chill. Serve with raw vegetables. Serves 8.

Approximate nutritional analysis per 1 cup veggies and ¼ cup dip serving:
Calories 93, Protein 6 g, Carbohydrates 15 g, Fat 2 g, Cholesterol 8 mg, Sodium 155 mg

BEAN PATÉ

2 cups (480 ml) ARROWHEAD MILLS Beans & Barley, cooked
¼ cup (60 ml) reserved cooking liquid from the beans
1 cup (240 ml) fresh parsley, minced
½ cup (120 ml) tahini
5 tbs (75 ml) lemon juice
¼ cup (60 ml) ARROWHEAD MILLS Olive Oil
1 clove garlic, crushed
½ tsp (3 ml) cumin
½ tsp (3 ml) onion powder
dash cayenne pepper or ¼ tsp (1 ml) chili powder
sea salt, optional
sliced black olives, optional

Purée the cooked beans, using the liquid as needed to make a smooth puree. Combine the purée with the remaining ingredients except the olives. The mixture should be thick. Chill, covered, at least 1 hour. Garnish with olives, if desired, and serve as an hors d'oeuvre with whole wheat bread or crackers. Yields 4 cups.

Approximate nutritional analysis per ¼ cup serving:
Calories 132, Protein 5 g, Carbohydrates 14 g, Fat 8 g, Cholesterol 0 mg, Sodium 4 mg

MILD SPINACH-N-CHESTNUT DIP

2 tbs (30 ml) fresh mint, minced
10-oz pkg (300 g) MORI-NU Silken
    Tofu, firm, drained
1 tbs (15 ml) lemon juice
2½ tsp (13 ml) garlic, minced
¼ tsp (1 ml) pepper
¼ cup (60 ml) green onion, chopped
½ cup (120 ml) water chestnuts,
    chopped, optional
salt to taste, optional

In a food processor or blender, combine first 6 ingredients until smooth. Whirl 30 seconds on high. Stir in water chestnuts and salt, if desired. Refrigerate 1 hour. Serve as a dip with raw vegetables or mound on your favorite greens. Top with diced tomatoes or pimiento. Yields 2½ cups.

Approximate nutritional analysis per ¼ cup serving:
Calories 42, Protein 3 g, Carbohydrates 6 g, Fat 1 g, Cholesterol 0 mg,
Sodium 36 mg

ALMOND PATÉ

1 cup (240 ml) minced onion
⅔ cup (160 ml) EAST WIND Almond
Butter
½ tsp (3 ml) cumin
½ cup (120 ml) toasted bread
crumbs
2 tbs (30 ml) parsley
1 tsp (5 ml) soy sauce
1 clove garlic, minced
½ tsp (3 ml) paprika
2-3 tbs (30-45 ml) mayonnaise

Combine all ingredients. Serve in a bowl or as a cracker and sandwich spread. Yields 2 cups.

Approximate nutritional analysis per 2 tbs serving:
Calories 103, Protein 3 g, Carbohydrates 5 g, Fat 8 g, Cholesterol 1 mg,
Sodium 59 mg

PEANUT BUTTER DIP

2 cups (480 ml) nonfat yogurt
¾ cup (180 ml) EAST WIND
    Peanut Butter
2 tbs (30 ml) lemon juice
5 tbs (75 ml) olive oil
1 tbs (15 ml) salt
2 tsp (10 ml) fresh grated ginger
    or 1 tsp (5 ml) powdered ginger
2 tsp (10 ml) black pepper
1 tsp (5 ml) chili powder
½ tsp (3 ml) cayenne pepper
½ tsp (3 ml) curry powder
water

NONDAIRY VARIATION:
2 cups (480 ml) soft tofu
1 tbs (15 ml) honey
water

In a blender or food processor, blend ingredients until smooth. Add a little water if it seems too thick. Chill for at least ½ hour before serving. Try this with broccoli and celery or your favorite dipping vegetable. Yields 3 cups.

    Nondairy Variation: Substitute tofu for the yogurt, add honey and water if a thinner consistency is desired.

Approximate nutritional analysis per 2 tbs serving:
Calories 90, Protein 2 g, Carbohydrates 4 g, Fat 7 g, Cholesterol .4 mg,
Sodium 289 mg

Approximate nutritional analysis per 2 tbs serving nondairy variation:
Calories 96, Protein 3 g, Carbohydrates 4 g, Fat 8 g, Cholesterol 0 mg,
Sodium 275 mg

MILD SPINACH-N-CHESTNUT DIP

CURRY-CASHEW SPREAD

½ cup (120 ml) cream cheese
½ cup (120 ml) EAST WIND
    Cashew Butter
½-1 tsp (3-5 ml) curry powder

Mash ingredients together. Try spread on fresh apple slices or celery sticks. Yields 1 cup.

Approximate nutritional analysis per 2 tbs serving:
Calories 156, Protein 4 g, Carbohydrates 5 g, Fat 14 g, Cholesterol 16 mg, Sodium 46 mg

MEDITERRANEAN ARTICHOKE & SMOKED SALMON DIP

14-oz jar (420 g) artichoke hearts,
    finely chopped
3 3-oz (270 g) HEALTH SEA Smoked
    Garlic Salmon Sausages, minced
½ cup (120 ml) Parmesan cheese
½ cup (120 ml) black olives,
    chopped
 juice of 1 lemon
1 cup (240 ml) mayonnaise
4 oz (120 ml) sun-dried tomato
    vinaigrette dressing
½ tsp (3 ml) fresh garlic

Mix all ingredients and bake in a 350°F (180°C) preheated oven until golden brown. Serve with chips, crackers, melba toast or bagel chips. May stuff into celery for hors d'oeuvres. Yields 3 cups.

Approximate nutritional analysis per 2 tbs serving:
Calories 128, Protein 4 g, Carbohydrates 3 g, Fat 12 g, Cholesterol 11 mg, Sodium 377 mg

MEDITERRANEAN ARTICHOKE & SMOKED SALMON DIP

CHAYOTE-GUACAMOLE SNACK

1 small FRIEDA'S Chayote
1 large ripe avocado, peeled,
    seeded and mashed
½ cup (120 ml) onion, chopped
½ cup (120 ml) sharp cheddar
    cheese, shredded
1 medium tomato, chopped
2 FRIEDA'S Fresh Serrano or
    Jalapeño Chiles, seeded and
    chopped
½ tsp (3 ml) salt
¼ tsp (1 ml) hot pepper sauce
¼ tsp (1 ml) ground black pepper
16 crisp tortilla chips
½-¾ cup (120-180 ml) sharp
    cheddar cheese, shredded
vegetable dippers and tortilla chips
    for dipping
fresh cilantro, optional

Quarter chayote; cook in a small amount of boiling water for about 15-20 minutes, or until very tender. Remove seed and peel; chop into blender or food processor bowl. Add avocado and blend until pureed. Add onion, ½ cup cheese, tomato, chiles and seasonings; blend for 5 seconds or just until mixed. Taste for seasoning. Line a 1-quart shallow casserole dish or pie plate with tortilla chips; spoon guacamole mixture over chips. Top with remaining cheese as desired. Place dish in a 350°F (180°C) oven for about 10 minutes or until cheese melts and bubbles. Serve immediately with more chips and vegetables and garnish with cilantro, if desired. Serves 8.

Approximate nutritional analysis per serving:
Calories 186, Protein 6 g, Carbohydrates 15 g, Fat 13 g, Cholesterol 15 mg, Sodium 351 mg

Overleaf: **CHAYOTE-GUACAMOLE SNACK**

ROASTED PEPPER & YOGURT SOUP

1¾ lbs (795 g) red bell peppers
1¼ lbs (570 g) yellow bell peppers
2 cups (480 ml) STONYFIELD FARM
   Nonfat Plain Yogurt
1 cup (240 ml) chicken stock
1 tbs (15 ml) fresh chervil, chopped
1 tbs (15 ml) fresh tarragon,
   chopped
1 tbs (15 ml) fresh basil, chopped
½ tsp (3 ml) salt, to taste
white pepper, to taste
1 tbs (15 ml) balsamic vinegar
1 lb (455 g) tiny salad shrimp,
   peeled, deveined and poached;
   or small scallops, poached
red and yellow bell peppers,
   julienne-cut, for garnish
STONYFIELD FARM Nonfat Plain
   Yogurt mixed with more chervil,
   tarragon and basil, for garnish

Preheat the broiler and place the broiler rack as close to the heat as possible. Use aluminum foil to line a cookie sheet with sides. Place washed and dried peppers on the foil and broil them, turning them with tongs every few minutes until they are charred all over. Be careful not to break the skins. Remove the charred peppers to a large bowl or bowls and let them cool.

When the peppers are cool, place a colander over a large bowl. Peel the peppers, catching the peeled peppers in the colander and the juices in the bowl. Discard the seeds and blackened skins.

Transfer the peppers and their juices to the bowl of a food processor fitted with a steel blade. Purée until smooth, then strain the purée through a sieve. Return the strained mixture to the food processor with the steel blade in place. Add the yogurt, chicken stock, chopped herbs, salt, pepper and vinegar. Process until blended. Chill.

Serve very cold, poured over the poached shrimp or scallops in individual soup bowls. Garnish with julienne peppers and yogurt-mixed chervil, tarragon and basil. Serves 6.

Approximate nutritional analysis per serving:
Calories 231, Protein 26 g, Carbohydrates 22 g, Fat 4 g, Cholesterol 140 mg, Sodium 750 mg

CREAMY BLUEBERRY BISQUE

2 cups (480 ml) fresh blueberries
2 cups (480 ml) water
⅓ cup (80 ml) granulated sugar
1 tbs (15 ml) brown sugar
1 cinnamon stick
1 lemon, thinly sliced
2 cups (480 ml) STONYFIELD FARM
   Nonfat Plain Yogurt
1 cup (240 ml) apple juice
STONYFIELD FARM Plain Yogurt,
   for garnish

Reserve a few blueberries for garnish. Place the remaining blueberries, water, sugars, cinnamon and lemon in a saucepan. Simmer, uncovered, for 15 minutes, then drain through a sieve into a bowl underneath. Chill the sieved liquid. Just before serving, whisk together liquid, yogurt and apple juice. Garnish each serving with a spoonful of yogurt and a few berries. Serves 6.

Approximate nutritional analysis per serving:
Calories 141, Protein 5 g, Carbohydrates 31 g, Fat .4 g, Cholesterol 1 mg, Sodium 67 mg

ROASTED PEPPER & YOGURT SOUP

COLD TOMATO DILL SOUP

2 tbs (30 ml) olive oil
2-3 medium onions, chopped
2-4 cloves garlic, crushed
6-8 tomatoes, peeled and chopped
2 cups (480 ml) chicken stock,
    homemade
½ tsp (3 ml) white pepper
3 tbs (45 ml) fresh dill, finely
    chopped
    or 1½ tsp (8 ml) dried dill
1 tsp (5 ml) sugar
2 cups (480 ml) STONYFIELD FARM
    Nonfat Plain Yogurt
1 cup (240 ml) buttermilk or
    skim milk
STONYFIELD FARM Nonfat Plain
    Yogurt, for garnish
dill or chives, chopped, for garnish

Heat the olive oil in a skillet over medium heat. Add the onions and garlic and sauté until soft but not brown. Add the tomatoes, chicken stock, white pepper, and dill. Cover and simmer for 15 minutes.

Cool the cooked mixture slightly, then process in a blender or food processor in batches. Add the sugar, yogurt and milk to the tomato mixture. Blend well. Chill. Adjust the seasonings, pour into individual bowls and garnish each with a dollop of yogurt sprinkled with chopped dill or chives. Serve very cold. Serves 8.

Note: Can be frozen before adding the sugar, yogurt and milk. After thawing, proceed with the recipe.

Approximate nutritional analysis per serving:
Calories 119, Protein 7 g, Carbohydrates 14 g, Fat 4 g, Cholesterol 2 mg, Sodium 282 mg

STRAWBERRY SOUP

STRAWBERRY SOUP

10-oz pkg (300 g) frozen
    unsweetened strawberries,
    thawed
2 tsp (10 ml) sugar
juice of ½ lemon
½ tsp (3 ml) almond extract
1 cup (240 ml) STONYFIELD FARM
    Low Fat Strawberry Yogurt
8 oz (240 ml) champagne

Purée the strawberries in a blender or food processor. Add the sugar, lemon juice and almond extract, then the yogurt and champagne. Blend until very smooth. Chill for at least 3 hours. Serve cold in small dessert dishes or cups with saucers. Serves 6.

Note: For a thicker soup, use 2 cups yogurt.

Approximate nutritional analysis per serving:
Calories 93, Protein 2 g, Carbohydrates 14 g, Fat .5 g, Cholesterol 2 mg, Sodium 27 mg

CUCUMBER-YOGURT SOUP

4 medium to large cucumbers, peeled
sprigs of fresh mint
2 cups (480 ml) skim milk
2 cups (480 ml) STONYFIELD FARM Nonfat Plain Yogurt
1-2 tbs (15-30 ml) honey
1 tsp (5 ml) chopped fresh dill
2-3 scallions, chopped
salt, to taste
pepper, to taste

Reserve a few cucumber slices and whole mint leaves for garnish. Chop remaining cucumbers into large pieces, then purée with the remaining mint and all the other ingredients in a blender or food processor. Chill for several hours. Serve cold, garnished with reserved mint leaves and cucumber slices. Serves 6.

Approximate nutritional analysis per serving:
Calories 112, Protein 9 g, Carbohydrates 19 g, Fat .6 g, Cholesterol 3 mg, Sodium 109 mg

ALBERT'S ORGANICS YELLOW POTATO-LEEK SOUP

3 organic celery stalks, sliced
1 medium organic white onion, sliced thin
2 medium organic leeks, sliced then rinsed
3 organic garlic cloves, sliced
2 tbs (30 ml) olive oil
3 medium organic yellow Finnish potatoes, unpeeled, cut into uniform chunks
3 large organic red potatoes, cut into uniform chunks
pinch fresh chopped parsley
2 tsp (10 ml) basil
2 bay leaves
2 tsp (10 ml) cumin
3 tbs (45 ml) shoyu soy sauce
½ tsp (3 ml) black pepper
pinch fresh chopped dill

Sauté celery, onion, leeks and garlic in oil for 2-3 minutes. Combine all ingredients, except fresh dill, in stockpot and cover with water. Simmer for 30-45 minutes, until potatoes are soft. Reserving ½-1 cup vegetables, blend soup into a purée using a blender, food processor or potato ricer (for more texture). Combine fresh dill and reserved vegetables with purée. Reheat and serve. Serves 6.

Approximate nutritional analysis per serving:
Calories 280, Protein 6 g, Carbohydrates 55 g, Fat 5 g, Cholesterol 0 mg, Sodium 551 mg

ALBERT'S ORGANICS YELLOW POTATO-LEEK SOUP

ALBERT'S ORGANICS GARNET YAM SOUP

3 medium organic carrots,
    sliced into uniform pieces
½ medium organic yellow onion,
    sliced into uniform pieces
1-2 tbs (15-30 ml) olive oil
3 medium organic garnet yams,
    cut into large pieces
1 small organic potato, sliced into
    uniform pieces
2 tbs (30 ml) soy sauce
1 tsp (5 ml) basil
cayenne, to taste
salt, optional

Sauté carrots and onion for 2-3 minutes in olive oil. Add yams and potato and cover with water. Simmer for 15-20 minutes until yams are soft. Add soy sauce, basil and cayenne. Salt to taste. Blend or food process until creamy. Add more water to adjust thickness. Serves 6.

Approximate nutritional analysis per serving:
Calories 260, Protein 5 g, Carbohydrates 55 g, Fat 3 g, Cholesterol 0 mg, Sodium 377 mg

INDIAN ROCK'S CURRY MUSHROOM SOUP

light vegetable oil spray
2 leeks, sliced and diced
pinch of curry powder, to taste
2 twists of fresh pepper from
    pepper mill
2 tbs (30 ml) flour
1 cup (240 ml) beef stock
1 cup (240 ml) skim milk
6 mushrooms, sliced (2 shiitake,
    2 portobello, 2 regular)
½ cup (120 ml) parsley, chopped

Lightly spray bottom of soup pot with vegetable oil. Sauté leeks until tender. Add curry powder, and pepper. Add flour and stir until blended. Add beef stock. Stir well. Add milk. Stir well. Simmer until reduced by half. Add sliced mushrooms. Simmer very gently for 5 minutes. Pour into bowls and top with chopped parsley. Serves 2.

Approximate nutritional analysis per ¾ cup serving:
Calories 186, Protein 10 g, Carbohydrates 34 g, Fat 2 g, Cholesterol 2 mg, Sodium 134 mg

WALNUT ACRES' LEMONY LENTIL SOUP

3 cups (720 ml) water
1 cup (240 ml) dried lentils
    (brown, green or red)
1 large onion, finely chopped
3½ cups (840 ml) WALNUT ACRES
    Vegetarian Broth
3 tbs (45 ml) WALNUT ACRES
    Organic Extra Virgin Olive Oil
2 tsp (10 ml) garlic, minced
freshly grated peel of 1 organic
    lemon
½ cup (120 ml) fresh lemon juice

Bring water, lentils, onion, broth, oil and garlic to a boil in a 3-quart pot. Reduce heat, partially cover and simmer 30 minutes or until lentils are tender. Stir in lemon peel and juice. Serve promptly or refrigerate up to 3 days. Serves 4.

Approximate nutritional analysis per serving:
Calories 312, Protein 15 g, Carbohydrates 38 g, Fat 11 g, Cholesterol 0 mg, Sodium 322 mg

WALNUT ACRES' LEMONY LENTIL SOUP

CREAM OF SQUASH-CILANTRO SOUP

SAFETY TIP: Be careful when blending hot ingredients in a closed blender, because they will explode with the pressure from the heat. Start the blender on slow with the lid slightly open, then turn to high speed and seal the lid, or use a hand blender and blend the soup in the cooking pot.

2 tbs (30 ml) extra virgin olive oil
4 cups (960 ml) buttercup or other winter squash or carrots, peeled and cubed
2 cups (480 ml) onion, chopped
1 cup (240 ml) celery, thinly sliced
¼ cup (60 ml) fresh cilantro, chopped
2 tbs (30 ml) fresh garlic, minced
4 cups (960 ml) water
1 tsp (5 ml) sea salt
¼ tsp (1 ml) coriander powder
½ cup (120 ml) SOLAIT Soy Beverage Powder

Warm a large skillet on medium heat for 30 seconds, then add the oil, squash, onion, celery, cilantro and garlic. Sauté for about 10 minutes, then add the water, sea salt, and coriander. Cook, covered, until the squash is done, then transfer to a blender. Add the soy milk powder, then blend for about 30 seconds or until the soup is mostly smooth with some small chunks. Serve while hot. Serves 4.

Approximate nutritional analysis per serving:
Calories 249, Protein 6 g, Carbohydrates 37 g, Fat 10 g, Cholesterol 0 mg, Sodium 629 mg

CREAMY TOMATO-ONION SOUP

¾ cup (180 ml) onions, chopped
3 tbs (45 ml) defatted chicken stock
2 cups (480 ml) fresh tomatoes, puréed or canned unsalted tomatoes
1 tsp (5 ml) sweet basil
2 medium garlic cloves, pressed or 1 tbs (15 ml) garlic powder
¼ tsp (1 ml) coarsely ground pepper
10½-oz pkg (315 g) MORI-NU Silken Soft or MORI-NU Lite Tofu , drained
pinch of salt, optional
margarine or butter, optional

In a medium saucepan, sauté onions in chicken stock until transparent. Add puréed tomatoes along with next 3 ingredients. Simmer 10-15 minutes. In a blender or a food processor, process tofu until smooth and stir into the tomato mixture. Simmer and serve hot. Serves 3.

Approximate nutritional analysis per 8 oz serving:
Calories 101, Protein 7 g, Carbohydrates 13 g, Fat 3 g, Cholesterol 0 mg, Sodium 14 mg

ALBERT'S ORGANICS SWEET CORN SOUP

2 qts (1.9 l) spring water
¼ cup (60 ml) wakame
4 ears fresh sweet corn, kernels
    removed
2 onions, diced
1 tsp (5 ml) safflower or light
    sesame oil
½ tsp (3 ml) sea salt
½ cup (120 ml) cooked brown rice
¼ cup (60 ml) light miso
parsley or cilantro, for garnish

In a large pot add water, wakame and bare corn cobs. Bring to a boil, simmer 20 minutes and remove cobs. Meanwhile, sauté the onions in oil and sea salt. Next, add sautéed onions, corn and rice to stock and simmer for 30 minutes. Dissolve miso in ½ cup of soup stock and add to soup. Simmer on low for 2 minutes and stir. Place in bowls and garnish with cilantro or parsley. Serves 8.

Approximate nutritional analysis per serving:
Calories 94, Protein 3 g, Carbohydrates 19 g, Fat 2 g, Cholesterol 0 mg, Sodium 442 mg

CREAM OF ASPARAGUS SOUP

1 lb (455 g) fresh asparagus,
    cut into 1-inch pieces
1 cup (240 ml) water
2 tbs (30 ml) butter
½ cup (120 ml) chopped onion
4 cups (960 ml) chicken stock
1 tbs (15 ml) unbleached
    all-purpose flour
2 cups (480 ml) STONYFIELD FARM
    Nonfat Plain Yogurt
cayenne pepper, to taste

Separate the asparagus tips from the stalks. Simmer the tips in water 5 minutes, then drain and reserve. Sauté the onion in 1 tbs butter. Add the asparagus stalks and sauté briefly. Add the chicken stock, bring to a boil and simmer for 5-8 minutes, or until the asparagus is tender. Purée the vegetable mixture in a blender, then return it to the pan.

In a separate pan, melt the remaining 1 tbs butter and blend in the flour; gradually blend in ½ cup of the hot stock. Add this mixture to the puréed vegetables and mix thoroughly. Simmer for 1 minute. Add the reserved asparagus tips. Stir in the yogurt and add cayenne pepper. Serve immediately. Do not boil after adding the yogurt or the mixture will curdle. Serves 6.

Approximate nutritional analysis per serving:
Calories 133, Protein 10 g, Carbohydrates 13 g, Fat 5 g, Cholesterol 12 mg, Sodium 621 mg

TURKISH YOGURT SOUP

½ cup (120 ml) barley
1 cup (240 ml) water
3 cups (720 ml) chicken stock
2 medium onions, chopped
2 tbs (30 ml) butter
¼ cup (60 l) fresh mint, chopped
    or 1 tbs (15 ml) dried mint
½ cup (120 ml) fresh parsley,
    chopped
1 tsp (5 ml) salt, or to taste
pinch of white pepper
2 cups (480 ml) STONYFIELD FARM
    Nonfat Plain Yogurt

Soak the barley in water overnight. Drain well. Boil the barley in the chicken stock for about 10 minutes or until tender. Meanwhile, cook the onions in the butter until soft. Stir the onions into the barley and stock. Add the mint, parsley, salt and pepper. Cover and simmer for 1 hour. Fold in the yogurt, heat through, do not boil after adding yogurt or soup will curdle. Serves 4.

Approximate nutritional analysis per serving:
Calories 260, Protein 15 g, Carbohydrates 34 g, Fat 8 g, Cholesterol 18 mg, Sodium 1272 mg

ALBERT'S ORGANICS SWEET CORN SOUP

YOGURT-CARROT SOUP

¼ cup (60 ml) butter
1 onion, chopped
2 cloves garlic, minced
½ tsp (3 ml) mustard seeds
½ tsp (3 ml) ground turmeric
½ tsp (3 ml) ground ginger
¼ tsp (1 ml) cayenne pepper
½ tsp (3 ml) salt
½ tsp (3 ml) ground cinnamon
½ tsp (3 ml) ground cumin
1 lb (455 g) carrots, peeled and
    thinly sliced
1 tbs (15 ml) lemon juice
3½ cups (840 ml) water
2 cups (480 ml) STONYFIELD FARM
    Nonfat Plain Yogurt
1 tbs (15 ml) honey
black pepper, optional
fresh parsley, chopped, for garnish

Melt the butter in a skillet and sauté the onion and garlic until they are golden. Add the mustard seeds, turmeric, ginger, cayenne, salt, cinnamon and cumin and sauté for several minutes, stirring constantly. Add the carrots and lemon juice, stir to combine and continue cooking for several more minutes. Add 2 cups of water. Cover and simmer for at least ½ hour or until the carrots are tender.

Purée the carrot mixture in a blender with the remaining 1½ cups of water. Pour the purée into a soup pot and stir in the yogurt with a whisk. Add the honey and heat the soup gently. Do not boil after adding the yogurt or the soup will curdle. Sprinkle with black pepper, if desired. Serve hot, garnished with parsley. Serves 4.

Approximate nutritional analysis per serving:
Calories 253, Protein 9 g, Carbohydrates 29 g, Fat 12 g, Cholesterol 33 mg, Sodium 519 mg

CREAM OF CARROT SOUP

3 cups (720 ml) vegetable bouillon
    or water
1 lb (455 g) carrots, cut into
    ⅛-inch slices
1 large onion, chopped
2 tbs (30 ml) margarine
4 tbs (60 ml) flour
3 cups (720 ml) Unsweetened
    WESTSOY
salt, to taste
pepper, to taste

Bring bouillon to a boil in a large pan. Add carrots and onion. Cover and cook until the carrots are tender, about 15 minutes. Drain, reserving cooking liquid. Purée carrots and onion in food processor or blender adding a little cooking liquid if necessary. In the large pan, melt margarine over medium heat and stir in flour, mixing well. Slowly stir in reserved cooking liquid and WestSoy. Cook, stirring until mixture thickens and begins to boil. Add puréed vegetables, salt and pepper to taste. Cook until warm. Serves 8.

Approximate nutritional analysis per serving:
Calories 90, Protein 3 g, Carbohydrates 11 g, Fat 4 g, Cholesterol 0 mg, Sodium 590 mg

CREAM OF CARROT SOUP

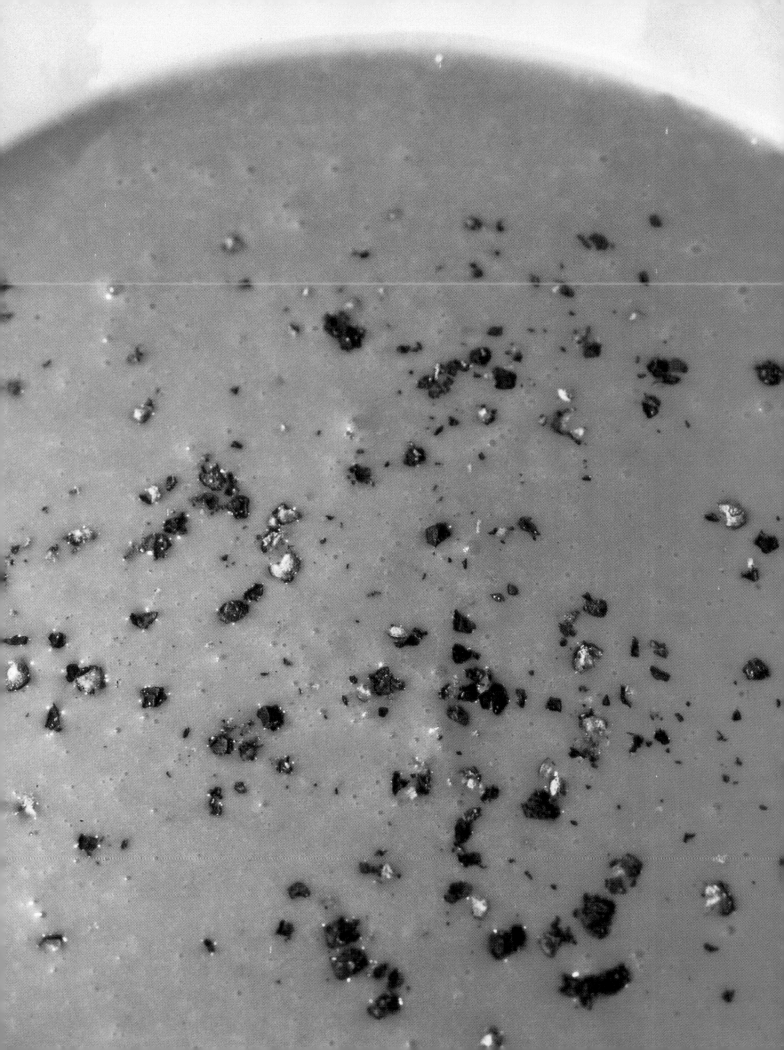

ALBERT'S ORGANICS ORGANIC CREAMY BROCCOLI SOUP

1 large organic carrot, chopped
　　into uniform pieces
1 small organic yellow onion,
　　chopped into uniform pieces
2 stalks organic celery, chopped
　　into uniform pieces
2 tbs (30 ml) olive oil
1 large bunch organic broccoli,
　　chopped into uniform pieces
water
1 clove garlic, pressed
½ inch fresh ginger, peeled and
　　grated
1 tsp (5 ml) cumin powder
1 tsp (5 ml) cardamom powder
3 tbs (45 ml) soy sauce, or to taste

In a large saucepan sauté carrots, onions and celery in olive oil for 2-3 minutes. Add broccoli. Sauté 1 minute, then add water to pot just to cover vegetables and simmer them for 10-15 minutes or until soft. Add garlic, ginger, cumin, cardamom and soy sauce. Process in blender or food processor until you have achieved the chunky or smooth texture you prefer. Serves 4.

Approximate nutritional analysis per serving:
Calories 107, Protein 4 g, Carbohydrates 9 g, Fat 7 g, Cholesterol 0 mg, Sodium 815 mg

HEARTY CLAM CHOWDER

5 medium potatoes, pared and
　　cut into ½-inch cubes
¾ cup (180 ml) green onions,
　　chopped, including tops
½ cup (120 ml) celery, diced
1 carrot, thinly sliced
¼ red or green pepper, diced
1 tsp (5 ml) garlic, minced
2 cups (480 ml) water
2 tbs (30 ml) margarine
1 tsp (5 ml) salt, or to taste
1 tsp (5 ml) Worcestershire sauce
dash of hot pepper sauce
2 6½-oz cans (390 g) minced clams
½ cup (120 ml) flour
2 cups (480 ml) Unsweetened
　　WESTSOY

Place potatoes, green onion, celery, carrot, bell pepper and garlic in large pan. Mix in water, margarine, salt, Worcestershire and hot pepper sauce. Bring to a boil, cover and cook 15 minutes over medium heat or until potatoes are tender. Drain clams, reserving liquid and adding water, if necessary, to make 1 cup. Combine clam liquid with flour and stir to make a smooth paste. Pour flour paste into vegetables and cook, stirring, until mixture thickens. Add clams and WestSoy. Continue cooking until chowder is hot, but do not boil. Serves 9.

Approximate nutritional analysis per serving:
Calories 180, Protein 10 g, Carbohydrates 28 g, Fat 4 g, Cholesterol 15 mg, Sodium 370 mg

HEARTY CLAM CHOWDER

CREAM OF CAULIFLOWER SOUP

4 cups (960 ml) vegetable bouillon
    or water
1 large cauliflower, divided
    into florets
4 tbs (60 ml) margarine
1½ cups (355 ml) celery, chopped
2 tbs (30 ml) minced onion
¼ cup (60 ml) flour
2 cups (480 ml) Unsweetened
    WESTSOY
salt, to taste
pepper, to taste

Bring bouillon to boil in large pan. Add cauliflower and cook until tender. Drain, reserving cooking broth. Coarsely chop about ⅓ of the florets. Purée remaining cauliflower in food processor or blender, adding some broth if necessary. In the same pan, melt margarine over medium heat and sauté celery and onion until tender, stirring often. Sprinkle flour over sautéed vegetables and stir well. Slowly stir in reserved broth and cook, stirring until mixture thickens and comes to a boil. Add puréed cauliflower and WestSoy and reheat, do not boil. Stir in chopped florets; add salt and pepper to taste. Serves 8

Approximate nutritional analysis per serving:
Calories 100, Protein 3 g, Carbohydrates 8 g, Fat 7 g, Cholesterol 0 mg, Sodium 400 mg

BLACK-EYED PEA SOUP

11-oz pkg (330 g) FRIEDA'S
    Black-Eyed Peas, cooked
    according to package directions,
    with cooking liquid
2 tbs (30 ml) cooking oil
1 cup (240 ml) minced celery
3 FRIEDA'S Leeks, sliced,
    white part only
2 cloves garlic, minced
4 cups (960 ml) beef broth
1 FRIEDA'S Bay Leaf
2 tbs (30 ml) FRIEDA'S Fresh
    Thyme, chopped
    or 1 tsp (5 ml) crushed dried
    thyme
2 tbs (30 ml) FRIEDA'S Fresh
    Cilantro, or parsley, chopped
1 tbs (15 ml) FRIEDA'S Fresh
    Marjoram, chopped
    or 1 tsp (5 ml) crushed dried
    marjoram
1 tbs (15 ml) lemon juice
salt, to taste
pepper, to taste
¼ tsp (1 ml) bottled hot pepper
    sauce
bacon, cooked and crumbled,
    for garnish, optional
FRIEDA'S Cilantro, or parsley,
    snipped, for garnish, optional

Set cooked black-eyed peas aside; do not drain. In a large saucepan or Dutch oven, heat oil; add celery, leeks and garlic. Sauté 5-8 minutes over medium heat. Stir in beef broth, bay leaf, thyme, cilantro, marjoram and lemon juice. Bring to boiling; reduce heat. Simmer, uncovered, 10 minutes. Remove bay leaf. Add beans and their liquid; process mixture in batches in food processor or blender. Return to pan; season to taste with salt, pepper and hot pepper sauce. Reheat until warmed. Garnish each serving with crumbled bacon and cilantro or parsley, if desired. Serves 6 as a main course.

Approximate nutritional analysis per serving:
Calories 274, Protein 15 g, Carbohydrates 43 g, Fat 6 g, Cholesterol 0 mg, Sodium 532 mg

BLACK-EYED PEA SOUP

CREAMY YOGURT-BEET SOUP

1 medium Vidalia onion, sliced
1 tbs (15 ml) butter or vegetable oil
16-oz can (480 g) beets, not drained
    or 2 cups (480 l) cooked fresh
    beets
2 cups (480 ml) chicken stock
2 cups (180 ml) STONYFIELD FARM
    Nonfat Plain Yogurt
1 cup (240 ml) low-calorie sour
    cream
1 tbs (15 ml) red or white wine
    vinegar
1 tbs (15 ml) fresh lemon juice
salt, to taste
pepper, to taste
additional STONYFIELD FARM
    Nonfat Plain Yogurt or sour
    cream, for garnish
fresh dill, coriander or pepper,
    for garnish

In a small skillet, sauté the onion in butter until soft. In a food processor, combine the beets, beet liquid (only if using canned beets), chicken stock and sautéed onion. Purée until smooth, in batches if necessary.

If the soup is to be served cold, simply whisk in the yogurt, sour cream, vinegar, lemon juice and salt and pepper, then chill. To serve soup warm, stir the beet mixture constantly while heating it up on top of the stove. When the mixture is hot but not boiling, slowly stir in the yogurt, sour cream, vinegar, lemon juice and salt and pepper. Do not boil or the yogurt will curdle. Soup may be garnished with a dollop of yogurt or sour cream and topped with fresh, chopped herbs or pepper. Yields 6 cups, serves 6.

Approximate nutritional analysis per serving:
Calories 163, Protein 9 g, Carbohydrates 16 g, Fat 7 g, Cholesterol 22 mg, Sodium 565 mg

WALNUT ACRES' ARMENIAN APRICOT-LENTIL SOUP

3 tbs (45 ml) WALNUT ACRES
    Organic Extra Virgin Olive Oil
1 large onion, finely chopped
2 large cloves garlic, finely chopped
⅓ cup (80 ml) WALNUT ACRES
    Organic Dried Unsulphured
    Apricots, chopped
⅓ cup (80 ml) dried peaches,
    chopped
1½ cups (355 ml) dried split red
    lentils, rinsed thoroughly
5 cups (1.2 l) WALNUT ACRES
    Vegetable Broth
3 tbs (45 ml) tamari or soy sauce
3 medium-size fresh, ripe plum
    tomatoes, peeled, seeded and
    chopped
1 tsp (5 ml) ground cumin
1 tsp (5 ml) dried thyme
1 tsp (5 ml) salt
1 tsp (5 ml) ground pepper
4 tbs (60 ml) fresh lemon juice
¾ cup (180 ml) fresh cilantro,
    chopped

In large soup pot, heat the oil over medium heat. Add the onion, garlic, dried apricots and peaches. Sauté, stirring occasionally, until the onion is soft, about 12 minutes. Add the lentils and vegetable broth. Bring to a boil. Reduce the heat and simmer, covered, until the lentils are tender, about 30 minutes. Stir in the soy sauce, tomatoes, cumin, thyme, salt and pepper. Simmer covered for another 10 minutes. Remove half the soup and purée it in a food processor. Return the purée to the pot. Stir a few times, then season the soup with the lemon juice and additional salt and pepper, if necessary. Simmer, stirring, for 2-3 minutes longer. Sprinkle with cilantro. Serves 10.

Approximate nutritional analysis per serving:
Calories 195, Protein 10 g, Carbohydrates 28 g, Fat 5 g, Cholesterol 0 mg, Sodium 644 mg

WALNUT ACRES' ARMENIAN APRICOT-LENTIL SOUP

FRENCH LENTIL SOUP

2 cups (480 ml) **OLD SAVANNAH DuPuy Lentils**
2 qts (1.9 l) water, plus more as needed
2 onions, chopped
4 garlic cloves, minced
2 bay leaves
½ tsp (3 ml) ground cinnamon
½ tsp (3 ml) ground cloves
2 tsp (10 ml) ground cumin
2 cups (480 ml) tomatoes, chopped or 1 cup (240 ml) tomato purée
4 pepperoncini peppers, diced
salt, to taste

Bring lentils and water to boil. Simmer 1 hour on very low heat. Add remaining ingredients, except salt. Add water as needed and simmer over very low flame 1 more hour. Add salt to taste.

Note: ordinary green lentils take longer to cook and have a less subtle flavor. This soup can be made in approximately 1 hour if cooked at higher temperatures, but the lentils will lose their shape. Serves 12.

Approximate nutritional analysis per serving:
Calories 135, Protein 10 g, Carbohydrates 25 g, Fat .6 g, Cholesterol 0 mg, Sodium 8 mg

PEA POD SPINACH SOUP

3 cups (720 ml) chicken broth
3 cups (720 ml) vegetable broth or additional chicken broth
1 tbs (15 ml) soy sauce
pinch ground red pepper (cayenne)
2-oz pkg (60 g) **FRIEDA'S SNO PEAS**, stringed and halved crosswise
2 cups (480 ml) spinach leaves, torn and stems removed
1 cup (240 ml) **FRIEDA'S Tofu**, drained and broken into chunks
½ cup (120 ml) **FRIEDA'S Enoki Mushrooms**
3 green onions, chopped
1 hard-cooked egg, chopped, optional

Heat broths in Dutch oven or 3-quart saucepan; add soy sauce and red pepper; simmer 2 minutes. Add snow peas, spinach leaves and tofu chunks. Cut off bottom ½ inch of enoki mushroom stems; add to soup with chopped onion. Simmer 1 minute. Serve soup in bowls, with some of the chopped egg sprinkled on top, if desired. Serves 7 as a first course.

Approximate nutritional analysis per serving:
Calories 73, Protein 8 g, Carbohydrates 4 g, Fat 3 g, Cholesterol 0 mg, Sodium 828 mg

WALNUT ACRES' BLACK BEAN SOUP

1 lb (455 g) WALNUT ACRES
   Organic Black Beans
2 smoked ham hocks
8 cups (1.9 l) water
1 tsp (5 ml) ground celery seed
1 tsp (5 ml) salt
2 cups (480 ml) WALNUT ACRES
   Beef Broth
1½ tbs (25 ml) WALNUT ACRES
   Organic Extra Virgin Olive Oil
1½ cups (355 ml) green peppers,
   cored, seeded and finely chopped
1½ cups (355 ml) onions,
   finely chopped
1½ tbs (25 ml) garlic, finely minced
1½ tsp (8 ml) ground cinnamon
pinch of ground cayenne, or to taste
2 16-oz cans (960 g) WALNUT ACRES
   Organic Whole Tomatoes,
   diced with juice
¼ cup (60 ml) red wine vinegar

Place beans, ham hocks, water, celery seed and salt in heavy kettle. Bring to boil; cover and simmer about 2½ hours or until beans are thoroughly tender. Remove ham hocks; set aside. Drain beans and reserve along with meat and cooking liquid. There should be about 6 cups of beans and several cups of liquid. Add enough broth to make 4 cups of liquid. Combine the beans with liquid in large bowl.

Heat oil in heavy kettle; add peppers, onions, garlic, cumin and cayenne. Cook, stirring until onions are wilted. Add tomatoes and vinegar. Let simmer about 15 minutes. Meanwhile, remove and discard skin and bones from ham hocks. Chop ham; set aside. Add bean mixture to cooked tomato mixture. Add chopped meat. Simmer until thoroughly heated. Serve in soup bowls. Serves 9.

Approximate nutritional analysis per serving:
Calories 174, Protein 10 g, Carbohydrates 21 g, Fat 6 g, Cholesterol 12 mg, Sodium 456 mg

MUIR GLEN SPICY BLACK BEAN SOUP

2 tsp (10 ml) vegetable oil
1 onion, chopped
1 clove garlic, minced or pressed
2 14½-oz cans (870 g) MUIR GLEN
   Organic Diced Tomatoes,
   undrained
3 15-oz cans (1.4 kg) black beans,
   drained, rinsed and puréed
1¾ cups (415 ml) vegetable or
   chicken broth
1 jalapeño chile, seeded and minced
2 tsp (10 ml) cumin seeds
¼ cup (60 ml) green onion,
   finely chopped
shredded cheese, for garnish,
   optional
plain nonfat yogurt, for garnish,
   optional
cilantro leaves, for garnish, optional

In 4-6 quart saucepan, combine oil, onion and garlic. Cook over medium heat, stirring frequently, until onion is tender. Add tomatoes, beans, broth, chile and cumin seeds. Bring to a boil; reduce heat and simmer, uncovered, about 10 minutes, or until flavors are blended. Stir in green onion. Ladle into bowls; garnish as desired. Serves 8

Approximate nutritional analysis per 1 cup serving:
Calories 261, Protein 17 g, Carbohydrates 44 g, Fat 2 g, Cholesterol 0 mg, Sodium 358 mg

MUIR GLEN SPICY BLACK BEAN SOUP

GARBANZO SOUP

1 tbs (15 ml) ARROWHEAD MILLS
   Unrefined Olive Oil
½ cup (120 ml) onion, chopped
4 cups (960 ml) cold water
½ cup (120 ml) ARROWHEAD
   MILLS Garbanzo Flour
2 tbs (30 ml) soy sauce
pinch garlic powder, optional
1 tsp (5 ml) sweet basil leaves,
   crushed

PROVENÇAL SEAFOOD SOUP

4 tbs (60 ml) SPECTRUM WORLD
   EATS Mediterranean Oil
4 cloves garlic, minced
6 ripe medium tomatoes
   or 28-oz can (840 g) diced
   tomatoes
pinch of salt
1 tbs (15 ml) SPECTRUM
   NATURALS Organic White Wine
   Vinegar plus 1 cup (240 ml) water
   or 1 cup (240 ml) dry white wine
1 cup (240 ml) chicken broth
   or water
2 lbs (910 g) assorted fresh firm-
   fleshed fish and shellfish,
   cut into large spoon-size pieces
8 tbs (120 ml) chopped Italian
   parsley
6 tbs (90 ml) chopped fresh basil
fresh ground pepper, to taste

Preheat heavy saucepan, then add oil and onion and sauté until soft. Add 1 cup cold water. Stir in flour until smooth. Stir in remaining water gradually. Add seasonings. Let cook over medium-low heat until slightly thickened, stirring occasionally, or over higher heat stirring constantly. Do not allow to boil. Serves 4.

Approximate nutritional analysis per serving:
Calories 106, Protein 4 g, Carbohydrates 13 g, Fat 5 g, Cholesterol 0 mg, Sodium 521 mg

PROVENÇAL SEAFOOD SOUP

Heat oil in a large casserole over medium-low heat. For 1 minute, sauté garlic, tomatoes and a pinch of salt. Add wine vinegar and simmer for 2 minutes. Add broth and return to a simmer. Add the seafood. Gently turn fish until just cooked through, no more than 5 minutes. Gently stir in herbs. Serves 4.

Approximate nutritional analysis per serving:
Calories 567, Protein 59 g, Carbohydrates 11 g, Fat 32 g, Cholesterol 175 mg, Sodium 363 mg

GARBANZO SOUP

ALBERT'S ORGANICS MISO SOUP WITH TOFU & SCALLIONS

2 oz (60 g) wakame, soaked
   and diced
6 cups (1.4 l) spring water
4 tsp (20 ml) miso
8 oz (240 g) fresh tofu, steamed
   and cubed
daikon radish, finely grated
2 scallions, thinly sliced

Add wakame to water, bring to a boil and simmer for 20-30 minutes. Place miso in suribachi (Japanese mortar and pestle) or small bowl and mix well with ¼ cup wakame broth. Stir miso into soup and simmer very low for 2-3 minutes. Do not boil, beneficial enzymes may be lost. Place cubed tofu in bowls and ladle in soup. Stir in ½-1 tbs grated daikon per bowl. Garnish with scallions. Serves 4.

Approximate nutritional analysis per serving:
Calories 61, Protein 6 g, Carbohydrates 4 g, Fat 3 g, Cholesterol 0 mg, Sodium 337 mg

THAI SEITAN SOUP

6 pieces dried galanga
27-oz can (810 ml) CHAOKOH
   Coconut Milk
16 oz (480 ml) vegetable stock
3 small whole chiles, hot
3 tbs (45 ml) cilantro stems,
   chopped
6 kaffir lime leaves, cut into
   large pieces
2 stalks lemon grass, bruised,
   cut into 1-inch pieces
1-3 tbs (15-45 ml) fish sauce,
   to taste, optional
8 oz (240 g) WHITE WAVE Seitan,
   cut into ¼x½-inch strips,
   discard marinade
1-3 tbs (15-45 ml) fresh lemon juice
½ cup (120 ml) mushrooms,
   coarsely chopped
¼ cup (60 ml) carrots,
   coarsely chopped
cilantro, chopped, for garnish

THAI SEITAN SOUP

Combine galanga, coconut milk, vegetable stock, chiles, cilantro, lime leaves, lemon grass and fish sauce. To bruise lemon grass, press hard with spoon or knife back; discard tops. Bring to a boil, reduce heat and simmer, uncovered, for 15 minutes. Add seitan, lemon juice, mushrooms and carrots to soup. Return to boil, lower heat and simmer for additional 10 minutes. Strain out the galanga, lime leaves and lemon grass and discard them. Garnish with chopped cilantro. Serves 6.

Approximate nutritional analysis per serving:
Calories 382, Protein 18 g, Carbohydrates 18 g, Fat 28 g, Cholesterol 2 mg, Sodium 181 mg

**ALBERT'S ORGANICS MISO SOUP
WITH TOFU & SCALLIONS**

ALMOST CHINESE HOT-AND-SOUR SOUP

2 cups (480 ml) vegetable stock
2 cups (480 ml) water
8 oz (240 g) WHITE WAVE Hard
  Tofu, slivered (2x¼x¼ inches)
2 cups (480 ml) Napa cabbage,
  slivered
½ cup (120 ml) fresh or
  reconstituted shiitake
  mushrooms, slivered
¼ cup (60 ml) carrots, grated
  coarsely
1 tsp (5 ml) ginger, peeled and
  minced
1 tbs (15 ml) soy sauce
¾ tsp (4 ml) salt
2 tbs (30 ml) white vinegar
⅛-¼ tsp (.5-1 ml) cayenne
2 tbs (30 ml) cornstarch
3 tbs (45 ml) water
cilantro, chopped scallions, garlic-
  chives or a squeeze of fresh
  lemon for garnish, optional

UDON IN SESAME-MISO BROTH

UDON IN SESAME-MISO BROTH

1 tbs (15 ml) sesame oil
2 slices fresh ginger root
½ cup (120 ml) onion, thinly sliced
½ cup (120 ml) celery, sliced
⅔ cup (160 ml) carrots, sliced
4 cups (960 ml) stock or water
⅓ cup (80 ml) sesame seeds, toasted
2 level tbs (30 ml) WESTBRAE
  Hatcho Miso
2 level tbs (30 ml) WESTBRAE Red
  Rice Miso
1 tbs (15 ml) mirin
1 lb (455 g) uncooked udon
4-5 qts (3.8-4.8 l) water, for noodles
scallions, slivered, for garnish

Boil stock and 2 cups water over medium-high heat. Add tofu, cabbage, shiitakes, carrots, ginger, soy sauce and salt. Return to boil, lower heat and simmer 4-5 minutes. Add vinegar and cayenne. Mix cornstarch and 3 tbs water together. Add to soup and cook for 1-2 minutes. Garnish with any of the suggested items and serve very hot. Serves 6.

Approximate nutritional analysis per serving:
Calories 72, Protein 4 g, Carbohydrates 9 g, Fat 2 g, Cholesterol 0 mg, Sodium 569 mg

ALMOST CHINESE HOT-AND-SOUR SOUP

Heat oil in medium-size pot. Sauté ginger until golden brown, then discard.

Sauté onion until translucent. Add celery and carrots, and sauté briefly. Add stock and bring to a boil. Reduce heat, cover, simmer until vegetables are tender.

While vegetables are cooking, thoroughly grind toasted seeds in a suribachi or mortar. Add the miso, mirin and ½ cup of broth. Purée with seeds, then add to soup. Cook udon in 4-5 qts of rapidly boiling water until just al dente (firm). Drain, rinse briefly in a cold bath and drain again. Divide noodles in 5 bowls.

Ladle hot miso broth over top of noodles to almost cover. Garnish with scallions and serve. Serves 5.

Note: For a summery variation, omit the sautéed vegetables, substitute 3 tbs white miso for the red miso and top the noodles and broth with a colorful assortment of lightly steamed or simmered vegetables.

Approximate nutritional analysis per serving:
Calories 434, Protein 18 g, Carbohydrates 68 g, Fat 12 g, Cholesterol 0 mg, Sodium 1593 mg

HEARTY KASHA-VEGETABLE SOUP

1 cup (240 ml) carrots, diced
1 cup (240 ml) celery, diced
1 cup (240 ml) cabbage, diced
1 medium onion, chopped
4 tbs (60 ml) olive oil
6 cups (1.4 l) chicken or beef stock
16-oz can (480 g) tomatoes
1 cup (240 ml) WOLFF'S Kasha
1 slightly beaten egg white
10-oz pkg (300 g) frozen cut
    green beans
10-oz pkg (300 g) frozen peas

Sauté carrots, celery, cabbage and onion in oil in large heavy pan for 10 minutes, stirring, until vegetables are soft. Add stock and tomatoes. Cook for 30 minutes, covered. Combine kasha and egg in small pan, cook over low heat, stirring until kasha is dry.

After soup has cooked, add kasha and cook 15 minutes longer. Add beans and peas and simmer soup 10 minutes longer. Correct seasoning. Soup will have a rich, thick consistency. Serves 6.

Approximate nutritional analysis per serving:
Calories 323, Protein 14 g, Carbohydrates 43 g, Fat 12 g, Cholesterol 0 mg, Sodium 1001 mg

WALNUT ACRES' MINESTRONE SOUP

WALNUT ACRES' MINESTRONE SOUP

2 qts (1.9 l) WALNUT ACRES
    Vegetarian Broth
½ lb (230 g) kidney beans or
    lima beans, dry
½ lb (230 g) fresh or frozen peas
1 small green cabbage,
    finely chopped
½ lb (230 g) fresh spinach leaves,
    shredded
4 carrots, finely chopped
4 stalks celery, finely chopped
1 yellow onion, finely chopped
4 garlic cloves, minced
½ cup (120 ml) raw WALNUT
    ACRES' Organic Brown Rice
1 tbs (15 ml) fresh parsley,
    finely chopped
½ tsp (3 ml) sage
salt, to taste
pepper, to taste
¼ cup (60 ml) WALNUT ACRES
    Organic Extra Virgin Olive Oil,
    optional

Soak beans overnight. Put all ingredients in a large stockpot. Bring to a boil, stirring occasionally. Reduce heat and simmer until beans are tender. This soup can be cooked in a crockpot for 8 hours on low. Serve with crusty French bread. Serves 10.

Approximate nutritional analysis per serving:
Calories 196, Protein 9 g, Carbohydrates 34 g, Fat .8 g, Cholesterol 0 mg, Sodium 407 mg

HEARTY KASHA-
VEGETABLE SOUP

KAMUT MACARONI MINESTRONE

1 tbs (15 ml) olive oil
1 small onion, chopped
2 cloves garlic, minced or pressed
1 cup (240 ml) cabbage, chopped
1 small zucchini
    or 1 cup (240 ml) green beans,
    chopped
1 small carrot, sliced
1 tomato, peeled, seeded and diced
    or 1 tbs (15 ml) tomato paste
1 cup (240 ml) cooked navy or great
    northern beans
¾-1 tsp (4-5 ml) salt
½ tsp (3 ml) pepper
1 bay leaf
1 tbs (15 ml) fresh basil, finely
    chopped
    or 1 tsp (5 ml) dried basil
1 tbs (15 ml) fresh parsley, finely
    chopped
    or 1 tsp (5 ml) dried parsley
4 cups (960 ml) water
1 cup (240 ml) KAMUT Elbows
½ cup (120 ml) grated Parmesan
    cheese

Add olive oil to a 2-quart soup pot and place over medium heat. Sauté the onion, then the garlic, cabbage, zucchini and carrot. Add the tomato, beans, salt, pepper, bay leaf, basil, parsley and water. Bring to a boil, add elbows and simmer for 12-15 minutes or just until the pasta is tender. Stir in ¼ cup of the Parmesan cheese. Sprinkle remaining cheese on each bowl as a garnish. Serves 4.

Approximate nutritional analysis per serving:
Calories 301, Protein 15 g, Carbohydrates 46 g, Fat 8 g, Cholesterol 10 mg, Sodium 648 mg

FRENCH ONION SOUP

FRENCH ONION SOUP

1 pkg GREEN HOUSE Bouquet
    Garni (includes thyme, bay leaf
    and Italian parsley)
4 cups (960 ml) onions, sliced
2 tbs (30 ml) fresh garlic, sliced
1 tbs (15 ml) olive oil
4 cups (960 ml) low-sodium
    chicken broth
fresh ground black pepper, to taste
4 ½-inch thick slices French bread
2 oz (60 g) reduced-fat Swiss cheese,
    grated

Finely chop thyme leaves to equal 1-2 tsp, chop Italian parsley and set aside.

Place the olive oil, onions, bay leaf and thyme in a nonstick saucepan and cook slowly until the onions turn light brown. This color is important as it provides a rich, sweet flavor. Add the garlic and cook for 5 minutes. Add the chicken broth and simmer 20 minutes. Stir in the parsley and pepper.

Divide soup into 4 ovenproof bowls. Top each serving with French bread and ½ oz cheese. Brown under broiler. Serve immediately. Serves 4.

Approximate nutritional analysis per serving:
Calories 290, Protein 11 g, Carbohydrates 27 g, Fat 7 g, Cholesterol 5 mg, Sodium 224 mg

CHICKEN SOUP

3-4 chicken quarters
½ onion, chopped
1 clove garlic, minced
2-3 carrots, sliced
1 cup (240 ml) celery, sliced
1 potato, cubed
1 tbs (15 ml) parsley
1½ tsp (8 ml) ZUMBRO Jerusalem
   Artichoke Flour
salt, to taste
pepper, to taste

Place chicken in soup pot and add enough water to cover. Add onion and garlic; cook, partially covered, over medium-high heat for about 45 minutes. Add carrots, celery, potato and parsley and cook another 30 minutes. Remove chicken from pot; separate chicken from bones, discarding skin, cartilage, etc. Skim fat from surface. Return chicken to pot. Five minutes before serving add flour, salt and pepper. Serves 3.

Approximate nutritional analysis per serving:
Calories 309, Protein 23 g, Carbohydrates 28 g, Fat 12 g, Cholesterol 77 mg, Sodium 133 mg

HOMESTYLE CHICKEN SOUP

6 cups (1.4 l) chicken broth
1 medium carrot, thinly sliced
1 stalk celery, thinly sliced
¼ cup (60 ml) WOLFF'S Kasha,
   medium granulation
1 cup (240 ml) cooked chicken,
   optional
2 tbs (30 ml) parsley, chopped
pinch pepper

Combine chicken broth, carrot, celery and kasha in saucepan. Heat to boiling. Reduce heat and simmer about 15 minutes or until vegetables are tender. Add remaining ingredients. Heat to boiling and serve. Serves 8.

Approximate nutritional analysis per serving:
Calories 56, Protein 5 g, Carbohydrates 6 g, Fat 1 g, Cholesterol 0 mg, Sodium 591 mg

CHICKEN-TORTILLA SOUP

4 cups (960 ml) low-sodium
   chicken broth
6 oz (180 g) boneless, skinless
   chicken breast, cut into
   ¼-inch strips
½ cup (120 ml) onion, sliced
½ cup (120 ml) red peppers, sliced
½ cup (120 ml) Passilla chiles or
   green peppers, sliced
1 cup (240 ml) Roma tomatoes,
   diced
2 cloves fresh garlic, chopped
¼ tsp (1 ml) cumin
1 jalapeño or serrano chile,
    chopped and seeded, optional,
    if spicy is desired
12 corn tortilla chips
2 tbs (30 ml) GREEN HOUSE Fresh
   Cilantro, chopped plus 4 sprigs,
   for garnish
2 tbs (30 ml) GREEN HOUSE Fresh
   Oregano, chopped

In a medium saucepan, bring chicken broth to a boil; add chicken strips and cook for 5 minutes, skimming the top. Add the vegetables and cook for 10 more minutes. Chop the oregano and cilantro, reserving 4 sprigs of cilantro for garnish. Add the fresh herbs at the last minute and serve, garnishing the bowls with a sprig of cilantro and 3 tortilla chips. Serves 4.

Approximate nutritional analysis per serving:
Calories 133, Protein 14 g, Carbohydrates 12 g, Fat 4 g, Cholesterol 23 mg, Sodium 132 mg

CHICKEN-TORTILLA SOUP

MUIR GLEN GAZPACHO

2 14½-oz cans (870 g) **MUIR GLEN Organic Diced Tomatoes, undrained**
14½-oz can (435 ml) **vegetable or chicken broth**
1 **red onion, minced**
1 **green bell pepper, chopped**
1 **cucumber, peeled and chopped**
1 **stalk celery, chopped**
1 **clove garlic, minced**
2 tbs (30 ml) **lemon juice**
¼ tsp (1 ml) **black pepper**

In large bowl, combine all ingredients. Cover and chill several hours. If desired, purée half of soup in blender or food processor, stir into remaining half. Serves 10.

Approximate nutritional analysis per serving:
Calories 37, Protein 2 g, Carbohydrates 6 g, Fat .3 g, Cholesterol 0 mg, Sodium 259 mg

R. W. KNUDSEN FAMILY GAZPACHO

1 qt (960 ml) **R. W. KNUDSEN FAMILY Tomato-Garlic Juice**
1 cup (240 ml) **fresh tomatoes, chopped**
1 cup (240 ml) **cucumber, chopped**
½ cup (120 ml) **red onion, chopped**
1 cup (240 ml) **croutons**
½ cup (120 ml) **Italian parsley**

Chill juice. Pour into 5 bowls; garnish with tomatoes, cucumber, onion, croutons and parsley. Serves 5.

Approximate nutritional analysis per serving:
Calories 100, Protein 3 g, Carbohydrates 21 g, Fat .6 g, Cholesterol 0 mg, Sodium 635 mg

ELEGANT ELEPHANT SOUP

1 **cucumber, coarsely chopped**
1 **green bell pepper, coarsely chopped**
1 **carrot, coarsely chopped**
1 jar **UNCLE DAVE'S Spicy Peanut Pasta Sauce**
½ cup (120 ml) **crushed tomatoes**
1 cup (240 ml) **chicken broth**

Combine chopped vegetables with sauce, tomatoes and chicken broth in a food processor or blender. Process just until vegetables are diced. Serve chilled. Serves 4.

Approximate nutritional analysis per serving:
Calories 158, Protein 7 g, Carbohydrates 17 g, Fat 8 g, Cholesterol 0 mg, Sodium 1379 mg

R. W. KNUDSEN FAMILY GAZPACHO

Overleaf: ELEGANT ELEPHANT SOUP

BLACK BEAN SALAD

3 cups (720 ml) black beans, cooked
2 cups (480 ml) corn, cooked
½ cup (120 ml) red onions, minced
1 cup (240 ml) red peppers, cut
½ cup (120 ml) cilantro, chopped
½ cup (120 ml) parsley
1 tsp (5 ml) chile peppers, crushed
3 cloves garlic, crushed
½ cup (120 ml) lime juice
½ cup (120 ml) OMEGA
    Flax Seed Oil
2 tsp (10 ml) cumin
1 tsp (5 ml) sea salt

BLACK BEAN SALAD

Combine beans, corn, onions, red peppers, cilantro, parsley and chile peppers. Mix garlic, lime juice, oil, cumin and sea salt. Pour dressing over salad and mix. Serves 7.

Approximate nutritional analysis per serving:
Calories 289, Protein 9 g, Carbohydrates 31 g, Fat 16 g, Cholesterol 0 mg, Sodium 315 mg

SOUTHWESTERN CHICKEN CAESAR SALAD

¼ cup (60 ml) chopped GREEN
    HOUSE Fresh Cilantro
¼ cup (60 ml) Ortega green chiles
1 cup (240 ml) Caesar salad
    dressing, low sodium, calorie
    and fat
8 cups (1.9 l) chopped romaine
    lettuce
4 4-oz (480 g) chicken breasts,
    grilled and cut in ½-inch strips
2 red peppers, lightly grilled and
    cut into 2-inch strips

Mix cilantro and chiles into salad dressing. Add to lettuce and toss together gently. Place ¼ mixture in the center of each of 4 large plates. Garnish salad with chicken and peppers and serve. Serves 4.

Approximate nutritional analysis per serving:
Calories 281, Protein 31 g, Carbohydrates 20 g, Fat 8 g, Cholesterol 75 mg, Sodium 100 mg

SOUTHWESTERN CHICKEN CAESAR SALAD

THAI CHICKEN NOODLE SALAD

4 cups (960 ml) cooked egg noodles
12-oz (360 g) cooked chicken breast,
    boneless, skinless
1 cup (240 ml) bean sprouts
½ cup (120 ml) shredded raw
    carrots
½ cup (120 ml) blanched snow peas
2 cups (480 ml) chopped iceberg
    lettuce
½ cup (120 ml) chopped red bell
    pepper, additional for garnish
¼ cup (60 ml) peanuts, dry roasted
    and unsalted

DRESSING:
1 cup (240 ml) seasoned rice vinegar
1 tbs (15 ml) chopped fresh garlic
1 tbs (15 ml) chopped fresh ginger
5 tsp (25 ml) sesame oil
1 tbs (25 ml) low-sodium soy sauce
¼ cup (60 ml) lime juice
6 tbs (90 ml) GREEN HOUSE
    Oriental Bouquet, equal parts
    of each herb
¼ tsp (1 ml) white pepper

Dressing: Mix all ingredients together.

Place all other ingredients in a large bowl and toss with 1 cup of the dressing. Serve in large bowls and garnish with chopped red peppers and herb leaves. Serves 4.

Approximate nutritional analysis per serving salad and ¼ cup dressing: Calories 480, Protein 33 g, Carbohydrates 54 g, Fat 16 g, Cholesterol 99 mg, Sodium 320 mg

THAI CHICKEN NOODLE SALAD

SESAME CHICKEN SALAD

3 cups (720 ml) cooked TEXMATI
    Rice
2 cups (480 ml) cooked chicken
    breast, sliced
¼ lb (115 g) snow peas,
    sliced into strips
1 medium cucumber, cut into strips
1 medium red pepper,
    cut into strips
½ cup (120 ml) sliced green onion
2 tbs (30 ml) toasted sesame seeds

SESAME DRESSING:
¼ cup (60 ml) chicken broth
1 tbs (15 ml) peanut oil
3 tbs (45 ml) white wine vinegar
3 tbs (45 ml) soy sauce
1 tsp (5 ml) sesame oil

Combine all salad ingredients; stir well. Toss with dressing. Serve at room temperature or slightly chilled. Serves 6.

Dressing: Combine all ingredients in jar; cover tightly and shake vigorously. Yields ¾ cup.

Approximate nutritional analysis per serving w/ dressing: Calories 328, Protein 34 g, Carbohydrates 28 g, Fat 8 g, Cholesterol 80 mg, Sodium 623 mg

CURRIED CHICKEN SALAD

**3 cups (720 ml) WOLFF'S Kasha,
    coarse or whole, uncooked**
6 cups (1440 ml) chicken broth
**2 cups (480 ml) diced cooked
    chicken**
1 large red apple, diced
½ cup (120 ml) raisins
2 green onions, sliced
¼ cup (60 ml) chopped celery
1 red bell pepper, chopped

HONEY VINAIGRETTE:
⅔ cup (160 ml) oil
¼ cup (60 ml) vinegar
2 tbs (30 ml) honey
2 tsp (10 ml) curry powder

Prepare kasha according to package directions, using chicken broth. When kasha is cool, combine all salad ingredients in a large bowl.

Dressing: In a small bowl, whisk together all ingredients until smooth. Pour over salad and toss gently. Serves 5.

Approximate nutritional analysis per serving:
Calories 682, Protein 41 g, Carbohydrates 55 g, Fat 35 g, Cholesterol 96 mg, Sodium 101 mg

CURRIED CHICKEN SALAD

WALDORF CHICKEN SALAD

2 tbs (30 ml) honey
2 tbs (30 ml) Dijon mustard
1 tbs (15 ml) poppy seeds
½ tsp (3 ml) grated fresh lemon peel
⅓ cup (80 ml) fresh lemon juice
⅓ cup (80 ml) salad oil
**12 dried apricots, moist packed
    preferred**
**4 cups (960 ml) bite-size pieces
    cooked chicken**
1 apple, cored and diced
¼ cup (60 ml) diced celery
¼ cup (60 ml) minced green onions
**⅓ cup (80 ml) sliced toasted
    almonds**

Stir together honey, mustard, poppy seeds, lemon peel, juice and oil. Add apricots and let stand 30 minutes. Remove apricots and set them aside. Add chicken and toss lightly. Refrigerate until ready to serve.

To serve: Add apple, celery, green onions and almonds to chicken mixture. Divide onto lettuce-lined plates and garnish with apricots. Serves 6.

Approximate nutritional analysis per serving:
Calories 363, Protein 29 g, Carbohydrates 21 g, Fat 19 g, Cholesterol 72 mg, Sodium 136 mg

Courtesy of The National Honey Board.

COLD CHICKEN WITH LIME DRESSING

1 lb (455 g) chicken breasts,
    cut in half
1 cup (240 ml) thinly sliced celery
1 cup (240 ml) diced red
    bell peppers
½ cup (120 ml) chopped scallions
⅓ cup (80 ml) chopped, dry roasted,
    unsalted peanuts
8 large romaine lettuce leaves,
    rinsed and drained

DRESSING:
½ cup (120 ml) CALIFORNIA
    CLASSICS Lime Oil
¼ tsp (1 ml) crushed dried
    red peppers
½ tsp (3 ml) ground cumin

Poach the chicken breasts in just enough water to cover. Bring to a boil over medium heat. Immediately reduce heat to low and simmer, covered for 15 minutes. Remove breasts and drain, cool and debone. Cut meat into ¼-inch strips.

   Dressing: Combine lime oil, dried red peppers and cumin with wire whisk.

   Put chicken strips, celery, red bell peppers and scallions in a large bowl. Add dressing to chicken and vegetables. Toss well and refrigerate for 1 hour. Do not marinate for longer than 3 hours. Sprinkle with peanuts just before serving on romaine leaves. Serves 4.

Approximate nutritional analysis per serving:
Calories 521, Protein 39 g, Carbohydrates 8 g, Fat 37 g, Cholesterol 96 mg, Sodium 117 mg

RASPBERRY CHICKEN SALAD

1-1½ lbs (455-683 g) chicken
    breasts, skinless, boneless
¼ cup (60 ml) plus 3 tbs (45 ml)
    CHESHIRE GARDENS Queen of
    Hearts Premium Raspberry
    Vinegar
¼-⅓ cup (60-80 ml) mayonnaise
¼ cup (60 ml) red onion
¼ cup (60 ml) red pepper
½ lb (230 g) mixed salad greens
berries, kiwi, avocado wedges or
    orange slices, for garnish

Place chicken breasts in heavy skillet, drizzle ¼ cup vinegar over them and poach for about 7 minutes on each side. Cool. Break into bite-size pieces, drizzle with 2 tbs vinegar, add mayonnaise, onions and pepper and serve over a bed of greens that have been tossed with remaining 1 tbs vinegar. Garnish with berries, kiwi or wedges of avocado alternating with orange. Serves 5.

Approximate nutritional analysis per serving:
Calories 315, Protein 36 g, Carbohydrates 7 g, Fat 15 g, Cholesterol 105 mg, Sodium 466 mg

COLEMAN WRANGLER STEAK & PASTA SALAD

1 lb (455 g) COLEMAN NATURAL
Chuck Blade Steak, grilled or
broiled, cut into bite-size cubes
12 oz (360 g) uncooked rotelli or
rotini pasta, cooked and drained
15-oz can (450 g) pinto beans,
rinsed and drained
15-oz can (450 g) red kidney beans,
rinsed and drained
1 cup (240 ml) chopped red onion
1 cup (240 ml) chopped green
bell pepper
1½ cups (355 ml) prepared
barbecue sauce
½ cup (120 ml) cider vinegar
2 tsp (10 ml) dry mustard
½ tsp (3 ml) ground black pepper

In large salad bowl, combine blade steak cubes, pasta, pinto and
kidney beans, onion and bell pepper; set aside. In medium bowl,
combine barbecue sauce, vinegar, dry mustard and pepper,
blending well. Pour over pasta salad; toss well to coat. Serves 8.

Approximate nutritional analysis per serving:
Calories 369, Protein 21 g, Carbohydrates 62 g, Fat 4 g, Cholesterol 25 mg,
Sodium 942 mg

COLEMAN WRANGLER STEAK & PASTA SALAD

COLEMAN THAI STEAK & RICE SALAD

1 lb (455 g) COLEMAN NATURAL
Chuck Blade or Top Sirloin
Steak, grilled or broiled, cut into
2-inch slices

DRESSING:
½ cup (120 ml) seasoned
rice wine vinegar
3 tbs (45 ml) olive oil
2 tbs (30 ml) soy sauce
1 tsp (5 ml) garlic powder
½ tsp (3 ml) ground ginger
½ tsp (3 ml) ground black pepper
2 tbs (30 ml) chopped fresh cilantro
leaves

SALAD:
1 cup (240 ml) long-grain rice,
cooked and cooled
½ cup (120 ml) chopped red
bell pepper
¼ cup (60 ml) thinly sliced
green onion
¼ cup (60 ml) shredded carrot
1 tbs (15 ml) toasted sesame seeds

In small bowl, combine dressing ingredients; set aside. In large
bowl, combine steak and salad ingredients. Pour on dressing and
toss to coat. Serves 4.

Approximate nutritional analysis per serving:
Calories 444, Protein 27 g, Carbohydrates 44 g, Fat 18 g, Cholesterol 50 mg,
Sodium 526 mg

COLEMAN THAI
STEAK & RICE SALAD

PASTA SALAD WITH SALMON SAUSAGE, ASPARAGUS, FRESH MOZZARELLA & BASIL

3 3-oz (270 g) **HEALTH SEA** Salmon
  Sausages, any flavor, diagonal
  bite-size slices
1 lb (455 g) fresh asparagus,
  trimmed, diagonal cut 3 inches
  and blanched
2 medium sun-ripened tomatoes,
  seeded and diced into
  ½-inch pieces
1 cup (240 ml) fresh vinaigrette
2 tbs (30 ml) fresh mint, chopped
8 oz (240 g) soft mozzarella,
  cut into bite-size pieces
8 oz (240 g) favorite pasta, blanched
7-oz jar (210 g) Mancini roasted
  peppers, drained and cut into
  ½-inch pieces
salt, to taste
pepper, to taste
Bibb lettuce, for serving
¼ cup (60 ml) fresh basil, chopped,
  plus sprigs for garnish
anchovies, optional
Parmesan cheese, optional

Assemble ingredients into 3-quart bowl. Toss with vinaigrette. Add salt and black pepper to taste. Serve pasta salad in Bibb lettuce cups and garnish with basil sprigs and anchovies and Parmesan, if desired. Serves 6.

Approximate nutritional analysis per serving:
Calories 424, Protein 24 g, Carbohydrates 26 g, Fat 26 g, Cholesterol 36 mg, Sodium 978 mg

SAVORY SALMON SALAD

SAVORY SALMON SALAD

¾-1 lb (340-455 g) salmon filet
1 tbs (15 ml) **CHESHIRE GARDEN**
  Savory Tarragon Blend Vinegar
1 tbs (15 ml) olive oil, optional
1 small onion, finely chopped
  or 3 large shallots or fresh
  chives, finely chopped
¼-⅓ cup (60-80 ml) mayonnaise,
  to taste
½ lb (230 g) lettuce, mixed red and
  green leaf, tossed with 1 tbs
  (15 ml) **CHESHIRE GARDEN**
  Savory Tarragon Vinegar

Drizzle vinegar over salmon, then olive oil and bake in a 350°F (180°C) oven for 10-15 minutes, until fish flakes. Cool. Mix with onion, shallots or chives and mayo. Serve over greens. Serves 3.

Approximate nutritional analysis per serving:
Calories 316, Protein 24 g, Carbohydrates 5 g, Fat 22 g, Cholesterol 73 mg, Sodium 174 mg

GRILLED CHILE-SHRIMP SALAD

½ lb (230 g) large raw shrimp,
    shelled and deveined, or scallops
½ cup (120 ml) water
¼ cup (60 ml) lime juice
1 tsp (5 ml) sesame oil
    or vegetable oil
2 tbs (30 ml) minced green onion
2 tbs (30 ml) minced FRIEDA'S
    Fresh Cilantro
1 FRIEDA'S Dried Habañero Chile,
    rehydrated and very finely
    minced
1 clove garlic, minced
2 cups (480 ml) shredded green
    or yellow zucchini
2 cups (480 ml) shredded carrot

Place shrimp or scallops in a nonmetal dish. Stir together water, lime juice, oil, onion, cilantro, habañero and garlic; pour over shrimp. Cover and chill for 2-6 hours.

To serve, preheat broiler or barbecue grill. Place shredded zucchini and carrot in steamer over simmering water. Cover and steam about 3-5 minutes or until tender. Drain shrimp; thread on skewers. Broil or grill 3-5 minutes or until pink and opaque. Serve shrimp over steamed vegetables. Serves 4 small salads.

Approximate nutritional analysis per serving:
Calories 104, Protein 13 g, Carbohydrates 9 g, Fat 2 g, Cholesterol 111 mg, Sodium 151 mg

GRILLED CHILE-SHRIMP SALAD

WARM SALAD OF SCALLOPS & HERBS BÉARNAISE

2 tbs (30 ml) olive oil
4 shallots, finely hopped
5 mushrooms, sliced thin
½ lb (455 g) washed and drained
    spinach
2 tbs (30 ml) CHESHIRE GARDEN
    Béarnaise Blend Vinegar, White
½ lb (230 g) scallops

Heat olive oil, sauté shallots in oil until golden. Add mushrooms and sauté until soft. Add spinach, cook covered until it wilts, then remove lid and simmer until liquid evaporates. Add béarnaise, raise heat until vinegar reduces by half, 1-2 minutes. Remove from skillet, add scallops, sear until browned, turn, and sear until browned on other side, 2-3 minutes per side. Slice one open; it should be opaque throughout. Serves 2 as a warm salad.

Approximate nutritional analysis per serving:
Calories 330, Protein 28 g, Carbohydrates 16 g, Fat 19 g, Cholesterol 45 mg, Sodium 675 mg

WARM SALAD OF SCALLOPS & HERBS BÉARNAISE

PURPLE POTATO SALAD NIÇOISE

2 cups (480 ml) chopped cooked
FRIEDA'S Purple Potatoes
6½-oz can (195 g) white albacore
tuna, drained and chunked
1 ripe tomato, seeded and chopped
½ cup (120 ml) sliced ripe olives
1 cup (240 ml) cooked cut
green beans
½ cup (120 ml) olive oil or salad oil
⅓ cup (80 ml) white wine vinegar
1 tbs (15 ml) FRIEDA'S Fresh
Tarragon
¼ tsp (1 ml) salt
¼ tsp (1 ml) pepper
lettuce leaves
2 hard-cooked eggs, quartered

In a large bowl, gently toss together cooked purple potatoes, tuna, tomato, olives and green beans. In a covered jar, shake together oil, vinegar, fresh tarragon, salt and pepper. Pour over salad and toss. Spoon onto lettuce-lined platter; garnish with cooked egg quarters. Serves 5.

Approximate nutritional analysis per serving:
Calories 377, Protein 14 g, Carbohydrates 20 g, Fat 28 g, Cholesterol 96 mg, Sodium 559 mg

CHINESE SEAFOOD SALAD

CHINESE SEAFOOD SALAD

½ lb (230 g) medium shrimp
in shells
1-2 tbs (15-30 ml) peanut oil or
salad oil for stir-frying
4-oz pkg (120 g) FREIDA'S Chinese
Long Beans
½ cup (120 ml) FREIDA'S
Water Chestnuts, sliced
1 red or green bell pepper,
cut into bite-size strips
¼ cup (60 ml) FREIDA'S
Black Radish, shredded
2 cups (480 ml) shredded Chinese
or napa cabbage
¼ lb (115 g) flaked cooked
crabmeat, optional
¼ cup (60 ml) red wine vinegar
2 tbs (30 ml) sesame or peanut oil
2 tbs (30 ml) soy sauce
1 tbs (15 ml) water
1 clove garlic, minced

Cook shrimp by boiling in water about 3 minutes, until pink. Remove shells and veins; rinse in cold water. Trim ends of Chinese long beans; cut into 2-inch lengths. Heat oil in wok or large skillet; add beans, water chestnuts and bell pepper; stir-fry for 3 minutes. Add black radish, cabbage, crab and shrimp to wok; toss 1 minute. Cover. Meanwhile, combine the remaining ingredients; toss with vegetables and seafood. Serve at once. Serves 3.

Approximate nutritional analysis per serving:
Calories 251, Protein 19 g, Carbohydrates 13 g, Fat 15 g, Cholesterol 147 mg, Sodium 934 mg

PURPLE POTATO SALAD NIÇOISE

SEAFOOD FAJITA SALAD

6 cups (1.4 l) shredded lettuce
½ lb (230 g) cooked bay shrimp, canned, frozen or fresh
½ lb (230 g) flaked cooked crab-meat, canned, frozen or fresh
1 small avocado, peeled, pitted and thinly sliced
1 cup (240 ml) julienne sticks of FRIEDA'S Jicama, peeled
1 red or yellow bell pepper, slivered
½ cup (120 ml) thinly sliced red onion
½ cup (120 ml) shredded cheddar or Monterey Jack cheese

SALSA DRESSING:
½ cup (120 ml) bottled or homemade salsa
¼ cup (60 ml) white wine vinegar
2 tbs (30 ml) FRIEDA'S Fresh Cilantro, chopped and additional sprigs, for garnish
warmed buttered tortillas, optional

Line 4 salad plates with shredded lettuce. Arrange shrimp, crab, avocado, jicama, bell pepper and onion on each salad plate. Sprinkle on cheese.

Dressing: Stir together salsa, vinegar and cilantro. Spoon over salads. Garnish salads with additional sprigs of cilantro, and serve with warm tortillas, if desired. Serves 4.

Approximate nutritional analysis per serving:
Calories 315, Protein 29 g, Carbohydrates 13 g, Fat 17 g, Cholesterol 178 mg, Sodium 653 mg

VITA-SPELT FETA SALAD

VITA-SPELT FETA SALAD

1 cup (240 ml) VITA-SPELT Kernels
2½ cups (590 ml) water
1 cup (240 ml) fresh parsley, chopped
4 cloves garlic, minced
3 tbs (45 ml) lemon juice
¼ cup (60 ml) feta cheese, in pieces
2 tbs (30 ml) currants
4 scallions, finely chopped
2 tsp (10 ml) fresh mint, chopped
3 tbs (45 ml) olive oil
¼ cup (60 ml) black olives
salt, to taste
pepper, to taste

Put Vita-Spelt in blender or processor until majority of kernels are broken into pieces. Do not over blend. Mixture should be the consistency of medium bulgur. Bring water to a boil. Add spelt and bring to boil again. Lower temperature and cover. Simmer for approximately 1 hour or until all water is absorbed. Be careful not to scorch the grain. Run cold water over grain, or allow to cool naturally. Toss all ingredients together thoroughly. Salt and pepper to taste. Chill before serving, to allow flavors to blend. Serves 6.

Approximate nutritional analysis per serving:
Calories 261, Protein 9 g, Carbohydrates 21 g, Fat 17 g, Cholesterol 37 mg, Sodium 517 mg

SEAFOOD FAJITA SALAD

SANTORINI SALAD WITH FETA

1 cup (240 ml) water
1⅓ cups (320 ml) Italian salad
  dressing
1 cup (240 ml) THE BIRKETT
  MILLS Whole Buckwheat Groats
1 cup (240 ml) plum tomatoes, diced
6-oz jar (180 g) marinated artichoke
  hearts, drained and coarsely
  chopped or marinated
  mushrooms, sliced
1 cup (240 ml) pitted kalamata
  olives or oil-cured black olives
⅓ cup (80 ml) green onion, sliced
⅓ cup (80 ml) red or orange sweet
  pepper, diced
⅓ cup (80 ml) fresh basil, chopped
⅓ cup (80 ml) flat-leaf parsley,
  minced
1 cup (240 ml) feta, diced
spinach or radicchio leaves

SANTORINI SALAD WITH FETA

In 2-qt saucepan, boil water and 1 cup salad dressing. Stir in buckwheat, reduce heat, cover pan, and simmer 15 minutes or until liquid is absorbed. Toss cooled buckwheat groats with remaining ⅓ cup salad dressing, tomatoes, artichoke hearts, olives, onions, pepper, herbs and feta. Serve on bed of spinach or radicchio. Serves 5.

Approximate nutritional analysis per serving:
Calories 617, Protein 13 g, Carbohydrates 40 g, Fat 48 g, Cholesterol 44 mg, Sodium 1529 mg

TORTELLONI WITH ROASTED EGGPLANT SALAD

1 pkg PUTNEY PASTA Parmesan
  and Cracked Black Peppercorn
  Tortelloni
1 pkg PUTNEY PASTA Sun Dried
  Tomato Basil Mozzarella
  Tortelloni
2 cups (480 ml) eggplant, small dice
3 tbs (45 ml) olive oil
6 garlic cloves, chopped
¼ cup (60 ml) golden raisins
1 tbs (15 ml) pine nuts, toasted
¼ cup (60 ml) fresh parsley,
  chopped
2 tbs (30 ml) balsamic vinegar
2 tsp (10 ml) honey
½ tsp (3 ml) salt
coarse ground black pepper, to taste
1 pt (480 ml) cherry tomatoes,
  halved
1 bunch scallions, thin sliced

Cook tortelloni according to package directions, lightly oil and chill.

In large bowl toss eggplant with olive oil and garlic. Transfer to a covered baking dish and bake for 30 minutes in a preheated 400°F (205°C) oven. Eggplant and garlic should be very soft and lightly browned. Allow to cool to room temperature.

Lightly mash eggplant and garlic mixture. Mix in raisins, pignolia nuts, parsley, balsamic vinegar, honey, salt and pepper. Toss eggplant mixture with pasta. Add cherry tomatoes and scallions. Adjust seasoning and serve. Serves 8.

Approximate nutritional analysis per serving:
Calories 280, Protein 12 g, Carbohydrates 41 g, Fat 8 g, Cholesterol 34 mg, Sodium 430 mg

TORTELLONI WITH ROASTED EGGPLANT SALAD

MEDITERRANEAN RAVIOLI SALAD

**2 pkgs PUTNEY PASTA Spinach
    and Feta Ravioli**
3 tbs (45 ml) olive oil
6 garlic cloves, minced
**1½ cups (355 ml) broccoli florets,
    blanched**
**1½ cups (355 ml) cauliflower florets,
    blanched**
1 cup (240 ml) cooked white beans
**2 oz (60 g) sun-dried tomatoes,
    oil packed, julienned**
2 bunches arugula leaves
1 tbs (15 ml) Romano cheese, grated
black pepper, to taste

VARIATION:
fresh grilled chicken or shrimp

Cook ravioli according to package directions, lightly oil and chill.
    In a large skillet heat olive oil. Add garlic and cook over a medium heat until lightly toasted. Add blanched broccoli, cauliflower, cooked white beans and sun-dried tomatoes. Sauté 3-4 minutes. Toss with cooked ravioli and arugula leaves. Top with grated Romano cheese and fresh ground black pepper. Serves 8.
    Variation: Add chicken or shrimp.

Approximate nutritional analysis per serving:
Calories 239, Protein 11 g, Carbohydrates 29 g, Fat 10 g, Cholesterol 31 mg, Sodium 356 mg

MEDITERRANEAN RAVIOLI SALAD

SPINACH & FETA PESTO RAVIOLI SALAD

**2 pkgs PUTNEY PASTA Spinach
    and Feta Ravioli**
**1 pkg PUTNEY PASTA Passionate
    Pesto Sauce**
**1 small Bermuda onion,
    cut into rings**
**½ cup (120 ml) frozen baby peas,
    thawed**
1 red bell pepper, diced
**1 tbs (15 ml) Parmesan cheese,
    grated**

Cook ravioli according to package directions. Drain ravioli and chill using cold water. Shake off any extra moisture.
    Toss ravioli with pesto sauce. Garnish with onion rings, peas, bell pepper and Parmesan cheese. Serves 6.

Approximate nutritional analysis per serving:
Calories 369, Protein 12 g, Carbohydrates 31 g, Fat 22 g, Cholesterol 41 mg, Sodium 587 mg

**SPINACH & FETA
PESTO RAVIOLI SALAD**

DILLED AGNOLOTTI SALAD

2 pkgs PUTNEY PASTA Broccoli &
    Aged Vermont Cheddar Agnolotti
½ lb (230 g) carrots, peeled and
    sliced thin
1 bunch asparagus, sliced
    on the bias
1 tsp (5 ml) fresh ginger, minced
1 tbs (15 ml) rice wine vinegar
1½ tsp (8 ml) soy sauce
1 tsp (5 ml) honey
2 tsp (10 ml) Dijon mustard
2 tbs (30 ml) olive oil
2 tbs (30 ml) fresh dill, chopped
salt, to taste
black pepper, to taste
2 tsp (10 ml) sesame seeds, toasted

Cook agnolotti according to package directions, lightly oil and chill.

Blanch carrots and asparagus in boiling salted water for 2 minutes, then chill.

In a mixing bowl, combine ginger, vinegar, soy sauce, honey and Dijon mustard. Whisk in olive oil. Add dill and adjust seasoning to taste. Combine pasta, carrots, asparagus, dressing and sesame seeds. Serve lightly chilled. Serves 6.

Variation: Add chicken breast, poached or grilled.

Approximate nutritional analysis per serving:
Calories 310, Protein 13 g, Carbohydrates 45 g, Fat 9 g, Cholesterol 42 mg, Sodium 615 mg

CURRIED TORTELLINI SALAD

2 pkgs PUTNEY PASTA Spinach
    Mozzarella and Walnut Tortellini
1½ tbs (25 ml) canola oil
½ cup (120 ml) Bermuda onion,
    diced
2 garlic cloves, minced
1 tsp (5 ml) curry powder
1 tbs (15 ml) honey
2 tsp (10 ml) balsamic vinegar
¼ cup (60 ml) raisins
¼ cup (60 ml) walnuts, halves
    and pieces
½ cup (120 ml) mandarin orange
    segments
salt, to taste
2 tbs (30 ml) fresh mint, torn

Cook tortellini according to package directions, lightly oil and chill.

In a large skillet heat oil then sauté onions and garlic until lightly browned. Add curry powder and gently heat for 1 minute. Add honey and balsamic vinegar, remove from heat then toss with pasta. Add raisins, walnuts and mandarin oranges. Adjust seasoning. Best served at room temperature or slightly chilled. Garnish with torn mint leaves. Serves 6.

Approximate nutritional analysis per serving:
Calories 240, Protein 9 g, Carbohydrates 31 g, Fat 9 g, Cholesterol 23 mg, Sodium 158 mg

CURRIED TORTELLINI SALAD

TEMPEH PASTA SALAD

½ lb (230 g) spaghetti
½ cup (120 ml) tofu mayonnaise
2 cloves garlic, crushed
2 tbs (30 ml) brown rice vinegar
1 tsp (5 ml) curry powder
1 green or red pepper, diced
1 medium zucchini, sliced
¼ lb (115 g) snow peas, blanched
    or raw
6.1-oz pkg SOY DELI Original or
    Marinated Pacific Tempeh
    Burgers, cubed
¼ cup (60 ml) fresh basil, minced
½ cup (120 ml) fresh parsley,
    chopped

Break spaghetti into thirds and cook to al dente.

In a small bowl whisk tofu mayonnaise, garlic, vinegar and curry powder. Gently mix with pasta. Add green pepper, zucchini, snow peas and the tempeh cubes. Top with a mixture of basil and parsley. Serve at room temperature. Serves 6.

Approximate nutritional analysis per serving:
Calories 196, Protein 8 g, Carbohydrates 23 g, Fat 9 g, Cholesterol 0 mg, Sodium 181 mg

PRIMAVERA PASTA SALAD

1½ tbs (25 ml) olive oil
1½ tbs (25 ml) butter or margarine
1½ cups (355 ml) broccoli florets
2 cloves garlic, minced
2 medium tomatoes, seeded and
    diced
¾ cup (180 ml) julienned zucchini
½ cup (120 ml) julienned carrot
¼ cup (60 ml) honey
¼ cup (60 ml) lemon juice
1½ tsp (8 ml) grated lemon peel
¾ tsp (4 ml) dried basil, crushed
¾ tsp (4 ml) dried oregano, crushed
salt, to taste
pepper, to taste
6 oz (180 g) linguine or fettuccine
    noodles, cooked
Parmesan cheese, grated

Heat oil and butter in large skillet over medium-high heat; add broccoli and garlic and stir-fry 2 minutes. Reduce heat to low and add tomatoes, zucchini, carrot, honey, lemon juice, lemon peel and seasonings. Simmer about 4 minutes or until vegetables are tender, stirring gently. Toss with noodles; cool. Sprinkle with Parmesan cheese. Serve at room temperature or chilled. Serves 6.

Approximate nutritional analysis per serving:
Calories 165, Protein 3 g, Carbohydrates 26 g, Fat 7 g, Cholesterol 8 mg, Sodium 44 mg

Courtesy of The National Honey Board.

PRIMAVERA PASTA SALAD

KAMUT MACARONI SALAD

DRESSING:
¾ cup (180 ml) olive oil
¼ cup (60 ml) red wine vinegar
2 cloves garlic, minced
1 tbs (15 ml) dried oregano
¼ tsp (1 ml) black pepper

8-oz pkg (240 g) KAMUT Macaroni
    or Rotelli/Rotini Pasta
1 cup (240 ml) cherry tomatoes
¼ cup (60 ml) parsley, chopped
½ cup (120 ml) black olives,
    chopped
½ cup (120 ml) celery, chopped
⅓ cup (80 ml) red onion, chopped

Mix ingredients for Dressing and allow to sit while preparing the salad.

Cook pasta, drain and cool. Add tomatoes, parsley, olives, celery and onions and mix. Pour Dressing over salad, toss gently and taste for seasoning. Serves 4.

Approximate nutritional analysis per serving:
Calories 619, Protein 9 g, Carbohydrates 56 g, Fat 44 g, Cholesterol 0 mg, Sodium 232 mg

KAMUT MACARONI SALAD

ITALIAN BEAN AND PASTA SALAD

2 cups (480 ml) ARROWHEAD
    MILLS Anasazi Beans
2 cups (480 ml) cooked spinach
    noodles or vegetable rotelli
½ cup (120 ml) chopped onion
1 medium chopped tomato
¼ cup (60 ml) chopped bell pepper
1 tbs (15 ml) ARROWHEAD MILLS
    Sesame Seeds
2 tbs (30 ml) ARROWHEAD MILLS
    Unrefined Olive Oil
2 tbs (30 ml) lemon juice
1 tsp (5 ml) garlic powder
¼ tsp (1 ml) oregano
¼ tsp (1 ml) basil
¼ tsp (1 ml) thyme
¼ tsp (1 ml) sea salt, optional

Gently mix all ingredients in a large mixing bowl. Refrigerate until cold and serve. Allowing the mixture to set for an hour before serving will enhance the flavor. Serves 4.

Approximate nutritional analysis per serving:
Calories 297, Protein 11 g, Carbohydrates 44 g, Fat 9 g, Cholesterol 0 mg, Sodium 16 mg

ITALIAN BEAN AND PASTA SALAD

KASHA AND BLACK BEAN COMBO

2 cups (480 ml) WOLFF'S Kasha,
    whole or coarse, prepared
    according to package directions,
    using chicken or vegetable broth
4 cups (960 ml) chicken or
    vegetable broth
8 oz (240 g) white cheddar or
    Monterey Jack cheese,
    ¼-inch cubed
15-oz can (450 g) black beans,
    drained and rinsed
½ cup (120 ml) thinly sliced celery
½ cup (120 ml) diced sweet
    red pepper
¼ cup (60 ml) diced green pepper
¼ cup (60 ml) sliced red onions
¼ cup (60 ml) chopped fresh basil
½ cup (120 ml) bottled or
    homemade Dijon vinaigrette
2 cups (480 ml) fresh spinach,
    cut into strips and additional
    leaves for garnish
4 slices bacon, fried crisp and
    crumbled

In a large nonmetal bowl, combine kasha, cheese, black beans, celery, peppers, onions and basil. Mix well, then add vinaigrette and toss. Cover and chill for at least 2 hours. Before serving, add spinach; toss. Arrange additional spinach leaves in salad bowl or on platter. Top with salad and sprinkle with bacon. Serves 5.

Approximate nutritional analysis per serving:
Calories 463, Protein 25 g, Carbohydrates 46 g, Fat 22 g, Cholesterol 53 mg, Sodium 587 mg

MARINATED PASTA SALAD

1 lb (455 g) uncooked pasta shells
⅓ cup (80 ml) MONTEBELLO Extra
    Virgin Olive Oil
⅓ cup (80 ml) red wine vinegar
½ tsp (3 ml) salt, optional
1 tsp (5 ml) CALIFORNIA CLASSICS
    Pesto Oil
1 large green bell pepper, minced
1 small red onion, minced
1 cup (240 ml) pimiento, drained
    and minced
½ cup (120 ml) minced fresh parsley
fresh black pepper
small cubes mozzarella, optional
handful toasted pine nuts, optional

Cook the shells until al dente, 5-8 minutes at the most. Drain the cooked shells in a colander, rinse under tepid water and shake to drain thoroughly. Transfer the still warm shells to a bowl and immediately toss with olive oil. Cover and chill at least 30 minutes. Add remaining ingredients and mix well. Serve very cold. Serves 8.

Approximate nutritional analysis per serving:
Calories 265, Protein 6 g, Carbohydrates 37 g, Fat 11 g, Cholesterol 0 mg, Sodium 8 mg

KASHA AND BLACK BEAN COMBO

SPRING GINGER SALAD

SALAD:
4 cups (960 ml) sliced bok choy,
    stem and leaves
2 tangerines, peeled & halved
2 large carrots, sliced diagonally
4 oz (120 g) bamboo shoots,
    rinsed and drained
4 tbs (60 ml) seasoned rice vinegar
1 tsp (5 ml) sesame oil
1 tsp (5 ml) minced garlic
2 tbs (30 ml) fresh ginger root
1 tsp (5 ml) fresh ground pepper

TOFU:
10½-oz pkg MORI-NU Silken Extra-
    Firm Tofu, sliced and cubed
1 tsp (5 ml) sesame oil

SPRING GINGER SALAD

Mix Salad ingredients and marinate overnight up to 2 days.

Sauté tofu in hot oil in nonstick wok or nonstick skillet. Cook about 8-10 minutes or until dark golden color on both sides. Cool on paper towel. Drain off excess liquid from salad. Add tofu to vegetables and serve. Serves 6.

Approximate nutritional analysis per 1 cup serving:
Calories 109, Protein 7 g, Carbohydrates 16 g, Fat 3 g, Cholesterol 0 mg, Sodium 99 mg

MARINATED GREEN BEAN & RED PEPPER SALAD

2 small red bell peppers
12 oz (360 g) green beans, blanched
½ of a 10½-oz pkg (158 g)
    MORI-NU Silken or Silken Lite
    Tofu, Ex-Firm, cubed
1 green onion, thinly sliced
3 tbs (45 ml) chopped parsley
⅓ cup (80 ml) extra-virgin olive oil
⅓ cup (80 ml) lemon juice
1 clove garlic, minced
½ tsp (3 ml) salt substitute
¼ tsp (1 ml) coarsely ground
    black pepper
½ tsp (3 ml) dry mustard
½ tsp (3 ml) oregano
½ tsp (3 ml) cumin

Roast bell peppers in broiler until skin is charred on all sides. Place in a plastic bag, let cool. Remove skin and seeds. Cut in thin strips.

In mixing bowl, combine pepper strips, green beans, tofu, green onion and parsley. In small mixing bowl, combine olive oil, lemon juice, garlic, salt substitute, pepper, mustard, oregano and cumin. Blend well.

Toss olive oil and seasonings with green bean mixture. Cover and refrigerate several hours to develop flavor. Serves 4.

Approximate nutritional analysis per serving:
Calories 149, Protein 4 g, Carbohydrates 10 g, Fat 10 g, Cholesterol 0 mg, Sodium 23 mg

MARINATED GREEN BEAN & RED PEPPER SALAD

WEHANI RICE SALAD

2 tbs (30 ml) olive oil
2 tbs (30 ml) lemon juice
1 tbs (15 ml) balsamic vinegar
2 cloves garlic, minced
½ tsp (3 ml) salt
½ tsp (3 ml) dried crushed
    rosemary leaves
1 cup (240 ml) fresh basil, minced
½ tsp (3 ml) ground black pepper
3 cups (720 ml) cooked LUNDBERG
    WEHANI Rice, still hot
2 bell peppers, 1 green and 1 red,
    seeded and finely chopped
½ cup (120 ml) carrots, diced small
1 medium tomato, seeded
    and finely chopped
1 small can sliced olives
¼ cup (60 ml) grated Parmesan
    cheese

In a container with lid, combine oil, lemon juice, vinegar, garlic, salt, rosemary, basil and pepper. Shake well. Pour over hot rice in a large bowl and toss lightly. Cover and let cool. Mix in remaining ingredients. Serve at room temperature or chill. Serves 6.

Approximate nutritional analysis per serving:
Calories 246, Protein 6 g, Carbohydrates 36 g, Fat 9 g, Cholesterol 3 mg, Sodium 332 mg

WEHANI RICE SALAD

COUSCOUS SALAD

¾ cup (180 ml) water
½ cup (120 ml) couscous
1 lb (455 g) cucumber, chopped
½ cup (120 ml) radishes, sliced
½ cup (120 ml) green onions,
    chopped
½ cup (120 ml) red peppers,
    chopped
½ cup (120 ml) tomatoes, chopped
5 tbs (75 ml) OMEGA Safflower Oil
4 tbs (60 ml) fresh lemon juice
2 tbs (30 ml) fresh mint
½ tsp (3 ml) thyme
½ tsp (3 ml) basil
½ tsp (3 ml) oregano
½ tsp (3 ml) tarragon

Boil water, add couscous and reduce heat. Simmer for 5 minutes. Let stand until cool. Mix couscous with vegetables. Prepare dressing with oil, lemon juice and the 5 herbs. Pour over salad and let sit 10 minutes before serving. Serves 4.

Approximate nutritional analysis per serving:
Calories 238, Protein 3 g, Carbohydrates 20 g, Fat 18 g, Cholesterol 0 mg, Sodium 17 mg

COUSCOUS SALAD

QUINOA TABOULI

¼ cup (60 ml) OMEGA
  Sunflower Oil
¼ cup (60 ml) lemon juice
1 clove garlic, crushed
1½ tsp (8 ml) herb seasoning blend
sea salt, to taste
1 cup (240 ml) uncooked quinoa,
  rinsed
2 cups (480 ml) boiling water
1 cup (240 ml) parsley, minced
3 tbs (45 ml) fresh mint, minced
½ cup (120 ml) scallions, chopped
¾ cup (180 ml) green bell pepper,
  chopped
1½ cups (355 ml) cucumber,
  chopped
1½ cups (355 ml) tomatoes, chopped
1 cup (240 ml) sunflower seed
  sprouts
4 leaves green leaf lettuce
1 cup (240 ml) plain nonfat yogurt
black olives, sliced, for garnish

Combine sunflower oil, lemon juice, garlic, herb seasoning blend and sea salt and set aside. Add quinoa to 2 cups of boiling water, cover and let simmer for 10 minutes or until water is absorbed. Remove quinoa from heat and let sit for 5 minutes, then transfer into a salad bowl to cool. Combine chopped vegetables, minced herbs and sunflower seed sprouts with quinoa. Add dressing and toss. Refrigerate for at least 1 hour before serving. Serve on lettuce leaves and top with yogurt and black olives, if desired. Serves 6.

Approximate nutritional analysis per serving:
Calories 370, Protein 13 g, Carbohydrates 33 g, Fat 23 g, Cholesterol .7 mg, Sodium 52 mg

QUINOA SALAD

1 tbs (15 ml) lemon grass, chopped
4 kefer lime leaves
1 dried red chile
2 cloves garlic, crushed
½ cup (120 ml) OMEGA
  Flax Seed Oil
½ cup (120 ml) OMEGA
  Safflower Oil
¼ cup (60 ml) lemon or lime juice
4 cups (960 ml) quinoa, cooked
½ cup (120 ml) fresh cilantro,
  chopped
1 green onion, chopped
sea salt, to taste
pepper, to taste

Blend lemon grass, lime leaves and chile pepper in blender for a couple of minutes until lemon grass turns into a coarse powder. Remove from blender. Add garlic, oils and lemon juice and blend again to make marinade. Mix cooked quinoa with marinade, cilantro and green onion. Adjust amount of marinade used as desired. Marinate overnight in the refrigerator. Serves 5.

Approximate nutritional analysis per serving:
Calories 642, Protein 9 g, Carbohydrates 49 g, Fat 47 g, Cholesterol 0 mg, Sodium 16 mg

QUINOA TABOULI

JASMINE RICE SALAD

6 cups (1.4 l) cooked FANTASTIC
FOODS Jasmine Rice

SAUCE:
3 cups (720 ml) water
3 stalks fresh lemon grass
    or 2 tbs (30 ml) dried lemon
    grass
¼ cup (60 ml) soy sauce
1 cup (240 ml) sugar, fruit source
    or ¾ cup (180 ml) honey
2 tbs (30 ml) grated fresh ginger
    or ½ tsp (3 ml) dried ginger
⅓ tsp (2 ml) cayenne or hot chile
    powder
2 limes, the juice and grated peel

1½ cups (355 ml) shredded coconut
1 cup (240 ml) finely chopped
    spinach
1 cucumber, thinly sliced and
    quartered
1 cup (240 ml) jicama, diced into
    ½-inch pieces
¼ red bell pepper, cut into
    1-inch thin strips
½ cup (120 ml) chopped green
    onions
½ cup (120 ml) snow peas
1 cup (240 ml) bean sprouts
1 cup (240 ml) peeled diced orange
½ cup (120 ml) chopped cilantro
1 cup (240 ml) chopped roasted
    peanuts

First boil the rice according to package directions. Cool. To quickly cool rice spread it in a thin layer on cookie sheets or in a large bowl.

In a saucepan combine water and lemon grass (lemon grass tea) and simmer for at least 8 minutes. Then set aside to cool. In a frying pan dry-roast the coconut by stirring over medium heat until toasted golden. Set aside the lemon grass tea and the roasted coconut to cool. Strain the lemon grass from the tea. To the tea, add all the rest of the Sauce ingredients and mix or blend well.

Assemble salad by gently tossing rice, coconut and vegetables with Sauce. Serve chilled. Garnish with chopped roasted peanuts when serving. Serves 8.

Approximate nutritional analysis per serving:
Calories 437, Protein 10 g, Carbohydrates 72 g, Fat 14 g, Cholesterol 0 mg, Sodium 527 mg

JASMINE RICE SALAD

RICE-VEGETABLE ASIAN SALAD

½ cup (120 ml) cauliflower florets
½ cup (120 ml) broccoli florets
½ cup (120 ml) carrots,
    cut into ½-inch slices
½ cup (120 ml) snow peas
½ cup (120 ml) onions,
    cut into ½-inch cubes
2 tbs (30 ml) soy sauce
2½ cups (590 ml) cooked ARROW
    HEAD MILLS Quick Brown Rice
1 tsp (5 ml) cider vinegar
dash ginger
dash lemon juice

VARIATION:
½ cup (120 ml) sliced water
    chestnuts
½ cup (120 ml) chopped mushrooms
½ cup (120 ml) bean sprouts
½ cup (120 ml) pineapple chunks

Place the vegetables in a heavy saucepan with the soy sauce. Cover and simmer over low heat for 5-7 minutes until the vegetables are barely tender. Set aside to cool and add the remaining ingredients. Chill before serving. Serves 4.

Variation: Add ½ cup (120 ml) each water chestnuts, chopped mushrooms, bean sprouts and pineapple.

Approximate nutritional analysis per serving:
Calories 159, Protein 5 g, Carbohydrates 33 g, Fat 1 g, Cholesterol 0 mg, Sodium 528 mg

FANTASTIC FOODS BROWN BASMATI RICE SALAD

DRESSING:
⅔ cup (160 ml) plain yogurt
2 tbs (30 ml) lemon juice
1 small clove garlic, minced
    or pressed
¼ tsp (1 ml) salt
1½ tsp (8 ml) dill weed

2 cups (480 ml) cooked and cooled
    FANTASTIC FOODS Brown
    Basmati Rice
⅓ cup (80 ml) chopped black olives
½ cup (120 ml) chopped fresh
    parsley
¼ cup (60 ml) chopped celery
¼ cup (60 ml) chopped red pepper
2 green onions, chopped
1 large tomato, chopped
½ cup (120 ml) fresh peas

Prepare Dressing and let stand while chopping vegetables. Mix vegetables with rice, add Dressing and toss. Serves 5.

Approximate nutritional analysis per 1 cup serving:
Calories 119, Protein 5 g, Carbohydrates 22 g, Fat 2 g, Cholesterol .6 mg, Sodium 223 mg

SESAME RICE SALAD

2 cups (480 ml) FANTASTIC FOODS
    White Jasmine Rice
4 cups (960 ml) water
2 garlic cloves, minced
1 tsp (5 ml) salt
2 tbs (30 ml) olive oil
5 tbs (75 ml) toasted sesame oil
4 tbs (60 ml) rice vinegar
4 tbs (60 ml) soy sauce
1 tsp (5 ml) minced fresh ginger
1½ cups (355 ml) fresh sugar snap
    peas or snow peas, blanched
1 medium red onion, minced
½ cup (120 ml) sliced water
    chestnuts
1 medium red bell pepper, cored,
    seeded and diced
2 tbs (30 ml) toasted sesame seeds,
    optional
salt, to taste
pepper, to taste

Cook rice as directed in water with the addition of garlic and salt. Set aside. To prepare the dressing, mix the olive oil, sesame oil, rice vinegar, soy sauce and ginger in a bowl. Toss together in another bowl the peas, onion, water chestnuts and red pepper, then add to the warm rice along with the dressing and the optional sesame seeds. Toss thoroughly, taste and adjust seasoning. Serve lukewarm or refrigerate until 30 minutes before serving. Serves 6.

Approximate nutritional analysis per serving:
Calories 384, Protein 6 g, Carbohydrates 55 g, Fat 16 g, Cholesterol 0 mg, Sodium 1044 mg

MEXICAN VEGETARIAN SALAD

1 medium FRIEDA'S Chayote,
    quartered
3 cups (720 ml) fresh torn
    spinach leaves
11-oz pkg (330 g) FRIEDA'S Fresh
    Garbanzo Beans, cooked and
    drained
1 ripe avocado, pitted, peeled and
    cut in chunks
1 cup (240 ml) shredded sharp
    cheddar cheese
½ cup (120 ml) sliced pitted olives
1 cup (240 ml) vinegar
½ cup (120 ml) salad oil
1 clove garlic, minced
½ tsp (3 ml) salt
½ tsp (3 ml) paprika
¼ tsp (1 ml) freshly ground pepper
pinch cayenne
FRIEDA'S Spicy Sprouts or Alfalfa
    Sprouts, optional

Cook chayote in a small amount of boiling water for about 15 minutes or until tender. Rinse pieces in cold water; peel and remove seeds. Cut into ½-inch chunks. In a large salad bowl toss together chayote, spinach, garbanzo beans, avocado, cheese and olives. In a jar place the vinegar, oil, garlic and seasonings; cover and shake well. Pour some over salad and toss. Top salad with sprouts if desired; serve with remaining dressing. Serves 6 as a sidedish salad.

Approximate nutritional analysis per serving w/ 1 tbs dressing:
Calories 282, Protein 11 g, Carbohydrates 21 g, Fat 19 g, Cholesterol 20 mg, Sodium 290 mg

MEXICAN VEGETARIAN SALAD

SESAME PASTA SALAD

12 oz (360 g) KAMUT BRAND
   Angel Hair Pasta
¼ cup (60 ml) Chinese sesame oil
4 tbs (60 ml) soy sauce
½ cup (120 ml) minced watercress
½-1 tsp (3-5 ml) minced garlic
1 tsp (5 ml) hot chile oil
sea salt, to taste
freshly ground pepper, to taste

Cook pasta to al dente stage, drain and toss with remaining ingredients. Chill salad for several hours before serving. Serves 6.

Approximate nutritional analysis per serving:
Calories 302, Protein 8 g, Carbohydrates 49 g, Fat 11 g, Cholesterol 0 mg, Sodium 687 mg

SPICY CUCUMBER-ORANGE SALAD

1 FRIEDA'S Hot House Cucumber,
   thinly sliced
1 large orange, peeled, thinly sliced
   and cut in quarters
½ of a red onion, thinly sliced and
   separated into rings
1 large FRIEDA'S Fresh Anaheim
   Chile, seeded and chopped
1 cup (240 ml) white vinegar
⅓ cup (80 ml) salad oil
1 tbs (15 ml) FRIEDA'S Fresh
   Oregano, chopped
   or 1 tsp (5 ml) crushed dried
   oregano
2 tsp (10 ml) FRIEDA'S Fresh Sage,
   chopped
   or ½ tsp (3 ml) ground dried
   sage
1 tbs (15 ml) FRIEDA'S Fresh
   Cilantro, chopped
½ tsp (3 ml) salt
1 tsp (5 ml) ground black pepper

In a deep glass bowl toss together the cucumber slices, orange pieces, onion and chile.

In a covered container place the vinegar, oil and remaining ingredients; shake together until blended. Pour over salad mixture; stir to coat all ingredients. Cover and chill 3 hours or overnight, stirring occasionally. Serve with a slotted spoon as a side-dish salad or relish. Marinade can be saved and used for salad dressing. Yields 3 cups salad, serves 3.

Approximate nutritional analysis per serving w/ 1 tbs marinade:
Calories 71, Protein 1 g, Carbohydrates 10 g, Fat 4 g, Cholesterol 0 mg, Sodium 52 mg

SPICY CUCUMBER-ORANGE SALAD

CURRIED SALAD

2 heads butter lettuce, salad ready
3 cups (720 ml) spinach, chopped
1 cup (240 ml) alfalfa sprouts
½ cup (120 ml) arugula, chopped
1 cup (240 ml) snow peas, cut
1 cup (240 ml) carrots, shredded
3 cups (720 ml) cooked chicken
  or tofu, cubed

DRESSING:
3 tbs (45 ml) OMEGA
  Apple Cider Vinegar
3 tbs (45 ml) nonfat yogurt
1 tbs (15 ml) maple syrup of honey
2 tsp (10 ml) curry powder
2 tsp (10 ml) basil
2 cloves garlic, crushed
1 tsp (5 ml) tamari or soy sauce
¼ tsp (1 ml) sea salt
¼ tsp (1 ml) black pepper
½ cup (120 ml) OMEGA Sesame Oil

ANNE'S AWESOME GREEK SALAD

ANNE'S AWESOME GREEK SALAD

DRESSING:
⅓ cup (80 ml) OMEGA NUTRITION
  Apple Cider Vinegar
⅓ cup (80 ml) OMEGA NUTRITION
  Garlic-Chile Flax Seed Oil
⅓ cup (80 ml) OMEGA NUTRITION
  Olive Oil
3 cloves garlic, minced
1 tsp (5 ml) dried ground oregano
2 tsp (10 ml) whole dried
  oregano leaf
sea salt, to taste
pepper, to taste

1 medium onion, sliced
1 large cucumber, cubed
5 medium tomatoes, diced
½ cup (120 ml) kalamata olives
1 cup (240 ml) feta cheese
1 green pepper, cubed

Combine lettuce pieces, spinach, sprouts, arugula, snow peas, carrots and chicken or tofu. Put in blender the vinegar, yogurt, syrup, curry, basil, garlic, tamari, salt and pepper. Blend while adding oil slowly. Pour Dressing over salad or serve separately. Serves 12 as an appetizer or side-dish salad.

Approximate nutritional analysis per serving:
Calories 203, Protein 20 g, Carbohydrates 5 g, Fat 11 g, Cholesterol 51 mg, Sodium 137 mg

Put Dressing ingredients in a jar and shake to mix well. Pour Dressing into large bowl; add vegetables, olives and cheese. Mix well. Serves 10.

Approximate nutritional analysis per serving:
Calories 231, Protein 5 g, Carbohydrates 9 g, Fat 21 g, Cholesterol 22 mg, Sodium 370 mg

CURRIED SALAD

JICAMA, ORANGE AND ONION SALAD

2 cups (480 ml) torn lettuce leaves
2 navel oranges, peeled and
    thinly sliced
4 thin slices red onion
1 cup (240 ml) FRIEDA'S Jicama,
    peeled and julienne sliced

CILANTRO-ORANGE DRESSING:
⅓ cup (80 ml) orange juice
½ tsp (3 ml) light olive oil
    or vegetable oil
1 tbs (15 ml) FRIEDA'S Fresh
    Cilantro, finely chopped
⅛-¼ tsp (.5-1 ml) chile powder

In a large salad bowl, place torn lettuce. Cut orange slices into quarters; toss into lettuce with onion and jicama. For dressing, shake together all ingredients in a shaker jar; toss with salad. Serves 4 side-dish salads, yields ⅓ cup dressing.

Approximate nutritional analysis per serving w/ dressing:
Calories 66, Protein 2 g, Carbohydrates 14 g, Fat .8 g, Cholesterol 0 mg,
Sodium 6 mg

**JICAMA, ORANGE
AND ONION SALAD**

NEW CAESAR-STYLE SALAD

3 ½-inch thick slices French bread,
    cubed
¼ cup (60 ml) lemon juice
1 tsp (5 ml) olive or vegetable oil
1 tsp (5 ml) anchovy paste
1 clove FRIEDA'S Elephant Garlic,
    peeled and finely minced
¼ tsp (1 ml) pepper
3 cups (720 ml) FRIEDA'S Limestone
    Lettuce, torn
3 cups (720 ml) romaine lettuce,
    torn
2 tbs (30 ml) grated Parmesan
    cheese

Sprinkle bread cubes on baking sheet; bake in 350°F (180°C) oven for 10-12 minutes or until toasted. Meanwhile, in a small bowl stir together lemon juice, oil, anchovy paste, garlic and pepper. Remove toasted bread from oven; place in a shallow bowl. Sprinkle 2 tbs of the dressing mixture over croutons; toss to coat.

    In a salad bowl toss together limestone and romaine lettuce. Add croutons, remaining dressing and Parmesan cheese; toss well. Serves 4 side-dish salads.

Approximate nutritional analysis per serving:
Calories 92, Protein 4 g, Carbohydrates 14 g, Fat 2 g, Cholesterol 3 mg,
Sodium 177 mg

AVOCADO & ROMAINE SALAD WITH RASPBERRY-RASPBERRY VINAIGRETTE

RASPBERRY-RASPBERRY VINAIGRETTE:
1 cup (240 ml) fresh raspberries
¼ cup (60 ml) SPECTRUM NATURALS Organic Raspberry Vinegar
½ cup (120 ml) SPECTRUM NATURALS High Oleic Super Canola
¾ tsp (4 ml) salt
fresh ground pepper, to taste
2 tsp (10 ml) fresh tarragon, minced, optional

2 small heads romaine lettuce, washed, dried, outer leaves removed
2 ripe Haas avocados, peeled and sliced

Vinaigrette: In a small mixing bowl, combine the raspberries and raspberry vinegar. Mash the berries with fork and allow them to macerate in the vinegar for approximately 10 minutes. Whisk the canola oil into the berry-vinegar mixture. Add the salt and pepper. Add the optional tarragon. Yields 1½ cups.

Arrange the lettuce and avocados attractively in a salad bowl. Spoon 6-8 tbs of the vinaigrette over the salad and serve immediately. The remaining dressing will keep for 2-3 days in the refrigerator. Serves 4.

Approximate nutritional analysis per serving:
Calories 246, Protein 3 g, Carbohydrates 10 g, Fat 24 g, Cholesterol 0 mg, Sodium 31 mg

AVOCADO & ROMAINE SALAD WITH RASPBERRY-RASPBERRY VINAIGRETTE

ARUGULA & TOMATO SALAD

4 vine-ripened tomatoes
1 red onion
2 pkgs GREEN HOUSE Fresh Arugula
2 cups (480 ml) canned cannellini or red kidney beans, rinsed and drained
2 tbs (30 ml) extra-virgin olive oil
1 clove fresh garlic, chopped
1 tbs (15 ml) balsamic vinegar
fresh ground black pepper

Slice the tomatoes and red onion in rings and place in alternate layers with the arugula and ½ cup beans on each of 4 plates. Mix the oil, garlic and vinegar and spoon over the salad. Finish with fresh ground pepper. Serves 4.

Approximate nutritional analysis per serving:
Calories 224, Protein 10 g, Carbohydrates 32 g, Fat 8 g, Cholesterol 0 mg, Sodium 225 mg

ARUGULA & TOMATO SALAD

ALBERT'S ORGANICS MIXED VEGETABLE SLAW

½ medium organic green cabbage
½ medium organic red cabbage
¼ medium organic red onion
1 large organic carrot
1 small organic beet
½ small red bell pepper

DRESSING:
¼-½ cup (60-120 ml) ANNIE'S
    Goddess Dressing
2 tbs (30 ml) ANNIE'S Balsamic
    Dressing
1 clove garlic, pressed
1 tbs (25 ml) dill weed
    or 3 tbs (45 ml) chopped fresh
    dill
1 tbs (15 ml) soy sauce

**ALBERT'S ORGANICS
MIXED VEGETABLE SLAW**

Grate the vegetables using food processor or by hand. Mix the Dressing ingredients well and stir into grated vegetables. Serves 4.

Approximate nutritional analysis per serving:
Calories 109, Protein 2 g, Carbohydrates 11 g, Fat 7 g, Cholesterol 0 mg, Sodium 457 mg

FAST FABULOUS COLESLAW

4 cups (960 ml) shredded green
    cabbage, packed
1½ cups (355 ml) shredded red
    cabbage, packed
1 cup (240 ml) finely grated carrot
1 cup minced red pepper
⅓ cup (80 ml) minced Vidalia
    or red onion
2 tbs (30 ml) minced fresh dill

DRESSING:
1 cup (240 ml) SPECTRUM
    NATURALS Canola Mayonnaise
2 tbs (30 ml) SPECTRUM
    NATURALS Apple Cider Vinegar
1 tbs (15 ml) maple syrup
1 tbs (15 ml) celery seed
sea salt, to taste
pepper, to taste

Prepare vegetables for salad by hand with sharp knife to make very thin shreds. Mince the red pepper, onion and dill, also by hand. Place vegetables in a large bowl.

Whisk together Dressing ingredients and pour over the vegetables, toss gently but well. Serve immediately or refrigerate until ready. Serves 16.

Approximate nutritional analysis per serving:
Calories 115, Protein .7 g, Carbohydrates 4 g, Fat 11 g, Cholesterol 8 mg, Sodium 923 mg

FAST FABULOUS COLESLAW

CHILLED DILLED CARROT SALAD

2 cups (480 ml) carrots, peeled
   and thinly sliced
½ cup (120 ml) diced shallots
   or red onions
1 tbs (15 ml) olive oil
1 tbs (15 ml) red wine vinegar
2-3 tbs (30-45 ml) GREEN HOUSE
   Fresh Dill, chopped
salt, to taste
pepper, to taste

Parboil carrots until tender yet crisp, about 2 minutes. Rinse under cold water and drain. Combine carrots and onions. Mix remaining ingredients in small bowl until well blended. Pour over carrot mixture and toss well. Refrigerate at least 3 hours to blend flavors. Serves 4.

Approximate nutritional analysis per serving:
Calories 46, Protein 1 g, Carbohydrates 9 g, Fat 1 g, Cholesterol 0 mg,
Sodium 157 mg

CHILLED DILLED CARROT SALAD

ROASTED HABAÑERO-BELL PEPPER SALAD

ROASTED HABAÑERO-BELL PEPPER SALAD

2 sweet red bell peppers
1 sweet yellow bell pepper
1 FRIEDA'S Fresh Habañero Chile*
lettuce leaves
½ cup (120 ml) thinly sliced
   red onion
½ cup (120 ml) FRIEDA'S Jicama,
   thinly julienne-sliced
½ cup (120 ml) shredded Monterey
   Jack cheese
⅓ cup (80 ml) orange juice
¼ cup (60 ml) olive oil
1 tbs (15 ml) FRIEDA'S Fresh
   Cilantro, chopped
1 clove garlic, quartered

*Note: Please use gloves to handle the habañero chile – it can burn your skin! Avoid touching face, nose, lips and eyes.

Preheat oven broiler to 500°F (260°C). Arrange peppers on a lightly oiled broiler pan; broil 4 inches from heat until charred on all sides, turning frequently with thongs. Remove from pan; place in a brown paper bag for 15 minutes to steam. Then peel off skins from peppers and chile. Set aside one red pepper and habanero chile.

   Slit remaining peppers; scrape out seeds. Cut into bite-size strips. Line 4 salad plates with lettuce leaves; arrange the bell pepper strips on each plate, along with red onion and jicama. Sprinkle on cheese.

   To prepare dressing, remove stems and seeds from reserved red pepper and chile. Chop both; place in a blender container or food processor bowl with orange juice, olive oil, cilantro and garlic. Cover and process until well blended and chile is puréed. Drizzle dressing over salads and serve.

   You can cover and chill salad and dressing separately up to 1 day ahead. Serves 4 as a side-dish salad, yields 1 cup dressing.

Approximate nutritional analysis per serving:
Calories 142, Protein 4 g, Carbohydrates 7 g, Fat 11 g, Cholesterol 13 mg,
Sodium 78 mg

ENSALADA DE TOMATILLO

½ cup (120 ml) salad oil
¼ cup (60 ml) white vinegar
3 cilantro sprigs, chopped
½ of a FRIEDA'S Jalapeño Chile, seeded and chopped
1 clove garlic, minced
1½ tsp (8 ml) FRIEDA'S Fresh Oregano, chopped
   or ½ tsp (3 ml) dried oregano, crushed
1½ tsp (8 ml) FRIEDA'S Fresh Basil, chopped
   or ½ tsp (3 ml) dried basil, crushed
shredded lettuce
2 cups (480 ml) zucchini chunks, ½-inch pieces
2 red tomatoes, cut into wedges
4 FRIEDA'S Tomatillos, peeled, washed and chopped
sliced green onion

Prepare dressing in a lidded jar by combining the salad oil, vinegar, cilantro, chopped jalapeño pepper, garlic, oregano and basil. Cover and shake well to blend. Arrange a bed of shredded lettuce on 4 salad plates. Top each salad with some of the zucchini, tomato wedges and diced tomatillo. Sprinkle with onion. Shake dressing again; drizzle over salads. Serves 4.

Approximate nutritional analysis per serving w/ 1 tbs dressing:
Calories 154, Protein 2 g, Carbohydrates 7 g, Fat 14 g, Cholesterol 0 mg, Sodium 115 mg

DILLED POTATO SALAD

DILLED POTATO SALAD

16 oz (480 g) red skin potatoes
1 cup (240 ml) plain nonfat yogurt
¼ cup (60 ml) whole grain mustard
¼ cup (60 ml) seasoned rice vinegar
½ cup (120 ml) diced red onion
½ cup (120 ml) diced celery
fresh ground pepper
4 tbs (60 ml) GREEN HOUSE Fresh Dill, chopped plus 4 sprigs for garnish

Boil potatoes in lightly salted water until tender. Set aside to cool. Cut the potatoes into quarters. Mix yogurt and the rest of the ingredients together. Add the potatoes. Chill. Garnish with sprigs of dill. Serves 4.

Approximate nutritional analysis per serving:
Calories 181, Protein 7 g, Carbohydrates 37 g, Fat 1 g, Cholesterol 1 mg, Sodium 258 mg

DRIED TOMATO-POTATO SALAD

1 lb (455 g) FRIEDA'S Baby Red
    or Baby White Potatoes,
    quartered and cooked according
    to package directions
3-oz pkg (90 g) FRIEDA'S Dried
    Tomatoes, reconstituted
1 FRIEDA'S Leek, trimmed and
    thinly sliced, white part only
⅓ cup (80 ml) light sour cream
2 tbs (30 ml) skim milk
2 tbs (30 ml) FRIEDA'S Fresh Basil,
    chopped
    or 2 tsp (10 ml) dried basil
1 tbs (15 ml) FRIEDA'S Fresh Dill,
    chopped
    or 1 tsp (5 ml) dill weed
1 clove garlic, minced
dash pepper
dash salt

In a large bowl, place potatoes. Sliver dried tomatoes; reserve ½ cup of the tomatoes for dressing. Add remaining tomatoes to potatoes, with leeks. Toss gently.

In a food processor or blender place reserved tomatoes, sour cream, milk, basil, dill, garlic, pepper and salt, if desired. Cover and process until smooth. Spoon onto salad; toss gently to coat. Serves 5 side-dish salads.

Approximate nutritional analysis per serving:
Calories 162, Protein 5 g, Carbohydrates 32 g, Fat 3 g, Cholesterol 6 mg, Sodium 375 mg

DRIED TOMATO-POTATO SALAD

EGGLESS EGG SALAD

10-oz pkg (300 g) MORI-NU Silken
    Lite Firm Tofu, drained
1 tsp (5 ml) apple cider vinegar
2 tsp (10 ml) prepared yellow
    mustard
1 tsp (5 ml) honey
½ tsp (3 ml) turmeric
2 tbs (30 ml) celery, diced
2 tbs (30 ml) onion, diced
1 tsp (5 ml) parsley, chopped
dash paprika
½ scant tsp (3 ml) white pepper

Crumble tofu into a small mixing bowl. Set aside. In a separate bowl, combine vinegar, mustard, honey and turmeric. Mix thoroughly and pour over crumbled tofu. Add celery, onion, parsley, paprika and pepper. Mix thoroughly. Refrigerate approximately 30 minutes to allow flavors to meld. Serves 3.

Approximate nutritional analysis per ½ cup serving:
Calories 77, Protein 9 g, Carbohydrates 4 g, Fat 2 g, Cholesterol 0 mg, Sodium 115 mg

Overleaf: EGGLESS EGG SALAD

ITALIAN PISTACHIO PILAF

3½ cups (840 ml) water
1 cup (240 ml) ARROWHEAD MILLS
   White Basmati Rice
½ tsp (3 ml) salt, optional
1 cup (240 ml) diced onions
1 cup (240 ml) diced red bell pepper
2 tbs (30 ml) fresh chopped garlic
2 cups (480 ml) flaked seitan,
   thinly sliced at a 45° angle
2 tsp (10 ml) salt, optional
3 tbs (45 ml) ground fennel
1 tsp (5 ml) ground black pepper
3 tbs (45 ml) olive oil
1 cup (240 ml) sliced scallions
1 cup (240 ml) chopped pistachios

Bring water to a simmer. Add rice and salt, if desired, and simmer for 10 minutes. Cover pot and turn off heat. Let sit until cooked, about 5 minutes.

Sauté onions, bell peppers, garlic, seitan, salt, fennel and black pepper in olive oil until vegetables are soft, about 10 minutes on medium heat. Add rice, scallions and pistachios. Serve hot with a vegetable as a light meal. Serves 8.

Approximate nutritional analysis per serving:
Calories 404, Protein 28 g, Carbohydrates 43 g, Fat 14 g, Cholesterol 0 mg, Sodium 25 mg

ORGANIC GOLDEN RICE CASSEROLE

juice of 1 lemon
2 cups (480 ml) SUNRIDGE FARMS
   Organic White Basmati Rice,
   cooked
½ tsp (3 ml) turmeric
2 cups (480 ml) steamed vegetables,
   any combination of peas, onions,
   broccoli, cauliflower, zucchini,
   carrots or mushrooms
8 oz (240 g) plain nonfat yogurt
½ cup (120 ml) toasted cashews,
   whole or in pieces
½ cup (120 ml) raisins

Preheat oven to 350°F (180°C). Combine lemon juice, rice and turmeric. Spread half of the rice in a buttered casserole dish. Layer with half the vegetables then follow with half the yogurt, cashews and raisins. Repeat and place in oven for about 30 minutes or until heated through. Serve piping hot; if desired, add butter, margarine or shoyu sauce. Serves 12.

Approximate nutritional analysis per serving:
Calories 190, Protein 5 g, Carbohydrates 37 g, Fat 3 g, Cholesterol .3 mg, Sodium 57 mg

ORGANIC GOLDEN RICE CASSEROLE

CONFETTI RICE

1 cup (240 ml) ARROWHEAD MILLS
   Indian Brown Basmati Rice
3 cups (720 ml) water or broth
   of your choice
1 tsp (5 ml) poultry seasoning
1 tsp (5 ml) sea salt, optional
1 cup (240 ml) julienne carrots
1 cup (240 ml) peas
1 cup (240 ml) slivered onions

Mix all ingredients in a 8x13-inch baking dish. Cover tightly. Bake at 350°F (180°C) for 1½ hours. Serves 4.

Approximate nutritional analysis per serving:
Calories 216, Protein 7 g, Carbohydrates 46 g, Fat 2 g, Cholesterol 0 mg, Sodium 13 mg

SPINACH-FETA RICE

1 cup (240 ml) LUNDBERG
   California Basmati Brown Rice
2¼ cups (540 ml) chicken broth
1 medium onion, chopped
1 cup (240 ml) sliced fresh
   mushrooms
2 cloves garlic, minced
vegetable cooking spray
1 tbs (15 ml) lemon juice
½ tsp (3 ml) dried oregano leaves
6 cups (1.4 l) shredded fresh spinach
4 oz (120 g) feta cheese, crumbled
black pepper

Combine rice and broth in saucepan. Bring to boil, stir. Reduce heat, cover and simmer 45 minutes, until water is absorbed. Cook onion, mushrooms and garlic in oil-sprayed skillet until tender. Stir in lemon juice and oregano. Add spinach, feta and pepper to rice; toss until spinach is wilted. Add mushrooms and onions. Serves 6.

Approximate nutritional analysis per serving:
Calories 195, Protein 8 g, Carbohydrates 30 g, Fat 5 g, Cholesterol 17 mg, Sodium 387 mg

CONFETTI RICE

GREEN LEAF BROWN RICE WITH GARLIC CHIVES

1 cup (240 ml) sliced baby leeks
    and/or scallions
1-2 tbs (15-30 ml) canola oil
1 cup (240 ml) brown rice
sea salt, to taste
2 cups (480 ml) water
black pepper, to taste
2 tbs (30 ml) garlic chives
2 tbs (30 ml) thyme, chopped
yogurt, to serve with

Lightly sauté leeks in canola oil until translucent. Add brown rice, sea salt to taste and water. Season with black pepper, bring to a boil and simmer about 45 minutes. When rice is cooked and fluffed, add garlic chives and chopped thyme. Serve with yogurt. Serves 6.

Approximate nutritional analysis per serving w/o yogurt:
Calories 202, Protein 4 g, Carbohydrates 40 g, Fat 4 g, Cholesterol 0 mg, Sodium 26 mg

ANTIPASTO RICE

1¾ cups (415 ml) water
½ cup (120 ml) tomato juice
1 cup (240 ml) LUNDBERG
    COUNTRYWILD Rice
1 tsp (5 ml) dried basil
1 tsp (5 ml) dried oregano
½ tsp (3 ml) salt
14-oz can (420 g) artichoke hearts,
    drained and quartered
7-oz jar (210 g) roasted red peppers,
    drained and chopped
2¼-oz can (68 g) sliced ripe
    black olives, drained
2 tbs (30 ml) snipped parsley
2 tbs (30 ml) lemon juice
½ tsp (3 ml) ground black pepper
2 tbs (30 ml) grated Parmesan
    cheese

Combine water, tomato juice, rice, basil, oregano and salt in a 3-quart saucepan. Bring to a boil. Stir. Reduce heat; cover and simmer 45 minutes or until liquid is absorbed. Stir in artichokes, red peppers, olives, parsley, lemon juice and black pepper. Cook 5 minutes longer. Sprinkle with cheese. Serves 8.

Approximate nutritional analysis per serving:
Calories 131, Protein 4 g, Carbohydrates 27 g, Fat 2 g, Cholesterol 1 mg, Sodium 522 mg

ANTIPASTO RICE

LEMON RICE

1 cup (240 ml) **LUNDBERG ROYAL** Rice
1 tsp (5 ml) **margarine**
1 clove garlic, minced
1 tsp (5 ml) **grated lemon peel**
⅓ tsp (2 ml) **ground black pepper**
2¼ cups (540 ml) **chicken broth**
2 tbs (30 ml) **snipped parsley**

Combine rice, margarine, garlic, lemon peel, pepper and broth in a 3-quart saucepan. Bring to a boil. Stir twice. Reduce heat; cover and simmer 45 minutes or until rice is tender and liquid is absorbed. Stir in parsley. Serves 6.

Approximate nutritional analysis per serving:
Calories 127, Protein 4 g, Carbohydrates 25 g, Fat .7 g, Cholesterol 0 mg, Sodium 261 mg

LEMON RICE

SPANISH SHORT GRAIN

1 tbs (15 ml) **olive oil**
1 bell pepper, chopped
1 large onion, chopped
2 cloves garlic, minced
1½ cups (355 ml) **LUNDBERG Short Grain Brown Rice, uncooked**
3 cups (720 ml) **liquid, tomato juice and broth or water**
14½-oz can (435 g) **chopped tomatoes, strained, with juice reserved**
pinch cayenne pepper, optional

Heat oil in 4-qt thick-walled skillet or saucepan with tight-fitting lid. Sauté bell pepper, onion and garlic in oil briefly. Add rice and stir. Add liquid, including juice from tomatoes, to equal 3 cups. Bring to boil, reduce heat to low, cover and simmer for 30 minutes. Add tomatoes, cover and continue cooking for another 15 minutes. Serve warm. Serves 6.

Approximate nutritional analysis per serving:
Calories 222, Protein 5 g, Carbohydrates 43 g, Fat 4 g, Cholesterol 0 mg, Sodium 11 mg

SPANISH SHORT GRAIN

SPANISH RICE

12 oz (360 g) **SURATA SOYFOODS CO-OP** Multi-Grain or Soy Tempeh
2 tbs (30 ml) water
2 tbs (30 ml) tamari
2 cloves minced garlic
¾ tsp (4 ml) onion powder
2 stalks celery, sliced
1 medium onion, chopped
1 medium bell pepper, chopped
2 tbs oil
1 cup (240 ml) brown rice
6 oz (180 g) tomato paste
8 oz (240 g) tomato sauce
3 cups (720 ml) water
½ tsp (3 ml) cayenne powder
½ tsp (3 ml) salt
⅛ tsp (.5 ml) black pepper
2 tsp (10 ml) oil

Combine first 5 ingredients in a medium-size stainless steel or glass mixing bowl. In a large skillet sauté the celery, onion and bell pepper in 2 tbs oil, until soft. Stir in the rice until lightly toasted. Add tomato paste, tomato sauce, water, cayenne, salt and pepper. Bring to a boil, reduce heat and cover. Simmer 1 hour. Brown tempeh mixture in 2 tsp oil and add to rice mixture. Serve immediately. Serves 6.

Approximate nutritional analysis per serving:
Calories 385, Protein 20 g, Carbohydrates 61 g, Fat 10 g, Cholesterol 0 mg, Sodium 1345 mg

SPANISH RICE

BANANA-GINGER RICE WITH DATES

2 cups (480 ml) water
2 tsp (10 ml) **SPECTRUM WORLD EATS** Caribbean Oil
4 tsp (20 ml) molasses
¼ tsp (1 ml) ground ginger
1½ tsp (8 ml) salt
1 cup (240 ml) long-grain white or brown rice
1 ripe banana, diced
½ cup (120 ml) chopped and pitted dates or raisins

In a heavy bottomed, 2-3-quart saucepan bring water, oil, molasses, ginger and salt to a boil. Add rice and stir well. Simmer covered for 15 minutes. Simmer for 5 more minutes with the lid slightly open.

Gently fold the banana and the dates into the rice. Allow to stand, covered, for 10 minutes, check seasoning and serve. Serves 4.

Approximate nutritional analysis per serving:
Calories 292, Protein 4 g, Carbohydrates 64 g, Fat 3 g, Cholesterol 0 mg, Sodium 806 mg

BANANA-GINGER RICE WITH DATES

BASMATI RICE PILAF

6-oz pkg (180 g) FRIEDA'S
   Basmati Rice
2 cups (480 ml) water
⅓ cup (80 ml) light or dark raisins
⅓ cup (80 ml) sliced green onion
1 tsp (5 ml) FRIEDA'S grated
   Fresh Ginger
¼ tsp (1 ml) ground cinnamon
pinch ground cloves or cardamom
½ cup (120 ml) FRIEDA'S Pignolias
   or slivered almonds

In a 2-quart saucepan, combine rice, water, raisins, onion, ginger, cinnamon and cloves. Bring to boiling; reduce heat. Simmer, cover, for 20-30 minutes, or until rice is tender. Stir in pignolias. Serves 6.

Approximate nutritional analysis per serving:
Calories 222, Protein 6 g, Carbohydrates 37 g, Fat 8 g, Cholesterol 0 mg, Sodium 3 mg

BASMATI RICE PILAF

WILD MAJUDRA

1 pkg FANTASTIC FOODS Wild Rice
3 cups (720 ml) water
½ cup (120 ml) lentils
1 onion, sliced in rings
¼ cup (60 ml) olive oil
1 red bell pepper, sliced
6 large mushrooms, sliced
½ cup (20 ml) cilantro leaves,
   chopped
salt

Rinse rice and add to water in a saucepan. Bring to a boil, reduce heat and simmer for 15 minutes. Add lentils to rice and continue cooking for about 40-45 minutes, until rice grains have popped open and lentils are tender. In a large skillet, sauté onions in olive oil for 15 minutes. Add red bell pepper and mushrooms and continue cooking for 10 more minutes. Add rice/lentil mixture to vegetables and cook briefly on high heat to absorb vegetable juices. Add cilantro, salt to taste and serve. Serves 6.

Approximate nutritional analysis per serving:
Calories 290, Protein 11 g, Carbohydrates 42 g, Fat 10 g, Cholesterol 0 mg, Sodium 8 mg

WILD MAJUDRA

ROYAL BLEND RICE PILAF

¾ cup (180 ml) chopped onion
2 tsp (10 ml) margarine, butter
 or vegetable oil
1½ cups (355 ml) chicken broth
6-oz pkg (180 g) TEXMATI ROYAL
 BLEND Rice
½ cup (120 ml) celery, diced
1 tbs (15 ml) minced parsley
½ tsp (3 ml) dried thyme
¼ tsp (1 ml) dried leaf sage
¼ tsp (1 ml) pepper

In large skillet, cook onion in margarine until golden. Add broth, rice and celery; bring to boil. Reduce heat, cover and simmer 15-20 minutes. Stir in parsley, thyme, sage, and pepper. Cover and let stand 10 minutes before serving. Serves 6.

Approximate nutritional analysis per serving:
Calories 131, Protein 4 g, Carbohydrates 24 g, Fat 2 g, Cholesterol 0 mg, Sodium 218 mg

BASMATI RICE WITH YOGURT

1 medium onion, chopped
1 clove garlic, minced
2 tbs (30 ml) butter
1¾ cups (415 ml) water
¾ tsp (4 ml) salt
1 cup (240 ml) FANTASTIC FOODS
 Basmati Rice
1 tsp (5 ml) dried mint
¼ cup (60 ml) chopped parsley
¼ cup (60 ml) green onions,
 chopped
½ cup (120 ml) plain nonfat yogurt

In saucepan on low heat sauté onion and garlic in butter until soft. Add water and salt and bring to a boil. Add rice, lower heat and simmer for 15 minutes or until all the water has been absorbed. Remove from heat. Add mint, parsley, green onions and yogurt and mix with rice. Serves 5.

Approximate nutritional analysis per serving:
Calories 213, Protein 5 g, Carbohydrates 38 g, Fat 5 g, Cholesterol 13 mg, Sodium 387 mg

BASMATI RICE WITH YOGURT

BROADWAY RICE FRY

¼ cup (60 ml) toasted sesame oil
2 tbs (30 ml) brown sugar
2 tbs (30 ml) soy sauce
2 cloves garlic, minced
½ cup (120 ml) unsalted peanuts
3 cups (720 ml) FANTASTIC FOODS
   cooked Arborio Rice
½ cup (120 ml) green peas
½ cup (120 ml) cooked black beans
2 green onions, thinly sliced
2 carrots, shredded
1 tsp (5 ml) crushed red pepper

Combine the toasted sesame oil, brown sugar and soy sauce in a skillet or wok and stir until homogenous. Add the minced garlic and peanuts. Sauté on medium heat until the brown sugar has melted. Take care not to scorch the sugar. Add cooked rice. Stir mixture until each kernel is coated with the sauce. Add peas, black beans, green onions and shredded carrots to rice and heat throughout. Add crushed red pepper and mix throughout the rice before serving. Serves 6.

Approximate nutritional analysis per 1 cup serving:
Calories 300, Protein 8 g, Carbohydrates 37 g, Fat 15 g, Cholesterol 0 mg, Sodium 349 mg

RUSSIAN HILL MUSHROOM SAUCE OVER ARBORIO RICE

1 cup (240 ml) FANTASTIC FOODS
   Creamy Mushroom Soup
½ cup (120 ml) hot tap water
½ cup (120 ml) low-fat milk
1 tbs (15 ml) butter
½ cup (120 ml) nonfat sour cream
salt, to taste
pepper, to taste
2 cups (480 ml) cooked FANTASTIC
   FOODS Arborio Rice

Combine the soup and the hot water in a small saucepan; whisk until smooth. Add the milk and butter to the mixture and whisk thoroughly. Heat on medium until the sauce thickens. Fold in the sour cream and mix evenly through the sauce. Season with salt and pepper. Serve over arborio rice. Serves 5.

Approximate nutritional analysis per 1 cup serving:
Calories 163, Protein 5 g, Carbohydrates 28 g, Fat 5 g, Cholesterol .9 mg, Sodium 235 mg

BROADWAY RICE FRY

FRIEDA'S QUINOA

8-oz pkg (240 g) FRIEDA'S Quinoa,
    black or white
14½-oz can (435 ml) chicken broth
1 cup (240 ml) water
¼ tsp (1 ml) salt
pinch pepper
butter, yogurt or soy sauce, optional

In a 2-quart saucepan, combine quinoa and broth and water. Bring to boiling; reduce heat. Simmer, covered, for 12-15 minutes, or until quinoa is tender and liquid is absorbed. Season with salt and pepper. Serve topped with butter, yogurt or soy sauce. Serves 7.

Approximate nutritional analysis per serving:
Calories 131, Protein 5 g, Carbohydrates 23 g, Fat 2 g, Cholesterol 0 mg, Sodium 270 mg

CURRIED WHOLE WHEAT COUSCOUS PILAF

1 small onion, chopped
1 clove garlic, minced
2 tbs (30 ml) butter
1 cup (240 ml) mushrooms, sliced
½ red bell pepper, chopped
½ cup (120 ml) fresh or frozen peas
½ cup (120 ml) green onions,
    chopped
1½ cups (355 ml) water or broth
¼ tsp (1 ml) salt
2 tsp (10 ml) curry powder
1 cup (240 ml) FANTASTIC FOODS
    Whole Wheat Couscous

In a covered saucepan on low heat, sauté onion and garlic in butter until soft. Add mushrooms, red bell pepper, peas and green onions and cook until nearly tender. Add water, salt and curry powder and bring to a boil. Add couscous, stir, reduce heat, cover and cook for 3-5 minutes or until liquid is absorbed. Serves 8.

Approximate nutritional analysis per ½ cup serving:
Calories 184, Protein 6 g, Carbohydrates 33 g, Fat 3 g, Cholesterol 8 mg, Sodium 105 mg

CURRIED WHOLE WHEAT COUSCOUS PILAF

CLASSIC VARNISHKAS WITH PASTA BOW KNOTS

KASHA PILAF:
2 tbs (30 ml) butter or margarine
½ cup (120 ml) chopped onions
½ cup (120 ml) sliced mushrooms
1 cup (240 ml) uncooked WOLFF'S
    Kasha
chicken or beef broth
2 tbs (30 ml) minced fresh parsley

Basic Kasha Pilaf (recipe below)
1 cup (240 ml) cooked pasta
    bow knots
2 tsp (10 ml) butter
minced parsley

Kasha Pilaf: In large skillet, melt butter and sauté onions and mushrooms. Prepare kasha according to basic directions on package, using chicken or beef broth as the liquid called for on package directions. Add the sautéed vegetables when the liquid is added and eliminate any additional butter or margarine. Before serving, fluff kasha with a fork and sprinkle with parsley. Yields 4 cups.

While pilaf is simmering, cook pasta in boiling salted water until just tender, about 12 minutes. Drain bows, return to pan and add butter. Combine with kasha and sprinkle with parsley before serving. Serves 4.

Approximate nutritional analysis per serving Classic Varnishkas:
Calories 300, Protein 9 g, Carbohydrates 46 g, Fat 10 g, Cholesterol 21 mg, Sodium 89 mg

Approximate nutritional analysis per 1 cup serving Kasha:
Calories 226, Protein 6 g, Carbohydrates 36 g, Fat 8 g, Cholesterol 16 mg, Sodium 69 mg

KAMUT WHOLE-GRAIN METHODS

3 cups (720 ml) water
½-1 tsp (3-5 ml) sea salt
1 cup (240 ml) KAMUT BRAND
    Grain, whole

Direct Heat Method: In a large saucepan, combine water and salt. Bring to a rolling boil and stir in grain. Bring to a boil again and boil for 2-3 minutes. Cover and simmer for 1½-2 hours or until the grain is tender and berries are plumped and a few have burst. Remove from heat and drain, if necessary, before using in recipes.

To reduce cooking time you may prepare grain by soaking it in water overnight. The next day, drain and then add to 3 cups boiling water. Cover and simmer as above.

Thermos Container Method : In a large saucepan, combine water and salt. Bring to a rolling boil and stir in grain. Bring to a boil again and boil for 2-3 minutes, then cover and simmer for 10 minutes. Pour mixture into a 1-quart wide-mouth thermos which you have preheated by pouring in warm water. Leave enough space at the top to allow for the grain to expand. Seal and let stand overnight or 8-10 hours. Drain, if necessary, before using in recipes. Serves 4.

Approximate nutritional analysis per serving:
Calories 110, Protein 4 g, Carbohydrates 25 g, Fat .5 g, Cholesterol 0 mg, Sodium 266 mg

CLASSIC VARNISHKAS WITH PASTA BOW KNOTS

KASHA ALMOND KUGEL

2 tbs (30 ml) butter or margarine
½ cup (120 ml) finely chopped onion
1 cup (240 ml) WOLFF'S Kasha,
    fine granulation
5 eggs
2 cups (480 ml) water
1 tsp (5 ml) salt
½ cup (120 ml) sugar
½ cup (120 ml) flour
1 tsp (5 ml) ground cinnamon
pinch ground nutmeg
15 pitted prunes, cooked, drained,
    cut into quarters
1 apple, peeled, cored and shredded
½ cup (120 ml) slivered almonds,
    chopped finely

Melt butter in medium skillet. Add onion and cook until tender, about 5 minutes. Toss kasha with 1 beaten egg and add to onion in pan. Stir and separate kasha as it cooks. Stir in water and salt and bring to a boil; cover, cook over low heat for 10 minutes. Cool.

Meanwhile, separate remaining 4 eggs. Beat whites until stiff; set aside. In large mixing bowl, beat yolks until thick. Gradually add sugar, beating after each addition. Add kasha mixture. In a medium bowl, combine flour, cinnamon, nutmeg, prunes and apple. Stir into batter. Add nuts. Fold in beaten egg whites. Spoon into well-greased and floured 9-inch Bundt pan or ring mold. Bake at 350°F (180°C) for 40-45 minutes. Cool 15 minutes before removing from pan. Serve warm. Serves 10.

Approximate nutritional analysis per serving:
Calories 262, Protein 8 g, Carbohydrates 41 g, Fat 9 g, Cholesterol 100 mg, Sodium 270 mg

KASHA ALMOND KUGEL

KNISHES

PASTRY:

2 cups (480 ml) all-purpose flour
½ tsp (3 ml) salt
1 egg or 2 egg whites
2 tbs (30 ml) vegetable oil
½ cup (120 ml) water
additional oil
additional flour and water
slightly beaten egg white

ONION FILLING:

1 cup (240 ml) onion, chopped
2 tbs (30 ml) butter or margarine
¾ cup (180 ml) cooked WOLFF'S Kasha
pinch pepper

CHICKEN FILLING:

1 cup (240 ml) diced cooked chicken
¾ cup (180 ml) cooked WOLFF'S Kasha
¼ cup (60 ml) finely chopped celery
3 tbs (45 ml) mayonnaise
½ tsp (3 ml) poultry seasoning
½ tsp (3 ml) lemon juice
dash salt

EGG FILLING:

¾ cup (180 ml) cooked WOLFF'S Kasha
3 hard-cooked eggs, chopped
3 tbs (45 ml) pickle relish
1 tbs (15 ml) minced onion
2 tsp (10 ml) prepared mustard

FRUIT AND NUT FILLING:

¾ cup (180 ml) WOLFF'S Kasha
⅓ cup (80 ml) chopped walnuts
⅓ cup (80 ml) diced dates
⅓ cup (80 ml) diced raisins
⅓ cup (80 ml) honey
1 tsp (5 ml) cinnamon
¼ tsp (1 ml) nutmeg

Pastry: Combine flour and salt in medium-size bowl. Make a well in the center. Add egg, oil and half of the water. Stir with a wooden spoon, adding remainder of water to make a smooth pliable dough. Turn dough out onto a lightly floured board; knead a few times. Brush dough with oil; cover with plastic wrap and let rest for about 1 hour.

At this point, dough may be refrigerated overnight. Roll dough on a floured board, to an 18-inch square or as thin as possible. Brush the dough with oil. Cut into 36 3-inch squares or rounds. Brush center of each with oil and fill with approximately 1 full tsp of filling; moisten edge with water; fold over; seal edges.

Place on lightly greased baking sheet. Brush top with beaten egg white. Bake at 375°F (190°C) for 12-15 minutes or until lightly browned. Yields 36 snack-size knishes.

Onion Filling: Sauté onion in butter or margarine; add kasha and seasoning. Use to fill knishes. Bake as above. Yields 1¼ cups.

Chicken Filling: Combine all ingredients and use to fill knishes. Bake as above. Yields 1¾ cups.

Egg Filling: Combine all ingredients and use to fill knishes. Bake as above. Yields 1½ cups.

Fruit and Nut Filling: Combine all ingredients and use to fill knishes. Bake as above. Yields 1½ cups.

Approximate nutritional analysis per Onion Knish:
Calories 46, Protein 1 g, Carbohydrates 7 g, Fat 2 g, Cholesterol 7 mg, Sodium 38 mg

Approximate nutritional analysis per Chicken Knish:
Calories 51, Protein 2 g, Carbohydrates 6 g, Fat 2 g, Cholesterol 8 mg, Sodium 41 mg

Approximate nutritional analysis per Egg Knish:
Calories 46, Protein 2 g, Carbohydrates 7 g, Fat 1 g, Cholesterol 21 mg, Sodium 49 mg

Approximate nutritional analysis per Fruit & Nut Knish:
Calories 64, Protein 1 g, Carbohydrates 11 g, Fat 2 g, Cholesterol 5 mg, Sodium 32 mg

KNISHES

Overleaf: FRIEDA'S QUINOA

CURRIED BAKED BEANS

1 lb (455 g) small dry white beans
6 cups (1.4 l) water
1 tsp (5 ml) salt
2 medium apples, cored and pared
½ cup (120 ml) golden raisins
1 small onion, minced
⅓ cup (80 ml) sweet pickle relish
⅔ cup (160 ml) DAWES HILL
   Buckwheat Honey
1 tbs (15 ml) prepared mustard
1 tsp (5 ml) curry powder, or to taste

Combine beans, water and salt in large saucepan. Let stand overnight. Bring to a boil over high heat. Reduce to low and simmer 2 hours, adding water if needed. Drain beans, reserving liquid.

Combine beans with remaining ingredients. Pour into 2½-quart casserole. Add enough bean liquid to barely cover. Bake, covered, at 300°F (150°C) for 1 hour. Remove cover; bake about 30 minutes, adding more liquid, if needed. Serves 10.

Approximate nutritional analysis per serving:
Calories 278, Protein 10 g, Carbohydrates 61 g, Fat .8 g, Cholesterol 0 mg, Sodium 298 mg

CURRIED BAKED BEANS

CHRISTMAS LIMAS & POTATOES

8-oz pkg FRIEDA'S Dried Christmas
   Lima Beans
2 cups (480 ml) cubed potatoes,
   white, yellow or sweet potatoes
½ cup (120 ml) chopped onion
4 cups (960 ml) water or
   chicken broth
1 tbs (15 ml) chopped FRIEDA'S
   Fresh Dill
½ tsp (3 l) salt
¼ tsp (1 ml) pepper

Place beans in a saucepan with water to cover. Bring to boiling; boil 2 minutes. Remove from heat; cover and let stand 1 hour. Drain beans; in same pan combine beans with potatoes, onion and water or broth. Bring to boiling; reduce heat. Simmer, partially covered, for 45-60 minutes, or until beans are tender. Drain well; stir in dill, salt and pepper. Serves 8 as a side dish.

Approximate nutritional analysis per serving:
Calories 182, Protein 8 g, Carbohydrates 38 g, Fat .3 g, Cholesterol 0 mg, Sodium 145 mg

CHRISTMAS LIMAS & POTATOES

RATTLESNAKE BEANS & BACON

8-oz pkg FRIEDA'S Rattlesnake Beans
6 strips bacon, chopped
1 cup (240 ml) chopped onion
2 cloves garlic, minced
2 cups (480 ml) water or chicken broth
1 tbs (15 ml) FRIEDA'S Fresh Sage, Basil or Oregano
½ tsp (3 ml) salt
¼ tsp (1 ml) pepper

In a saucepan cover beans with water; bring to a boil. Boil 2 minutes; remove from heat. Cover and let stand 1 hour. Drain; set aside. In a 3-quart saucepan or deep skillet cook bacon with onion and garlic until bacon is crisp; drain off fat. Add water or broth, drained beans and desired chopped herb; bring to a boil. Reduce heat; simmer, covered, for 30-45 minutes, or until beans are tender. Drain off any excess liquid; stir in salt and pepper. Serves 6 as a side dish.

Approximate nutritional analysis per serving:
Calories 103, Protein 6 g, Carbohydrates 12 g, Fat 4 g, Cholesterol 5 mg, Sodium 281 mg

BAKED BLACK BEANS WITH SOUR CREAM

4 MILL VALLEY Tostada Bowls
1 cup (240 ml) black beans, uncooked
2 tbs (30 ml) oil
3 medium onions, thinly sliced
2 medium cloves garlic, minced
1 jalapeño chile, finely chopped
3 tbs (45 ml) finely chopped cilantro
1 tsp (5 ml) salt
½ cup (120 ml) low-fat sour cream

Soak beans overnight in cold water or do a quick soak by bringing them to a boil in water to cover beans, boiling for 2 minutes, covering and letting stand 1 hour. Drain soaked beans and put them in a large saucepan. Add enough water to cover generously. Bring to a boil and simmer uncovered until tender, about 1½-2 hours.

Heat oil in skillet. Add onions and cook over low heat until soft but not brown. Add garlic, chile and 2 tbs chopped cilantro and cook 1 minute longer. Remove from heat. Preheat oven to 350°F (180°C). Drain beans, reserving ½ cup cooking liquid. Put beans in an oiled, small baking dish. Add reserved liquid and onion mixture. Add salt. Bake 30-40 minutes or until liquid is absorbed.

Preheat tostada bowls for 3-5 minutes in the oven and fill with black beans. Top each serving with 2 tbs sour cream and a sprinkle of the remaining chopped cilantro. Serves 4.

Approximate nutritional analysis per serving:
Calories 290, Protein 7 g, Carbohydrates 33 g, Fat 16 g, Cholesterol 12 mg, Sodium 584 mg

BAKED BLACK BEANS WITH SOUR CREAM

NAVY BEAN TARRAGON

1 tbs (15 ml) olive oil
1 cup (240 ml) finely diced onions
1 cup (240 ml) quartered
   mushrooms
1 cup (240 ml) thinly sliced scallions
1 cup (240 ml) thinly sliced leeks
¾ tsp (4 ml) dry tarragon leaf
1½ cups (355 ml) cooked navy beans
½ cup (120 ml) white wine
¼ cup (60 ml) SOLAIT Powder
4½ tsp (23 ml) dark miso
1 tbs (15 ml) fresh lemon juice
3 tbs (45 ml) diced red bell pepper,
   optional
3 tbs (45 ml) sliced scallions,
   optional

Heat a sauté pan on medium heat for 1 minute and add oil, onions, mushrooms, scallions, leeks and tarragon leaf; sauté until the onions are transparent. Add the beans. Blend the white wine, soy beverage powder, dark miso and fresh lemon juice together until smooth. Add this mixture to the sautéed vegetables and simmer gently for 5 minutes. Serve as is or over cooked pasta or grain. Garnish with either or both scallions and red bell pepper, if desired. Serves 5.

Approximate nutritional analysis per serving:
Calories 209, Protein 9 g, Carbohydrates 31 g, Fat 5 g, Cholesterol 0 mg, Sodium 241 mg

NAVY BEAN TARRAGON

BLACK BEANS & COUSCOUS

1 cup (240 ml) OLD SAVANNAH
   Black Beans, soaked overnight
1-2 bay leaves
6-8 cloves garlic, minced
2 tsp (10 ml) oregano dried
1 tsp (5 ml) cumin
pepper, to taste
red pepper, optional
1 tbs (15 ml) baking soda
1 tsp (5 ml) salt
1 cup (240 ml) raw couscous,
   steamed

In saucepan, place beans and bay leaves in enough water to cover beans and bring to a boil. Reduce heat and simmer for 1½ hours or until beans are tender. Add garlic, oregano, cumin, pepper and red pepper. Add additional water so that beans remain covered. Simmer 30 minutes more, or until beans are softened, add baking soda and salt, mix well. Correct seasoning to taste. Continue to cook until the soup thickens to desired consistency. Adjust with additional water if necessary. Meanwhile, steam couscous. Serve couscous with a ladle of black beans. Serves 6.

Approximate nutritional analysis per serving:
Calories 226, Protein 9 g, Carbohydrates 46 g, Fat .4 g, Cholesterol 0 mg, Sodium 638 mg

BLACK BEANS & COUSCOUS

STIR-FRY LENTILS & BEANS

¼ cup (60 ml) sesame oil
½ cup (120 ml) diced onion
½ cup (120 ml) diced celery
1 cup (240 ml) sliced mushrooms
2 cups (480 ml) cooked
    ARROWHEAD MILLS Red Lentils
1 cup (240 ml) cooked ARROWHEAD
    MILLS Adzuki Beans
½ cup (120 ml) fresh mung bean
    sprouts
½ cup (120 ml) sliced water
    chestnuts
2 tsp (10 ml) low-sodium tamari
    sauce
½ tsp (3 ml) marjoram
¼ tsp (1 ml) nutmeg
¼ tsp (1 ml) garlic powder
¼ tsp (1 ml) onion powder

Heat the oil in a large skillet or wok and sauté the onion, celery and mushrooms until brown. Add remaining ingredients and cook, stirring until heated through. Serves 6.

Approximate nutritional analysis per serving:
Calories 225, Protein 10 g, Carbohydrates 27 g, Fat 9 g, Cholesterol 0 mg, Sodium 105 mg

QUICK STEUBEN STIR-FRY WITH RICE

½ cup (120 ml) chopped scallions
    or onions
⅓ cup (80 ml) chopped celery
½ cup (120 ml) chopped green
    pepper
2 cloves minced garlic
3 tbs (45 ml) cooking oil
2-3 cups (480-720 ml) cooked OLD
    SAVANNAH Steuben Yellow Eye
    Beans
½ cup (120 ml) organic tomato purée
½ tsp (3 ml) dry basil
salt, to taste
pepper, to taste
¼ cup (60 ml) grated carrots
2 cups (480 ml) cooked brown rice,
    optional

Sauté scallions, celery, green pepper and garlic in oil for 1-2 minutes, to soften. Add beans and stir-fry for a minute or 2 more, then add tomato purée, basil, salt and pepper. Continue to cook over medium heat, stirring frequently, for about 10 minutes. Correct seasoning. Place in serving dish and garnish with grated carrots. Can be served next to or over rice. Serves 4.

Approximate nutritional analysis per serving:
Calories 339, Protein 11 g, Carbohydrates 48 g, Fat 12 g, Cholesterol 2 mg, Sodium 19 mg

QUICK STEUBEN STIR-FRY WITH RICE

CHESTNUT HILL HAYSTACK EDIBOWLS

8 MILL VALLEY Beans 'n' Rice Tostada Bowls, warmed in oven
1 batch Lil's Sombrero Sauce (recipe below)
1 head shredded lettuce
4 chopped tomatoes
2 cups (480 ml) tofu sour cream or shredded soy cheddarlike cheese
6-oz can (180 g) chopped black olives
2 cups (480 ml) homemade or prepared salsa, heated
4 chopped scallions
1 chopped green pepper

LIL'S SOMBRERO SAUCE:
2 large onions
1 green pepper
1 clove garlic
2 celery ribs
1 tsp (5 ml) salt
1 tsp (5 ml) oregano
1 tsp (5 ml) cumin, optional
28-oz can (840 g) tomato purée
40-oz can (1.2 kg) kidney beans, drained
15½-oz can (465 g) kidney beans, drained

MARROW BEANS WITH RICE

8-oz pkg (240 g) FRIEDA'S Dried Marrow Beans
1 tbs (15 ml) vegetable oil
1 cup (240 ml) chopped onion
2 cloves garlic, minced
1 fresh FRIEDA'S Anaheim Chile, seeded and minced
3 cups (720 ml) chicken broth or water
2 tomatoes, chopped
1 cup (240 ml) FRIEDA'S Wild Rice, brown or white rice
1 bay leaf
1 tbs (15 ml) chopped FRIEDA'S Basil
1 tsp (5 ml) grated orange peel
½ tsp (3 ml) salt
¼ tsp (1 ml) pepper

Place warmed tostada bowls on individual serving plates. Fill tostada bowls with ingredients in order given. Serves 8.

Lil's Sombrero Sauce: Chop onions, green pepper, garlic and celery in food processor, then sizzle in a skillet in a few drops of water, stirring to avoid burning. Beans may be puréed or left whole. Combine all ingredients and cook over low heat for about 30 minutes. Leftover sauce may be frozen. Serves 16.

Approximate nutritional analysis per edibowl:
Calories 370, Protein 11 g, Carbohydrates 48 g, Fat 17 g, Cholesterol 0 mg, Sodium 980 mg

MARROW BEANS WITH RICE

In a large saucepan, cover beans with water. Bring to a boil; boil 2 minutes. Remove from heat; cover and let stand 1 hour. Drain beans; in same pan heat oil. Sauté onion, garlic and chile in oil for 5 minutes or until vegetables are tender. Stir in drained beans, broth or water, tomatoes, rice, bay leaf, basil and orange peel. Bring mixture to a boil. Reduce heat; cover, simmer for 45-50 minutes, or until beans and rice are tender and all liquid is absorbed. Remove bay leaf; stir in salt and pepper.
Serves 6 as a main dish.

Approximate nutritional analysis per serving:
Calories 250, Protein 13 g, Carbohydrates 45 g, Fat 3 g, Cholesterol 0 mg, Sodium 189 mg

YELLOW-EYE & SQUASH STEW

8-oz pkg FRIEDA'S Dried Yellow
    Eye Beans
1 tbs (15 ml) olive oil
1 cup (240 ml) chopped onion
1 red or green bell pepper
2 cloves garlic, minced
14½-oz can (435 ml) chicken broth
2 cups (480 ml) water
2 cups (480 ml) diced tomatoes
1 lb (455 g) FRIEDA'S Table Queen,
    Acorn, Butternut, Banana or
    Pumpkin Squash, peeled, seeded
    and cut into 1-inch chunks
1 tbs (15 ml) chopped FRIEDA'S
    Fresh Oregano
2 tsp (10 ml) chopped FRIEDA'S
    Fresh Thyme
½ tsp (3 ml) salt
¼ tsp (1 ml) pepper

Place beans in a 2-quart saucepan. Cover with 2 inches of water and bring to a boil. Cook for 2 minutes; remove from heat. Cover; let stand for 1 hour. Drain beans. In a large Dutch oven heat oil; sauté onion, bell pepper and garlic for 5-10 minutes or until vegetables are tender. Stir in drained beans, broth, water, tomatoes, squash, oregano and thyme. Bring to a boil; reduce heat. Simmer, partially covered, for 1-1½ hours or until beans are tender. Stir in salt and pepper. Serves 6 as a main dish.

Approximate nutritional analysis per serving:
Calories 132, Protein 7 g, Carbohydrates 20 g, Fat 3 g, Cholesterol 0 mg, Sodium 405 mg

APPALOOSA BEANS & CORN

8-oz pkg (240 g) FRIEDA'S Dried
    Appaloosa Beans
1 tbs (15 ml) vegetable oil
1 cup (240 ml) chopped onion
2 cloves garlic, minced
2 cups (480 ml) chicken broth
    or water
1½ cups (355 ml) niblet corn
2 tsp (10 ml) FRIEDA'S Fresh Sage,
    chopped
½ tsp (3 ml) salt
¼ tsp (1 ml) pepper

Place beans in a 2-quart saucepan. Cover with 2 inches of water and bring to a boil. Cook for 2 minutes; reduce heat. Simmer partially covered about 2 hours or until beans are just tender, making sure water does not cook out. Drain beans. Remove beans from pan and set them aside.

    In same saucepan heat oil; sauté onion and garlic for 5 minutes or until vegetables are tender. Stir in drained beans, broth, corn and sage. Cook 10-15 minutes, or until mixture is heated through. Stir in salt and pepper. Serves 4 as a main dish.

Approximate nutritional analysis per serving:
Calories 175, Protein 7 g, Carbohydrates 30 g, Fat 4 g, Cholesterol 0 mg, Sodium 145 mg

APPALOOSA BEANS & CORN

CURRIED GARBANZO BEANS & RICE

2 tbs (30 ml) olive oil
1 medium onion, chopped
1 medium green bell pepper, diced
2 15-oz cans (900 g) AMERICAN PRAIRIE Organic Garbanzo Beans, drained and rinsed
2-4 cloves garlic, finely chopped
2 tsp (10 ml) curry powder
½ cup (120 ml) water
14-oz can (420 g) plum tomatoes, chopped, reserving liquid
2 10-oz pkgs (600 g) frozen chopped spinach, thawed and squeezed dry
sea salt, to taste

In large saucepan, heat oil. Add onion and green pepper; cook over medium heat, stirring occasionally, 3-5 minutes. Add garbanzo beans, garlic, curry and water; bring to a simmer, cover and cook 5 minutes. Stir in tomatoes and their liquid. Add spinach and cover and cook 10 minutes. Salt to taste. Serve over cooked rice. Serves 6.

Approximate nutritional analysis per serving:
Calories 265, Protein 11 g, Carbohydrates 44 g, Fat 7 g, Cholesterol 0 mg, Sodium 512 mg

LENTIL CURRY

1½ cups (355 ml) lentils, washed and drained
6 cups (1.4 l) water
1 tbs (15 ml) vegetable oil
1 cup (240 ml) chopped onion
2 cloves garlic, minced
1 tsp (15 ml) curry powder
1 tsp (5 ml) cumin seeds
2 14½-oz cans (870 g) MUIR GLEN Organic Diced Tomatoes, undrained
1 green apple, diced
½ cup (120 ml) seedless raisins
salt, to taste
pepper, to taste
3 cups (720 ml) cooked couscous or rice
2 tbs (30 ml) chopped fresh cilantro or parsley

In large saucepan, combine lentils and water. Bring to a boil; reduce heat to low and simmer, partially covered, 45-50 minutes, or until lentils are tender, occasionally skimming off foam and stirring to prevent sticking.

In large skillet, heat oil over medium heat. Add onion, garlic, curry powder and cumin seeds; cook until onion is tender. Stir in tomatoes, apple and raisins. Season with salt and pepper. When lentils are tender, stir into onion mixture; cook, covered, about 15 minutes, until apple is tender. Serve over hot cooked couscous, garnished with cilantro. Serves 6.

Approximate nutritional analysis per serving:
Calories 379, Protein 19 g, Carbohydrates 70 g, Fat 3 g, Cholesterol 0 mg, Sodium 217 mg

CURRIED GARBANZO BEANS & RICE

SPICY BLACK BEANS WITH TOMATO & CILANTRO

2 cups (480 ml) dry black beans
1 red onion, diced
4 cloves garlic, minced
1 tbs (15 ml) **SPECTRUM WORLD EATS Southwestern Oil**
salt, to taste
pepper, to taste
1 medium ripe tomato, diced
4 tbs (60 ml) cilantro, chopped
1 tbs (15 ml) lime juice

Measure the beans into a 4-quart saucepan and cover with water. Bring to a boil for 2 minutes. Remove from heat and let stand for 1 hour or more.

Meanwhile, prepare the other ingredients.

Drain the beans then cover them with clear cold water. Bring to a simmer, add onions, garlic and oil. Simmer gently for 40 minutes or until tender. Season with salt and pepper. Continue to simmer until beans are thoroughly cooked, adding more water if necessary. Stir in tomato, cilantro and lime juice. Correct seasoning and serve. Serves 4.

Approximate nutritional analysis per serving:
Calories 171, Protein 9 g, Carbohydrates 27 g, Fat 4 g, Cholesterol 0 mg, Sodium 5 mg

SPICY BLACK BEANS WITH TOMATO & CILANTRO

LENTIL LOAF

2 cups (480 ml) cooked **ARROWHEAD MILLS Lentils**, red or green
1 cup (240 ml) cooked **ARROWHEAD MILLS Medium Brown Rice**
1 cup (240 ml) cooked **ARROWHEAD MILLS Bulgur Wheat**
1 cup (240 ml) **ARROWHEAD MILLS Garbanzo Flour** mixed with
⅔ cup (180 ml) cold water
½-1 cup (120-240 ml) chopped nuts
1 tbs (15 ml) soy sauce
1 tsp (5 ml) sea salt, optional
1 tsp (5 ml) sage
1 tbs (15 ml) **ARROWHEAD MILLS Unrefined Vegetable Oil**

Drain the cooked lentils and grains. Mix all ingredients together. Spoon into a loaf pan. Bake at 350°F (180°C) for 30-45 minutes. Serve with any leftover gravy over top. Serves 6.

Approximate nutritional analysis per serving:
Calories 306, Protein 15 g, Carbohydrates 42 g, Fat 10 g, Cholesterol 0 mg, Sodium 184 mg

LENTIL LOAF

TOASTED GARBANZO PATTIES

1½ cups (355 ml) ARROWHEAD
    MILLS Garbanzo Flour
1 cup (240 ml) water
1 medium onion, chopped finely
½ cup (120 ml) ARROWHEAD
    MILLS Oat Flakes
½ cup (120 ml) ground pecans
    or other nuts
1 tbs (15 ml) parsley
1 tsp (5 ml) savory
1 tsp (5 ml) salt
toasted sesame oil or other oil

Mix the flour and water. Let sit while preparing remaining ingredients. Combine all other ingredients together, mxing well. When mixture is quite thick, shape into patties. Fry lightly on both sides. Flatten patties fairly thin while cooking. Serves 6.

Approximate nutritional analysis per serving:
Calories 207, Protein 8 g, Carbohydrates 28 g, Fat 9 g, Cholesterol 0 mg, Sodium 49 mg

SOYBEAN-LENTIL-RICE LOAF

1 cup (240 ml) cooked ARROWHEAD
    MILLS Soybeans
1 cup (240 ml) cooked ARROWHEAD
    MILLS Lentils
1 cup (240 ml) cooked ARROWHEAD
    MILLS Medium Brown Rice
¾ cup (180 ml) soy milk, water,
    stock or gravy
1 medium onion, finely chopped
2 cloves garlic, finely chopped
2 egg whites, beaten
¼ cup (60 ml) tomato purée,
    additional for serving
2 stalks celery, chopped
2 tsp (10 ml) sea salt, optional
1 cup (240 ml) ARROWHEAD MILLS
    Wheat Germ
½ tsp (3 ml) onion powder
½ tsp (3 ml) chile powder

In a large mixing bowl, mash soybeans and lentils well. Add the rest of the ingredients and mix well. Turn into an oiled loaf pan. Bake in preheated oven for 1 hour. Serve as is or top with additional tomato purée. Serves 4.

Approximate nutritional analysis per serving:
Calories 287, Protein 20 g, Carbohydrates 41 g, Fat 6 g, Cholesterol 0 mg, Sodium 104 mg

TOASTED GARBANZO PATTIES

BAKED BARLEY & BEAN CASSEROLE

2 cups cooked and mashed
   ARROWHEAD MILS Beans,
   of choice
1 cup (240 l) precooked
   ARROWHEAD MILLS
   Bits-O-Barley
1 cup (240 ml) soy milk
½ cup (120 ml) ARROWHEAD
   MILLS Raw Wheat Germ
2 tbs (30 ml) ARROWHEAD MILLS
   Low Fat Soy Flour
1 tbs (15 ml) ARROWHEAD MILLS
   Unrefined Vegetable Oil
¼ cup (60 ml) onion, minced
   and sautéed
3 tbs (45 ml) prepared mustard
½ cup (120 ml) honey
½ cup (120 ml) ketchup
½ tsp (3 ml) garlic powder
½ tsp (3 ml) onion powder
½ tsp (3 ml) chile powder
sea salt, to taste, optional

Preheat oven to 350°F (180°C). Mix all ingredients together. Let stand for 30 minutes. Turn into an oiled casserole dish and bake for 40 minutes. Serves 6.

Approximate nutritional analysis per serving:
Calories 298, Protein 10 g, Carbohydrates 58 g, Fat 5 g, Cholesterol 0 mg, Sodium 641 mg

BAKED BARLEY & BEAN CASSEROLE

Overleaf: YELLOW-EYE & SQUASH STEW

PASTA & NOODLES

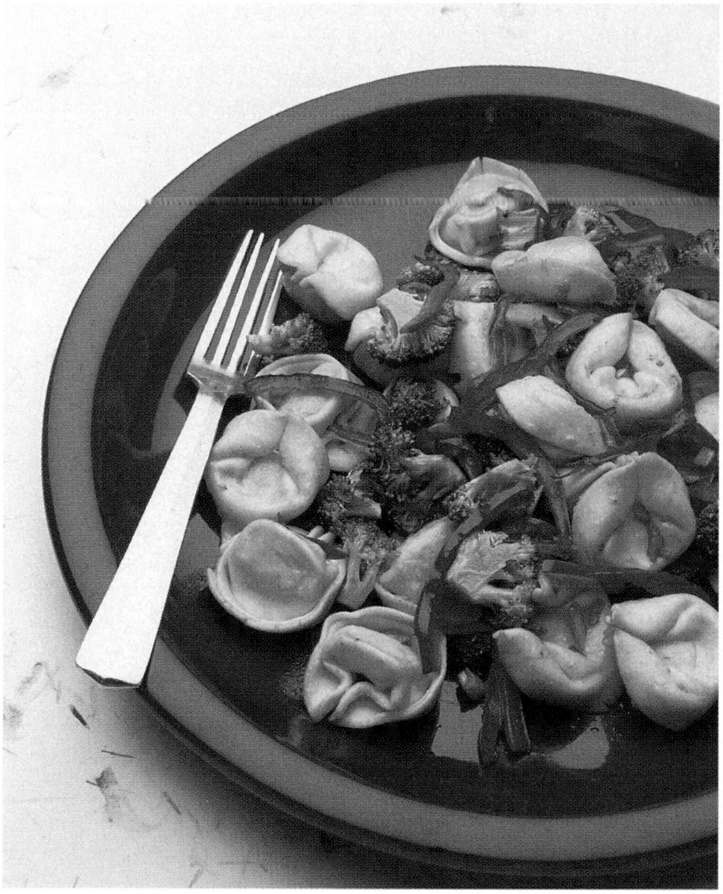

HOMEMADE KAMUT PASTA

A good homemade pasta has minimal liquid and thus yields a light and pleasing, rather than heavy and dense, noodle. However, if you are making ravioli, make a softer and moister dough to prevent it from tearing when you mold the pasta around the filling.

**2 cups (480 ml) KAMUT BRAND Flour
or 1 cup (240 ml) KAMUT BRAND Flour, plus 1 cup (240 ml) unbleached white flour
2 large eggs
2-4 tbs (30-60) ml water**

Hand Mixing Method: Place flour(s) on a large work surface, shape into a mound and make a well in the top. Barely combine the egg and 2 tbs water in a small bowl and pour into the well. Work the mixture with your hands, folding the flour over the egg until a dry dough is formed. If more water is needed, add only a few drops at a time. Knead this stiff dough with your hands for 10 minutes or until very smooth. Put the dough in a plastic bag and let it rest at room temperature for 30 minutes.

Mixer Method Using Dough Hook: Place the flour, eggs and 2 tbs water in a mixer and knead on low speed for 8-10 minutes. If necessary, add just enough additional water to form a stiff dough. With hands, form into a round ball, wrap in plastic and let rest for 30 minutes.

Hand Rolling Dough: Divide the dough into 4 balls and form each into a rectangular shape. Roll the dough, stretching it with each roll. If necessary, sprinkle it with a little extra flour to prevent from sticking. Repeat rolling for about 10 times or until the dough is paper-thin and translucent. Repeat with remaining dough. Let sheets dry up to 30 minutes; do not allow them to become brittle. Roll each sheet up like a jelly roll and cut it with a sharp knife into the desired shape.

Machine Rolling: Divide dough into 4 pieces. With hands, pat and flatten each piece into a rectangle about the width of the rolling bars and thin enough to insert into the pasta machine's widest setting. Roll the dough through the machine. Fold it in thirds and roll it through again. Now proceed through all the settings, making the dough thinner and thinner each time. Cut the dough sheets into 8-inch lengths, then using the cutting bars on the machine, cut into desired shape.

To Cook: For each 4 oz of pasta, bring 1 quart of water to a boil and use 1 tsp salt per quart of water. Unroll each strand of pasta into the pot and boil about 2-3 minutes or until al dente. Fresh pasta cooks in less time than dried pasta.

To Store: If pasta is not cooked immediately, cover with plastic wrap, refrigerate and cook within 48 hours; or hang until dry, then store in plastic.

Recipe yields 16 oz pasta.

Approximate nutritional analysis per 2 oz serving:
Calories 126, Protein 5 g, Carbohydrates 25 g, Fat 2 g, Cholesterol 47 mg, Sodium 14 mg

PASTA WITH PESTO

¾ lb (340 g) pasta
1 pkg GREEN HOUSE Fresh Basil,
  leaves only
⅓ cup (80 ml) pine nuts or walnuts
2 cloves garlic, peeled
⅓ cup (80 ml) olive oil
½ cup (120 ml) Parmesan cheese,
  freshly grated
2 tbs (30 ml) hot water

Bring large pot of water to a boil. Cook pasta according to package directions while you prepare the pesto.

Place basil along with nuts and garlic in a food processor or blender and process until finely chopped. With the machine running, pour in the olive oil in a thin stream. Add the cheese, salt and pepper to taste, and process briefly to combine. Thin with 2 tbs hot water. Toss pesto with hot pasta, cooked and drained, and serve. Serves 4.

Approximate nutritional analysis per serving:
Calories 557, Protein 20 g, Carbohydrates 31 g, Fat 44 g, Cholesterol 10 mg, Sodium 235 mg

PASTA PEAS & PESTO

1 pkg PUTNEY PASTA Parmesan &
  Cracked Black Peppercorn
  Tortelloni
1 pkg PUTNEY PASTA Sun Dried
  Tomato Basil & Mozzarella
  Tortelloni
1 pkg PUTNEY PASTA Passionate
  Pesto Sauce
½ cup (120 ml) baby frozen peas,
  defrosted
2 tbs (30 ml) pine nuts, toasted
1 red bell pepper, julienned
1 tbs (15 ml) Romano cheese, grated

Cook tortelloni according to package directions, lightly oil and chill. Toss with pesto and sauce. Mix in peas. Garnish with nuts, red pepper and Romano cheese. Serves 8.

Approximate nutritional analysis per serving:
Calories 344, Protein 14 g, Carbohydrates 34 g, Fat 17 g, Cholesterol 35 mg, Sodium 407 mg

PASTA WITH PESTO

PASTA WITH DELFTREE SHIITAKE MUSHROOMS & ASPARAGUS

1 tbs (15 ml) butter
1 tbs (15 ml) olive oil
1 tbs (15 ml) onion, finely chopped
1 lb (455 g) DELFTREE Shiitake
    Mushrooms, sliced
1 lb (455 g) asparagus, tips only
½ cup (120 ml) chicken broth
pinch salt
3 tbs (45 ml) dry sherry or Madeira
1 cup (240 ml) heavy cream
1 tsp (5 ml) chopped fresh tarragon
    or ½ tsp (3 ml) dry tarragon
salt, to taste
freshly ground pepper, to taste
½ lb (230 g) tagliatelle or other
    broad noodle, freshly cooked

Heat butter and olive oil in a large deep skillet over medium heat until butter is foaming. Add chopped onion and stir for 1 minute. Add shiitakes and asparagus tips and toss. Add chicken broth, salt lightly and cook partially covered for 5-6 minutes until shiitake and asparagus are barely cooked.

Increase heat to high, add sherry and cook until most of the liquid has evaporated from the pan. Add cream and tarragon and cook, shaking pan over heat until cream thickens slightly and vegetables are tender. Season with salt and freshly ground black pepper to taste, and toss with freshly cooked pasta. Serves 5.

Approximate nutritional analysis per serving:
Calories 336, Protein 6 g, Carbohydrates 27 g, Fat 24 g, Cholesterol 86 mg, Sodium 127 mg

ORIENTAL RIGATONI WITH CHICKEN

8 oz (240 g) rigatoni, cooked
    and drained
1 lb (455 g) chicken breasts, skinless
    and boneless
1 tsp (5 ml) vegetable oil
pinch cayenne pepper
1 bunch green onion, cut 1-inch
    diagonals
1½ cups (355 ml) pineapple juice
1 tbs (15 ml) fresh ginger root
1 tbs (15 ml) honey
1 tbs (15 ml) butter or margarine
1 tbs (15 ml) lemon juice
1 tbs (15 ml) fresh cilantro, chopped
    or 1 tsp (5 ml) dried cilantro
1 tbs (15 ml) pine nuts, toasted

Prepare pasta according to package directions, drain. Brush the chicken with the vegetable oil and season with the cayenne pepper. Bake at 350°F (180°C) until cooked through, about 30 minutes. During the last 10 minutes, place the green onions in the pan. Combine the pineapple juice, ginger and honey in a small saucepan. Bring to a boil over medium-high heat and reduce by half. Whisk in the butter or margarine and the lemon juice. Toss together the pasta with the chicken and scallions and add the sauce. Garnish with the cilantro and pine nuts and serve immediately. Serves 4.

Approximate nutritional analysis per serving:
Calories 477, Protein 35 g, Carbohydrates 64 g, Fat 8 g, Cholesterol 74 mg, Sodium 110 mg

Courtesy of The National Honey Board.

RAVIOLI SICILIAN STYLE

2 pkgs PUTNEY PASTA Garlic
 and Herb Ravioli
4 garlic cloves, minced
⅓ cup (80 ml) extra-virgin olive oil
½ lb (230 g) broccoli rabe, trimmed,
 ½-inch sliced
¼ cup (60 ml) white wine
1 cup (240 ml) garbanzo beans,
 cooked
⅓ cup (80 ml) oil-cured olives,
 pitted and cut into large pieces
¼ tbs (4 ml) red pepper flakes
1 tbs (15 ml) capers
2 tbs (30 ml) fresh parsley, chopped
2 tbs (30 ml) fresh basil, julienne
3 oz (90 g) Pecorino Romano cheese,
 grated
coarse ground fresh black pepper,
 to taste

Cook ravioli according to package directions.

In a large skillet, sauté garlic in olive oil until lightly toasted. Add broccoli rabe and cook for 2 minutes then add white wine. Cover and simmer for 3 minutes. Add garbanzo beans, olives, red pepper flakes and capers. Simmer covered for an additional 2 minutes then remove from heat. Toss mixture with pasta, parsley, basil, cheese and black pepper. Serve at once. Serves 6.

Approximate nutritional analysis per serving:
Calories 371, Protein 14 g, Carbohydrates 32 g, Fat 21 g, Cholesterol 34 mg, Sodium 453 mg

AGNOLOTTI WITH TOASTED GARLIC & BROCCOLI

2 pkgs PUTNEY PASTA Broccoli and
 Aged Vermont Cheddar Agnolotti
6 garlic cloves, minced
2 tsp (10 ml) olive oil
2 cups (480 ml) broccoli florets,
 blanched
2 tbs (30 ml) butter, unsalted
1 tsp (5 ml) poppy seeds, optional
1½ tbs (25 ml) Parmesan cheese,
 grated
2 tbs (30 ml) parsley, chopped
fresh ground black pepper, to taste
juice from ½ lemon

Cook agnolotti according to package directions.

In a large skillet toast garlic in olive oil. Add blanched broccoli, butter and poppy seeds,if desired. Toss lightly. Add cooked agnolotti and combine over a medium heat for 1 minute. Transfer to a bowl and toss with Parmesan cheese, parsley, pepper and lemon juice. Serve immediately. Serves 6.

Approximate nutritional analysis per serving:
Calories 286, Protein 13 g, Carbohydrates 35 g, Fat 12 g, Cholesterol 49 mg, Sodium 436 mg

AGNOLOTTI WITH TOASTED GARLIC & BROCCOLI

TORTELLONI WITH FRESH TOMATO SAUCE & ARUGULA

4 garlic cloves, minced
3 tbs (45 ml) olive oil
1 pkg PUTNEY PASTA Magnificent
   Marinara Sauce
2 cups (480 ml) arugula leaves,
   trimmed, washed and rough
   chopped
salt, to taste
pepper, to taste
1 pkg PUTNEY PASTA Parmesan
   and Cracked Black Peppercorn
   Tortelloni
1 pkg PUTNEY PASTA Sun Dried
   Tomato Basil & Mozzarella
   Tortelloni
¼ cup (60 ml) Pecorino Romano,
   grated
¼ cup (60 ml) Parmesan cheese

In a heavy skillet over medium heat, sauté the garlic in olive oil until it just begins to brown. Add marinara sauce and cook for 3-4 minutes. Add arugula, turn down heat and allow leaves to wilt. Adjust seasoning and remove from heat. Keep warm.

Cook tortelloni according to package directions. Toss tortelloni with sauce and grated cheeses. Serve at once. Serves 4.

Approximate nutritional analysis per serving:
Calories 594, Protein 29 g, Carbohydrates 67 g, Fat 23 g, Cholesterol 80 mg, Sodium 969 mg

BROCCOLI AND RED PEPPER TORTELLINI

3 tbs (45 ml) olive oil
1 lb (455 g) broccoli florets
2 large sweet red peppers, julienned
3-4 cloves garlic, crushed
2-3 tbs (30-45 ml) CHESHIRE
   GARDEN Italia Piccante Vinegar
1 lb (455 g) cheese tortellini, cooked
   according to package directions
   and drained

Heat the olive oil in a heavy skillet. Sauté the broccoli and peppers until they are slightly tender, about 3-4 minutes. Add the garlic and cook 1 minute more. Add the vinegar, raise heat and cook 1 minute more. Stir in tortellini and heat thoroughly, about 1 minute. Serves 4.

Approximate nutritional analysis per serving:
Calories 375, Protein 17 g, Carbohydrates 37 g, Fat 19 g, Cholesterol 147 mg, Sodium 288 mg

BROCCOLI AND RED PEPPER TORTELLINI

PENNE PEPPER PASTA

3 cups (720 ml) penne pasta, uncooked
3 peppers, red, yellow and green, cut into strips
2 scallions, trimmed and finely chopped
1 tbs (15 ml) CALIFORNIA CLASSICS Garlic Oil
¼ cup (60 ml) fresh basil, finely chopped
1 tbs (15 ml) paprika
3 tbs (45 ml) CALIFORNIA CLASSICS Balsamic Vinegar
½ cup (120 ml) kalamata olives
1½ tbs (25 ml) MONTEBELLO Extra-Virgin Olive Oil
black pepper, to taste
grated mozzarella

In a large pot of boiling water cook penne until al dente, about 6-8 minutes. Drain in a colander and rinse well with cold water. Transfer to a large bowl and set aside.

Sauté peppers, scallions, garlic oil, chopped basil and paprika in a pan until peppers are soft and glistening. Remove from heat and add balsamic vinegar. Spoon pepper mixture over pasta and toss with olives and extra-virgin olive oil. Season with pepper and grated mozzarella. Serves 6.

Approximate nutritional analysis per serving:
Calories 281, Protein 7 g, Carbohydrates 43 g, Fat 9 g, Cholesterol 0 mg, Sodium 456 mg

SMOKEY CHIPOTLE PASTA

1 tbs (15 ml) olive or vegetable oil
1 cup (240 ml) slivered zucchini or yellow squash
1 cup (240 ml) slivered red or green bell pepper
1½ cups (355 ml) low-sodium chicken or beef broth
⅓ cup (80 ml) chopped onion
1 clove garlic, minced
3-oz pkg (90 g) FRIEDA'S Dried Tomatoes, rehydrated and chopped
¼ cup (60 ml) FRIEDA'S Chipotle Chiles, rehydrated and minced
¼ cup (60 ml) FRIEDA'S Fresh Cilantro, chopped and additional sprigs for garnish
1 tbs (15 ml) FRIEDA'S Fresh Oregano, chopped
   or 1 tsp (5 ml) crushed dried oregano
¼ tsp (1 ml) pepper
½ cup (120 ml) niblet corn, low sodium
1¾ cups (415 ml) cooked or grilled julienne strips of chicken breast
½ lb (230 g) pasta of choice, cooked and drained

In a large skillet, heat oil. Sauté zucchini and bell pepper 3 minutes, turning often. In blender container or food processor bowl, place half of the broth, onion, garlic, half of the tomatoes, minced chipotle chile, cilantro, oregano and pepper. Cover and process until smooth. Add mixture to skillet with remaining broth and tomato pieces, corn and chicken pieces. Simmer over low heat until heated through. Toss with drained cooked pasta; garnish with fresh cilantro sprigs. Serves 4.

Approximate nutritional analysis per serving:
Calories 305, Protein 26 g, Carbohydrates 37 g, Fat 7 g, Cholesterol 52 mg, Sodium 495 mg

PENNE PEPPER PASTA

PASTA DE ARBOL

4 oz (120 g) fusilli or corkscrew pasta
3-oz pkg (120 g) FRIEDA'S Dried Tomatoes, rehydrated and chopped
8-oz can (240 ml) tomato sauce, low sodium
1-2 FRIEDA'S Chile de Arbol, r ehydrated
1½ tbs (25 ml) vegetable oil
1 cup (240 ml) slivered red, yellow or green bell pepper
1 cup (240 ml) slivered zucchini or yellow squash
½ cup (120 ml) thinly sliced red onion
1 clove garlic, minced
1 tbs (15 ml) FRIEDA'S Fresh Cilantro, chopped
¼ tsp (1 ml) pepper

Cook pasta according to package directions.

Meanwhile, in a food processor or blender process half of the chopped dried tomatoes with tomato sauce and chile de arbol until smooth. In a medium skillet, heat oil. Sauté bell pepper, zucchini, onion and garlic for 3 minutes or until vegetables are crisp-tender. Add tomato mixture, remaining chopped tomatoes, cilantro and pepper; heat through. Drain pasta; toss with tomato mixture. Serves 2.

Approximate nutritional analysis per serving:
Calories 479, Protein 16 g, Carbohydrates 82 g, Fat 13 g, Cholesterol 0 mg, Sodium 923 mg

SUNNY TORTELLINI

2 cups (480 ml) nonfat plain yogurt
¼ cup (60 ml) finely chopped sun-dried tomatoes
2 scallions chopped
½ tsp (3 ml) dried thyme
freshly ground black pepper, to taste
dash of tamari or soy sauce
1 lb (455 g) cheese-filled spinach tortellini
1 large onion, chopped
2 shallots, chopped
2 cloves garlic, crushed
3-5 tbs (45-75 ml) vegetable oil
1½ lbs (683 g) mushrooms, sliced

Boil water for the tortellini. Combine the yogurt, tomatoes, scallions, thyme, pepper and tamari. Mix well and set aside. Cook the tortellini according to package directions.

While tortellini are cooking, sauté the onion, shallots and garlic in oil. Add the mushrooms and continue cooking, stirring occasionally, for 15-20 minutes or until wilted.

When the tortellini are done, drain them and return them to a pot. Add the mushroom mixture immediately and toss. Add the yogurt mixture, stirring to coat the pasta and mushrooms. Serve immediately. Serves 4.

Approximate nutritional analysis per serving:
Calories 447, Protein 23 g, Carbohydrates 48g, Fat 20 g, Cholesterol 149 mg, Sodium 413 mg

SUNNY TORTELLINI

VEGETABLE PASTA PRIMAVERA

1 lb (455 g) pasta, uncooked

WHITE SAUCE:
4 cups (960 ml) water
4 vegetable bouillon cubes
1½ cups (355 ml) SOLAIT Instant
    Soy Beverage
4 rounded tbs (60 ml) cornstarch

¼ cup (60 ml) canola oil
1½ cups (355 ml) broccoli flowers
1½ cups (355 ml) sliced carrots
1 cup (240 ml) diced celery
1½ cups (355 ml) onions,
    cut in wedges
1½ cups (355 ml) cauliflower
1 cup (240 ml) peas

Cook pasta according to package directions and drain.

Meanwhile blend White Sauce ingredients and cook in saucepan on medium heat. Stir until thickened.

In large skillet sauté vegetables in canola oil until al dente. Pour White Sauce over vegetable mix. Place pasta on plate, pour vegetables and sauce on top. Serves 8.

Approximate nutritional analysis per serving:
Calories 309, Protein 11 g, Carbohydrates 41 g, Fat 12 g, Cholesterol .1 mg, Sodium 421 mg

MEXICAN MACARONI

1 medium onion, finely chopped
2 cloves garlic, minced
1 green pepper, chopped
2 tbs (30 ml) butter
2 tbs (30 ml) olive oil
15-oz can (450 ml) tomato sauce
15-oz can (450 g) stewed tomatoes,
    slightly cut up
1 tsp (5 ml) Italian seasoning
1 tsp (5 ml) salt
½ tsp (3 ml) garlic powder
½ tsp (3 ml) cumin
1 tsp (5 ml) celery seed
¼ tsp (1 ml) whole chile seeds
1 lb (455 g) ground turkey
8 oz (240 g) VITA-SPELT Macaroni,
    cooked

In a medium saucepan, sauté onion, garlic and pepper in butter and oil until onions are almost clear. Add tomato sauce and stewed tomatoes. Bring mixture to a boil and add Italian seasoning, salt, garlic powder, cumin, celery seed and whole chile seeds. Lower heat and simmer.

In the meantime, brown turkey, drain excess fat before adding to the tomato mixture. Simmer mixture to reach desired consistency, at least 1-2 hours.

When sauce is ready, mix with cooked macaroni. Serve while hot or bake in a 3-quart casserole at 350°F (180°C) for 15 minutes. Serves 6.

Approximate nutritional analysis per serving:
Calories 336, Protein 21 g, Carbohydrates 31 g, Fat 14 g, Cholesterol 66 mg, Sodium 816 mg

VEGETABLE PASTA-YOGURT TOSS

2 tbs (45 ml) olive oil
3 cloves garlic, minced
3-4 carrots, peeled and
   cut diagonally
1 medium onion, sliced
¼ head red cabbage, shredded
1 red bell pepper, cored,
   seeded and chopped
1 tsp (5 ml) caraway seeds
¼ cup (60 ml) water
1 tsp (5 ml) cider vinegar
1 lb spinach pasta, any kind
¾ cup (180 ml) sliced mushrooms
1 tsp (5 ml) dried dill
¼ tsp (1 ml) white pepper

SAUCE:
1 tbs (15 ml) olive oil
1 tbs (15 ml) butter
1 cup (240 ml) STONYFIELD FARM
   Nonfat Plain Yogurt
1 tbs (15 ml) cornstarch
1 cup (240 ml) grated sharp
   cheddar cheese

Heat olive oil over medium-high heat in a large skillet. Add the garlic and cook until softened. Add the carrots and sauté for 2-3 minutes. Add the onion, red cabbage, chopped bell pepper and caraway seeds. Sauté for 1 minute. Add the water and vinegar; stir to combine. Continue cooking; when water boils and begins to steam, cover the pan and reduce the heat to medium-low. Cook for 10 minutes.

Meanwhile, cooking pasta according to package directions.

Add the mushrooms, dill, white pepper to the cabbage mixture. Cover and cook for 5 more minutes.

To make the Sauce, combine the olive oil, butter, yogurt and cornstarch in a small saucepan. Stir constantly over medium-low heat. Add the cheese gradually while continuing to stir. Simmer gently for 1 minute.

When the pasta is done, drain it and return it to the cooking pot. Add the vegetables and toss. Add the yogurt sauce and toss again. Serve immediately. Serves 4.

Approximate nutritional analysis per serving:
Calories 744, Protein 28 g, Carbohydrates 103 g, Fat 25 g,
Cholesterol 39 mg, Sodium 312 mg

VEGETABLE PASTA-YOGURT TOSS

PEANUT BUTTER SPAGHETTI

1 garlic clove, minced
½ cup (120 ml) diced onion
½ cup (120 ml) green pepper, diced
2 tbs (30 ml) vegetable oil
2 tomatoes, diced
1 cup (240 ml) tomato sauce
½ cup (120 ml) EAST WIND
    Peanut Butter
½ tsp (3 ml) oregano
½-1 cup (120-240 ml) water
12 oz (360 g) cooked pasta

Sauté garlic, onions, and green peppers in oil until onion is translucent. Stir in next four ingredients. Bring to slow boil, gradually adding the water to reach a pourable consistency. Serve over hot pasta. Serves 6.

Approximate nutritional analysis per serving:
Calories 280, Protein 7 g, Carbohydrates 28 g, Fat 16 g, Cholesterol 0 mg, Sodium 265 mg

SWEET AND SOUR KAMUT PASTA

8-oz pkg (240 g) EDEN KAMUT
    Spirals
15-oz can (450 g) EDEN Kidney
    Beans, drained
15-oz can (450 g) EDEN Black Beans,
    drained
1 red pepper, diced
2 bunches green onions, diced
3 tbs (45 ml) dried basil

DRESSING:
⅓ cup (80 ml) EDEN Brown Rice or
    Red Wine Vinegar
⅓-½ cup (80-120 ml) EDEN
    Olive Oil
¼ cup (60 ml) EDEN Barley Malt
⅓ cup (80 ml) EDEN Shoyu
    Soy Sauce

Cook spirals as package directs, rinse, drain. Add drained beans, diced red pepper, green onions and basil. Prepare Dressing, mix into pasta and serve. Serves 6.

Approximate nutritional analysis per serving:
Calories 453, Protein 17 g, Carbohydrates 72 g, Fat 13 g, Cholesterol 0 mg, Sodium 1162 mg

PEANUT BUTTER SPAGHETTI

INDIAN ROCK'S PASTA E PISELLI

½ cup (120 ml) chopped onions
4 slices bacon
2 tbs (30 ml) butter
1 cup (240 ml) low-sodium
  chicken broth
1 lb (455 g) shelled peas
1 lb (455 g) fettucini
1 cup (240 ml) grated Parmesan
  cheese

Sauté onions and bacon in butter. Remove bacon and place on paper towel to drain. Add chicken broth to pan along with peas and cover. Cook over a very low flame with the lid on the pan until the onions are limp and the liquid almost gone.

Cook fettucini and drain while the onions are cooking. Both should be finished at the same time, about 20 minutes. Crumble bacon and combine onions and peas with the fettucini. Sprinkle in Parmesan cheese and toss. Serves 8.

Approximate nutritional analysis per serving:
Calories 235, Protein 13 g, Carbohydrates 26 g, Fat 9 g, Cholesterol 20 mg, Sodium 390 mg

INDIAN ROCK'S PASTA E PISELLI

PASTA E FAGIOLI WITH BASIL

olive oil spray
1 medium onion, chopped
4 cloves garlic, chopped
½ lb (230 g) mushrooms, sliced
1 red bell pepper, chopped
2 stalks celery, sliced
2 14½-oz cans (870 g) low-sodium
    ready-cut tomatoes with juice
2 15-oz cans (900 g) cannellini,
    red kidney or great northern
    beans, rinsed and drained
½ lb (230 g) spinach leaves,
    coarsely chopped
1 pkg GREEN HOUSE Fresh Basil,
    chopped, some for garnish
salt, to taste
pepper, to taste
1 lb (455 g) ziti, cooked al dente
grated Parmesan cheese, optional

Coat a nonstick skillet with olive oil cooking spray. Sauté onion, garlic, mushrooms, bell pepper and celery for 5 minutes, or until soft. Reduce heat and add tomatoes with juice, and beans. Add water (optional) to reach desired consistency. Cover and simmer for 15 minutes. Add spinach, basil, salt and pepper. Simmer 15 more minutes. Toss with additional chopped basil to taste and serve over hot pasta with Parmesan cheese, if desired. Serves 8.

Approximate nutritional analysis per serving:
Calories 384, Protein 19 g, Carbohydrates 75 g, Fat 2 g, Cholesterol .5 mg, Sodium 199 mg

HOT & SWEET CHINESE NOODLES

2 tbs (30 ml) SPECTRUM WORLD
    EATS Asian Oil
3 tbs (45 ml) SPECTRUM
    NATURALS Toasted Sesame Oil
3 tbs (45 ml) tamari soy sauce
1 tbs (15 ml) balsamic vinegar
1 tbs (15 ml) SPECTRUM
    NATURALS Organic Brown
    Rice Vinegar
2 tbs (30 ml) dark molasses
pinch of salt
1 lb (455) long Chinese egg noodles
4 tbs (60 ml) cilantro, chopped
2 green onions, chopped

Bring 4 quarts of salted water to a boil. Meanwhile, combine the oils, tamari, vinegars, molasses and salt in a bowl. Stir well. Cook the noodles for 2 minutes until they rise to the top of the water. Drain the noodles well and toss them in seasoned oils. Add the cilantro and green onions. Correct the seasoning and serve hot or cold. Serves 8.

Approximate nutritional analysis per serving:
Calories 167, Protein 3 g, Carbohydrates 18 g, Fat 10 g, Cholesterol 19 mg, Sodium 393 mg

PASTA E FAGIOLI WITH BASIL

CHINESE-STYLE NOODLES WITH TOFU & VEGETABLES

12-oz pkg (360 g) **NASOYA Chinese Style Noodles**
1½ cups (355 ml) **vegetable or chicken stock**
¼ tsp (1 ml) **salt**
3 tbs (45 ml) **soy sauce or oyster sauce**
1 tbs (15 ml) **arrowroot or cornstarch**
½ tbs (8 ml) **vegetable oil**
1 lb (455 g) **NASOYA Tofu, cut into ½-inch cubes**
2 medium **tomatoes, cut into ¼-inch cubes**
1 cup (240 ml) **celery, sliced thin**
3 **scallions, 2-inch lengths, julienned**
parsley or scallions for garnish

Cook noodles as package directs.

Place broth and salt in a saucepan and bring to a boil. Add precooked noodles, heat 2-3 minutes, then drain, reserving broth. Keep noodles warm. Combine broth, soy sauce and arrowroot and put aside.

Add oil to hot wok or frying pan. Add tofu and stir-fry 2 minutes. Add vegetables and fry 2 minutes. Cover and cook 2 minutes more. Add broth mixture and stir until thickened. Turn off heat. Place noodles in serving dish. Pour vegetables, tofu and broth over noodles. Top with parsley or scallions and serve. Serves 5.

Approximate nutritional analysis per serving:
Calories 315, Protein 15 g, Carbohydrates 51 g, Fat 5 g, Cholesterol 0 mg, Sodium 862 mg

PIQUANT PRAWNS WITH TOMATO & LINGUINE

6 qts (3.8 l) **water**
1 tbs (15 ml) **salt**
½ cup (120 ml) **SPECTRUM NATURALS Cold Pressed Extra Virgin Olive Oil**
6 cloves **garlic, peeled and minced**
3 tbs (45 ml) **SPECTRUM NATURALS Organic Red Wine Vinegar**
14½-oz can (435 g) **MUIR GLEN Organic Diced Tomatoes**
1 tsp (5 ml) **red chile flakes**
1 lb (455 g) **large prawns, shelled and deveined**
8 oz (240 g) **linguine**
5 tbs (75 ml) **fresh basil, chopped**
5 tbs (75 ml) **fresh parsley, chopped**
salt, to taste
fresh ground pepper, to taste

Bring water to the boil with the salt. Meanwhile warm the olive oil in a large sauté pan. Add the garlic and gently begin to cook. Add the vinegar and tomatoes and continue to cook over low heat. Stir in the chile flakes. Add the prawns and simmer until just cooked through, turning often, about 5 minutes. Remove from the heat and set aside. Cook the pasta, drain and toss together with tomato sauce and cooked prawns. Add the basil and parsley. Season to taste and serve immediately. Serves 4.

Approximate nutritional analysis per serving:
Calories 460, Protein 28 g, Carbohydrates 21 g, Fat 29 g, Cholesterol 221 mg, Sodium 411 mg

PIQUANT PRAWNS WITH TOMATO & LINGUINE

FRIED UDON & VEGETABLES

14-oz pkg (420 g) NASOYA
   Japanese Noodles
1 tsp vegetable oil
1 medium onion, cut into slices
1 celery stalk, cut into slices
1 carrot, cut into matchsticks
tamari, to taste
sesame oil, to taste

Cook noodles as package directs. Heat a small amount of oil in skillet. Add onion and sauté for 2-3 minutes. Add celery and carrot and sauté for 3-4 minutes. Place noodles on top of vegetables and cover skillet. Reduce heat and cook until vegetables are tender. Remove cover and season with tamari and sesame oil. Mix and sauté for 3-4 minutes longer. Serves 5.

Approximate nutritional analysis per serving:
Calories 226, Protein 9 g, Carbohydrates 47 g, Fat 2 g, Cholesterol 0 mg, Sodium 456 mg

NORTH COAST-STYLE RAVIOLI WITH MUSSELS

1 pkg PUTNEY PASTA Garlic and
   Herb Ravioli
1⅓ tbs (20 ml) olive oil
1 tsp (5 ml) garlic, minced
½ Bermuda onion, julienned
1 tsp (5 ml) curry powder
16 fresh mussels, cleaned
12 oz (360 ml) fresh clam broth
½ red bell pepper, julienned
½ yellow bell pepper, julienned
1 fresh jalapeño pepper,
   cut into rings
1 tomato, peeled, seeded and diced
2 tbs (30 ml) parsley, chopped
dash salt

Cook ravioli according to package directions. In olive oil sauté garlic and onions lightly; add curry powder. Add mussels and clam broth; steam mussels until barely open. Add peppers, tomato, parsley and salt. Cook until mussels are fully opened. Serve atop cooked ravioli. Serves 2.

Approximate nutritional analysis per serving:
Calories 694, Protein 46 g, Carbohydrates 76 g, Fat 22 g, Cholesterol 122 mg, Sodium 1037 mg

NORTH COAST-STYLE RAVIOLI WITH MUSSELS

LINGUINE WITH HONEY-SAUCED PRAWNS

8 oz (240 g) prawns, peeled and
   deveined
¼ cup (60 ml) julienned carrots
¼ cup (60 ml) julienned celery
¼ cup (60 ml) green onions,
   diagonally sliced
3 cloves garlic, minced
1 tbs (15 ml) olive oil
¼ cup (60 ml) water
2 tbs (15 ml) honey
2 tsp (10 ml) cornstarch
½ tsp (3 ml) salt
pinch crushed dried red chiles
pinch rosemary
2½ cups (590 ml) warm, cooked
   linguine

In medium skillet, stir-fry prawns, carrot, celery, green onion and garlic in oil about 3 minutes or until shrimp start to turn pink. Combine remaining ingredients, except linguine, in a small bowl and mix well. Add to vegetable mixture; stir-fry about 1 minutes or until sauce thickens. Serve over linguine. Serves 2.

Approximate nutritional analysis per serving:
Calories 512, Protein 33 g, Carbohydrates 74 g, Fat 9 g, Cholesterol 221 mg, Sodium 810 mg

Courtesy of The National Honey Board.

SHRIMP WITH HONEY CREAM SAUCE & SPINACH PASTA

2 tbs (30 ml) olive oil
1 lb (455 g) medium shrimp, peeled
   and deveined
2 tbs (30 ml) chopped shallots
½ cup (120 ml) dry white wine
½ cup (120 ml) heavy cream
2 tbs (30 ml) honey
½ cup (120 ml) fresh plum t
   omatoes, diced, seeded and
   peeled or canned plum tomatoes,
   diced and drained
2 tbs (30 ml) fresh chopped basil
salt, to taste
pepper, to taste
½ lb (230 g) spinach fettucini,
   cooked and drained
basil sprigs, for garnish, optional

Heat olive oil in large skillet over medium-high heat. Add shrimp and shallots, tossing lightly, until shrimp are just opaque. Remove shrimp and keep warm. Add wine to pan; boil until liquid is reduced by half, stirring and scraping sides of pan. Add cream and reduce heat to medium; cook until slightly thickened. Add honey, tomatoes and chopped basil; stir to blend. Return shrimp to sauce and season with salt and pepper to taste. Arrange equal portions of fettucini and shrimp mixture on warm serving plates. Garnish with basil sprigs, if desired. Serves 4.

Approximate nutritional analysis per serving:
Calories 547, Protein 32 g, Carbohydrates 54 g, Fat 20 g, Cholesterol 262 mg, Sodium 290 mg

Courtesy of The National Honey Board.

LINGUINE WITH HONEY-SAUCED PRAWNS

STIR-FRIED NOODLES WITH SHRIMP

12-oz pkg (360 g) NASOYA Chinese
    Style Noodles
½ lb (230 g) Chinese cabbage
4 tbs (60 ml) vegetable oil
1 lb (455 g) uncooked shrimp,
    shelled, deveined and sliced in
    half lengthwise
1 tsp salt, total
1 tbs (15 ml) Chinese rice wine
    or sherry
1 tsp (5 ml) honey or
    other sweetener
1 tbs (15 ml) low-sodium soy sauce
½ cup (120 ml) low-sodium
    vegetable or chicken stock

Cook noodles as package directs. Wash cabbage and slice each stalk lengthwise into ⅛-inch wide strips. Heat a wok or skillet. Pour in half the oil. On medium heat, add shrimp and stir-fry 1 minute or until they turn pink. Add ½ tsp salt and rice wine, stir, then transfer to a plate and set aside. Pour the rest of the oil into the hot pan and stir-fry cabbage for 2 minutes. Add ½ tsp salt, honey, noodles, soy sauce and stock and boil briskly for 3 minutes or until liquid has evaporated. Add shrimp and cook, stirring for 30 seconds. Serve at once. Serves 5.

Approximate nutritional analysis per serving:
Calories 408, Protein 27 g, Carbohydrates 45 g, Fat 12 g,
Cholesterol 177 mg, Sodium 639 mg

EGG FOO YUNG

1 pkg WESTBRAE Brown Rice
    Ramen
4 eggs, well beaten
1 carrot, shredded
½ cup (120 ml) thinly sliced
    green onions
pinch garlic powder
2 tbs (30 ml) oil
1 cup (240 ml) water
1 tbs (15 ml) cornstarch or
    arrowroot

Break the ramen into pieces and cook as directed on package; set aside broth packet for later use. Drain, rinse and drain again.
    Combine ramen, eggs, carrot, green onions and garlic powder. Heat the oil in large nonstick frying pan, using just enough to coat the pan; add remaining oil as needed. Using ¼-½ cup of the mixture for each portion, form patties and fry until set and lightly browned, turning once. Remove to a heated platter and keep warm. In a small pan combine contents of broth packet with water and cornstarch. Cook, stirring constantly, over medium heat until sauce boils and thickens. Spoon over patties and serve. Serves 6.

Approximate nutritional analysis per serving:
Calories 143, Protein 6 g, Carbohydrates 13 g, Fat 8 g, Cholesterol 125 mg,
Sodium 293 mg

STIR-FRIED NOODLES WITH SHRIMP

SHRIMP & SHELLS

1¼ cups (295 ml) small shell pasta,
 uncooked
¼ lb (115 g) fresh snow peas
½ lb (230 g) cooked medium shrimp
2-3 tbs (30-45 ml) olive oil
1 clove garlic, minced
1-2 tbs (15-30 ml) GREEN HOUSE
 Fresh Dill, minced
⅓ cup (80 ml) Parmesan cheese,
 freshly grated

Cook pasta shells, rinse with cool water and drain. Steam peas, until crisp-tender. Combine shrimp, olive oil, garlic and dill in small skillet and cook until hot. Add pasta, peas and Parmesan cheese and toss to coat. Serves 2.

Approximate nutritional analysis per serving:
Calories 423, Protein 35 g, Carbohydrates 24 g, Fat 20 g,
Cholesterol 234 mg, Sodium 568 mg

FETTUCINI PRIMAVERA WITH BÉCHAMEL SAUCE

1 head broccoli, thinly cut
2 cloves garlic, minced
1 small red onion, sliced
3 tbs (45 ml) extra-virgin olive oil
1 large red pepper, thinly sliced
10 large mushrooms, thinly sliced
1 cup (240 ml) frozen baby peas,
 thawed
½ cup (120 ml) black olives, sliced
½ cup (120 ml) fresh basil,
 cut into strips
3 cups (720 ml) Béchamel Sauce,
 recipe below
12 oz (360 g) fettucini pasta
basil flowers, for garnish

RICE DREAM BÉCHAMEL
(CREAM) SAUCE:
1 large yellow onion, finely chopped
1-2 cloves garlic, minced
6 tbs (90 ml) butter, ghee or olive oil
9 tbs (135 ml) whole wheat or
 brown rice flour
splash of white wine or lemon juice,
 optional
1½ cups (355 ml) Original
 RICE DREAM
¾ cup (180 ml) water or
 vegetable stock
pinch dried dill
½-¾ tsp (3-4 ml) sea salt
pinch white pepper

In a medium pan, sauté broccoli, garlic and red onion in olive oil for 5 minutes. Add red pepper and mushrooms; sauté over medium heat for 5-10 minutes more, depending upon how well cooked you like your vegetables. Stir in peas; cook a few more minutes until mixture is hot. Add olives and basil; cover and set aside.

Béchamel Sauce: In a heavy saucepan, over a low flame, sauté onions and garlic in butter until soft and translucent. Sprinkle in flour and stir frequently for 5 minutes. Slowly add wine, Rice Dream, water and seasonings. Whisk until well blended. Increase heat and allow mixture to come briefly to a boil. Reduce heat to low and simmer for 5 minutes, stirring often. Taste, adjust seasoning and/or sauce thickness by adding more water or flour in small increments. Serve immediately or allow to cool and refrigerate for later use. Yields 3 cups

Cook pasta following package directions. Serve immediately topped with sautéed vegetables and Béchamel Sauce. Garnish with basil flowers. Serves 6.

Approximate nutritional analysis per serving:
Calories 554, Protein 15 g, Carbohydrates 88 g, Fat 16 g, Cholesterol 31 mg,
Sodium 504 mg

KAMUT PASTA & SALMON HOT DISH

8-oz pkg (240 g) KAMUT Fettuccine
    Noodles cooked al dente, drained
1 tbs (15 ml) olive or canola oil
½ cup (120 ml) asparagus tips and
    pieces, cut diagonally in ½-inch
    lengths, or zucchini, thinly sliced
½ cup (120 ml) green or red pepper,
    cut into ½-inch chunks
¼ cup (60 ml) green onion, sliced
1 garlic clove, minced
6-oz can (180 g) salmon, drained
1 cup (240 ml) frozen peas, thawed
2 tbs (30 ml) fresh parsley
    or 2 tsp (10 ml) dried parsley
½ tsp (3 ml) dried basil
½ cup (120 ml) plain low-fat
    yogurt
2-3 tbs (30-45 ml) Parmesan cheese,
    grated

Cook fettucini noodles. Meanwhile, heat oil in a large skillet. Add asparagus or zucchini, pepper, onion and garlic and sauté until crisp-tender. Add salmon in chunks, peas, parsley, and basil. Sauté until mixture is heated through and peas are soft. Drain pasta and add yogurt. Toss salmon mixture with pasta. Top with Parmesan cheese. Serves 4.

Approximate nutritional analysis per serving:
Calories 452, Protein 32 g, Carbohydrates 58 g, Fat 12 g, Cholesterol 44 mg, Sodium 582 mg

PASTA WITH SEAFOOD & SHALLOTS

¼ cup (60 ml) olive or cooking oil
½ lb (230 g) scallops or fish fillets,
    cut into ½-inch chunks, fresh or
    frozen and thawed
½ lb (230 g) shelled shrimp, fresh
    or frozen and thawed
4 FRIEDA'S Shallots, peeled and
    sliced
1 clove garlic, minced
⅓ cup (80 ml) dry white wine
¼ cup (60 ml) butter or margarine
1 tbs (15 ml) lemon juice
salt, to taste
pepper, to taste
7-oz can (210 g) minced clams,
    drained
½ lb (230 g) hot cooked linguine or
    fettucini, drained
2 tbs (30 ml) chopped parsley

In a large skillet, heat oil; sauté scallops or fish chunks, shrimp, shallots and garlic in oil about 3 minutes or until shrimp turn pink. Add wine all at once; bring to a boil. Reduce heat and simmer 2 minutes more. Add butter, lemon juice, salt and pepper to taste, and clams, stirring until butter melts. Add pasta and parsley and toss well to combine. Serve at once. Serves 4.

Approximate nutritional analysis per serving:
Calories 468, Protein 31 g, Carbohydrates 21 g, Fat 27 g, Cholesterol 178 mg, Sodium 417 mg

KAMUT PASTA & SALMON HOT DISH

COUSIN VERA'S PASTA WITH CHICKEN CATCH

1 green bell pepper
1 red bell pepper
1 cup (240 ml) chopped broccoli
1 carrot
3 lbs (1.4 g) chicken breast
2 tbs (30 ml) olive oil
1 medium onion
2 cloves garlic, minced
25-oz jar (750 ml) UNCLE DAVE'S Marinara with Mushrooms
1 lb (455 g) linguine, cooked and drained
2 tbs (30 ml) chopped parsley

Cut vegetables and chicken in bite-size pieces. Heat oil over medium-high heat. Add chicken and brown all over. Remove from pan. Sauté onion and garlic until onion is limp. Add chopped vegetables and cook 2 minutes, or steam vegetables separately, add marinara and cook for another 2 minutes. Serve warm over linguine. Garnish with chopped parsley. Serves 6.

Approximate nutritional analysis per serving:
Calories 498, Protein 60 g, Carbohydrates 38 g, Fat 10 g, Cholesterol 131 mg, Sodium 158 mg

CHINESE CHICKEN NOODLES WITH SESAME SAUCE

8 oz (240 g) FRIEDA'S Fresh Chinese Noodles
2 tbs (30 ml) soy sauce
2 tbs (30 ml) dry sherry
1½ tbs (25 ml) sesame paste or tahini
1 tbs (15 ml) sesame oil or salad oil
2 tbs (30 ml) sesame seeds
1 tbs (15 ml) peanut oil or salad oil for frying
1 cup (240 ml) FRIEDA'S Leeks, sliced or onions
½ cup (120 ml) FRIEDA'S Bamboo Shoots, sliced
4 chicken breasts, boneless and skinless, cut into bite-size strips
1 cup (240 ml) zucchini squash, bias-sliced

Cook noodles according to package directions; drain.

Combine sauce ingredients: stir together the soy sauce, sherry, sesame paste, sesame oil and sesame seeds; set aside.

In wok, heat oil; add leeks, bamboo shoots and chicken pieces. Stir-fry 3 minutes. Remove from wok; add more oil if necessary. Stir-fry zucchini for 2 minutes. Add chicken mixture and cooked, drained noodles back to wok; pour sauce over all. Toss mixture to coat with sauce; cover. Cook 3 minutes or until heated through. Serves 4.

Approximate nutritional analysis per serving:
Calories 539, Protein 39 g, Carbohydrates 44 g, Fat 23 g, Cholesterol 68 mg, Sodium 965 mg

COUSIN VERA'S PASTA WITH CHICKEN CATCH

PASTA ALLA BOLOGNESE

1 lb (455 g) lean ground beef
1 lb (455 g) mild Italian sausage
1 cup (240 ml) chopped onion
½ cup (120 ml) finely shredded carrot
½ cup (120 ml) chopped celery
3 cloves garlic, minced
28-oz can (840 g) MUIR GLEN Organic Whole Peeled Tomatoes, undrained
15-oz can (450 g) MUIR GLEN Organic Tomato Sauce
½ cup (120 ml) dry red wine
¼ cup (60 ml) chopped fresh parsley
1 ½ tsp (8 ml) basil leaves, crushed
½ tsp oregano
½ tsp (3 ml) salt
¼ tsp (1 ml) pepper
2 lb (910 g) cooked shells, penne or rigatoni, hot

In large saucepan over medium heat, cook ground beef, sausage, onion, carrot, celery and garlic until meat is browned. Drain. Stir in whole peeled tomatoes, tomato sauce, wine, parsley, basil, oregano, salt and pepper. Reduce heat to low and simmer, uncovered, 40-45 minutes, or until thickened. Serve over hot cooked pasta. Serves 12.

Approximate nutritional analysis per serving:
Calories 387, Protein 22 g, Carbohydrates 29 g, Fat 19 g, Cholesterol 66 mg, Sodium 713 mg

TUSCAN-STYLE TORTELLINI WITH ASPARAGUS

1 ½ lbs (683 g) asparagus, fresh trimmed, ½-inch sliced
6 oz (180 ml) heavy cream
3 tbs (45 ml) butter, unsalted
2 tbs (30 ml) lemon zest, from 3 lemons
¼ cup (60 ml) lemon juice, fresh
¾ tsp (4 ml) salt
½ tsp (3 ml) red pepper flakes
2 pkgs PUTNEY PASTA Tri-Color Tortellini
2 tbs (30 ml) Pecorino Romano cheese, grated
⅓ cup (80 ml) parsley, rough chopped

Blanch asparagus in boiling salted water for 2 minutes. Remove asparagus from water and quickly cool in cold water. In a large skillet, scald cream and butter over medium heat. Stir in lemon zest, lemon juice, salt and red pepper flakes. Remove from heat and set aside.

Cook tortellini according to package directions.

Return skillet to heat, toss sauce with asparagus, pasta, Romano cheese and parsley. Serve immediately. Serves 4.

Approximate nutritional analysis per serving:
Calories 457, Protein 17 g, Carbohydrates 40 g, Fat 28 g, Cholesterol 119 mg, Sodium 835 mg

TUSCAN-STYLE TORTELLINI WITH ASPARAGUS

COLEMAN MEDITERRANEAN STEAK & PASTA SUPPER

4 tsp (20 ml) olive oil, divided
1 lb (455 g) COLEMAN NATURAL
   Beef Top Sirloin Steak, cut into
   bite-size cubes
½ cup (120 ml) chopped onion
1 medium green bell pepper, seeded
   and cut into 1½-inch long thin
   strips
2 cloves garlic, minced
¼ cup (60 ml) lightly packed fresh
   basil leaves, chopped
15-oz can (450 g) ready-cut tomatoes
   and juice
2 tsp (10 ml) granulated sugar
4 oz (120 g) rotini pasta,
   cooked and drained
3 tbs (45 ml) Parmesan cheese

In large skillet with cover, heat 2 tsp oil over medium heat. Add meat and brown, stirring to cook quickly; about 3 minutes. Remove meat from pan, drain and set aside. Using same skillet, add remaining 2 tsp oil and sauté onion and bell pepper for about 3 minutes. Stir in garlic and basil, cook 1 minute. Add tomatoes with their juice and the sugar, bring to a boil. Cover, reduce heat and simmer for 5 minutes. Stir in rotini and meat, heat through. Sprinkle with cheese and serve. Serves 4.

Approximate nutritional analysis per serving:
Calories 372, Protein 30 g, Carbohydrates 34 g, Fat 13 g, Cholesterol 59 mg, Sodium 855 mg

EGG NOODLES WITH YOGURT-VEGETABLE SAUCE

1 tbs (15 ml) butter or oil for frying
1 small onion, chopped
1 clove garlic, finely chopped
½ cup (120 ml) sliced mushrooms
½ cup (120 ml) peeled and
   diced carrots
1 ear of corn, sliced off the cob
   or ¾ cup (180 ml) frozen corn
1 cup (240 ml) diced cooked turkey
   and/or ham, optional
tamari or soy sauce, to taste
2 cups (480 ml) STONYFIELD FARM
   Nonfat Plain Yogurt, at room
   temperature
12-oz pkg (360 g) egg noodles
butter, optional
paprika
thinly sliced zucchini, for garnish,
   optional

Heat the butter in an ovenproof skillet. Working with one ingredient at a time, and stirring after each addition, add the onion, garlic, mushrooms, carrots and corn. Sprinkle in a small amount of water as vegetables cook so they don't become too dry. Add the meat, if desired, and stir in. Add the tamari and stir again. When the vegetables are tender, remove from heat, add the yogurt and stir to blend. Then place the pan of vegetables in a warm oven to blend the flavors while you cook the noodles.

Cook the egg noodles according to package directions. Drain, place in a serving dish and dot with butter. Cover with the yogurt-vegetable sauce and sprinkle with paprika. Garnish with zucchini, if desired. Serves 3.

Approximate nutritional analysis per serving:
Calories 607, Protein 27 g, Carbohydrates 105 g, Fat 7 g, Cholesterol 109 mg, Sodium 157 mg

EGG NOODLES WITH YOGURT-VEGETABLE SAUCE

BURGUNDY "SPAGHETTI"

1 lb (455 g) ground beef or turkey
1 medium onion, chopped
3 tbs (45 ml) safflower oil
3 cups (720 ml) tomato sauce
½ cup (120 ml) mushrooms, sliced
1 cup (240 ml) burgundy wine
2 cloves garlic, minced
½ tsp (3 ml) oregano
½ tsp (3 ml) basil
½ tsp (3 ml) rosemary
½ tsp (3 ml) marjoram
1 bay leaf, optional
½ tsp (3 ml) salt
¼ tsp (1 ml) black pepper
12 oz (240 g) dry VITA-SPELT
     Angel Hair Pasta
2 cups (480 ml) low-fat cheese,
     shredded

Sauté the ground meat and onion in oil until meat is browned. Drain excess fat. Add all ingredients except pasta and cheese. Simmer on low at least 1 hour, stirring occasionally, until desired thickness is reached.

In the meantime, add pasta to boiling water. Watch pasta carefully. Cook just until pasta separates, approximately 2-3 minutes. You may separate pasta carefully with a fork as it cooks. Drain pasta well. Turn into sauce with approximately 1½ cups of the cheese. Transfer to a covered casserole dish. If you wish, you may cover and refrigerate at this point. Before serving, heat oven to 325°F (165°C). Sprinkle remaining cheese, cover and bake for approximately 45 minutes. Uncover and continue baking for 30 minutes. Garlic bead and red wine go well with this meal. Serves 6.

Approximate nutritional analysis per serving:
Calories 410, Protein 29 g, Carbohydrates 29 g, Fat 19 g, Cholesterol 62 mg, Sodium 696 mg

SPANISH PASTA ROLL

PASTA:
1¼ cups (295 ml) VITA-SPELT
     Whole Grain Flour
2 tbs (30 ml) butter, melted
2 eggs, beaten
dash of salt

FILLING:
2 cups (480 ml) ricotta cheese
4 oz (120 g) canned green chiles,
     chopped
¼ cup (60 ml) fresh cilantro,
     chopped
¼ tsp (1 ml) oregano
¼ tsp (1 ml) salt
⅛-¼ tsp (.5-1 ml) red pepper,
     to taste
¾ cup (180 ml) corn kernels
¾ cup (180 ml) tomato, chopped
¼ cup (60 ml) green onion, chopped
¼ tsp (1 ml) garlic powder

Preheat oven to 375°F (190°C). Prepare pasta by making a well in the flour and pouring in butter, eggs and salt. Mix thoroughly and roll into ball. Keep dough covered while preparing the filling.

Add all the filling ingredients together. Stir just until everything is coated and mixed. Roll out dough on a floured surface to a 12x16-inch baking dish. Spread evenly with filling and roll like a jelly roll. Seal edges with water. Bake for approximately 25 minutes. Serves 4.

Approximate nutritional analysis per serving:
Calories 436, Protein 25 g, Carbohydrates 46 g, Fat 19 g, Cholesterol 147 mg, Sodium 479 mg

SPANISH PASTA ROLL

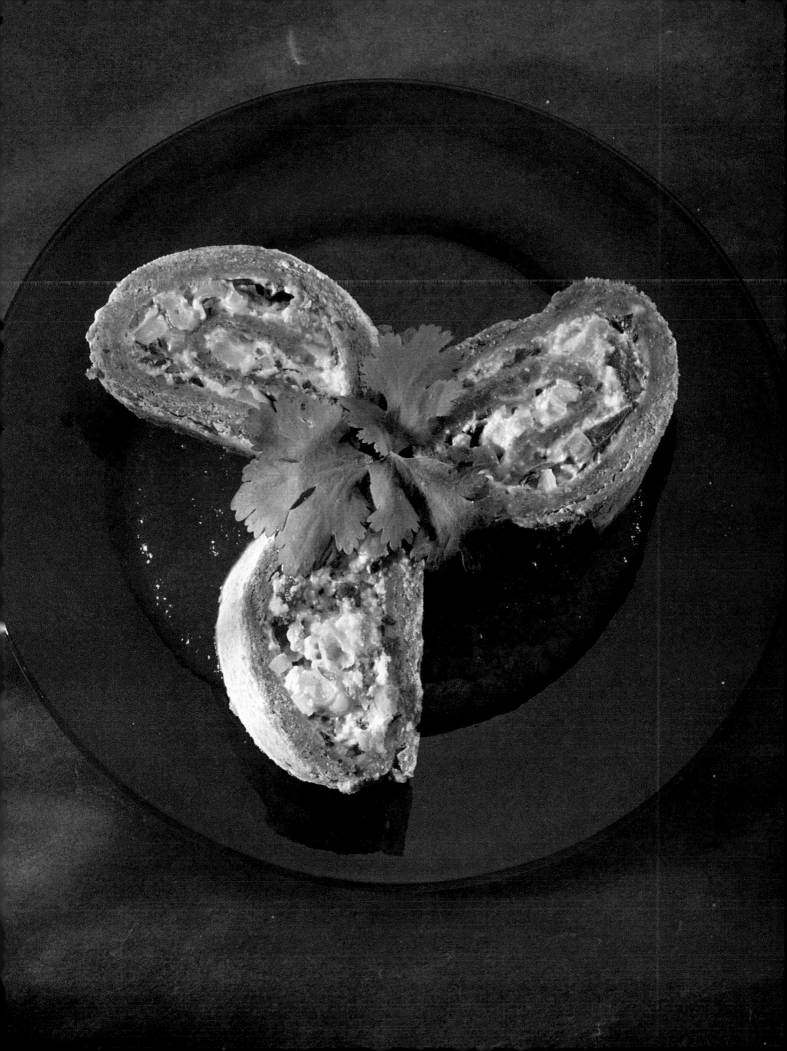

CANNELLONI

8 shells, cannelloni or manicotti
15-oz carton (450 g) part-skim
   ricotta cheese
1½ cups (355 ml) grated low-fat
   mozzarella cheese
¼ cup (60 ml) freshly grated
   Parmesan cheese
1 egg, slightly beaten
2 tbs (30 ml) fresh parsley, chopped
dash nutmeg
26-oz jar (780 ml) MUIR GLEN
   Organic Pasta Sauce
   or 3 cups (720 ml) homemade
   pasta sauce

Cook cannelloni shells according to package directions; rinse with cool water and drain well. Combine ricotta cheese, ½ cup mozzarella cheese, Parmesan cheese, egg, parsley and nutmeg. Spoon ricotta filling into shells. Preparation may be covered and refrigerated several hours at this point. Pour 1½ cups pasta sauce in bottom of 12x18-inch glass baking dish. Lay filled shells over sauce; cover with remaining sauce. Cover with aluminum foil; bake at 375°F (190°C) for 30 minutes, or until sauce is bubbling. Sprinkle with remaining 1 cup grated mozzarella cheese. Bake, uncovered, another 5-10 minutes, or until cheese has melted. Serves 4.

Approximate nutritional analysis per serving:
Calories 465, Protein 33 g, Carbohydrates 10 g, Fat 19 g, Cholesterol 107 mg, Sodium 938 mg

SEAFOOD D'ITALIA

2 tbs (30 ml) butter
1 medium onion, finely chopped
4 large mushrooms, sliced thin
6 cloves garlic, crushed
2 tbs (30 ml) olive oil
1 tbs (15 ml) capers
½ tsp (3 ml) oregano
2 tbs (30 ml) chopped chives
8½-oz can (255 g) artichoke hearts,
   drained
8 oz (240 g) scallops
8 oz (230 g) whole raw shrimp,
   peeled and deveined
2 tbs (30 ml) CHESHIRE GARDEN
   Blenda d'Italia Vinegar or
   Lemon Italia Vinegar
1 lb (455 g) fettucini

Sauté onions, mushrooms and garlic in olive oil and butter until soft. Add capers, herbs, pepper, artichokes, scallops and shrimp and continue to simmer until seafood is cooked, 5-7 minutes at medium heat. Stir in vinegar and cook 1 minute more. Serve over fettucini, cooked al dente. Serves 8.

Approximate nutritional analysis per serving:
Calories 340, Protein 19 g, Carbohydrates 48 g, Fat 8 g, Cholesterol 72 mg, Sodium 160 mg

SEAFOOD D'ITALIA

SPAGHETTI-SAUSAGE CASSEROLE

1 large onion
1 lb (455 g) chopped KNOX
  MOUNTAIN FARM
  Not-So-Sausage, prepared
  according to package directions
1 tbs (15 ml) olive oil
28-oz (840 ml) can tomato sauce
1 cup (240 ml) grated cheddar
  cheese, dairy or soy
1 lb (455 g) spaghetti, cooked

Sauté chopped Not-So-Sausage and onion in oil. Place spaghetti on bottom of casserole dish. Add sautéed mix on top of spaghetti. Pour sauce over everything. Top with cheese and bake for 20 minutes at 350°F (180°C). Serves 8.

Approximate nutritional analysis per serving:
Calories 532, Protein 39 g, Carbohydrates 64 g, Fat 8 g, Cholesterol 15 mg, Sodium 333 mg

MACARONI AND CHEESE

8 oz (240 g) macaroni
4 tbs (60 ml) margarine
4 tbs (60 ml) flour
2 cups (480 ml) Unsweetened
  WESTSOY
8 oz (240 g) shredded cheddar
  cheese alternative
2 oz (60 g) sliced pimentos
1 tsp (5 ml) prepared mustard
salt, to taste
pepper, to taste
paprika, optional

Preheat oven to 350°F (180°C). Cook macaroni in boiling water until tender and drain well.

Meanwhile, melt margarine in a medium-size saucepan, add flour, stirring to combine. Slowly add soy milk and cook, stirring until mixture thickens and begins to boil. Remove from heat and stir in shredded cheese alternative, pimentos, mustard, salt and pepper to taste. Add drained macaroni, mixing well.

Turn into a lightly greased 2-quart baking dish. Sprinkle with paprika, if desired, and bake 30-40 minutes until bubbly around edges and golden brown on top. Serves 6.

Approximate nutritional analysis per serving:
Calories 230, Protein 10 g, Carbohydrates 25 g, Fat 10 g, Cholesterol 0 mg, Sodium 380 mg

TEMPEH LASAGNA

12-oz pkg (360 g) SURATA
    SOYFOODS CO-OP
    Italiano Tempeh
4 cups (960 ml) Italian-style
    tomato sauce
1½ lbs (683 g) SURATA SOYFOODS
    CO-OP Soft Tofu
¼ cup (60 ml) olive oil
¼ cup (60 ml) fresh lemon juice
1 tsp (5 ml) salt
1 tsp (5 ml) oregano
2 tbs (30 ml) fresh basil
9 large lasagne noodles, cooked
1 cup (240 ml) low-fat mozzarella,
    grated

Grate tempeh, combine with tomato sauce and set aside.

Combine and blend soft tofu, olive oil, lemon juice, salt, oregano and basil. Place a layer of cooked noodles into a lightly oiled 9x13-inch pan. Cover bottom with ⅓ of the tempeh sauce. Place another layer of noodles, spread with ½ of the tofu mixture and ½ of the remaining tempeh mixture. Add another layer of noodles, the remaining tofu and the rest of the tempeh sauce. Top with mozzarella. Bake in preheated 350°F (180°C) oven for 20 minutes covered, uncover pan and bake another 20 minutes. Serves 6.

Approximate nutritional analysis per serving:
Calories 353, Protein 23 g, Carbohydrates 34 g, Fat 15 g, Cholesterol 8 mg, Sodium 1037 mg

TOFU LASAGNA

10 oz (300 g) spinach, optional
1 medium onion, chopped
½ lb (230 g) mushrooms, sliced
1 clove garlic
2 tbs (30 ml) vegetable oil
1½ lbs (683 g) NASOYA Firm or
    Soft Tofu, mashed
½ cup (120 ml) grated Parmesan or
    Romano cheese
2 beaten eggs, optional
2 tbs (30 ml) parsley, chopped
½ tsp (3 ml) salt
    or 1 tbs (15 ml) soy sauce
¼ tsp (1 ml) pepper
16-oz pkg (480 g) NASOYA Egg Roll
    Wrappers
3 cups (720 ml) low-fat spaghetti
    sauce
¼ cup (60 ml) grated low-fat
    mozzarella, Swiss or Monterey
    Jack cheese

If you are using spinach, wash, chop and steam lightly. Set aside. Sauté onion, mushrooms and garlic in oil. Set aside. In a bowl, mix together tofu, Parmesan cheese, eggs, parsley, salt and pepper. Mix together the sautéed vegetables and tofu mixture. Oil an 8x11-inch baking dish. Place a row of egg roll wrappers on the bottom. Build layers, alternating wraps, tofu mixture, spaghetti sauce, spinach, and grated cheese. The final layer should be sauce. Cover with aluminum foil; bake in preheated oven at 350°F (180°C) for 40 minutes. Remove foil, bake another 10 minutes and serve. Serves 6.

Approximate nutritional analysis per serving:
Calories 510, Protein 25 g, Carbohydrates 63 g, Fat 18 g, Cholesterol 16 mg, Sodium 1459 mg

GOLDEN TOMATO-VEGETABLE RISOTTO

3½ cups (840 ml) chicken broth,
    low sodium
3-oz pkg (90 g) FRIEDA'S Dried
    Yellow Tomatoes
2 tbs (30 ml) olive oil
2 cups (480 ml) diced vegetables,
    such as zucchini, carrots, red or
    green bell peppers, asparagus
    or mushrooms
1 clove FRIEDA'S Elephant Garlic,
    minced
6-oz pkg (180 g) FRIEDA'S Risotto
1 tbs (15 ml) FRIEDA'S Fresh Herbs,
    such as Basil, Chervil, Chives,
    Sage, Marjoram or Oregano,
    chopped
⅓ cup (80 ml) grated Parmesan or
    Romano cheese
pepper, to taste

In a medium saucepan, bring broth to a boil; add tomatoes. Reduce heat and simmer 2 minutes. Drain tomatoes out, reserving liquid in saucepan; keep broth warm. Sliver tomatoes; set aside.

In a large saucepan or deep skillet, heat olive oil. Sauté vegetables and garlic for 3-5 minutes or until vegetables are tender. Stir in risotto and tomatoes to coat well with olive oil. Add 1 cup of the hot broth; cook over medium heat, stirring constantly, until broth is nearly absorbed. Repeat adding broth and cooking liquid until rice is tender, and nearly all liquid has cooked away, about 18-25 minutes. Remove from heat; stir in herbs, Parmesan cheese and season to taste with pepper. Serves 4.

Approximate nutritional analysis per serving:
Calories 209, Protein 8 g, Carbohydrates 33 g, Fat 7 g, Cholesterol 4 mg, Sodium 437 mg

NORTH BEACH RISOTTO SAFFRON

5 cups (1.2 l) vegetable broth
½ tsp (3 ml) powdered saffron
½ cup (120 ml) minced shallots
¼ lb (115 g) unsalted butter
1 garlic clove, minced
1½ cups (355 ml) FANTASTIC
    FOODS Arborio Rice, dry
½ cup (120 ml) dry white wine
1 cup (240 ml) artichoke hearts,
    cooked and julienned, or fresh
    asparagus, cooked firm and cut
    into 1-inch lengths or broccoli
    florets, cooked firm
1 cup (240 ml) shredded Parmesan
    cheese
salt, to taste
black pepper, to taste

In a saucepan, bring the vegetable broth to a boil over high heat. Lower heat and keep the broth at a bare simmer during the rest of the cooking time. Remove ½ cup of the broth, stir the saffron into it and set aside.

In a separate 2½-quart saucepan, sauté the minced shallot until translucent in 7 tbs butter. Add the garlic and rice. Sauté until opaque and pearl-like for 1-2 minutes. Stir in white wine and cook. Stir constantly for about 3 minutes until the wine has evaporated.

Add ½ cup of the simmering broth to the rice, stirring constantly with a wooden spoon and waiting until the broth is absorbed before adding more. Continue adding broth ½ cup at a time until rice is cooked but still al dente, or firm to the bite. Use saffron-flavored broth after the first 15 minutes of cooking. All broth may not be needed. This will take 20-25 minutes. Never let rice stick to the bottom of the pan.

Stir in the artichoke hearts, cheese and 1 tbs butter 1-2 minutes before the rice is done. Add salt and pepper to taste. Serves 6.

Approximate nutritional analysis per ½ cup serving:
Calories 242, Protein 8 g, Carbohydrates 31 g, Fat 8 g, Cholesterol 23 mg, Sodium 473 mg

RISOTTO & VEGETABLES

2 tbs (30 ml) butter
1 tbs (15 ml) olive oil
½ cup (120 ml) chopped onion
⅓ cup (80 ml) celery, diced fine
⅓ cup (80 ml) carrot, diced fine
½ tsp (3 ml) salt, or to taste
1½ cups (355 ml) **RICE SELECT**
    Risotto Rice
2 cups (480 ml) chicken broth,
    heated
2 cups (480 ml) water, heated
1 medium zucchini, finely diced
¾ cup (180 ml) frozen peas, thawed
⅓ cup (80 ml) Parmesan cheese

Combine 1 tbs butter and the olive oil in large heavy saucepan. Add onions and cook until golden. Add celery and carrots; cook for 2-3 minutes. Add salt and rice stirring to coat. Add 3 cups of liquid, 1 cup at a time, using all of the broth then water; cook and stir until all liquid is absorbed before adding the next cup. Add diced zucchini. Add peas with the remaining water, stirring it in ½ cup at a time (all may not be needed), until last liquid is absorbed. Rice should be tender, yet firm, with a creamy sauce. Remove from heat; stir in remaining 1 tbs butter and Parmesan cheese. Serves 6.

Approximate nutritional analysis per serving:
Calories 178, Protein 6 g, Carbohydrates 28 g, Fat 6 g, Cholesterol 10 mg, Sodium 405 mg

HAZELNUT MUSHROOM RISOTTO

7 oz (210 g) shiitake mushrooms,
    sliced
3½ oz (105 g) black trumpet
    mushrooms, sliced
14 oz (420) white mushrooms, sliced
5 tbs (75 ml) shallots, minced
5 tbs (75 ml) **OMEGA Hazelnut Oil**
17½ oz (525 g) Italian Arborio rice
27 oz (810 ml) chicken stock
4 sprigs thyme
3½ oz (105 g) hazelnuts, chopped
3½ oz (105 g) Parmesan cheese
sea salt, to taste
pepper, to taste

Sauté mushrooms and shallots in a large pan with 2 tbs hazelnut oil over moderate heat. Add rice, stir. Slowly add half the chicken stock, little by little, until liquid is absorbed. Mix in sliced mushrooms, thyme and cook with a little additional stock until mushrooms are done. Cool risotto on baking sheet. For serving, heat the rest of the chicken stock in sauté pan, add risotto. Stir in chopped hazelnuts. Mix in Parmesan cheese, salt and pepper. Blend in the rest of hazelnut oil for a nice shine and flavor. Serves 10.

Approximate nutritional analysis per serving:
Calories 373, Protein 12 g, Carbohydrates 49 g, Fat 17 g, Cholesterol 8 mg, Sodium 432 mg

HAZELNUT MUSHROOM RISOTTO

POTATO-GARBANZO GNOCCHI

2 cups (480 ml) boiling water
2 cups (480 ml) ARROWHEAD `
    MILLS Potato Flakes
½ cup (120 ml) ARROWHEAD
    MILLS Garbanzo Flour
¼ cup (60 ml) ARROWHEAD MILLS
    Rice Flour
1 tsp (5 ml) non-alum baking
    powder, optional
1 tsp (5 ml) garlic powder
pinch cayenne or red pepper
1 tbs (15 ml) smoked nutritional
    yeast, optional
1 tsp (5 ml) sea salt, optional

Combine water and potato flakes quickly. They will set up firmly and be somewhat dry. Stir in the remaining ingredients. Drop by the teaspoonful into hot oil and deep fry until golden brown. Omitting the baking powder will result in denser gnocchi. Serves 4.

Approximate nutritional analysis per serving:
Calories 240, Protein 6 g, Carbohydrates 37 g, Fat 8 g, Cholesterol 0 mg, Sodium 31 mg

CREAMY POLENTA WITH FRESH THYME

3 cups (720 ml) water
⅔ cup (160 ml) polenta, yellow
    cornmeal
½ cup (120 ml) whole milk
2 tbs (30 ml) GREEN HOUSE Fresh
    Thyme
2 tbs (30 ml) grated Parmesan
    cheese
salt, to taste
pepper, to taste
2 medium zucchini
2 medium tomatoes
1 small eggplant
1 medium green pepper
olive oil, for grilling

In a medium saucepan bring water to a boil and add the polenta. Reduce heat and simmer for 10 minutes. Add the milk and fresh thyme and cook for an additional 5 minutes. Add the cheese and season with salt and pepper if you wish. Cut vegetables crosswise in halves, season with pepper, brush lightly with olive oil and grill. Divide into even portions and serve over polenta. Serves 3.

Approximate nutritional analysis per serving:
Calories 196, Protein 8 g, Carbohydrates 35 g, Fat 4 g, Cholesterol 9 mg, Sodium 119 mg

FRUIT & KAMUT NOODLE BAKE

4 oz (120 g) KAMUT Fettucini
    Noodles, cooked and drained
1 egg, beaten
½ cup (120 ml) skim milk
1 tbs (15 ml) unsaturated
    margarine, melted
½ cup (120 ml) dried apricots,
    chopped
¼ cup (60 ml) raisins
½ tsp (3 ml) sea salt

Combine all ingredients and mix. Prepare a 1-quart casserole dish or 8x8-inch glass pan with vegetable spray. Pour ingredients into the pan. Bake in 350°F (180°C) oven for 40 minutes or until lightly brown. This recipe may be doubled. Serves 2.

Approximate nutritional analysis per serving:
Calories 226, Protein 7 g, Carbohydrates 44 g, Fat 5 g, Cholesterol 47 mg, Sodium 332 mg

TERRY'S VEGGIE BURGERS

½ cup (120 ml) sunflower seeds, toasted
½ cup (120 ml) OMEGA NUTRITION Pumpkin Seed Spread
½ cup (120 ml) grated carrots
1 cup (240 ml) rolled oats
½ cup (120 ml) onions, chopped
1 cup (240 ml) alfalfa sprouts
2 tsp (10 ml) sesame seeds
¼ tsp (1 ml) sea salt
⅛-¼ tsp (.5-1 ml) herbs of choice, optional
2 tsp (10 ml) OMEGA NUTRITION NUTRI-FLAX
¼ cup (60 ml) water
1 tsp (5 ml) miso
2 tbs (30 ml) water
2 tbs (30 ml) OMEGA NUTRITION Coconut Butter

Toast sunflower seeds in dry frying pan over low-medium heat, stirring constantly until browned. Remove from pan and set aside. Combine in medium-size bowl: pumpkin seed spread, carrots, rolled oats, onions, sprouts, sunflower and sesame seeds, sea salt and herbs. In a bowl, stir together Nutri-Flax and ¼ cup water; in another, mix miso with 2 tbs water. Add both to vegetable mixture; mix well, using hands. Form into ½-inch patties. In frying pan over medium heat, melt 2 tbs Coconut Butter. Cook patties until crispy and golden brown. Use more Coconut Butter to prevent sticking, if needed. Serves 6.

Approximate nutritional analysis per serving:
Calories 318, Protein 13 g, Carbohydrates 16 g, Fat 23 g, Cholesterol 0 mg, Sodium 129 mg

BULGUR PATTIES

½ cup (120 ml) ARROWHEAD MILLS Bulgur Wheat
½ cup (120 ml) onion, chopped
1 cup (240 ml) boiling water
2 tbs (30 ml) ARROWHEAD MILLS Unrefined Vegetable Oil
1 tsp (5 ml) chicken broth seasoning powder, to taste
pinch garlic powder
½ tsp (3 ml) non-alum baking powder
¾ cup (180 ml) ARROWHEAD MILLS Garbanzo Flour mixed with ½ cup (120 ml) cold water

Add bulgur and onion to boiling water. Stir, cover and simmer until water is absorbed, 5-10 minutes. Add remaining ingredients. Shape into patties and heat on hot oiled griddle. Brown on both sides. Yields 4 patties.

Approximate nutritional analysis per serving:
Calories 222, Protein 7 g, Carbohydrates 31 g, Fat 9 g, Cholesterol 0 mg, Sodium 78 mg

WALNUT ACRES' BEAN CAKE PARMESAN

½ cup (120 ml) **WALNUT ACRES Garbanzo Beans, dried**
½ cup (120 ml) **WALNUT ACRES Great Northern Beans, dried**
1 tsp (5 ml) **fresh garlic, minced**
1 small onion, minced
1 large egg
½ cup (120 ml) **sesame seeds**
1 tsp (5 ml) **baking powder**
⅓ cup (80 ml) **cornstarch**
1 tsp (5 ml) **coriander**
1 tsp (5 ml) **cumin**
½ cup (120 ml) **spaghetti sauce**
8 oz (240 g) **WALNUT ACRES' Organic Mozzarella Cheese**
3 tbs (45 ml) **cooking oil**

Rinse beans and place in a 1-quart bowl. Cover dried garbanzo and Great Northern beans with water and let soak overnight. Drain water from the beans. In a small food processor, grind beans to a fine texture. Add all above ingredients except spaghetti sauce, mozzarella cheese and cooking oil to the beans.

Add cooking oil to a 12-inch Teflon fry pan and heat for 2 minutes over medium heat. Spoon in bean mixture, pancake style, and flatten with back of spoon to form a patty, ¼-inch thick and 4 inches in diameter. Repeat with the remainder of the batter. Fry patties until golden brown over medium heat for approximately 10 minutes, turn and fry again until golden brown. Remove from pan and place in a flat casserole dish. Top with spaghetti sauce and mozzarella cheese. Bake in a 350°F (180°C) preheated oven for 15 minutes, until the cheese melts and sauce is hot. Yields 7 patties.

Approximate nutritional analysis per patty:
Calories 360, Protein 19 g, Carbohydrates 29 g, Fat 20 g, Cholesterol 44 mg, Sodium 353 mg

WALNUT ACRES' BEAN CAKE PARMESAN

7-GRAIN VEGETABLE & BROWN RICE LOAF

2 cups (480 ml) raw cashew nuts, unsalted
1 box cooked ARROWHEAD MILLS Quick Brown Rice Vegetable & Herb
1 cup (240 ml) cooked ARROWHEAD MILLS 7 Grain Cereal
2 cups (480 ml) soy milk
1 large onion, chopped
¾ cup (180 ml) ARROWHEAD MILLS Wheat Germ
4 tbs (60 ml) ARROWHEAD MILLS Canola Oil
2 tbs (30 ml) soy sauce
1 tsp (5 ml) sea salt, optional
4 tbs (60 ml) minced parsley
½ tsp (3 ml) thyme
½ tsp (3 ml) ground celery seed
½ tsp (3 ml) ground sage
1 tsp (5 ml) onion powder
1 tsp (5 ml) garlic powder

Chop nuts fine, or run through a food grinder. Add the remaining ingredients and mix well. Place in a baking dish and bake at 350°F (180°C) uncovered for 1 hour or until done. Serves 8.

Approximate nutritional analysis per serving:
Calories 442, Protein 14 g, Carbohydrates 44 g, Fat 26 g, Cholesterol 0 mg, Sodium 352 mg

7-GRAIN VEGETABLE & BROWN RICE LOAF

SHEPHERD'S FALL VEGETABLE PIE

¾ cup (180 ml) cubed tofu
1 tbs (15 ml) soy sauce
1 tbs (15 ml) cornstarch
1½ cups (355 ml) STONYFIELD FARM Plain Low Fat Yogurt
2 cups (480 ml) peeled carrots, cut in large dice
1 cup (240 ml) unpeeled parsnips, cut in large dice
2 cups (480 ml) winter squash, cut in large dice
1 tbs (15 ml) butter
2 cups (480 ml) sliced mushrooms
1 small red pepper, sweet or hot, diced
1 clove garlic, minced
1 tsp (5 ml) ground ginger
½ tsp (3 ml) salt
2 tbs (30 ml) cornstarch
¼ tsp (1 ml) kelp powder, optional
pinch cayenne pepper
1 cup (240 ml) skim milk
¾ cup (180 ml) Jarlsberg or Swiss cheese
unbaked 10-inch pie crust

Preheat oven to 375°F (190°C).

Combine the tofu and soy sauce; set aside. Add 1 tbs cornstarch to the yogurt in a small bowl and set aside. Steam the carrots, parsnips and squash until tender.

Melt the butter in a nonstick skillet; add mushrooms, red pepper, garlic, ginger and salt and sauté until the mushrooms and pepper are tender. Do not brown. Combine 2 tbs cornstarch, optional kelp powder, cayenne and milk, and add to the mushroom mixture. Bring to a boil, stirring constantly, and boil for 1 minute.

Remove from heat and stir in the cheese. Fold in the tofu, then stir in the yogurt mixture. Add the steamed vegetables and transfer the mixture to an ungreased 10-inch deep-dish pie plate. Top with the unbaked crust, and slash the crust to let steam escape. Bake for 35-40 minutes or until crust is lightly browned. Serves 4-6.

Approximate nutritional analysis per serving:
Calories 401, Protein 16 g, Carbohydrates 37 g, Fat 22 g, Cholesterol 35 mg, Sodium 669 mg

MEATLESS SHEPHERD'S PIE

½ cup (120 ml) uncooked
ARROWHEAD MILLS Lentils
2 cups (480 ml) water
1 bay leaf
1 cup (240 ml) boiling water
½ cup (120 ml) ARROWHEAD
MILLS Bulgur Wheat
½ tsp (3 ml) garlic powder
¼ tsp (1 ml) sea salt
½ cup (120 ml) low-fat mozzarella
cheese, grated
1 medium onion, finely chopped
16-oz can (480 g) tomatoes, drained
1½ cups (355 ml) ARROWHEAD
MILLS Potato Flakes
2 cups (480 ml) boiling water
¼ tsp (1 ml) sea salt, optional

Cook lentils in water with bay leaf about 15 minutes or until tender, drain. Remove bay leaf. While cooking lentils, pour boiling water over bulgur wheat, garlic powder and salt, set aside for 10 minutes. Preheat oven to 350°F (180°C). Layer in the bottom of an oiled 8x8-inch oven dish in the following order: bulgur wheat, lentils, mozzarella cheese, onion and tomatoes. Mix potato flakes, water and salt and layer on top of the tomatoes. Bake for 30 minutes. Serves 4.

Approximate nutritional analysis per serving:
Calories 276, Protein 16 g, Carbohydrates 48 g, Fat 4 g, Cholesterol 8 mg, Sodium 284 mg

CHILE RELLENO CASSEROLE

1 lb (455 g) soft tofu, rinsed
2 7-oz cans (420 g) diced green chiles
1 cup (240 ml) shredded Monterey
Jack cheese
6 egg whites
2 eggs
⅔ cup (160 ml) nonfat milk
1 cup (240 ml) all-purpose flour
1 tsp (5 ml) baking powder
½ tsp (3 ml) ground cumin
1 cup (240 ml) shredded cheddar
cheese
28-oz can (840 ml) MUIR GLEN
Organic Chunky Tomato Sauce
¼ cup (60 ml) chopped fresh
cilantro

Coarsely mash tofu; drain in colander 10 minutes. Combine tofu, diced green chiles and Monterey Jack cheese and spread on bottom of lightly greased 12x8-inch baking dish. In large bowl of electric mixer, whip egg whites and whole eggs on high speed until thick and foamy. Add milk, flour, baking powder and cumin; beat until smooth. Pour egg mixture over chiles; sprinkle with cheddar cheese.

Bake, uncovered, at 375°F (190°C) for 25-30 minutes, or until golden brown. Meanwhile, heat tomato sauce in medium saucepan over low heat until hot through. Stir in cilantro; serve immediately with casserole. Serves 6.

Approximate nutritional analysis per serving:
Calories 340, Protein 22 g, Carbohydrates 30 g, Fat 14 g, Cholesterol 85 mg, Sodium 620 mg

VEGETARIAN TOSTADAS

4 MILL VALLEY Tostada Bowls
1 cup (240 ml) nonfat refried beans,
    warmed
1 avocado, mashed and minced
    with red onion, to taste and
    lime juice, to taste
¾ cup (180 ml) finely shredded
    lettuce or other tender greens
2 green onions, finely chopped
½ cup (120 ml) grated Monterey
    Jack cheese or cheddar cheese
½ cup (120 ml) salsa verde or
    salsa ranchera

Preheat tostada bowls for 3-5 minutes in a 350°F (180°C) oven and fill with beans, avocado, lettuce, a sprinkling of onions, cheese and a dollop of salsa. Place on a bed of lettuce and serve. Serves 4.

Approximate nutritional analysis per serving:
Calories 310, Protein 10 g, Carbohydrates 31 g, Fat 18 g, Cholesterol 13 mg, Sodium 472 mg

TEMPEH-STUFFED ZUCCHINI

3-4 medium-large zucchini

FILLING:
12-oz pkg (360 g) SURATA
    SOYFOODS CO-OP Multi-Grain
    or Soy Tempeh
6 tbs (90 ml) tamari
1 tsp (5 ml) dried basil
pinch oregano
½ tsp (3 ml) black pepper
½ cup (120 ml) onion, minced
2 cloves garlic, minced
3 tbs (45 ml) plus 1 tbs (15 ml) oil
1 cup (240 ml) soft bread crumbs
½ cup (120 ml) parsley, minced
1½ cups (355 ml) tomatoes

Wash and trim ends from the zucchini. Slice into ¾-inch thick circles; using sharp knife, remove centers, leaving ¼-inch ring of shell. Reserve pulp for filling. Parboil for 2 minutes.

Combine first 7 Filling ingredients and sauté the mixture in 3 tbs oil. Add the zucchini pulp, chopped, and 1 tbs oil. Sauté until pulp softens. Remove from heat and stir in bread crumbs, parsley and tomatoes. Place drained zucchini rings in an oiled flat 9x13-inch pan. Heap filling in centers and bake at 375°F (190°C) for 20 minutes. Serves 6.

Approximate nutritional analysis per serving:
Calories 372, Protein 18 g, Carbohydrates 42 g, Fat 15 g, Cholesterol 0 mg, Sodium 1199 mg

TEMPEH-STUFFED ZUCCHINI

TEMPEH-STUFFED BELL PEPPERS

12-oz pkg (360 g) SURATA
   SOYFOODS CO-OP Soy or
   Multi-Grain Tempeh, grated
2 tbs (30 ml) tamari
1 tbs (15 ml) vinegar
2 tbs (30 ml) oil
1 medium onion, chopped
1 clove garlic, pressed
1 cup (240 ml) tomatoes, chopped
1½ cups (355 ml) rice, cooked
¼ tsp (1 ml) black pepper
½ tsp (3 ml) basil
1½ cups (355 ml) water
2 large bell peppers, cut in half
   with seeds removed
1 cup (240 ml) vegetable stock
   or 1 tsp (5 ml) vegetable bouillon
   granules dissolved in 1 cup
   (240 ml) water
1 cup (240 ml) tomato sauce

Combine in a 2-quart mixing bowl tempeh, tamari and vinegar. Sauté in a heavy skillet 2 tbs oil, onion and garlic. Add tempeh mixture, tomatoes, rice, black pepper, basil.

In a large saucepan bring to boil 1½ cups water. Drop bell peppers into boiling water and remove immediately after 3 minutes; drain at once.

Set parboiled peppers in oiled baking dish. Stuff peppers with filling. Mix together stock and tomato sauce. Pour over filled peppers. Cover with aluminum foil. Bake at 350°F (180°C) for 30-40 minutes, basting peppers with tomato sauce occasionally. Remove foil cover for last 10 minutes of baking. Serve hot. Serves 4 as a side dish.

Approximate nutritional analysis per serving:
Calories 584, Protein 34 g, Carbohydrates 90 g, Fat 11 g, Cholesterol 0 mg, Sodium 1349 mg

SEITAN IRISH STEW

2 cups (480 ml) diced ARROWHEAD
   MILLS Seitan
1 cup (240 ml) rutabagas, peeled
   and cut into ½-inch cubes
1 cup (240 ml) onions, ½-inch cubed
1 cup (240 ml) carrots, washed not
   peeled, diced or roll cut
1 cup (240 ml) potatoes, peeled and
   cut into ½-inch cubes
2 bay leaves
½ tsp (3 ml) rosemary
½ tsp (3 ml) fresh chopped garlic
½ tsp (3 ml) basil
1 tbs (15 ml) fresh chopped parsley
4 tsp (20 ml) sesame oil,
   or oil of choice
2 cups (480 ml) water
5 tsp (25 ml) tamari soy sauce
½ cup (120 ml) celery, chopped
4 tbs (60 ml) water
4-5 tbs (60-75 ml) arrowroot

Place first 11 ingredients in a 2-quart saucepan. Sauté on medium heat for about 8 minutes, stirring occasionally to prevent burning. Add 2 cups water and tamari and bring mixture to a simmer. Cook for another 10 minutes, or until the vegetables are tender-crisp. Add celery at the end of the cooking process to help retain color. In a separate bowl, mix water and arrowroot well. Turn heat off under stew and vigorously stir in arrowroot mixture. Turn heat on to medium and stir constantly until mixture thickens. Serves 4.

Variation: To serve stew over noodles, rice or mashed potatoes, eliminate potatoes in stew and replace with frozen green peas, added at the same time as the celery.

Approximate nutritional analysis per serving:
Calories 284, Protein 21 g, Carbohydrates 38 g, Fat 6 g, Cholesterol 0 mg, Sodium 708 mg

SEITAN

1 cup plus 6 tsp (270 ml)
    ARROWHEAD MILLS Seitan Mix
1 cup (240 ml) water, room
    temperature

SEITAN MIX BROTH:
8 cups (1.9 l) water
½ cup (120 ml) low-sodium
    soy sauce
1 cup (240 ml) tomato juice
1 tbs (15 ml) food yeast
2 fresh onions, chopped
seasonings, to taste

Add seitan mix to water in mixing bowl. Stir, then knead until well mixed and elastic, about 5 minutes. Form dough into a 2½-inch thick log form and let rest 5 minutes while preparing Broth. Cut into 1-inch pieces before immersing into Broth.

    Seitan Mix Broth: Combine all ingredients in a saucepan. Bring broth to a boil, add seitan pieces and simmer until most of the liquid is gone. Serves 4.

Approximate nutritional analysis per serving:
Calories 203, Protein 22 g, Carbohydrates 26 g, Fat 1 g, Cholesterol 0 mg, Sodium 1240 mg

TOFU RAGOUT PROVENÇAL

10½ oz (315 g) tofu
3 cloves garlic, crushed
3 tbs (45 ml) fresh lemon juice
½ tbs (8 ml) fresh rosemary
½ cup (120 ml) OMEGA Olive Oil
1 lb (455 g) eggplants
1 lb (455 g) tomatoes
½ lb (230 g) zucchini
black olives, optional
½ cup (120 ml) vegetable broth
½ tsp (3 ml) oregano
½ tsp (3 ml) thyme
½ tsp (3 ml) basil
½ tsp (3 ml) tarragon
½ tsp (3 ml) marjoram
½ tsp (3 ml) sea salt
½ tsp (3 ml) pepper

Cut the tofu into small cubes. Mix fresh-pressed garlic, lemon juice, rosemary and 2 tbs olive oil. Marinate tofu in this dressing for 2 hours, stirring occasionally. Cut the eggplant lengthwise, salt them and let sit for 5 minutes. Cut the tomatoes and zucchini into chunks. Dry the eggplant halves, cut into chunks and sauté them in the rest of the olive oil. Remove the eggplant and sauté zucchini. Return eggplant to pan with tomatoes and marinated tofu. Add the vegetable broth and the spices. Cover the ragout and cook at moderate heat for approximately 5 minutes or until tofu is hot. Serves 6.

Approximate nutritional analysis per serving:
Calories 243, Protein 6 g, Carbohydrates 11 g, Fat 21 g, Cholesterol 0 mg, Sodium 222 mg

TOFU RAGOUT PROVENÇAL

TEMPEH ÉTOUFFEE

12-oz pkg (360 g) SURATA
    SOYFOODS CO-OP Soy, Multi-
    Grain or Italiano Tempeh, cubed
2 cups (480 ml) chopped tomatoes,
    with juice
    or 16 oz (480 g) canned stewed
    tomatoes
¼ tsp (1 ml) dry mustard
    or 1 tsp (5 ml) prepared mustard
2 tsp (10 ml) Tabasco
    or 1 tsp (5 ml) cayenne pepper
1 bunch green onions, chopped
1 green bell pepper, chopped
1 yellow onion, chopped
2 cloves garlic, minced
½-¾ cup (120-180 ml) water
2 tsp (10 ml) thyme
1 tbs (15 ml) dry basil
2 tbs (30 ml) dry parsley
2 tbs (30 ml) soy sauce
2 tbs (30 ml) lemon juice
2 tbs (30 ml) flour

TEMPEH ÉTOUFFEE

Place everything, except the flour, in a pot; bring to a boil. Stir in the flour. Simmer ½ hour. Serve over rice. Serves 4.

Approximate nutritional analysis per serving w/o rice:
Calories 355, Protein 24 g, Carbohydrates 50 g, Fat 8 g, Cholesterol 0 mg, Sodium 588 mg

TEMPEH CURRY

1 small onion, chopped
1 tbs (15 ml) oil
12-oz pkg (360 g) SURATA
    SOYFOODS CO-OP Soy or Multi-
    Grain Tempeh, cubed
1 cup (240 ml) water
¼ cup (60 ml) soy sauce
2 tbs (30 ml) flour
2 tsp (10 ml) curry powder
1 tsp (5 ml) marjoram
1 large peeled, chopped tomato
10-oz can (300 g) pineapple chunks,
    drained
1 cup (240 ml) cooked peas

In a large pot, sauté onion in oil on medium-high heat until onions are clear. Add tempeh, water, soy sauce, flour, curry powder and marjoram. Bring to a simmer and stir until thickened. Add tomato, pineapple and peas. Serve over rice or noodles. Serves 4.

Approximate nutritional analysis per serving w/o rice:
Calories 419, Protein 24 g, Carbohydrates 57 g, Fat 12 g, Cholesterol 0 mg, Sodium 36 mg

TEMPEH CURRY

WHEATBALL STROGANOFF

1 box KNOX MOUNTAIN FARM
   Wheat Ball Mix, prepared into
   25 balls
⅓ cup (80 ml) Italian bread crumbs
4 tbs (3 ml) olive oil
2 cups (480 ml) mushrooms
1 large onion
1 small green pepper
spices of choice
1 lb (455 g) tofu
1 cup (240 ml) water

VARIATION:
2 cups (480 ml) nonfat yogurt or
   low-fat sour cream

Roll cooled wheat balls in Italian bread crumbs. Fry in 2 tbs olive oil until crispy. Set aside. In skillet sauté mushrooms, onion and green pepper in 2 tbs olive oil. In blender, mix with spices of choice, tofu and water. Pour over the sautéed vegetables. Simmer until thick. Pour over wheat balls and serve at once.
Yields 25 wheat balls.

Variation: For a more traditional stroganoff, use nonfat plain yogurt or low-fat sour cream instead of the tofu and water.

Approximate nutritional analysis per wheat ball:
Calories 87, Protein 7 g, Carbohydrates 7 g, Fat 3 g, Cholesterol 0 mg, Sodium 57 mg

Approximate nutritional analysis per wheat ball variation w/ yogurt:
Calories 84, Protein 7 g, Carbohydrates 8 g, Fat 3 g, Cholesterol .4 mg, Sodium 71 mg

Approximate nutritional analysis per wheat ball variation w/ sour cream:
Calories 99, Protein 7 g, Carbohydrates 8 g, Fat 5 g, Cholesterol 7 mg, Sodium 64 mg

FIVE-SPICE TOFU WITH PEANUT SAUCE

1 medium onion, chopped
1 clove garlic, minced
1 tsp (5 ml) grated ginger root
1 crushed dried chile pepper
1 tbs (15 ml) oil
2 cups (480 ml) hot water
1 cup (240 ml) unsweetened
   grated coconut
½ cup (120 ml) peanut butter
1 tbs (15 ml) tamari
3 6.1-oz pkgs (549 g) SOY DELI
   Baked Five-Spice Tofu,
   1-inch cubed

Sauté onion, garlic, ginger root and dried chile pepper in oil until onion is clear. Blend water, coconut, peanut butter and tamari in a blender or food processor. Add to the onions and stir well as it thickens. Add tofu to the sauce and heat through. Serve over brown rice. Serves 4.

Approximate nutritional analysis per serving w/o rice:
Calories 514, Protein 37 g, Carbohydrates 30 g, Fat 30 g, Cholesterol 0 mg, Sodium 1764 mg

FIVE-SPICE TOFU WITH PEANUT SAUCE

VEGAN LONDON BROIL

2 boxes ARROWHEAD MILLS
   Seitan Quick Mix
8 cups (1.9 l) water
1½ cups (355 ml) tamari soy sauce
7-inch strip kombu sea vegetable
6 thin slices fresh ginger
bordelaise or miso sauce

Place seitan in an 8-inch square cake pan. Allow to rest until it takes the shape of the pan. Place this pan inside a second, large pan that is half-filled with water. Cover the larger pan. Bake in a preheated oven at 375°F (190°C) for 1 hour. When the seitan is done, remove from the pan. Divide into 8 equal pieces.

To 8 cups of water, add tamari, kombu, ginger and seitan steaks in a pot. Cover, bring to a simmer and cook for about 45 minutes.* You may leave the cooked steaks in the stock for several hours, if you wish. Remove steaks from stock and drain. To serve, brush with a little sauce and broil so they will be lightly browned. Serve steaks hot with additional sauce. Serves 6.

*Note: If you are using a pressure cooker, reduce liquid by one half and cook for 20-25 minutes.

Approximate nutritional analysis per serving w/o sauce:
Calories 444, Protein 60 g, Carbohydrates 45 g, Fat 3 g, Cholesterol 0 mg, Sodium 4180 mg

SEITAN & ONIONS

3 cups (720 ml) half moon-sliced
   onions
3 4-oz pieces (360 g) ARROWHEAD
   MILLS Seitan, cooked
3 tbs (45 ml) vegetable oil
¼ tsp (1 ml) ground black pepper,
   optional
2 tbs (30 ml) tamari soy sauce
1¼ cups (295 ml) vegetable stock
   or water

Slice onions and set aside. Sauté seitan in oil at high heat to brown. When the seitan starts to brown, add the onions and sauté a few minutes, then add the rest of the ingredients, lower heat, cover and cook until liquid is reduced to almost nothing. Serve while hot. Serves 2.

Approximate nutritional analysis per serving:
Calories 313, Protein 20 g, Carbohydrates 27 g, Fat 15 g, Cholesterol 0 mg, Sodium 707 mg

SEITAN & ONIONS

MUSHROOM-MISO CORNUCOPIA

2 cups (480 ml) finely diced onions
2 cups (480 ml) whole button or
    medium mushrooms
2 cups (480 ml) fresh Brussels
    sprouts, stems cut off and halved
2 cups (480 ml) ARROWHEAD
    MILLS Seitan, flaked
    (thinly sliced at a 45° angle)
2 tbs (30 ml) regular sesame oil,
    or oil of choice
1 tsp (5 ml) salt, optional
½ tsp (3 ml) ground black pepper,
    optional
1 tsp (5 ml) tarragon leaves
3 cups (720 ml) miso sauce

Sauté vegetables and seitan in oil with spices at medium heat for about 5 minutes. Add miso sauce and continue to cook until hot. Serve as is or over grain, pasta or toast. Serves 4.

Approximate nutritional analysis per serving:
Calories 543, Protein 32 g, Carbohydrates 80 g, Fat 13 g, Cholesterol 0 mg, Sodium 3043 mg

SIZZLING SAVORY TOFU STEAKS

3 tbs (45 ml) shoyu
1 tsp (5 ml) garlic powder
1 tsp (5 ml) ginger powder, optional
1 lb (480 g) WHITE WAVE Tofu,
    hard, sliced into ½-inch steaks
1 tbs (15 ml) vegetable oil, soy
    or canola

Whisk together shoyu, garlic and ginger in a small bowl. Dip the tofu steaks in the sauce mixture. Cook in an oiled pan over medium-high heat for 10 minutes until browned, turning tofu after 5 minutes. Serves 3.

Approximate nutritional analysis per serving:
Calories 270, Protein 25 g, Carbohydrates 9 g, Fat 18 g, Cholesterol 0 mg, Sodium 1049 mg

SIZZLING SAVORY TOFU STEAKS

UNREAL VEAL PARMESAN

1 box KNOX MOUNTAIN FARM
    Wheat Ball Mix, cooked into
    8 burgers
½ cup (120 ml) Italian bread
    crumbs
1 cup (240 ml) tomato sauce,
    warmed
¼ cup (60 ml) Parmesan cheese

After boiling the burgers, drain and cool. Press burgers into bread crumbs and bake on an oiled 9x13-inch pan for 25 minutes at 350°F (180°C). Remove from oven and cover with hot tomato sauce and top with Parmesan cheese. Return to the oven until the cheese has melted. Let sit for 10 minutes before serving. Yields 8 burgers.

Approximate nutritional analysis per serving:
Calories 213, Protein 21 g, Carbohydrates 28 g, Fat 2 g, Cholesterol 3 mg, Sodium 578 mg

TEMPEH SOYSAGE

2-3 tbs (30-45 ml) oil
12-oz pkg (360 g) SURATA
    SOYFOODS CO-OP Italiano
    Tempeh, grated
2-3 tbs (30-45 ml) soy sauce
2 cloves garlic, minced
    or ½ tsp (3 ml) garlic powder
1½ tsp (8 ml) fennel seeds
    or ¾ tsp (4 ml) ground fennel
2 tsp (10 ml) oregano
½ tsp (3 ml) thyme
½ tsp (3 ml) sage

Heat oil in a fry pan and add all ingredients. Sauté until browned, about 10-15 minutes. Use as a pizza topping or add to spaghetti sauce or lasagne. Serves 4.

Approximate nutritional analysis per serving:
Calories 221, Protein 17 g, Carbohydrates 13 g, Fat 12 g, Cholesterol 0 mg, Sodium 525 mg

TEMPEH SOYSAGE

SEA BASS WITH TOMATO & DILL RELISH

2 cups (480 ml) diced tomatoes
½ cup (120 ml) diced red onion
½ cup (120 ml) diced cucumber
¼ cup (60 ml) GREEN HOUSE
    Fresh Dill, chopped
½ cup (120 ml) seasoned
    rice vinegar
2 tbs (30 ml) fresh lemon juice
2 tbs (30 ml) hazelnut oil or salad oil
fresh ground white pepper, to taste
4 small new potatoes, boiled,
    leave skin on
1 lb (455 g) sea bass or halibut
    steak, grilled

Toss all ingredients except bass in a salad bowl and leave to blend in the refrigerator for at least 1 hour. Meanwhile grill or broil fish. Serve relish over fish. Serves 4.

Approximate nutritional analysis per serving:
Calories 301, Protein 25 g, Carbohydrates 32 g, Fat 9 g, Cholesterol 60 mg, Sodium 113 mg

**SEA BASS WITH
TOMATO & DILL RELISH**

STEAMED SALMON WITH QUICK SPECTRUM SPICY ASIAN MARINADE

MARINADE:
½ cup (120 ml) AYLA'S ORGANICS
    Garlic and Onion Salad Dressing
4 tbs (60 ml) SPECTRUM
    NATURALS Unrefined Toasted
    Sesame Oil
4 tsp (20 ml) tamari soy sauce
1 tsp (5 ml) SPECTRUM WORLD
    CUISINE Asian Seasoning Oil

4 6-oz (720 g) salmon filets,
    skin and bones removed
4 tsp (20 ml) fresh ginger,
    finely minced
salt, to taste
fresh ground pepper, to taste
sprigs of cilantro for garnish

Begin by boiling the water for a Chinese bamboo steamer. In a stainless steel or glass bowl, whisk together the ingredients for the marinade. Place each piece of salmon into a shallow bowl small enough to fit each steamer basket. Spoon 3 tbs of marinade over each filet. Sprinkle the fresh ginger over each filet.

Place the bowls into the steamer baskets and stack them over the boiling water. Cover and let steam for approximately 5 minutes. When the fish is cooked, remove from the steam, season with salt and pepper, garnish with the sprigs of cilantro and serve immediately. Serves 4.

Alternately, if you don't have a steamer, place each filet on an ample square of aluminum foil with marinade and ginger. Seal foil into a packet. Bake in 400°F (205°C) oven for 10-12 minutes until fish is steaming hot and cooked through. Season to taste.

Approximate nutritional analysis per serving:
Calories 384, Protein 34 g, Carbohydrates 2 g, Fat 26 g, Cholesterol 94 mg, Sodium 472 mg

**STEAMED SALMON WITH
QUICK SPECTRUM SPICY ASIAN MARINADE**

SALMON: TECHNIQUES & MARINADES

4 6-oz (720 g) Maine steelhead
   salmon steaks

HONEY LEMON MARINADE:
4 tbs (60 ml) extra-virgin olive oil
2 tsp (10 ml) Dijon mustard
1 tbs (15 ml) mirin*
1 tbs (15 ml) honey
juice from ½ lemon
2 tbs (30 ml) fresh basil, slivered
sea salt, to taste
freshly ground pepper, to taste

SESAME MARINADE:
4 tbs (60 ml) sesame oil
2 tbs (30 ml) tamari
2 tbs (30 ml) lime juice
1 clove garlic, minced
3 scallions, chopped

Cooking Maine Steelhead Salmon: Before cooking, check for and remove the pin bones, there won't be many. Cook salmon with the skin on - it will come off filet easily before serving. Cut the filet into pieces to marinate. Salmon should be cooked approximately 10 minutes per inch of thickness. Measure the maximum thickness of your fish. The higher the cooking temperature, the shorter the cooking time; don't be afraid to check. Salmon is done when it is light pink throughout and flakes easily with fork. Avoid overcooking, which dries out the fish.

To Grill: A Griffo Grill is indispensable here. Place filets skin side down on Griffo Grill over medium-hot fire. Cover grill if possible and cook without turning. If you use a marinade and it will cover your fish, rake coals to each side so they are not directly under fish.

To Pan Sauté: Cut filet to fit your pan, if necessary. Warm a small amount of marinade in a skillet. Add fish skin side down, cover and cook without turning.

To Broil: Place filets skin side down in a broiling pan and drizzle with marinade. Broil 3-6 inches from heat.

Marinades: Marinades keep fish moist and provide flavor and variety. When broiling or grilling, lightly coat salmon with Honey Lemon Marinade or Sesame Marinade.

To prepare marinades, combine all ingredients. Marinate fish from 30 minutes to 3 hours. Serves 4.

Not included in nutritional analysis due to unavailability of nutrient data.

Approximate nutritional analysis per serving w/ Sesame Marinade:
Calories 374, Protein 35 g, Carbohydrates 3 g, Fat 25 g, Cholesterol 94 mg, Sodium 591 mg

Approximate nutritional analysis per serving w/ Honey Lemon Marinade:
Calories 386, Protein 34 g, Carbohydrates 6 g, Fat 25 g, Cholesterol 94 mg, Sodium 108 mg

Courtesy of Sea Run Holdings, Inc.

SMOKED SALMON-STUFFED CABBAGE

1 whole cabbage, core removed
1 medium onion, minced
½ stick butter
6 HEALTH SEA Dill Sausages,
    in ¼-inch dice
salt, to taste
black pepper, to taste
2 hard-boiled eggs, chopped
1 tbs fresh dill, chopped
    or ½ tsp dried dill
2 cups (480 ml) chicken stock
3 cups (720 ml) tomato sauce
½ cup (120 ml) low-calorie
    sour cream
2 tbs (30 ml) cider vinegar

Cook cabbage in salted water. Peel away each outer leaf as it becomes done. Chop and reserve the middle ½ of the cabbage after cooking. Sauté onion in butter until soft, add chopped cabbage, sausage, salt, black pepper. Cook until tender. Cool mixture. Fold in chopped egg and dill.

Spoon mixture into the whole leaves, taking time to seal in leaves completely. Place in casserole, cover with chicken stock, tomato sauce, sour cream and vinegar. Simmer slowly for approximately 1½ hours until tender. Serves 6.

Approximate nutritional analysis per serving:
Calories 271, Protein 23 g, Carbohydrates 20 g, Fat 13 g, Cholesterol 91 mg, Sodium 2010 mg

GRILLED AHI WITH MANGO-PEACH SALSA

¼ cup (60 ml) mint leaves
¼ cup (60 ml) cilantro
¼ cup (60 ml) red onions
4 tbs (60 ml) lime juice
2 tbs (30 ml) fresh ground ginger
1 tbs (15 ml) minced serrano chile
1 cup (240 ml) R. W. KNUDSEN
    FAMILY Mango Peach Juice
1 large ripe mango
4 6-oz (720 g) Ahi tuna steaks

Mix all ingredients together except for the mango and tuna. Marinate the fish overnight in half the mixture. Heat coals in barbecue. Peel and cut mango into cubes; add to the other half of the marinade. Broil tuna steaks 6-8 minutes turning once. Spoon mango salsa over fish and serve at once. Serves 4.

Approximate nutritional analysis per serving:
Calories 383, Protein 52 g, Carbohydrates 18 g, Fat 11 g, Cholesterol 83 mg, Sodium 99 mg

GRILLED AHI WITH MANGO-PEACH SALSA

MAIN COURSES

BAKED FISH IN WINE

2 lbs (910 g) filet of sole
½ cup (120 ml) IL CLASSICO White
    Pepper Chablis Cooking Wine
1 medium onion, chopped
2 tsp (5 ml) parsley
½ tsp (3 ml) salt
2 bay leaves, crushed

Wash fish, pat dry and place in 2-quart greased casserole. Pour remaining ingredients over fish. Cover and bake at 375°F (190°C) for 25 minutes or until the fish flakes when pierced with a fork. Serves 4.

Approximate nutritional analysis per serving:
Calories 248, Protein 43 g, Carbohydrates 12 g, Fat 3 g, Cholesterol 109 mg, Sodium 452 mg

MOROCCAN-STYLE SALMON

1 small onion, sliced
2 garlic cloves, minced
1 tbs (15 ml) olive oil
28-oz can (840 g) tomatoes, whole,
    peeled, coarsely chopped,
    liquid reserved
4 tsp (20 ml) honey
1 tsp (5 ml) grated fresh lemon peel
¾ tsp (4 ml) ground cumin
1½ tsp (8 ml) lemon juice
salt, to taste
black pepper, to taste
cayenne pepper, to taste
24-36 oz (720-1080 g) salmon filets
2 tbs (30 ml) chopped, toasted
    almonds
2 tbs (30 ml) chopped cilantro
3 cups (720 ml) cooked couscous,
    or rice

Sauté onions and garlic in olive oil in a medium skillet over medium-high heat until golden. Stir in tomatoes, tomato liquid, honey, lemon peel and cumin. Simmer 10-15 minutes. Stir in lemon juice and season with salt, pepper and cayenne, to taste. Meanwhile, season salmon filets with salt and pepper. Broil 4-6 inches from heat, allowing 10 minutes per inch of thickness, measured at thickest part. Place each filet on a dinner plate. Top with tomato sauce; sprinkle with almonds and cilantro. Serve with couscous. Serves 4.

Approximate nutritional analysis per serving:
Calories 525, Protein 42 g, Carbohydrates 50 g, Fat 17 g, Cholesterol 94 mg, Sodium 440 mg

Courtesy of The National Honey Board.

MOROCCAN-STYLE SALMON

PESCADO A LA VERACRUZANA

2 tbs (30 ml) vegetable oil
½ cup (120 ml) chopped onion
½ cup (120 ml) chopped green
   bell pepper
¼ cup (60 ml) chopped Anaheim
   pepper
2 cloves garlic, minced
15-oz can (450 ml) MUIR GLEN
   Organic Tomato Sauce
½ cup (120 ml) chopped green olives
¼ cup (60 ml) capers
2 bay leaves
½ tsp (3 ml) lime juice
1½ lbs (683 g) sea bass or red
   snapper filets

Heat oil in large skillet over medium heat. Add onion, green pepper, Anaheim pepper and garlic; cook until tender. Stir in tomato sauce, olives, capers, bay leaves and lime juice. Bring to a boil; reduce heat to low. Add fish filets to skillet. Cover and simmer 10-15 minutes or until fish flakes easily with fork. Remove bay leaves and serve immediately. Serves 6.

Approximate nutritional analysis per serving:
Calories 228, Protein 27 g, Carbohydrates 8 g, Fat 9 g, Cholesterol 60 mg, Sodium 819 mg

PESCADO A LA VERACRUZANA

GRILLED SALMON SAUSAGE ON FOCACCIA WITH SAUTÉED PEPPERS

1 HEALTH SEA Plain Salmon
   Sausage
¼ cup (60 ml) balsamic vinaigrette
½ cup (120 ml) combination onion,
   red and green peppers, julienned
1 tsp (5 ml) garlic, minced
1 tbs (15 ml) fresh basil, julienned
4 leaves radicchio
2½ oz (75 g) soft low-fat mozzarella,
   sliced ¼-inch thick
2 slices focaccia bread, 1-inch thick

Quickly grill sausage 3-8 minutes, basting frequently with vinaigrette, until lightly browned and hot. In skillet, sauté onions, peppers, garlic and basil in remaining vinaigrette for 1-2 minutes. Add radicchio, heat for 30 seconds stirring quickly. Remove radicchio, add mozzarella to mixture and melt under broiler. Arrange radicchio and salmon sausage on toasted focaccia. Top with the sautéed vegetables/melted cheese mixture. Great with mustard. Serves 2.

Approximate nutritional analysis per serving:
Calories 243, Protein 21 g, Carbohydrates 23 g, Fat 8 g, Cholesterol 36 mg, Sodium 792 mg

GRILLED SALMON SAUSAGE ON FOCACCIA WITH SAUTÉED PEPPERS

LEMON-BROILED SALMON SAUSAGE

4 6-oz (720 g) **HEALTH SEA Salmon
    Sausages, cut in 2-inch diagonal
    pieces**
1 tsp (5 ml) salt
1 tsp (5 ml) fresh tarragon
1 tsp (5 ml) fresh basil
6 tbs (90 ml) melted butter
6 tbs (90 ml) lemon juice
½ tbs (8 ml) Worcestershire sauce

Preheat broiler. Place sausages on a broiling tray. Whisk together remaining ingredients, pour over sausages and marinate 5 minutes. Remove ½ the liquid before broiling. Broil 3-4 minutes, 3-5 inches from heat, basting occasionally. Turn sausages. Broil and baste another 3-4 minutes. Serve with rice or in a sandwich. Serves 4.
   Variation: Grill whole mushrooms with sausages.

*Approximate nutritional analysis per serving w/o mushrooms:
Calories 251, Protein 17 g, Carbohydrates 8 g, Fat 18 g, Cholesterol 77 mg,
Sodium 1641 mg*

MUSTARD-GLAZED GRILLED SALMON SAUSAGE

GLAZE:
½ cup (120 ml) Dijon mustard
¼ cup (60 ml) white wine
1 tsp (5 ml) garlic, minced
2 tbs (30 ml) brown sugar
1 tbs (15 ml) lemon juice

TEQUILA SALSA:
4 medium tomatoes,
    seeded and diced
½ cup (120 ml) fresh green
    chile peppers, chopped
1 cup (240 ml) tomato juice
juice of 3 limes
2 tbs (30 ml) virgin olive oil
2 medium onions, minced
6 garlic cloves, minced
2 tbs (30 ml) fresh red chile peppers,
    chopped
¼ cup (60 ml) cilantro, minced
1 oz (30 ml) tequila
salt, to taste
fresh cracked black pepper, to taste

6 **HEALTH SEA Salmon Sausages**

Combine ingredients for glaze; and salsa.
   Grill salmon sausages 2-8 minutes, turning and brushing on Glaze every minute or so. Remove when lightly browned and hot. Cut into thin slices. Serve with Tequila Salsa. Both are spicy. Adjust to your taste. Serves 8.

*Approximate nutritional analysis per serving w/ 1 generous tbs glaze:
Calories 223, Protein 20 g, Carbohydrates 21 g, Fat 6 g, Cholesterol 30 mg,
Sodium 1328 mg*

MUSTARD-GLAZED GRILLED SALMON SAUSAGE

STEAMED HALIBUT WITH GARLIC & GINGER

6 tbs (90 ml) SPECTRUM WORLD
   EATS Thai Oil
1 tbs (15 ml) garlic, finely minced
2 tsp (10 ml) ginger, finely minced
2 tbs (30 ml) soy sauce or first press
   fish sauce (nam pla)
1 tbs lime juice
4 6-oz (720 g) halibut filets or other
   firm white fish, skinless and
   boneless
16 large cilantro leaves
lime wedges for garnish

BAKED DILLED SALMON ON RICE

BAKED DILLED SALMON ON RICE

olive oil cooking spray
1 medium onion, chopped
3 cloves garlic, minced
3 medium tomatoes, diced
½ lb (230 g) mushrooms, sliced
3 tbs (45 ml) lemon juice
3 tbs (45 ml) GREEN HOUSE
   Fresh Dill, chopped
salt, to taste
pepper, to taste
2 cups (480 ml) cooked brown rice
4 6-oz (720 g) salmon filets

Gently warm Thai oil in a small skillet. Add garlic and ginger, cook slowly over low heat for 2 minutes. Add the soy sauce and lime juice, stir well. Simmer 1 minute more. Remove from heat. Arrange the fish filets in a steamer basket, simmer until just cooked through, no more than 5 minutes. Place filets onto 4 warm plates and spoon the finished sauce over them. Garnish with fresh cilantro and lime wedges. Serves 4.

Approximate nutritional analysis per serving:
Calories 372, Protein 36 g, Carbohydrates 1 g, Fat 25 g, Cholesterol 54 mg, Sodium 263 mg

Coat a nonstick skillet with olive oil cooking spray. Sauté onion, garlic, tomatoes and mushrooms for 5 minutes or until softened. Add lemon juice and fresh dill. Remove from heat. Add salt and pepper to taste. Spray a baking dish with olive oil spray. Spread rice evenly over the bottom. Top rice with salmon. Cover each filet with vegetable mixture. Cover pan with foil. Bake for 20 minutes at 350°F (180°C). Serves 4.

Approximate nutritional analysis per serving:
Calories 405, Protein 42 g, Carbohydrates 34 g, Fat 12 g, Cholesterol 65 mg, Sodium 230 mg

THAI-FLAVORED SCALLOPS WITH GREEN BEANS

¾ lb (340 g) sea scallops or
    peeled shrimp
2 cups (480 ml) green beans,
    chopped
2 tbs (30 ml) CALIFORNIA
    CLASSICS Peanut Oil
1 small jalapeño pepper,
    chopped finely
½ red bell pepper, cut into strips
1 tbs (15 ml) CALIFORNIA
    CLASSICS Garlic Oil
⅓ cup (80 ml) loosely packed
    chopped fresh cilantro
    or ½ tsp (3 ml) CALIFORNIA
    CLASSICS Pesto Oil

Peel off tough muscle on one side of scallops, if present; pat scallops dry between paper towels.

Place beans in microwave dish. Add 2 tbs water; cover and cook on high for 8 minutes. Drain off water.

Heat skillet until very hot; if skillet is not hot enough, scallops will give off water and boil instead of browning. Add peanut oil and stir-fry scallops just until they are no longer translucent; remove from skillet and set aside. Add jalapeño, beans, red pepper and garlic oil; stir-fry for 2 minutes. Return scallops to skillet; sprinkle with cilantro or pesto oil and toss all ingredients for an additional ½ minute. Serves 4.

Approximate nutritional analysis per serving:
Calories 203, Protein 15 g, Carbohydrates 7 g, Fat 13 g, Cholesterol 27 mg, Sodium 192 mg

THAI-FLAVORED SCALLOPS WITH GREEN BEANS

SWEET & SOUR FISH

1 cup (240 ml) carrots, julienned
½ cup (120 ml) thinly sliced celery
½ cup (120 ml) thinly sliced onion
2 tsp (10 ml) vegetable oil
½ cup (120 ml) orange juice
¼ cup (60 ml) honey
1 tsp (5 ml) grated fresh ginger root
½ tsp (3 ml) salt
pinch black pepper
pinch cayenne pepper
1½ lbs (683 g) halibut steaks or
    snapper filets

Stir-fry vegetables in oil in medium skillet until crisp-tender. Add orange juice, honey and seasonings; bring mixture to a boil. Arrange fish in 13x9x2-inch oiled baking pan. Spoon vegetable mixture over fish. Bake covered at 425°F (220°C) allowing 10 minutes per inch of thickness of fish or until fish flakes when tested with a fork. Serves 4.

Approximate nutritional analysis per serving:
Calories 307, Protein 36 g, Carbohydrates 26 g, Fat 6 g, Cholesterol 54 mg, Sodium 383 mg

Courtesy of The National Honey Board.

SWEET & SOUR FISH

CREAM OF RYE SALMON LOAF

16-oz can (480 g) salmon with liquid
½ cup (120 ml) ROMAN MEAL
    Cream of Rye
2 tbs (30 ml) fresh chopped parsley
    or 1 tsp (5 ml) dry parsley flakes
2 tbs (30 ml) finely chopped onion
1 tsp (5 ml) prepared mustard
2 eggs, beaten
1 cup (240 ml) skim milk

Combine and bake in greased loaf pan at 350°F (180°C) for 35-40 minutes Serves 6.

Approximate nutritional analysis per serving:
Calories 171, Protein 19 g, Carbohydrates 6 g, Fat 7 g, Cholesterol 96 mg, Sodium 515 mg

ROAST CHICKEN WITH FRESH SAGE

1 pkg GREEN HOUSE Fresh Sage,
    chopped
10 gloves garlic, chopped
3-lb (1.4 kg) roasting chicken
juice of 1 lemon
salt, to taste
pepper, to taste

Mix fresh sage and garlic. Remove giblets and stuff sage mixture under the skin of the chicken. Place chicken in a shallow baking dish. Squeeze lemon juice in body cavity and over chicken. Season with salt and pepper to taste. Bake at 375°F (190°C) for 1 hour and 15 minutes until golden brown. Serves 4.

Approximate nutritional analysis per serving:
Calories 661, Protein 99 g, Carbohydrates 4 g, Fat 25 g, Cholesterol 304 mg, Sodium 293 mg

ROAST CHICKEN WITH FRESH SAGE

ROASTED CHICKEN IN HONEY-CHIPOTLE SAUCE WITH BAKED PLANTAINS

3-lb (1.4 kg) roasting chicken
pepper

HONEY-CHIPOTLE SAUCE:
4 FRIEDA'S Dried Chipotle Chiles,
 reconstituted, drained and
 minced
⅔ cup (160 ml) lime juice
¼ cup (60 ml) honey
2 tbs (30 ml) FRIEDA'S Fresh
 Cilantro, minced
1 tsp (5 ml) ground cumin
1 tsp (5 ml) peanut oil
1 tsp (5 ml) Dijon mustard
2 cloves garlic, minced

4 FRIEDA'S Plantains,
 yellow-skinned

Wash chicken; pat dry. Sprinkle with pepper; place on roasting rack in a shallow roasting pan. Cover; bake in 350°F (180°C) oven for 45 minutes. Meanwhile, prepare the sauce.

Honey-Chipotle Sauce: In food processor or blender, process chiles with lime juice, honey, cilantro, cumin, peanut oil, mustard and garlic until well combined. Halve plantains lengthwise; arrange in a lightly oiled baking dish. Brush plantains liberally with Sauce mixture; cover and place in oven with bird, allowing approximately 45 minutes to cook. After the first 45 minutes, uncover chicken; brush with some of the sauce. Continue roasting chicken uncovered, with plantains, for 15-30 minutes more or until done, brushing chicken frequently with sauce. Recover bird if skin becomes too brown. Serve chicken and plantains drizzled with remaining sauce. Serves 4.

Approximate nutritional analysis per serving:
Calories 650, Protein 68 g, Carbohydrates 56 g, Fat 18 g, Cholesterol 202 mg, Sodium 782 mg

ROASTED CHICKEN IN HONEY-CHIPOTLE SAUCE WITH BAKED PLANTAINS

SESAME CHICKEN WITH MANGO SWEET & SOUR SAUCE

MANGO SWEET & SOUR SAUCE:
2 tbs (30 ml) SPECTRUM
   NATURALS Organic Unrefined
   Toasted Sesame Oil
1 tsp (5 ml) minced garlic
1 tsp (5 ml) minced ginger
4 tbs (60 ml) SPECTRUM
   NATURALS Organic Mango
   Vinegar
4 tbs (60 ml) honey
1 tbs (15 ml) tamari soy sauce
1 tsp (5 ml) arrowroot

SESAME CHICKEN:
4 tsp (20 ml) SPECTRUM
   NATURALS Organic Canola Oil
4 boneless, skinless, free-range
   chicken breasts
1 bunch green onions,
   cut into 1-inch long pieces
1 large ripe mango, peeled and
   cut into 1-inch cubes
freshly ground pepper
2 tsp (10 ml) sesame seeds

Mango Sweet and Sour Sauce: Heat the sesame oil in a 10-inch skillet over medium heat. Add the garlic and ginger and sauté for 30 seconds. Add the vinegar, honey and tamari sauce. Bring to a boil and stir constantly for 30 seconds more. Remove from the heat and transfer to a small container. Reserve. Yields ½ cup.

Sesame Chicken: Rinse out the pan and return to heat. Add canola oil. When the oil is hot, add the chicken breasts and sauté gently, about 4 minutes. Turn the chicken breasts and add the green onions. Continue to cook for 2 minutes longer and then add the mango. Continue to cook until the chicken is done. Toss the mango and the onion during this time until they are cooked through. Remove from the heat and pour off any excess fat from the pan. Combine arrowroot with cooled Mango Sweet and Sour Sauce. Pour the Sauce over the chicken and return to the heat for several minutes.

Remove from the heat and arrange the chicken, mango and onions equally among 4 plates. Cover each breast with the remaining Sauce, season with pepper and sprinkle with sesame seeds. Serve immediately. Serves 4.

Approximate nutritional analysis per serving:
Calories 384, Protein 28 g, Carbohydrates 34 g, Fat 16 g, Cholesterol 72 mg, Sodium 324 mg

**SESAME CHICKEN WITH
MANGO SWEET & SOUR SAUCE**

SOY-HONEY CHICKEN

½ cup (120 ml) DAWES HILL
   Wildflower Honey
½ cup (120 ml) tamari soy sauce
⅓ cup (80 ml) dry sherry or water
1 tsp (5 ml) grated fresh ginger root
   or 2 tsp (10 ml) ground ginger
1 medium clove garlic, crushed
2½-lb (1.1 kg) broiler-fryer chicken,
   cut into serving-size pieces

Combine honey, soy sauce, sherry, ginger root and garlic in a small bowl. Place chicken in large glass baking dish. Pour honey marinade over chicken, turning chicken to coat. Cover dish and place in refrigerator. Marinate at least 6 hours, turning to coat 2 or 3 times.

Remove chicken from marinade; reserve marinade. Arrange chicken on oven roasting pan. Cover with foil. Bake at 350°F (180°C) for 30 minutes. Bring reserved marinade to a boil in small saucepan over medium heat; simmer at slow boil for 3 minutes. Set aside.

Uncover chicken; brush with marinade. Bake uncovered, 30-45 minutes longer or until juices run clear and chicken is no longer pink, brushing occasionally with marinade. Serves 4.

Approximate nutritional analysis per serving:
Calories 491, Protein 63 g, Carbohydrates 39 g, Fat 9 g, Cholesterol 198 mg, Sodium 2276 mg

SOY-HONEY CHICKEN

RATATOUILLE-TOPPED CHICKEN

1 tbs (15 ml) olive oil
1 medium onion, chopped
2 cloves garlic, minced
½ red bell pepper, chopped
½ green bell pepper, chopped
1 small eggplant, cubed
14-oz can (420 g) chopped tomatoes
1 yellow squash, sliced
1 zucchini, sliced
2 tbs (30 ml) GREEN HOUSE
   Fresh Oregano
pepper, to taste
4 chicken breasts, boneless, skinless
olive oil cooking spray
½ lb (230 g) favorite pasta, cooked
   and drained

Coat a nonstick skillet with olive oil. Add onions, garlic, peppers and eggplant. Sauté 10 minutes until soft. Add the next 5 ingredients. Cover and simmer for 15 minutes. Preheat oven to 350°F (180°C). While sauce is simmering, brown chicken breasts in skillet sprayed with olive oil cooking spray, about 3 minutes on each side. Place in baking dish, set aside and keep warm. Cover chicken with sauce, cover with foil and bake 15 minutes. Serve over pasta. Serves 4.

Vegetarian Variation: Omit chicken and serve over rice or pasta.

Approximate nutritional analysis per serving w/ chicken:
Calories 478, Protein 37 g, Carbohydrates 64 g, Fat 9 g, Cholesterol 66 mg, Sodium 241 mg

Approximate nutritional analysis per serving w/o chicken:
Calories 337, Protein 11 g, Carbohydrates 64 g, Fat 5 g, Cholesterol 0 mg, Sodium 180 mg

BAKED CHICKEN OR TURKEY WITH POULTRY BOUQUET

cooking spray
1 tbs (15 ml) olive oil
½ cup (120 ml) onion, diced
½ cup (120 ml) celery, diced
1 tbs (15 ml) fresh garlic, chopped
6 oz (180 g) mushrooms, crimini or portabello, if available
1 pkg GREEN HOUSE Poultry Bouquet, leaves chopped
1½ lbs (683 g) chicken breasts or turkey breast, boneless and skinless
fresh ground black pepper, to taste
2 cups (480 ml) broccoli florets, steamed

Preheat oven to 350°F (180°C). Spray nonstick skillet with cooking spray. Heat half the oil, add onion, celery and garlic and sauté for 5 minutes. Add the mushrooms and half the herbs and cook another 2 minutes. Transfer to a shallow baking dish. Add remaining oil to the skillet and brown the poultry, about 2 minutes per side. Place poultry over mushroom mixture and cover with foil. Bake for 15 minutes. Serve poultry on a bed of the mushroom mix, season with black pepper to taste and sprinkle with remaining chopped fresh herbs. Serve broccoli on the side. Serves 4.

Approximate nutritional analysis per serving:
Calories 263, Protein 39 g, Carbohydrates 7 g, Fat 8 g, Cholesterol 93 mg, Sodium 110 mg

ROSEMARY-LEMON CHICKEN

1 lb (455 g) baby red potatoes
1 lb (455 g) carrots, peeled
4 chicken breasts, skin removed
½ cup (120 ml) lemon juice
1 tsp (5 ml) lemon peel, finely grated
2 tbs (30 ml) honey
2 tbs (30 ml) vegetable oil
2 tbs (30 ml) GREEN HOUSE Fresh Rosemary, leaves chopped

ROSEMARY-LEMON CHICKEN

Parboil potatoes and carrots about 5 minutes. Rinse in cool water, drain and set aside. Marinate chicken in rest of ingredients for 30 minutes to several hours. Cover and bake at 375°F (190°C) for 30 minutes. Remove cover, add potatoes and carrots and bake for another 20 minutes. Serves 4.

Approximate nutritional analysis per serving:
Calories 412, Protein 30 g, Carbohydrates 50 g, Fat 11 g, Cholesterol 66 mg, Sodium 116 mg

BAKED CHICKEN OR TURKEY WITH POULTRY BOUQUET

APRICOT & GINGER CHICKEN

1 cup (240 ml) R. W. KNUDSEN
   FAMILY Apricot Nectar
2 tbs (30 ml) honey
½ cup (120 ml) soy sauce
2 tbs (30 ml) fresh ground ginger
4 cloves garlic, crushed
1 tsp (5 ml) chile oil, optional
3 lbs (1.4 kg) chicken, cut up

APRICOT & GINGER CHICKEN

Mix first 6 ingredients together. Cover chicken with half of the marinade and marinate 2 hours or longer.

Preheat oven to 375°F (190°C). Bake chicken, with half the marinade, uncovered in an ovenproof dish. Bring the other half of the marinade to a boil and simmer until it thickens. Use this to baste chicken. Bake until done, basting frequently. Serves 6.

Approximate nutritional analysis per serving:
Calories 544, Protein 44 g, Carbohydrates 13 g, Fat 34 g,
Cholesterol 170 mg, Sodium 1536 mg

**Opposite: ARUGULA-STUFFED
CHICKEN ROLLS**

ARUGULA-STUFFED CHICKEN ROLLS

4 boneless chicken breasts
1 pkg GREEN HOUSE Fresh
   Arugula, heavy stems removed
fresh ground black pepper
2 tbs (30 ml) butter or margarine
½ cup (120 ml) chicken broth
½ cup (120 ml) dry white wine
½ lb (230 g) mushrooms, sliced
4 green onions, sliced

Lay chicken breasts skin side down. Pound each to an even ½-inch thickness. Divide arugula into 4 portions and place one portion on each breast. Roll breast jelly roll-style and secure with toothpicks. Season with pepper. Sauté in 1 tbs butter until golden brown, about 4 minutes. Add broth, wine, mushrooms and green onions. Reduce heat, cover and simmer until meat is no longer pink inside, 10-12 minutes.

Transfer chicken to a warm platter and keep warm. Bring cooking liquid, mushrooms and green onions to a boil until reduced by half. Add 1 tbs butter, stir until butter is melted. Pour sauce over chicken. Serves 4.

Approximate nutritional analysis per serving:
Calories 224, Protein 29 g, Carbohydrates 4 g, Fat 8 g, Cholesterol 84 mg,
Sodium 238 mg

WEHANI RICE-STUFFED CHICKEN BREASTS

4 chicken breast halves,
   boneless and skinless
½ tsp (3 ml) ground black pepper
¼ tsp (1 ml) salt
1 cup (240 ml) cooked LUNDBERG
   WEHANI Rice
¼ cup (60 ml) minced tomato
¼ cup (60 ml) shredded mozzarella
   cheese
1 tbs (15 ml) chopped fresh basil
   or 2 tbs (30 ml) dry basil
vegetable cooking spray

Pound chicken breasts until ¼-inch thick. Season insides of meat with ¼ tsp pepper and salt. Combine rice, tomato, cheese, basil and remaining ¼ tsp pepper. Spoon rice mixture on top of chicken; fold over and secure sides with wooden toothpicks soaked in water. Wipe off outside of chicken breasts with paper towel.

   Coat a large skillet with cooking spray and place over medium-high heat until hot. Cook chicken 2 minutes on each side or until just golden brown. Transfer chicken to shallow baking pan. Bake at 350°F (180°C) for 20 minutes. Serves 4.

Approximate nutritional analysis per serving:
Calories 223, Protein 30 g, Carbohydrates 12 g, Fat 5 g, Cholesterol 79 mg, Sodium 337 mg

WEHANI RICE-STUFFED CHICKEN BREASTS

JAMAICAN JERK CHICKEN

1 FRIEDA'S Dried Habañero Chile,
   reconstituted, seeded and
   coarsely chopped
2 tbs (30 ml) prepared yellow
   mustard
2 tbs (30 ml) FRIEDA'S Fresh
   Rosemary
2 tbs (30 ml) FRIEDA'S Fresh Basil,
   torn
2 tbs (30 ml) FRIEDA'S Fresh Thyme
⅓ cup (80 ml) chopped green onion
1 clove garlic, quartered
1 tsp (5 ml) salt
¼ tsp (1 ml) pepper
2 tbs (30 ml) lime juice
4 chicken breasts, bone-in, or thighs
   with legs attached, skinless

In a small food processor or blender, mix chopped chile and all ingredients except chicken; blend well. Arrange chicken in a nonmetal dish. Brush ¾ of the mixture over the chicken; cover. Refrigerate chicken and leftover chile mixture for 2-6 hours.

   Arrange chicken pieces on broiler pan or grill. Grill or broil chicken, 4 inches from heat, for 25-30 minutes, or until juices run clear, turning once and brushing with remaining chile mixture. Serves 4.

Approximate nutritional analysis per serving:
Calories 146, Protein 28 g, Carbohydrates 3 g, Fat 2 g, Cholesterol 68 mg, Sodium 923 mg

JAMAICAN JERK CHICKEN

PACIFIC CHICKEN, SHRIMP & KIWI FRUIT KEBABS

LIME-GINGER MARINADE:
6 tbs (90 ml) lime juice
3 tbs (45 ml) honey
2 tbs (30 ml) rice vinegar
2 tbs (30 ml) olive oil
1½ tsp (8 ml) chopped cilantro
1 tsp (5 ml) grated fresh ginger root
¼ tsp (1 ml) red hot pepper flakes

½ lb (230 g) chicken breasts,
  boneless and skinless,
  cut into 16 1-inch pieces
1 large red bell pepper, cored and
  cut into 16 pieces
1 small red onion, cut into 16 pieces
6 whole New Zealand kiwi fruits,
  peeled and quartered
16 peeled frozen shrimp

Lime-Ginger Marinade: Whisk together ingredients until well combined.

Toss chicken, peppers and onions with Lime-Ginger Marinade; marinate 1-2 hours in refrigerator. When ready to cook, toss kiwi fruit and shrimp with other ingredients to coat with Marinade. Divide ingredients among 8 skewers.* Grill or broil, 3-4 minutes per side, turning skewers once, until chicken and shrimp are cooked through. Serves 4.

*Note: If using wooden skewers, soak in water for 15 minutes prior to assembling meat and vegetables.

Approximate nutritional analysis per serving:
Calories 294, Protein 20 g, Carbohydrates 38 g, Fat 8 g, Cholesterol 80 mg, Sodium 99 mg

Courtesy of The National Honey Board.

MOROCCAN CHICKEN TAJINE

MOROCCAN CHICKEN TAJINE

8 chicken thighs, skinless
¼ cup (60 ml) honey
1 large onion, chopped
3 cloves garlic, minced
2 cinnamon sticks, 3 inches each
1 lemon, juiced
2 tsp (10 ml) turmeric
½ cup (120 ml) dried apricots,
  quartered

Arrange chicken thighs in bottom of Dutch oven. Pour honey over chicken; sprinkle with onion and then with minced garlic. Add cinnamon sticks and sprinkle with lemon juice and turmeric. Top with apricot quarters and bake in 350°F (180°C) for about 1 hour or until fork can be inserted in chicken with ease. Remove cinnamon sticks from chicken mixture and serve with rice or couscous. Serves 4.

Approximate nutritional analysis per serving w/o rice:
Calories 290, Protein 29 g, Carbohydrates 33 g, Fat 6 g, Cholesterol 115 mg, Sodium 123 mg

Courtesy of The National Honey Board.

BLACK JAPONICA WITH CHICKEN & ROSEMARY

2 cloves garlic, minced
2 tbs (30 ml) olive oil
1 cup (240 ml) LUNDBERG BLACK
    JAPONICA Rice
½ lb (230 g) mushrooms, sliced
8 oz (240 g) chicken breast, boneless
    and skinless, cut into pieces
1 bouillon cube
½ tsp (3 ml) rosemary
½ tsp (3 ml) black pepper
1 cup (240 ml) water
½ cup (120 ml) sherry, optional

In a deep 4-quart saucepan, with tight-fitting lid, sauté garlic in olive oil briefly. Add rice and sauté until rice is coated in oil. Turn heat to medium-high. Add mushrooms and cook until tender. Add chicken and cook for 5 minutes. Add remaining ingredients, turn heat to low, cover and simmer for 45 minutes. Serves 4.

Approximate nutritional analysis per serving:
Calories 318, Protein 20 g, Carbohydrates 43 g, Fat 13 g, Cholesterol 33 mg, Sodium 241 mg

BLACK JAPONICA WITH CHICKEN & ROSEMARY

ITALIAN CHICKEN & RICE

cooking oil spray
2 whole chicken breasts, deboned
    and cut into slices
½ lb (230 g) zucchini, thinly sliced
½ cup (120 ml) chopped green onion
16-oz can (480 g) tomatoes,
    chopped, liquid reserved
3 cups (720 ml) cooked TEXMATI
    Light Brown Rice
¼ cup (60 ml) chopped parsley
½ tsp (3 ml) salt
¼ tsp (1 ml) pepper
pinch of oregano

Coat large skillet with cooking oil spray. Sauté chicken until lightly browned. Add zucchini; cook until crisp-tender. Stir in remaining ingredients. Cover, reduce heat, simmer 15 minutes or until heated through. Serve 4.

Approximate nutritional analysis per serving:
Calories 409, Protein 18 g, Carbohydrates 77 g, Fat 3 g, Cholesterol 23 mg, Sodium 335 mg

ITALIAN CHICKEN & RICE

ARTICHOKE CHICKEN

2 tbs (30 ml) butter
1½ cups (360 g) mushrooms, sliced
13¾-oz can (413 ml) chicken broth
16-oz jar (480 g) marinated
    artichoke hearts, juice reserved
3 chicken breasts, split, skinned
    and boned
1 cup (240 ml) STONYFIELD FARM
    Plain Nonfat Yogurt

In a medium-size frying pan, melt butter. Add the mushrooms and sauté until wilted.

In a large skillet, mix the chicken broth with the juice from the artichoke hearts; bring to a boil. Add the chicken, cover and poach for 20 minutes, turning the chicken occasionally. Remove the chicken from the pan and place it in a covered dish to keep it warm. Reduce the liquid in the pan by half. Add the artichoke hearts and mushrooms and stir. Reduce heat and add the yogurt mixing gently. Pour over the warm chicken. Serve with rice pilaf. Serves 6.

Approximate nutritional analysis per serving w/o rice:
Calories 162, Protein 19 g, Carbohydrates 14 g, Fat 4 g, Cholesterol 35 mg, Sodium 429 mg

CHICKEN IN RED CURRY SAUCE

2 tbs (30 ml) curry powder
1 tbs (15 ml) ground coriander
2 tsp (10 ml) paprika
½ tsp (3 ml) turmeric
pinch salt
4 tsp (20 ml) SPECTRUM WORLD
    EATS Thai Oil
4 free-range chicken breasts,
    skinless
2 tbs (30 ml) SPECTRUM
    NATURALS Unrefined Peanut or
    Sesame Oil
1 small onion, minced
1 tbs (15 ml) fresh ginger, minced
2 cloves garlic, minced
1 cup (240 ml) water
salt, to taste
fresh ground pepper, to taste

Combine curry powder, coriander, paprika, turmeric and pinch of salt in a 2-quart bowl. Whisk in Thai oil. Add the chicken breasts and coat them evenly. Cover and refrigerate for at least 30 minutes. In a large skillet, heat peanut oil. Add onion and sauté 3 minutes. Add ginger and garlic. Cook 2 minutes more. Add the chicken breasts and the marinade. Add water, cover and simmer 4 minutes. Remove from heat and correct the seasonings, serve piping hot over plain rice. Serves 4.

Approximate nutritional analysis per serving w/o rice:
Calories 232, Protein 27 g, Carbohydrates .5 g, Fat 13 g, Cholesterol 68 mg, Sodium 77 mg

ARTICHOKE CHICKEN

INDIAN ROCK'S INCREDIBLE LOW-FAT CHICKEN POT PIE

4-5 lb (1.8-2.3 kg) chicken
1 lb (455 g) fresh pearl onions
1 lb (455 g) carrots, cut into
　½-inch chunks
1 lb (455 g) asparagus
1 lb (455 g) fresh or frozen peas
1 tsp (5 ml) olive oil
1 tsp (5 ml) butter
½ lb (230 g) yellow finn potatoes,
　peeled and thinly sliced
1 lb (455 g) celery root, peeled and
　thinly sliced
1 cup (240 ml) parsnips, peeled and
　thinly sliced
2 leeks, white only, thinly sliced
2 garlic cloves
sprig of fresh thyme
¾ cup water
3 cups (720 ml) chicken stock
salt, to taste
pepper, to taste

PASTRY CUT-OUTS:
1 cup (240 ml) flour
1 tsp (5 ml) sugar
½ tsp (3 ml) salt
4 tbs (60 ml) unsalted butter,
　softened
3 tbs (45 ml) low-calorie sour cream
1½ tsp water

Roast chicken until done, about 1 hour. Allow to cool.

Pastry Cut-Outs: Place flour in a large bowl or on work surface. Spoon sugar and salt over it. Cut butter into flour until mixture is the texture of cornmeal. Spoon sour cream and 1½ tsp water over top. Mix with fork to incorporate sour cream. Using your hands form dough into a ball. Refrigerate 1 hour before rolling out. Roll dough and cut into desired shapes. Place on baking sheet. Freeze for 15 minutes. Bake 10-12 minutes at 425°F (220°C).

While chicken is cooking and dough is resting in refrigerator, bring a large pot of water to a boil. Cook pearl onions 5-7 minutes. Drain and run under cold water. When cool enough, peel and set aside. Cook carrots until crisp-tender. Cook asparagus 3 minutes and drain.

To make sauce, combine olive oil, butter, potatoes, celery root, parsnips, leeks, garlic, thyme, ¾ cup water. Cover and simmer until water is almost evaporated, 15-20 minutes. Add the chicken stock and bring to a simmer. Cook covered until vegetables are very tender. Discard the thyme. Transfer to food processor or blender. Process until smooth. Season with salt and pepper. Remove meat from chicken and discard skin and bones.

Combine chicken and vegetable sauce and add peas; transfer to a casserole. Bake 30 minutes or until bubbly. Take out of oven and arrange Pastry Cut-Outs over top. Serves 10.

Approximate nutritional analysis per serving:
Calories 451, Protein 47 g, Carbohydrates 37 g, Fat 13 g,
Cholesterol 142 mg, Sodium 705 mg

**INDIAN ROCK'S INCREDIBLE
LOW-FAT CHICKEN POT PIE**

CHICKEN SALTIMBOCCA

6 4-oz pieces (720 g) chicken breast, pounded into cutlets
6 thin slices prosciutto, cut to match chicken cutlets
1 cup (240 ml) cooked spinach, well drained
3 cloves garlic, crushed
2 tbs (30 ml) Parmesan or Romano cheese, grated
3 tbs (45 ml) CHESHIRE GARDEN Blenda d'Italia or Italia Piccante Vinegar
3 tbs (45 ml) olive oil

Lay out the chicken cutlets with the prosciutto on top.

Mix spinach, garlic, cheese and 1 tbs Blenda d'Italia. Place a dollop of the mixture on the center of each cutlet, fold, and skewer with toothpicks.

Heat the oil in a heavy skillet, brown the rolled cutlets in oil, turning until cooked through, 6-8 minutes per side.

Add remaining 2 tbs Blenda d'Italia and raise the heat. Deglaze pan by scraping the browned food and mixing it into the vinegar. Use as sauce. Serves 6.

Approximate nutritional analysis per serving:
Calories 250, Protein 34 g, Carbohydrates 2 g, Fat 11 g, Cholesterol 84 mg, Sodium 408 mg

GREEK ISLAND CHICKEN

4 chicken breast halves, skinless
2 tbs (30 ml) olive oil
1 onion, chopped
3 cloves garlic, minced
1 red bell pepper, cut into strips
1 cup (240 ml) dried tomato halves
1½ cups (355 ml) dry white wine
⅓ cup (80 ml) sliced pitted black olives
1 lemon, sliced
1½ tsp (8 ml) cinnamon
1 tsp (5 ml) honey
½ tsp (3 ml) pepper
salt, to taste
dried parsley, chopped, for garnish

In large skillet, cook chicken breasts in olive oil over medium heat, about 5 minutes, turning once. Add onion, garlic and red pepper. Cook, stirring often, about 4 minutes until onions are limp. With kitchen shears, halve tomato pieces; stir into skillet with remaining ingredients except parsley. Cover and simmer 15 minutes. Remove cover and cook 5 more minutes until chicken is tender and sauce is slightly reduced. Sprinkle with chopped parsley. Serve over rice pilaf, if desired. Serves 4.

Approximate nutritional analysis per serving:
Calories 323, Protein 30 g, Carbohydrates 16 g, Fat 10 g, Cholesterol 68 mg, Sodium 444 mg

Courtesy of The National Honey Board.

CHICKEN SALTIMBOCCA

GINGER TURKEY STIR-FRY

2 cups (480 ml) boiling water
1 cup (240 ml) cracked bulgur wheat
⅓ cup (80 ml) water
2 tbs (30 ml) fresh lemon juice
2 tbs (30 ml) honey
1 tsp (5 ml) grated fresh ginger root
1 tbs (15 ml) low-sodium soy sauce
1 large clove minced garlic
2 tbs (30 ml) cornstarch
1 tbs (15 ml) vegetable oil
2 cups (480 ml) diagonally
    sliced carrots
2 cups (480 ml) broccoli florets
2 cups (480 ml) sliced mushrooms
8-oz can (240 g) sliced water
    chestnuts
1 lb (455 g) turkey breast cutlets,
    cut ½x2-inch strips

Pour boiling water over cracked wheat and let stand 1 hour; drain
    Combine water, lemon juice, honey, ginger, soy sauce and garlic. Dissolve cornstarch in mixture; set aside.
    Heat oil over high heat in wok or large skillet. Add carrots; stir-fry 3 minutes or until tender-crisp. Add broccoli, mushrooms and water chestnuts; stir-fry about 2 more minutes. Remove from pan.
    Stir-fry turkey until lightly browned. Add sauce and cook, stirring constantly, until thickened and translucent. Add vegetables; heat throughout. Serve over cracked wheat. Serves 4.

Approximate nutritional analysis per serving:
Calories 315, Protein 29 g, Carbohydrates 44 g, Fat 4 g, Cholesterol 63 mg, Sodium 160 mg

Courtesy of The National Honey Board.

LUNDBERG BLACK JAPONICA STIR-FRY

2 tbs (30 ml) teriyaki sauce
½ lb (230 g) chicken breast,
    boneless and skinless,
    cut into bite-size pieces
1 tbs (15 ml) oil
2-4 cups (480-960 ml) vegetables,
    fresh or frozen, cut into
    bite-size pieces
1 cup (240 ml) LUNDBERG BLACK
    JAPONICA Rice, cooked

Sprinkle teriyaki over chicken bits. Let stand for 10 minutes. Heat oil in wok or deep heavy fry pan on medium-high heat. Stir-fry chicken bits for 5-10 minutes and remove from pan. Stir-fry vegetables until tender-crisp. Add rice and continue to stir-fry. Add cooked chicken briefly. Serves 4.

Approximate nutritional analysis per serving:
Calories 316, Protein 21 g, Carbohydrates 50 g, Fat 9 g, Cholesterol 33 mg, Sodium 69 mg

TURKEY FAJITAS

½ lb (230 g) breast of turkey
5 tsp (25 ml) vegetable oil, divided
1 tbs (15 ml) lemon juice
1 clove garlic, crushed
¾ tsp (4 ml) chile pepper
½ tsp (3 ml) dried oregano leaves
½ large yellow bell pepper,
    cut into 1-inch pieces
8 strips green bell pepper
1 medium tomato, cut into
    12 wedges
4 MILL VALLEY Tostada Bowls
salsa for topping

Cut turkey into thin slices and then into strips about ¾-inch wide. In medium bowl, combine 3 tsp of the oil, with the lemon juice, garlic, chile pepper and oregano. Add turkey and stir to coat. Let stand ½ hour.

Heat remaining 2 tsp oil in large nonstick skillet over medium-high heat. Add yellow and green peppers; stir-fry 2 minutes. Add turkey strips and stir-fry another 3 minutes. Stir in tomato; heat 1 minute more.

Preheat tostada bowls for 3-5 minutes in a 350°F (180°C) oven and fill with ingredients. Top with salsa. Serves 4.

Approximate nutritional analysis per serving:
Calories 245, Protein 19 g, Carbohydrates 18 g, Fat 11 g, Cholesterol 47 mg, Sodium 43 mg

TURKEY FAJITAS

MICROWAVE STIR-FRY WITH CHICKEN

1 tbs (15 ml) oil
1 tbs (15 ml) butter
3 medium onions, quartered
1 green pepper, cut into
    ¼-inch strips
3 cups (720 ml) cabbage, sliced thin
1 cup (240 ml) carrots,
    sliced diagonally
¼ cup (60 ml) sliced green onions
1 cup (240 ml) cauliflower florets
1 cup (240 ml) ANDY BOY
    Broccoli Florets
3 stalks celery, sliced diagonally
10-oz pkg (300 g) frozen pea pods
½ cup (120 ml) cooked chicken
½ cup (120 ml) sliced mushrooms

Put oil, butter and onions into a 3-quart casserole. Microwave uncovered on high for 3 minutes until hot. Mix in peppers, cabbage, carrots, onions, cauliflower, broccoli, celery and pea pods. Microwave on high, covered, for 4 minutes. Add chicken and mushrooms. Microwave uncovered for 4-6 minutes more. Serves 6.

Approximate nutritional analysis per serving:
Calories 126, Protein 7 g, Carbohydrates 16 g, Fat 5 g, Cholesterol 13 mg, Sodium 57 mg

**MICROWAVE STIR-FRY
WITH CHICKEN**

STUFFED PEPPERS

4 medium green peppers
olive oil cooking spray
¾ lb (360 g) lean ground turkey
1 medium onion, chopped
2 cloves garlic, minced
½-1 tsp (3-5 ml) black pepper, t
  o taste
2 tbs (30 ml) GREEN HOUSE
  Fresh Tarragon, chopped
2 cups (480 ml) cooked rice
8-oz can (240 ml) tomato sauce
4 tbs (60 ml) Parmesan cheese,
  grated

VEGETARIAN VARIATION:
2 cups (480 ml) canned black beans,
  rinsed and drained

STUFFED PEPPERS

Cut off pepper tops and remove seeds. Chop tops, discarding stem. Set aside. Bring large saucepan of water to boil. Immerse peppers; boil 5 minutes. Drain and set aside. Spray large, nonstick fry pan with olive oil spray and sauté chopped pepper tops, turkey, onion, garlic, black pepper and fresh tarragon until turkey is browned. Add rice and all but 4 tbs of tomato sauce. Mix well. Fill peppers with mixture. Place in baking dish. Top with 4 tbs tomato sauce and Parmesan. Serves 4.

Vegetarian Variation: Omit turkey and add beans.

Approximate nutritional analysis per serving w/ turkey:
Calories 358, Protein 24 g, Carbohydrates 41 g, Fat 11 g, Cholesterol 61 mg, Sodium 168 mg

Approximate nutritional analysis per vegetarian serving :
Calories 336, Protein 15 g, Carbohydrates 65 g, Fat 3 g, Cholesterol 4 mg, Sodium 332 mg

TURKEY MEATBALLS WITH LEMON SAUCE

1 cup (240 ml) cooked WOLFF'S
  Kasha, any granulation
1 beaten egg
1 tsp (5 ml) Worcestershire sauce
1 tsp (5 ml) grated lemon peel
1½ lbs (683 g) ground raw turkey
2 tbs (30 ml) cooking oil
1 cup (240 ml) chicken or
  turkey broth
¼ cup (60 ml) plain low-fat yogurt
1 tbs (15 ml) cornstarch
1 tbs (15 ml) lemon juice
1 small carrot, finely shredded
1 green onion, diced

Prepare kasha according to package directions, using chicken broth variation. In a mixing bowl combine prepared kasha with next 4 ingredients; blend well. Shape into 12 balls. In large skillet, heat oil and brown turkey meatballs on all sides. Add broth; cover and simmer 20 minutes. Use slotted spoon to transfer turkey meatballs to serving dish. In a small bowl, combine yogurt, cornstarch and lemon juice. Combine with pan juices in skillet and cook until sauce is thickened and bubbly. Add carrot and onion. Pour sauce over turkey meatballs. Serves 4.

Approximate nutritional analysis per serving:
Calories 166, Protein 17 g, Carbohydrates 5 g, Fat .6 g, Cholesterol 74 mg, Sodium 141 mg

SPICED BEEF WITH BLACK BEANS & PLANTAINS

4 tbs (60 ml) vegetable oil

2 lbs (910 g) boneless chuck steaks, cut into ½-inch cubes

2 14½-oz cans (870 ml) low-sodium beef broth

1 bay leaf

1½ cups (355 ml) chopped onion

¼ tsp (1 ml) pepper

1 FRIEDA'S Fresh Anaheim Chile, seeded and finely chopped

1-2 FRIEDA'S Fresh or Dried Serrano, Jalapeño or Pasilla Chile; if dried, rehydrate

½ clove FRIEDA'S Elephant Garlic, minced
or 4 cloves garlic, minced

2 FRIEDA'S Ripe Plantains, yellow or black, peeled and chopped

1 cup diced tomatoes

2 tsp (10 ml) capers

11-oz pkg (330 g) FRIEDA'S Black Beans, cooked and drained

2-oz jar (60 g) chopped pimentos, drained

3 cups (720 ml) hot cooked rice

Heat 2 tbs vegetable oil in a large Dutch oven; add chuck steak. Brown meat on all sides; drain off fat. Add beef broth, bay leaf, ½ of the onion and pepper. Bring to a boil; reduce heat. Cover and simmer 1-1½ hours or until meat is very tender. Transfer meat to a plate with slotted spoon, reserving juices; cover.

Measure 1½ cups juices (add water if necessary). In a large skillet, heat 1 tbs oil. Add chiles, remaining onions and garlic; sauté 2 minutes. Add 1 tbs more oil and plantains; sauté 5 minutes. Stir in measured juices, tomatoes and capers. Bring to a boil; reduce heat and simmer, covered 15 minutes. Add meat and cooked black beans to the chile mixture and cook until heated through. Taste for seasoning. Spoon mixture into serving dish; sprinkle on pimento. Serve over hot cooked rice. Serves 6.

Approximate nutritional analysis per serving:
Calories 774, Protein 68 g, Carbohydrates 73 g, Fat 24 g,
Cholesterol 153 mg, Sodium 320 mg

SPICED BEEF WITH BLACK BEANS & PLANTAINS

CHILE COLORADO CON CARNE
Red Chile Stew

CHILE COLORADO
  (Red Chile Sauce):
3-oz pkg (90 g) FRIEDA'S Chile New Mexico
3 cups (720 ml) water
¼ cup (60 ml) FRIEDA'S Shallots, finely chopped
½ tsp (3 ml) dried oregano, crumbled
cumin, to taste
garlic, to taste
salt, to taste

2 lbs (910 g) tender, lean stew meat, beef or pork
2 tbs (30 ml) cooking oil
1 cup (240 ml) FRIEDA'S Shallots, coarsely chopped
3 cups (720 ml) CHILE COLORADO
1 cup (240 ml) water

THICKER CHILE VARIATION:
1 tbs (15 ml) butter
1 tbs (15 ml) flour
pinch of salt, optional
1 cup (240 ml) skim milk

Chile Colorado Sauce: Break off stems and crack the chile pods, shaking out most of the seeds. Rinse pods and towel or drain them dry. Retain the light orange seams. They have lots of flavor. Cover and soak the cleaned pods with boiling water. Allow at least 30 minutes for pods to soften, although they will be fine if left to soak overnight.

When the pods are light red and spongy, include the water they have soaked in and purée the pods in a blender for 1½ minutes. In a ricer or sieve, over a container, stir the purée continuously with a wooden spoon until all that remains is a residue of seeds and fragments of chile skin. The resulting pure chile purée will have the color and texture of a smooth tomato sauce. Add all other ingredients to the chile purée and season to taste. Simmer for at least 10 minutes to cook the chile. The flavor will improve over time as the spices and chile blend. Yields 3½ cups sauce.

Chile Colorado Sauce can be spooned over a fried egg served on a grilled tortilla for huevos rancheros or simply stirred into a pot of beans. It also keeps well in your refrigerator or can be successfully frozen and thawed.

Brown meat in a small amount of cooking oil. When nicely browned, remove meat from pan and drain off all but 1 tbs of fat. Sauté shallots in this oil and then return meat to the pan and add the Chile Colorado Sauce and water. Cook over medium-low flame until the meat is tender and the gravy is a consistency that suits you. Serves 6.

Variation: Should you care to thicken chile, in a small saucepan, over low flame, melt butter and stir in flour and salt, if desired. Remove from flame as this mixture begins to bubble. Add milk and stir with a wire whisk over low flame until smooth and thick. Add this carefully, 1 spoonful at a time, stirring well, until the chile is as thick as you wish.

Approximate nutritional analysis per serving chile:
Calories 340, Protein 37 g, Carbohydrates 5 g, Fat .2 g, Cholesterol 18 mg, Sodium 380 mg

Approximate nutritional analysis per serving chile variation:
Calories 367, Protein 39 g, Carbohydrates 7 g, Fat 20 g, Cholesterol 130 mg, Sodium 411 mg

Approximate nutritional analysis per ¼ cup serving Chile Colorado Sauce:
Calories 20, Protein 1 g, Carbohydrates .8 g, Fat 1 g, Cholesterol 7 mg, Sodium 27 mg

FRIEDA'S BLACK BEAN CHILE CON CARNE

2 tbs (30 ml) vegetable oil
1 lb (455 g) lean ground beef, pork or turkey
¾ cup (180 ml) chopped red or brown onions
¾ cup (180 ml) chopped carrot
1 cup (240 ml) chopped green or red bell peppers
1 clove FRIEDA'S Elephant Garlic, peeled and minced
28-oz can (840 g) diced tomatoes, juices reserved
2 14½-oz cans (870 ml) low-sodium beef broth
1 bay leaf
1-2 FRIEDA'S Fresh or Dried, rehydrated Chiles, such as Chipotle, Jalapeño, Serrano, Yellow or Anaheim
½ tsp (3 ml) salt
¼ tsp (1 ml) ground cumin
1 cup (240 ml) niblet corn
11-oz pkg (330 g) FRIEDA'S Black Beans, cooked and drained

ACCOMPANIMENTS:
shredded cheese
diced avocado
chopped onions
hot corn or flour tortillas
tortilla chips

In Dutch oven heat oil. Sauté beef until browned. Drain, reserving 2 tbs drippings in pan. Sauté onion, carrot, bell pepper and garlic until tender; drain off excess fat. Add tomatoes and their juices, broth, browned meat, bay leaf, chiles, salt and cumin. Bring to boiling; reduce heat. Simmer 30 minutes. Stir in corn and black beans; simmer 5 minutes more or until chile is desired consistency. Serve with desired accompaniments. Yields 10 cups.

Approximate nutritional analysis per serving w/o accompaniments:
Calories 316, Protein 24 g, Carbohydrates 29 g, Fat 12 g, Cholesterol 45 mg, Sodium 388 mg

BURGUNDY BEEF STEW

BURGUNDY BEEF STEW

2 lbs (910 g) lean beef stew meat, cubed
2 tbs (30 ml) low-sodium soy sauce
6 carrots, cut into chunks
2 cups (480 ml) red or white rose potatoes, peeled and cut into chunks
2 large onions, sliced
2 cloves garlic, minced
¼ tsp (1 ml) black pepper
1 cup (240 ml) dry red wine
1 cup (240 ml) mushrooms, quartered
1 tbs (15 ml) GREEN HOUSE Fresh Marjoram, minced
1 tsp (5 ml) GREEN HOUSE Fresh Thyme, minced

Place beef in a large covered casserole dish and stir in soy sauce. Add carrots, onions, celery, potatoes, garlic, pepper and wine. Cover and bake at 325°F (165°C) for 1½ hours. Add mushrooms, stir gently, cover and bake 1 hour longer. Stir in fresh marjoram and fresh thyme and bake for 15 minutes. Flour or cornstarch can be added to thicken the sauce. Serves 6.

Approximate nutritional analysis per serving:
Calories 355, Protein 40 g, Carbohydrates 28 g, Fat 6 g, Cholesterol 98 mg, Sodium 323 mg

THAI-STYLE SKILLET SUPPER

1 lb (455 g) lean ground beef,
　turkey or pork
5 cups (1.2 l) assorted vegetables:
　celery, green pepper, bamboo
　shoots, mushrooms, bok choy,
　green onions, water chestnuts,
　fresh spinach, bean sprouts
¾ cup (180 ml) honey French
　salad dressing
2 tbs (30 ml) cornstarch
¼ cup (60 ml) water or broth
3 tbs (45 ml) soy sauce
½ tsp (3 ml) ground ginger
hot pepper sauce, or ground
　red pepper, to taste

In large skillet or wok, brown beef over high heat. Drain fat. Add vegetables. Cook, stirring constantly, 2 minutes or until vegetables are tender-crisp. Add French dressing and cornstarch mixed with water and soy sauce. Continue cooking until thickened and clear. Season with ginger and hot pepper sauce to taste. Serve over white rice. Serves 6.

Approximate nutritional analysis per serving w/o rice:
Calories 440, Protein 25 g, Carbohydrates 10 g, Fat 34 g, Cholesterol 75 mg, Sodium 774 mg

Courtesy of The National Honey Board.

GRILLED LAMB CHOPS WITH HERB-YOGURT MARINADE

MARINADE:
½ pkg GREEN HOUSE Pasta
　Bouquet, leaves chopped
　(approx. 1 tbs [15 ml] each Basil,
　Rosemary & Oregano)
1 tbs (15 ml) fresh garlic, chopped
1 cup (180 ml) nonfat plain yogurt
1 tbs (15 ml) Worcestershire sauce
pinch fresh ground black pepper

4 lean loin lamb chops,
　trimmed of fat
2 cups (480 ml) cooked spinach,
　fresh or frozen

Mix Marinade ingredients together in a glass or ceramic bowl. Add the lamb chops and coat them well. Cover and refrigerate overnight.

　Prepare barbecue. When coals are medium-hot, remove lamb chops from marinade, keeping them well coated. Grill over medium coals for 5 minutes per side for medium-rare. Serve ½ cup spinach with each chop. Serves 4.

Approximate nutritional analysis per serving:
Calories 184, Protein 23 g, Carbohydrates 10 g, Fat 6 g, Cholesterol 58 mg, Sodium 194 mg

GRILLED LAMB CHOPS WITH HERB-YOGURT MARINADE

LAMB KEBABS WITH MINT

½ cup (120 ml) GREEN HOUSE
    Fresh Mint, chopped
1 cup (240 ml) plain low-fat yogurt
2 tbs (30 ml) Dijon mustard
3 cloves garlic, minced
2 tbs (30 ml) lemon juice
salt, to taste
pepper, to taste
14 oz (420 g) boneless leg of lamb,
    cubed
4 plum tomatoes, halved
4 small zucchini, cut into
    1-inch chunks
2 cups (480 ml) cooked couscous
    or brown rice

Mix fresh mint, yogurt, mustard, garlic, lemon juice, salt and pepper in a medium-size bowl. Add lamb pieces and refrigerate overnight. Preheat broiler or barbecue. Thread lamb with tomatoes and zucchini onto skewers,* reserving marinade. Place in broiler or on grill. Cook until desired doneness, turning and basting with marinade, approximately 7-10 minutes. Serve over couscous or brown rice. Serves 4.

*Note: If using wooden skewers, soak for 15 minutes prior to assembly.

Approximate nutritional analysis per serving:
Calories 395, Protein 38 g, Carbohydrates 36 g, Fat 11 g, Cholesterol 95 mg, Sodium 227 mg

ROAST LAMB & GLAZE

½ cup (120 ml) CHESHIRE
    GARDEN Herbes de Provence
    Vinegar, red
1 tbs (15 ml) brown sugar
3 cloves crushed garlic
7-8 lb (3.1-3.6 kg) leg of lamb

In a heavy saucepan, heat vinegar, brown sugar and garlic until reduced by half. Brush this glaze directly over the leg of lamb and set in roasting pan, fat side up. Roast until meat thermometer plunged into the center of the large end of the leg registers 140°F (60°C) (medium) or about 1½ hours at 350°F (180°C). Let lamb rest 15-20 minutes before carving. Serve with gravy made from the drippings. Serves 12.

Approximate nutritional analysis per serving:
Calories 457, Protein 45 g, Carbohydrates .7 g, Fat 29 g, Cholesterol 164 mg, Sodium 117 mg

LAMB KEBABS WITH MINT

MOROCCAN COUSCOUS
Lamb Stew

1 tbs (15 ml) olive oil
1 lb (455 g) lean boneless lamb,
    cut into 1-inch cubes
1 medium onion, sliced
1½ cups (355 ml) water or
    chicken broth
1 cup (240 ml) sliced carrots
1 cup (240 ml) diced tomatoes
1 tsp (5 ml) ground cinnamon
½ tsp (3 ml) ground coriander
¼ tsp (1 ml) cayenne pepper
¼ tsp (1 ml) saffron, optional
¼ tsp (1 ml) pepper
11-oz pkg (330 g) FRIEDA'S
    Garbanzo Beans
    or 15-oz can (450 g) garbanzo
    beans, rinsed and drained
3 cups (720 ml) chopped or
    shredded cabbage
1 cup (240 ml) cubed zucchini or
    yellow summer squash
6-oz pkg (180 g) FRIEDA'S Couscous
2 cups (480 ml) water
⅔ cup (160 ml) raisins

MOROCCAN COUSCOUS

In a Dutch oven, heat oil; sauté lamb and onions until browned. Stir in broth, carrots, tomatoes and seasonings. Bring to a boil; reduce heat. Simmer, covered, for 1 hour. Stir in garbanzos, cabbage and zucchini; simmer 30 minutes more. Meanwhile, in a 1-quart saucepan combine couscous, water and raisins. Bring to a boil; reduce heat. Simmer 5 minutes. Fluff couscous with fork. Serve lamb stew over couscous. Serves 4.

Approximate nutritional analysis per serving:
Calories 777, Protein 59 g, Carbohydrates 97 g, Fat 19 g, Cholesterol 122 mg, Sodium 130 mg

JACKSON WONDER BEANS & PORK

8-oz pkg FRIEDA'S Dried Jackson
    Wonder Beans
1 tbs (15 ml) vegetable oil
1 lb (455 g) lean boneless pork,
    cut into 1-inch cubes
1 cup (240 ml) chopped onion
2 cloves garlic
2½-2¾ cups (590-660 ml) water
    or broth
1½ cups (355 ml) diced carrots
1½ tbs (25 ml) minced FRIEDA'S
    Fresh Sage, Rosemary or
    Oregano
½ tsp (3 ml) salt
¼ tsp (1 ml) pepper

Cover beans with water in a large saucepan and bring to a boil. Boil 2 minutes; remove from heat. Cover; let stand 1 hour. Drain beans and set aside. In same saucepan heat oil; sauté pork with onion and garlic until meat is browned and vegetables are tender. Stir in broth, beans, carrots and herbs. Bring to a boil; reduce heat. Simmer, covered, for 1-1½ hours, or until meat and beans are tender. Stir in salt and pepper. Serves 5.

Approximate nutritional analysis per serving:
Calories 353, Protein 36 g, Carbohydrates 34 g, Fat 8 g, Cholesterol 72 mg, Sodium 282 mg

JACKSON WONDER BEANS & PORK

PORK & POSOLE STEW

2 tbs (30 ml) vegetable oil
2 lbs (910 g) lean pork, cut into
  ½-inch cubes
1½ cups (355 ml) chopped onion
4 cloves garlic, minced
2 cups (480 ml) water
8-oz pkg FRIEDA'S Blue or
  White Posole
7-10 FRIEDA'S Dried Red Chile de
  Arbol, rehydrated and chopped
1 tbs (15 ml) chopped fresh thyme
1 tbs (15 ml) chopped fresh oregano
2 bay leaves
1 tsp (5 ml) cumin seed
½ tsp (3 ml) salt
¼ tsp (1 ml) pepper
salsa or red chile sauce, of choice
shredded green cabbage

PORK & POSOLE STEW

In a Dutch oven heat oil; sauté meat with onion and garlic for 10 minutes or until browned. Drain off excess fat. Add water, posole, chiles, thyme, oregano, bay leaves, cumin seed, salt and pepper. Bring to a boil; reduce heat. Simmer, covered, for 2-3 hours or until pork and posole are tender. Serve topped with salsa and shredded cabbage. Serves 6.

Approximate nutritional analysis per serving:
Calories 360, Protein 45 g, Carbohydrates 17 g, Fat 4 g, Cholesterol 120 mg, Sodium 334 mg

COLEMAN BEEF & BOK CHOY STIR-FRY

SAUCE:
⅓ cup (80 ml) prepared thick
  teriyaki sauce
2 tsp (10 ml) dry sherry
½ tsp (3 ml) granulated sugar

2 tbs (30 ml) peanut oil, divided
1 lb (455 g) COLEMAN NATURAL
  Top Round Steak, 1-inch thick,
  slightly frozen, cut across the
  grain cut into thin slices
1 medium red onion, cut into
  ½-inch wedges
1 bok choy, sliced thin
8 oz (240 g) pea pods,
  stems removed
1 cup (240 ml) sliced mushrooms
½ cup (120 ml) toasted slivered
  almonds

In a small bowl, combine all Sauce ingredients; set aside.
    Heat wok over high heat until hot. Add 1 tbs oil and stir-fry meat until browned, about 2 minutes. Remove meat from pan. Add remaining tbs oil to wok and stir-fry red onion and bok choy for 2 minutes. Stir in meat and sauce mixture, cover and cook for 2 minutes. Add pea pods and mushrooms and sauté for 2 minutes more. Sprinkle with almonds and serve immediately. Serves 4.

Approximate nutritional analysis per serving:
Calories 405, Protein 32 g, Carbohydrates 21 g, Fat 23 g, Cholesterol 50 mg, Sodium 143 mg

COLEMAN BEEF & BOK CHOY STIR-FRY

COLEMAN TUSCAN STEAK WITH SUN-DRIED TOMATOES

**4 5-oz (600 g) COLEMAN NATURAL
Beef Top Round Steaks,
cut 1-inch thick**

MARINADE:
½ cup (120 ml) red wine, Cabernet
   Sauvignon or Pinot Noir
½ cup (120 ml) sun-dried tomatoes
   packed in oil, drained
¼ cup (60 ml) lightly packed fresh
   basil leaves
3 tbs (45 ml) olive oil
4 cloves garlic, chopped
2 tsp (10 ml) mixed peppercorns,
   crushed
1 tsp (5 ml) salt

In food processor or blender combine Marinade ingredients and process until thick. Pour into glass bowl or sealable plastic bag. Add meat, turning to coat. Cover and refrigerate for a minimum of 30 minutes or overnight.

Remove meat from Marinade and grill over medium coals for 10-15 minutes per side, or broil 4 inches from source of heat for 10-15 minutes per side. Serves 4.

Approximate nutritional analysis per serving:
*Calories 332, Protein 28 g, Carbohydrates 5 g, Fat 21 g, Cholesterol 62 mg,
Sodium 710 mg*

**COLEMAN TUSCAN STEAK
WITH SUN-DRIED TOMATOES**

COLEMAN JAMAICAN JERKED RIB EYE STEAK

JAMAICAN RUB:
1 tbs (15 ml) garlic powder
1 tbs (15 ml) onion flakes
2 tsp (10 ml) granulated sugar
2 tsp (10 ml) salt
2 tsp (10 ml) thyme leaves
2 tsp (10 ml) ground ginger
2 tsp (10 ml) allspice
1 tsp (5 ml) ground black pepper
1 tsp (5 ml) ground cinnamon
½ tsp (3 ml) cayenne pepper
¼ tsp (1 ml) ground nutmeg

**4 ½-lb (910 g) COLEMAN NATURAL
Beef Ribeye Steaks,
cut 1-inch thick**

In small bowl, combine Rub ingredients. Sprinkle each side of the steaks with 1-2 tsp of the rub mixture. Grill over medium coals for 7-10 minutes per side or broil 4 inches from source of heat for 7-10 minutes per side. Serves 4.

Approximate nutritional analysis per serving:
*Calories 360, Protein 40 g, Carbohydrates 4 g, Fat 20 g, Cholesterol 100 mg,
Sodium 820 mg*

COLEMAN TEX-MEX STEAK FAJITA STICKS

MARINADE:

3 tbs (45 ml) fresh lime juice
2 tbs (30 ml) olive oil
2 tbs (30 ml) tequila or orange juice
2 tsp (10 ml) ground cumin
1 tsp (5 ml) dried oregano leaves, crushed
1 tsp (5 ml) chile powder
1 tsp (5 ml) salt

1 lb (455 g) COLEMAN NATURAL Skirt or Top Round Steak, cut into 8x1-inch strips
1 small red onion, cut into wedges
1 small yellow bell pepper, cut into 1-inch squares
1 small green bell pepper, cut into 1-inch squares
4 fresh Anaheim chiles, seeded and cut into 1-inch pieces
8 8-inch flour tortillas
½ cup (120 ml) green chile salsa
¼ cup (60 ml) low-fat sour cream

In small bowl, combine Marinade ingredients. Pour into glass bowl or sealable plastic bag. Add meat, cover and marinate while preparing vegetables.

Remove meat from marinade and thread onion, peppers, chiles and meat onto skewers*. Grill over medium coals for 4 minutes per side or until cooked to taste. Slide meat and vegetables off skewer into flour tortillas and serve with salsa and a dollop of sour cream. Serves 4.

*Note: If using wooden skewers, soak in water for 15 minutes prior to assembling meat and vegetables.

Approximate nutritional analysis per serving:
Calories 481, Protein 30 g, Carbohydrates 51 g, Fat 18 g, Cholesterol 56 mg, Sodium 1086 mg

COLEMAN TEX-MEX STEAK FAJITA STICKS

Overleaf: COLEMAN JAMAICAN JERKED RIB EYE STEAK

BEANS AND ESCAROLE

3 qts (2.9 l) water
3 lbs (1.4 kg) fresh green escarole, washed
1 garlic clove, chopped
4 tbs (60 ml) olive oil
14-oz can (420 g) AMERICAN PRAIRIE Organic Great Northern Beans, rinsed, reserve liquid
sea salt, to taste
pepper, to taste

Bring water to a boil and drop in washed escarole. Cook until tender. Drain in a colander. In medium-large saucepan, sauté garlic in olive oil until garlic turns light brown. Add greens to pan and sauté for 10 minutes. Add rinsed beans and ½ cup bean liquid and simmer for another 10 minutes. Season with sea salt and pepper to taste. Serve with loaf of bread on the side. Serves 8 as a side dish.

Approximate nutritional analysis per serving w/o bread:
Calories 148, Protein 6 g, Carbohydrates 16 g, Fat 7 g, Cholesterol 0 mg, Sodium 39 mg

BEANS AND ESCAROLE

BRAISED FENNEL WITH PANCETTA

1 bulb FRIEDA'S Fennel
1 cup (240 ml) water or chicken broth
2 strips pancetta or bacon, diced
¼ cup (60 ml) chopped onion
1 clove garlic, minced
salt, to taste
pepper, to taste
FRIEDA'S Pignolias (pine nuts) , chopped and toasted, for garnish

Trim fennel, discarding woody stems and reserving some of the fernlike leaves for garnish. Cut fennel into ¼-inch thick slices, then slice crosswise. In a medium saucepan, bring water or broth to boil. Add fennel pieces; reduce heat, simmer, partially covered for 10-15 minutes or until tender.

Meanwhile, sauté pancetta or bacon slowly; add onion and garlic. Cook about 5 minutes or until onion is tender; drain well. Drain cooked fennel; stir in pancetta mixture. Season with salt and pepper. Spoon mixture onto a serving platter. Sprinkle with pignolias and garnish with some of the reserved fennel leaves. Serves 4 as a side dish.

Approximate nutritional analysis per serving:
Calories 41, Protein 2 g, Carbohydrates 5 g, Fat 2 g, Cholesterol 3 mg, Sodium 81 mg

BRAISED FENNEL WITH PANCETTA

454

STEAMED DANDELION GREENS

2 bunches FRIEDA'S Dandelion
   Greens, trimmed and
   washed well
2 tsp (10 ml) olive oil
¼ cup (60 ml) low-sodium chicken
   or beef broth
1 tbs (15 ml) FRIEDA'S Fresh Basil,
   chopped
salt, to taste
pepper, to taste

ITALIAN-STYLE GREENS:
½ lb (230 g) Italian sausage,
   cooked and crumbled

Trim off bottom third of stems; wash leaves and remaining stems well. Chop into bite-size pieces. In a large saucepan or skillet, heat oil. Add chopped greens, broth and basil. Cover and cook over medium heat for 10-15 minutes or until tender. Add salt and pepper to taste. Serves 4.

Italian-Style Greens: Cook greens with sausage, crumbled. Drain well to serve.

Approximate nutritional analysis per serving:
Calories 40, Protein 1 g, Carbohydrates 3 g, Fat 3 g, Cholesterol 0 mg, Sodium 28 mg

Approximate nutritional analysis per serving Italian-Style Greens:
Calories 236, Protein 9 g, Carbohydrates 4 g, Fat 20 g, Cholesterol 43 mg, Sodium 442 mg

ALBERT'S ORGANICS STEAMED GREENS WITH GINGER-TAMARI DRESSING

1 lb (455 g) kale, collard, mustard,
   dandelion, daikon or
   turnip greens
1 cup (240 ml) water
1 tbs (15 ml) tamari
1 tbs (15 ml) toasted sesame oil
1 tbs (15 ml) mirin*
grated ginger, to taste

Clean greens well and separate leaves from stems. Bring water to boil and add stems and boil until tender. Remove and drain. Add leaves to boiling water, stirring until bright green, 1 minute or less. Do not overcook. Chop stems and leaves.

Combine tamari, toasted sesame oil, mirin and grated ginger, to taste, for dressing. Pour dressing on hot greens. Serves 4.

*Not included in nutritional analysis due to unavailability of nutrient data.

Approximate nutritional analysis per serving:
Calories 90, Protein 4 g, Carbohydrates 12 g, Fat 4 g, Cholesterol 0 mg, Sodium 306 mg

ALBERT'S ORGANICS STEAMED BROCCOLI WITH TOFU DRESSING

½ lb (240 g) tofu
⅓ cup (80 ml) tahini
⅓ cup (80 ml) light miso
¾ cup (180 ml) spring water
2 tbs (30 ml) umeboshi vinegar
3 cloves minced garlic
2 minced shallots
2 lbs (910 g) broccoli
¼ tsp (1 ml) sea salt

Steam tofu and drain. Blend all ingredients, except broccoli and sea salt, until there is a smooth dressing consistency. Separate the broccoli stems from the florets. Peel away the tough skin on stems; cut stems and florets into bite-size pieces. In a steamer, place water to cover and sea salt. Steam stems until tender and florets until bright green. Pour dressing over broccoli and serve. Serves 4.

Approximate nutritional analysis per serving:
Calories 241, Protein 13 g, Carbohydrates 20 g, Fat 15 g, Cholesterol 0 mg, Sodium 505 mg

HERBED STEAMED VEGETABLES

1 pkg GREEN HOUSE
    Veggie Bouquet
2 lbs (910 g) assorted vegetables;
    green or yellow squash, sweet
    red bell peppers, green beans
    and cauliflower
4 medium or 8 small new potatoes
2 tbs (30 ml) olive oil
    or 1¾ oz (153 g) fresh grated
    Parmesan cheese
fresh ground black pepper

Chop herbs. Cut the vegetables and potatoes into 1-inch pieces and place them in a steamer; sprinkle with half of the herbs and steam for 5 minutes or until potatoes are tender. Remove when cooked and toss in a large bowl with the rest of the herbs and the oil or cheese. Serve immediately. Serves 4.

Approximate nutritional analysis per serving:
Calories 239, Protein 11 g, Carbohydrates 42 g, Fat 4 g, Cholesterol 10 mg, Sodium 261 mg

HERBED STEAMED VEGETABLES

SUNCHOKE SUCCOTASH

2 tbs (30 ml) cooking oil
2 cups (480 ml) FRIEDA'S
    Sunchokes, chopped
1 cup (240 ml) FRIEDA'S
    Lima Beans, cooked
1 cup (240 ml) FRIEDA'S
    Haricot Verts, cut, or green or
    yellow wax beans
1 cup (240 ml) chopped red or
    green bell pepper
½ cup (120 ml) niblet corn
2 tbs (30 ml) butter or margarine
½ tsp (3 ml) salt
¼ tsp (1 ml) pepper
2 tbs (30 ml) chopped parsley
2 tbs (30 ml) FRIEDA'S Fresh Herbs,
    chopped, such as Basil, Chives,
    Chervil, Savory, Thyme or
    Rosemary

In a large skillet, heat oil. Sauté sunchokes for 5 minutes. Add lima beans, haricot verts, bell pepper and corn. Cook 5 minutes more, stirring frequently. Add butter; stir in remaining ingredients; heat through. Serves 4 as a side dish.

Approximate nutritional analysis per serving:
Calories 232, Protein 8 g, Carbohydrates 32 g, Fat 9 g, Cholesterol 10 mg, Sodium 227 mg

PEAS, PEARLS & CARROTS MEDLEY

11-oz pkg (330 g) FRIEDA'S
    Green Peas
10-oz pkg (300 g) FRIEDA'S Red,
    Gold or White Pearl Onions
1 bunch FRIEDA'S Baby Carrots,
    peeled if desired and trimmed
    or 1 cup (240 ml) half-slices of
    carrots
1 tbs (15 ml) butter or margarine
1 tbs (15 ml) FRIEDA'S Fresh Basil,
    chopped
    or 1 tsp (5 ml) crushed dried
    basil
2 tsp (10 ml) FRIEDA'S Fresh Thyme
    or Dill, chopped
    or ½ tsp (3 ml) crushed dried
    herb
salt, to taste
pepper, to taste

Cook green peas according to package directions. Boil pearl onions in their skins for 3-5 minutes or until nearly tender. Add baby carrots to the peas during the last 8 minutes of cooking. Drain pearl onions and rinse well in cold water. Slice off stem end and slip off skins. Halve any large onions. Drain peas and carrots; place in a serving bowl with onions. In pea saucepan; melt butter; stir in herbs. Drizzle over vegetables; sprinkle with salt and pepper. Toss well and serve. Serves 6.

Approximate nutritional analysis per serving:
Calories 83, Protein 3 g, Carbohydrates 13 g, Fat 2 g, Cholesterol 0 mg, Sodium 74 mg

PEAS, PEARLS & CARROTS MEDLEY

GINGERED ASPARAGUS

¾ cup (180 ml) OMEGA Apple
    Cider Vinegar
1½ tbs (25 ml) fresh ginger, grated
2 tbs (30 ml) maple syrup
1 lb (455 g) fresh asparagus
1 clove garlic, finely minced
3-4 tbs (45-60 ml) OMEGA
    Sesame Oil
1 tsp (5 ml) soy sauce
½ tsp (3 ml) sea salt

Combine vinegar, ginger and maple syrup and bring to a boil. Cook uncovered over medium heat 10-15 minutes. Set aside.

Cut off ½ inch of each lower stalk of asparagus. Bring water to a boil. Cook asparagus until tender 5-8 minutes. Remove from heat and rinse with cold water.

Combine garlic, oil, salt and soy sauce with vinegar mixture. Arrange asparagus on a plate. Cover with marinade and refrigerate 1-2 hours before serving. Serves 6 as a side dish.

Approximate nutritional analysis per serving:
Calories 96, Protein 2 g, Carbohydrates 8 g, Fat 7 g, Cholesterol 0 mg, Sodium 237 mg

ALBERT'S ORGANICS MARINATED GARDEN VEGETABLES

½-1 lb (230-455 g) green beans
½-1 lb (230-455 g) yellow squash
½-1 lb (230-455 g) broccoli
½-1 lb (230-455 g) cauliflower
½-1 lb (230-455 g) green peas
½-1 lb (230-455 g) red or yellow
    bell pepper
½-1 lb (230-455 g) lemon or
    regular cucumbers

MARINADE:
⅔ cup (160 ml) extra-virgin olive oil
⅓ cup (80 ml) lemon juice
⅓ cup (80 ml) balsamic vinegar
1 tbs (15 ml) Dijon mustard
2 tbs (30 ml) minced onion
3 cloves garlic, minced
1 tsp (5 ml) sea salt
1 tsp (5 ml) basil
1 tsp (5 ml) oregano

Lightly steam beans, squash, broccoli, cauliflower, green peas. Chop raw veggies, bell peppers and cucumbers, into medium bite-size pieces. Place all veggies in a shallow bowl.

Blend all Marinade ingredients together and pour over veggies. Marinate, refrigerated, for at least 2 hours. Serves 8.

Approximate nutritional analysis per serving:
Calories 229, Protein 4 g, Carbohydrates 15 g, Fat 19 g, Cholesterol 0 mg, Sodium 336 mg

GINGERED ASPARAGUS

GINGERED CARROTS

1 bunch green onions, chopped,
  white and green parts separated
1 lb (4355 g) carrots, peeled
  and sliced
2 tbs (30 ml) OISHII Ginger Tamari
  Soy Sauce
½ cup (120 ml) chicken broth
2 tsp (10 ml) cornstarch mixed with
  1 tbs (15 ml) water

Trim root ends off green onions. Slice into ¼-inch pieces. Microwave carrots on high with 2 tbs water in a covered microwave dish for about 6 minutes or until carrots are crisp-tender; drain off excess water. Heat skillet. Add ginger tamari soy sauce and white part of green onions; stir-fry 1 minute. Reduce heat and add carrots and chicken broth; cover and simmer until carrots are completely cooked. Thicken with cornstarch/water mixture. Garnish with onion tops. Serves 4 as a side dish.

Approximate nutritional analysis per serving:
Calories 79, Protein 3 g, Carbohydrates 17 g, Fat .5 g, Cholesterol 0 mg, Sodium 550 mg

INDIAN ROCK'S TASTY MARINATED FIDDLEHEADS

1¼ lb (569 g) fresh fiddleheads
¼ lb (115 g) fresh peppers,
  hot or mild
¼ lb (115 g) fresh wild leeks,
  ramps or shallots
1¼ cups (295 ml) apple cider
  or wine vinegar
fine-cut fresh herbs, including basil,
  tarragon, thyme, rosemary,
  chives
1¼ tbs (25 ml) sugar
salt, to taste
1¼ cups (295 ml) extra-virgin
  olive oil

Rinse fiddleheads in cold water to remove any remaining chaff or dirt. Blanch for 1 minute in boiling water. Remove from heat, drain and rinse in cold water. Clean and chop peppers. Cut up wild leeks. Pour vinegar over cooled fiddleheads in a glass bowl. Add cut-up peppers, wild leeks, herbs, sugar and salt. Stir to wet all ingredients. Add olive oil and stir again. Refrigerate 24 hours before serving. Serves 6.

*Approximate nutritional analysis per serving:
Calories 225, Protein 3 g, Carbohydrates 14 g, Fat 18 g, Cholesterol 0 mg, Sodium 8 mg

* Note: All olive oil will not be consumed.

GINGERED CARROTS

MARINATED VEGETABLE MEDLEY

1 cup (240 ml) bias-sliced carrots
1 cup (240 ml) chopped
    broccoli florets
2 FRIEDA'S Japanese Eggplants,
    cut into ½-inch chunks
    or 1 small regular eggplant,
    cut into ½-inch chunks
1½ cups (355 ml) FRIEDA'S Jicama,
    peeled and sliced
1 red bell pepper, seeded and
    julienned
½ cup (120 ml) sliced green onions

MARINADE:
1 cup (240 ml) olive oil or salad oil
¾ cup (180 ml) white wine vinegar
1 FRIEDA'S Bay leaf
4 FRIEDA'S Fresh Basil Leaves,
    whole
1 tbs (15 ml) FRIEDA'S
    Fresh Rosemary, chopped
    or 1 tsp (5 ml) crushed dried
    rosemary
¼ tsp (1 ml) whole black
    peppercorns
½ tsp (3 ml) salt

**PEPERONATA OF EGGPLANT
WITH FRESH THYME**

PEPERONATA OF EGGPLANT WITH FRESH THYME

1 cup (240 ml) diced eggplant
1 cup (240 ml) sliced onion
2 tbs (30 ml) olive oil
1 tbs (15 ml) chopped fresh garlic
1 cup (240 ml) diced red
    bell peppers
2 cups (480 ml) diced Roma
    tomatoes
8 pitted olives, kalamata or niçoise,
    if available
2 tbs (30 ml) GREEN HOUSE
    Fresh Thyme, chopped
fresh ground black pepper
8 oz (240 g) pasta

In a steamer basket, place carrots, broccoli and Japanese eggplant chunks over simmering water. Steam 5 minutes. Place steamed vegetables in a nonmetal bowl; add jicama, bell pepper strips and green onion; toss well.

Combine all Marinade ingredients in a shaker jar; cover and shake well to blend. Pour Marinade over vegetables; stir to coat well. Cover and refrigerate 4-24 hours, stirring occasionally. To serve, remove vegetables from marinade with slotted spoon. Keeps up to 1 week in refrigerator. Serves 8.

Approximate nutritional analysis per serving:
Calories 120, Protein 2 g, Carbohydrates 11 g, Fat 7 g, Cholesterol 0 mg, Sodium 148 mg

Dice eggplant, lightly salt and place on a paper towel to drain. In a thick-bottomed saucepan, cook the onions in the olive oil until light brown. Add the garlic and eggplant and cook for 5 minutes. Add the peppers and tomatoes and cook for 10 minutes. Take off the stove and add the olives, chopped fresh thyme and fresh ground black pepper. Cook pasta and serve with peperonata over it. Serves 4.

Variation: Peperonata may also be served cold or at room temperature, inside an omelet, on top of grilled bread or just by itself with crusty bread.

Approximate nutritional analysis per serving:
Calories 311, Protein 9 g, Carbohydrates 48 g, Fat 10 g, Cholesterol 49 mg, Sodium 77 mg

RATATOUILLE

1 eggplant, sliced into 1-inch slices
¼ cup (60 ml) CALIFORNIA
 CLASSICS Garlic Oil
1-2 tbs (15-30 ml) CALIFORNIA
 CLASSICS Pesto Oil
2 onions, peeled and quartered
1 red pepper, remove seeds and
 chop roughly
1 green pepper, remove seeds and
 chop roughly
2 zucchini, sliced diagonally
4 tomatoes, chopped roughly
salt, to taste
pepper, to taste

Chop eggplant slices, roughly. In frying pan, heat oils over medium heat. Add onions. Cover and cook gently until onion is soft but not colored. Add peppers, zucchini and eggplant. Cover and sauté gently for 15 minutes stirring occasionally. Add tomatoes and salt and pepper. Cook covered for 10 minutes. Serve hot or chilled. Serves 4.

Approximate nutritional analysis per serving:
Calories 258, Protein 4 g, Carbohydrates 21 g, Fat 18 g, Cholesterol 0 mg, Sodium 19 mg

TAMARILLO RATATOUILLE

1½ cups (355 ml) chicken broth
1 small eggplant, peeled and diced
4 FRIEDA'S Tamarillos, any variety,
 peeled and diced
1½ cups (355 ml) sliced mushrooms
1 red, golden or orange bell pepper,
 chopped
1 clove FRIEDA'S Elephant Garlic,
 minced
 or 3 cloves regular garlic, minced
2 tbs (30 ml) FRIEDA'S Fresh Basil,
 chopped
1 tbs (15 ml) FRIEDA'S Fresh
 Oregano, chopped
salt, to taste
pepper, to taste
2 tbs (30 ml) grated Parmesan
 cheese

In a large saucepan or Dutch oven, combine broth, eggplant, tamarillos, mushrooms, bell pepper, garlic, basil and oregano. Bring mixture to a boil; reduce heat. Simmer, partially covered, for 30 minutes or until vegetables are tender. Season to taste; serve topped with grated Parmesan cheese. Serves 6.

Approximate nutritional analysis per serving:
Calories 59, Protein 3 g, Carbohydrates 10 g, Fat 1 g, Cholesterol 2 mg, Sodium 52 mg

RATATOUILLE

GRILLED DELFTREE SHIITAKE MUSHROOMS WITH GARLIC, GINGER & SOY SAUCE

1 lb (455 g) DELFTREE Shiitakes,
    stems removed
1 tsp (5 ml) minced ginger
1 tsp (5 ml) minced garlic
1 tsp (5 ml) sugar
3 tbs (45 ml) soy sauce
2 tbs (30 ml) dry sherry
4 tbs (60 ml) peanut oil

Prepare a grill or preheat the broiler to high.

In a bowl, combine the mushrooms with the remaining ingredients and toss thoroughly to combine. Set aside to marinate for 15 minutes.

Skewer each shiitake through the cap horizontally with a bamboo skewer.* Grill the mushrooms for about 2 minutes on each side, until lightly browned and tender. Serve hot. Serves 5 as an hors d'oeuvre.

*Note: If using wooden skewers, soak in water for 15 minutes prior to assembling.

Approximate nutritional analysis per serving:
Calories 159, Protein 2 g, Carbohydrates 15 g, Fat 11 g, Cholesterol 0 mg, Sodium 621 mg

ALBERT'S ORGANICS ARAME, SHIITAKE MUSHROOMS, CABBAGE & CARROTS

1 cups (240 ml) arame,
    soaked 3-5 minutes
1 onion, diced
2 tsp (10 ml) toasted sesame oil
½ tsp (3 ml) sea salt
6-10 dried shiitakes, soaked,
    diced and stems removed
¼ cup spring water
1 carrot, diced
2 cups (480 ml) Napa cabbage, diced
3 tbs (45 ml) tamari
2 tbs (30 ml) mirin*
3 scallions, sliced

Place arame in saucepan with enough water to cover. Bring to boil and simmer 20 minutes. In a skillet, sauté onion in 1 tsp oil with salt and shiitake. Add ¼ cup spring water, cover and cook 10 minutes. Add carrots and cabbage, and sauté. Then add drained arame with remaining oil, tamari and mirin. Stir and simmer 5 minutes. Toss in scallions. Serves 4 as a side dish.

Not included in nutritional analysis due to unavailability of nutrient data.

Approximate nutritional analysis per serving:
Calories 92, Protein 3 g, Carbohydrates 17 g, Fat 3 g, Cholesterol 0 mg, Sodium 1379 mg

GRILLED DELFTREE SHIITAKE MUSHROOMS WITH GARLIC, GINGER & SOY SAUCE

SWEET & HOT MARINATED MUSHROOMS

⅓ cup (80 ml) honey
¼ cup (60 ml) white wine vinegar
¼ cup (60 ml) dry white wine or
    vegetable broth
2 tbs (30 ml) vegetable oil
1 tbs (15 ml) soy sauce
1 tbs (15 ml) sesame oil
1 clove garlic, minced
1 small green onion, chopped
1 tsp (5 ml) grated fresh ginger root
½ tsp (3 ml) grated orange peel
¼ tsp (1 ml) ground red pepper
1 lb (455 g) fresh small button
    mushrooms
parsley sprigs, for garnish, optional
orange wedges for garnish, optional

Combine honey, vinegar, wine, vegetable oil, soy sauce, sesame oil, garlic, green onion, ginger root, orange peel and red pepper in small saucepan. Cook and stir mixture over low heat until hot. Place mushrooms in heatproof bowl; pour hot marinade over mushrooms. Cover and marinate 3 hours in refrigerator, stirring occasionally. Arrange mushrooms in serving dish; garnish with parsley sprigs and orange wedges, if desired. Serves 5.

Approximate nutritional analysis per serving:
Calories 175, Protein 2 g, Carbohydrates 24 g, Fat 9 g, Cholesterol 0 mg, Sodium 211 mg

Courtesy of The National Honey Board.

DELFTREE TEMPURA

¾ cup (180 ml) cornstarch
¼ cup (60 ml) flour
1 tsp (5 ml) baking powder
½ tsp (3 ml) salt
¼ tsp (1 ml) pepper
1 egg, slightly beaten
½ cup (120 ml) water
corn oil for frying
¼ lb (115 g) DELFTREE Shiitake
    Mushrooms

Mix dry ingredients; add egg and water and mix again. Heat ¼ inch corn oil in skillet for frying, approximately 375°F (190°C). Dip mushrooms in batter and fry until golden brown. Drain on paper towel and serve. Serves 2.
    Variation: Add sautéed garlic, oregano or spice of your choice to batter.

Approximate nutritional analysis per serving:
Calories 365, Protein 5 g, Carbohydrates 65 g, Fat 9 g, Cholesterol 94 mg, Sodium 812 mg

DELFTREE TEMPURA

INDIAN ROCK'S PURÉED BUTTERNUT SQUASH

4 lbs (1.8 kg) butternut squash
1 large onion
1 clove garlic, peeled and diced
2 cloves shallots, peeled and diced
12 sliced black olives
2 tbs (30 ml) sweet butter
¼ cup (60 ml) light cream
¼ tsp (1 ml) nutmeg
3 twists of fresh ground pepper

Peel the squash and cut into even-size slices. Remove the seeds. Steam until tender in the basket of a double boiler, about 15 minutes. Sauté onions, garlic, shallots and olives in butter. Process squash in a food processor. Add onion, garlic, shallots, olives and butter to the squash in food processor. Add cream and flavor with nutmeg and pepper. Process until the squash is puréed. Serve hot. Serves 8.

Approximate nutritional analysis per serving:
Calories 161, Protein 3 g, Carbohydrates 28 g, Fat 6 g, Cholesterol 16 mg, Sodium 73 mg

SQUASH-N-APPLE SAUTÉ

2 FRIEDA'S Sweet Dumplings or
    Golden Nugget Squash
2 tbs (30 ml) butter or margarine
2 large Jonathan or Delicious
    apples, cored and chopped
1 FRIEDA'S Leek, sliced,
    white part only
2 tbs (30 l) white or rosé wine
¼ tsp (1 ml) ground cinnamon
pinch ground black pepper
pinch ground allspice

Halve each squash; cook halves, covered in a small amount of boiling water for 15 minutes. Meanwhile, in a large skillet melt butter. Add apples and leek slices and sauté for 5 minutes. Add wine and seasonings, cook 3 minutes more. Reserving shells, scoop out squash and mash; blend with apple mixture in skillet. Spoon mixture back into squash shells and serve immediately. Serves 4.

Approximate nutritional analysis per serving:
Calories 220, Protein 3 g, Carbohydrates 43 g, Fat 6 g, Cholesterol 16 mg, Sodium 71 mg

SQUASH-N-APPLE SAUTÉ

INDIAN ROCK'S SPAGHETTI SQUASH

1 spaghetti squash
1 tbs (15 ml) olive oil
2 garlic cloves, finely chopped
fresh basil leaves, shredded
¾ cup (180 ml) plum tomatoes,
   cut up

Preheat oven to 375° F (190° C). Cut open the squash, discard seeds and remove the long vibrant yellow strings of squash meat that look like pasta. Toss the squash strings with olive oil, garlic, basil and tomatoes. Bake, covered, until tender, approximately 30-45 minutes. Serves 4.

Approximate nutritional analysis per serving:
Calories 85, Protein 2 g, Carbohydrates 12 g, Fat 4 g, Cholesterol 0 mg, Sodium 30 mg

GRILLED SUMMER VEGETABLES

3 tbs (45 ml) olive oil
3 tbs (45 ml) CHESHIRE GARDEN
   Vinegar, such as French
   Tarragon, Purple Ruffles Basil,
   Lemon Basil, Chive Blossom or
   Piccolo Basil
2 Japanese eggplants,
   halved lengthwise
2 zucchini, halved lengthwise
2 yellow squash, halved lengthwise
4 slices red onion, ½-inch thick
1 sweet red pepper, quartered
   and seeded

Whisk oil into vinegar. Brush vegetables with vinaigrette. Prepare barbecue at medium-high heat. Grill vegetables until tender, about 4 minutes per side. Serves 8 as a side dish.

Approximate nutritional analysis per serving:
Calories 73, Protein 1 g, Carbohydrates 6 g, Fat 5 g, Cholesterol 0 mg, Sodium 3 mg

INDIAN ROCK'S SPAGHETTI SQUASH

GRILLED VEGETABLES, EXOTIC STYLE

4 cups (1.4 l) FRIEDA'S Delicata,
   Table Queen, Sweet Dumpling or
   Golden Nugget Squash, halved
   and seeded
1 lb (455 g) FRIEDA'S Baby Red or
   small Yellow Finnish Potatoes
1 Japanese eggplant, stem removed,
   halved lengthwise
½ lb (230 g) FRIEDA'S Baby Carrots,
   trimmed and peeled, if desired
2 cups (480 ml) FRIEDA'S Plantains,
   peel on and quartered
leaves from 1 FRIEDA'S Cactus,
   thorns removed and cut into
   1-inch wide strips
6 oz (180 g) FRIEDA'S Gold, Red or
   White Pearl Onions, peeled
   according to package directions
6 oz (180 g) FRIEDA'S Fresh
   Shiitakes or whole oyster
   mushrooms, stems removed

BASTING SAUCE:
¼ cup (60 ml) olive or vegetable oil
¼ cup (60 ml) lime juice
2 cloves garlic, minced
2 tbs (30 ml) FRIEDA'S Fresh Mint,
   minced
1 tbs (15 ml) FRIEDA'S Fresh
   Oregano, minced
¼ tsp (1 ml) salt
¼ tsp (1 ml) pepper

Chopped fresh mint, garnish
oregano leaves, for garnish

Precook squash, potatoes, eggplant, baby carrots, plantains, cactus leaves and pearl onions until not quite tender.

Meanwhile, mix oil, lime juice, garlic, herbs and seasonings of Basting Sauce until well combined.

Drain vegetables well; arrange on grill* over medium-hot coals or on lightly oiled broiler pan from preheated broiler. Brush mushrooms and vegetables liberally with Basting Sauce and turn once. Remove vegetables from grill and peel plantains. Spoon remaining Sauce over veggies to serve. Sprinkle on chopped mint and oregano. Serves 4.

*Note: Small shiitakes or oyster mushrooms and pearl onions can be threaded on skewers for easier handling and to prevent accidental "fall-throughs" on grill. If using wooden skewers, soak them in water for 15 minutes before assembling them.

Approximate nutritional analysis per serving:
Calories 530, Protein 11 g, Carbohydrates 100 g, Fat 16 g, Cholesterol 0 mg, Sodium 273 mg

GRILLED VEGETABLES, EXOTIC STYLE

POLENTA FANTASTICA DI VEGETALE AL FORNO
Polenta with Grilled Vegetables

MUSHROOM-TOMATO SAUCE:
FANTASTIC FOODS Creamy
Mushroom Soup Cup
2 8-oz cans (480 ml) MUIR GLEN
Organic Tomato Sauce
or 2 cups (480 ml) homemade
tomato sauce
1 tbs (15 ml) olive oil
4 Roma tomatoes, cut into large
1-inch chunks
1 tsp (5 ml) dry cracked oregano or
Italian herb blend
½ tsp (3 ml) dry thyme
pinch ground basil
¼ tsp (1 ml) black pepper
2 garlic cloves, minced
½ cup (120 ml) green olives,
sliced lengthwise
salt, to taste

GRILLED VEGETABLES:
2 small zucchini squash
2 small yellow summer squash
1 small eggplant
juice from 2 lemons
2 cobs yellow corn
3 baby artichokes, cleaned
2 Anaheim or New Mexico peppers,
sliced lengthwise
2 large processor carrots,
a woody-type carrot
or 2 cups (480 ml) baby tender
carrots
1 bunch young asparagus
1 bulb garlic, roasted
1 cup (240 ml) extra-virgin olive oil
or regular olive oil
2 branches fresh rosemary
4 porcini mushrooms
or 2 cups (480 ml) white
mushrooms

POLENTA FANTASTICA:
1 pkg FANTASTIC FOODS Polenta
Parmesan cheese, shredded

Mushroom-Tomato Sauce: Prepare mushroom soup cup according to package directions. Pour the tomato sauce into a 2-quart saucepan. Add the prepared mushroom soup, olive oil and chunked tomatoes. Bring to a simmer and add herbs, black pepper and minced garlic. Simmer, covered for 15 minutes and then add olives and simmer for 5 minutes. Keep warm until ready to serve. Salt to taste. Serves 6.

Grilled Vegetables: Prepare vegetables as follows: Slice squash and eggplant in ¼-inch pieces on the bias. Blanch in microwave for approximately 1 minute in a covered dish. Brush lightly with lemon juice and reserve. Wrap cleaned corncobs in wax paper and microwave for 1 minute. Cut through corncobs to make 1-inch-thick cob coins. Slice artichokes (brush with lemon juice immediately after slicing), and Anaheim peppers lengthwise. Blanch for 1 minute in a covered dish in the microwave. Cut carrots in half and lengthwise in ¼ inch pieces. Blanch in a covered dish for 2 minutes. Precooking the vegetables is optional, except for hard woody carrots, tough asparagus and corn.

Mash 4 soft roasted garlic cloves into the olive oil. Whisk the remaining lemon juice into the oil. Baste all veggies and fungi in a large marinating pan with a basting brush. Clip the rosemary into 2-inch pieces. Brush the rosemary also. Place all the veggies on the grill. Top the veggies with the rosemary and let the rosemary heat up on the vegetables. You want the volatiles of the rosemary to be picked up by the vegetables.

Grill so that the grill marks are apparent on the vegetables. Doneness will vary due to grill area, warmth and type of vegetables or mushrooms. When done hold on coolest part of grill or in a 200°F (93°C) oven until ready to serve.

Polenta Fantastica: Prepare polenta according to package directions. Then refrigerate the polenta until ready to grill. Cut polenta into 6 slices or squares. For a more fanciful look use a large star-shaped cookie cutter or any other shape. Grill the polenta to heat through, turn, cook other side.

To Serve: Place the grilled polenta in the center of the plate. Pile the vegetables on the polenta. Design with color in mind. Use the artichoke as a side vegetable. Top the vegetables with the Sauce. Garnish with the mushrooms. Lightly sprinkle shredded Parmesan. Serves 6.

Approximate nutritional analysis per serving sauce:
Calories 95, Protein 2 g, Carbohydrates 14 g, Fat 4 g, Cholesterol 0 mg, Sodium 387 mg

*Approximate nutritional analysis per serving grilled vegetables:
Calories 209, Protein 7 g, Carbohydrates 29 g, Fat 10 g, Cholesterol 0 mg, Sodium 75 mg

*Not all olive oil will be consumed.

Approximate nutritional analysis per serving Polenta Fantastica:
Calories 202, Protein 7 g, Carbohydrates 22 g, Fat 10 g, Cholesterol 20 mg, Sodium 462 mg

MEXICAN VEGETABLE SAUTÉ

2 tbs (30 ml) vegetable oil
½ cup (120 ml) chopped onions
1-2 cloves FRIEDA'S Elephant
 Garlic, peeled, halved and
 thinly sliced
1-2 Fresh or Dried FRIEDA'S Chiles,
 such as Jalapeño, Serrano,
 Chipotle, Fresno, Anaheim or
 Yellow, rehydrated if dried,
 seeded and cut into thin strips
1½ cups (355 ml) cooked potatoes
 or yams, diced, or uncooked
 FRIEDA'S Plantains, peeled
 and diced
1½ cups (355 ml) diced zucchini
 or chayote squash
½ cup (120 ml) whole kernel corn
1 tbs (15 ml) chopped FRIEDA'S
 Fresh Cilantro
salt, to taste
pepper, to taste

Heat oil in a large skillet; sauté onion, garlic and chiles over medium-low heat for 3-5 minutes, or until garlic is tender; do not allow vegetables to burn. Add potatoes and squash; sauté 5-10 minutes more or until squash is tender. Add corn and cilantro; season to taste. Cook until warmed through. Serves 5.

Approximate nutritional analysis per serving:
Calories 141, Protein 3 g, Carbohydrates 21 g, Fat 6 g, Cholesterol 0 mg, Sodium 59 mg

PURPLE POTATOES AU GRATIN

3 tbs (45 ml) olive or cooking oil
1 cup (240 ml) chopped onions
1 tbs (15 ml) chopped FRIEDA'S
 Fresh Thyme
 or 1 tsp (5 ml) crushed dried
 thyme
½ tsp (3 ml) salt
¼ tsp (1 ml) pepper
1 lb (455 g) FRIEDA'S Purple
 Potatoes, peeled and thinly sliced
1 cup (240 ml) beef or chicken broth
½ cup (120 ml) finely shredded
 Swiss or Jarlsberg cheese

In a large skillet, heat oil. Sauté onions in oil 5 minutes over medium-low heat. Remove ½ of the onions; reserve. Stir in fresh thyme, salt and pepper to skillet. Add raw potatoes; mix well. Transfer mixture to an oiled 1½-quart shallow baking dish; pour broth over potatoes. Bake covered, in a 350°F (180°C) oven for 50-60 minutes or until broth is absorbed. Top with reserved onions and cheese; bake 5 minutes more. Serves 4 as a side dish.

Approximate nutritional analysis per serving:
Calories 262, Protein 7 g, Carbohydrates 27 g, Fat 14 g, Cholesterol 12 mg, Sodium 326 mg

SAUTÉED PLANTAINS & SWEET POTATOES

2 tbs (30 ml) butter or margarine
2 tbs (30 ml) cooking oil
2 cups (480 ml) sweet potatoes or
    yams, cooked and sliced
2 FRIEDA'S Plantains, peeled and
    chopped
½ cup (120 ml) chopped green onion
½ cup (120 ml) cooked ham,
    chopped, optional
1 clove garlic, minced
½ cup (120 ml) chicken or
    beef broth
2 tbs (30 ml) butter or margarine
1-2 tbs (15-30 ml) chopped FRIEDA'S
    Fresh Thyme, Chervil, Dill or
    Savory
salt, to taste
pepper, to taste

In a large skillet, melt 2 tbs butter and cooking oil until hot. Add potatoes, plantains, onions, ham, if desired, and garlic. Cook, stirring frequently, about 5 minutes. Add broth; cover and simmer 10 minutes or until plantains are tender. Add remaining butter and desired fresh herbs; season to taste with salt and pepper. Serves 6 as a side-dish.

Approximate nutritional analysis per serving:
Calories 275, Protein 3 g, Carbohydrates 41 g, Fat 13 g, Cholesterol 21 mg, Sodium 156 mg

**SAUTÉED PLANTAINS
& SWEET POTATOES**

POTATOES WITH SHALLOT-GARLIC-ONION RELISH

8-oz pkg (240 g) FRIEDA'S Pearl
    Onions, Red, White or Gold,
    peeled
    or 1 cup (240 ml) chopped brown
    onions
6 FRIEDA'S Shallots, peeled and
    thinly sliced
1 clove FRIEDA'S Elephant Garlic,
    peeled and finely minced
1 cup (240 ml) beef or chicken broth
2 tbs (30 ml) chopped fresh parsley
¼ tsp (1 ml) pepper
1½ lbs (683 g) FRIEDA'S Yellow
    Finnish, Yukon Gold, Purple or
    New Baby Potatoes, sliced
    ¼-inch thick

If using pearl onions, halve peeled onions. Place in a medium saucepan with shallots, garlic and broth. Bring to a boil; reduce heat to simmer. Cover and braise 5 minutes, or until vegetables are very tender. Uncover and simmer 5-10 minutes more, or until nearly all liquid has disappeared. Stir in parsley and pepper; set aside.

Cook potatoes in boiling water to cover for 10-15 minutes. Drain well; serve hot with relish Serves 4.

Approximate nutritional analysis per serving:
Calories 204, Protein 6 g, Carbohydrates 45 g, Fat .7 g, Cholesterol 0 mg, Sodium 168 mg

POTATOES WITH SHALLOT-GARLIC-ONION RELISH

MASHED POTATO BOATS

5 large potatoes
¾ cup (180 ml) SOLAIT Powder
onion, to taste
salt, to taste
garlic powder, to taste
water
½ cup (120 ml) chopped onions
½ cup (120 ml) red bell pepper
½ cup (120 ml) diced celery
3 tbs (45 ml) canola oil
margarine or butter, to taste,
    optional
½ cup (120 ml) nutritional yeast
paprika

Bake potatoes at 350°F (180°C) until soft. Scoop potato pulp into a bowl, leaving skins intact for boat. Mash pulp. Add Solait Powder, onion, salt and garlic powder, to taste. If too stiff, add water.

Sauté onions, red bell peppers and celery in canola oil. Add onion mixture to mashed potatoes. Add margarine and yeast, if desired. Place mashed mixture back into skins, sprinkle with paprika. Reheat if necessary, covered, in hot oven until piping hot. Serve with main dish and green or orange vegetable. Serves 5.

Approximate nutritional analysis per serving:
Calories 441, Protein 11 g, Carbohydrates 73 g, Fat 12 g, Cholesterol 0 mg, Sodium 153 mg

MASHED POTATOES WITH GRAVY

1 qt (960 ml) water
4 medium baking potatoes,
    peeled and cubed
2-5 tbs (30-75 ml) butter or
    margarine
½ tsp (3 ml) sea salt
pinch black pepper
⅓ cup (80 ml) Original
    RICE DREAM

HERBED GRAVY:
2 tbs (30 ml) oleic safflower
    or canola oil
⅓ cup (80 ml) whole wheat
    pastry flour
1 cup (240 ml) Original
    RICE DREAM
1 tbs (15 ml) soy sauce
1 cup (240 ml) water
½ tsp (3 ml) sea salt
1 tsp (5 ml) dried crushed sage
¼ tsp (1 ml) thyme
¼ tsp (1 ml) marjoram
pinch black pepper

Bring water to boil and add potatoes. Reduce heat and cook until potatoes are soft and easily pierced with a fork, about 15 minutes. Drain well and place in medium mixing bowl. Add butter, salt, pepper and Rice Dream. Using an electric or hand mixer, mash potatoes until thick, smooth and creamy. Adjust seasonings to taste. Serve topped with hot Herbed Gravy. Serves 4.

Herbed Gravy: In a 2-quart saucepan, heat oil over medium heat. Add flour and stir often for 2 minutes. Remove from heat and allow to cool for several minutes. In a separate bowl, combine remaining ingredients. Whisk together with the flour/oil, half at a time to avoid lumping. Bring to boil over medium heat, stirring often. Reduce heat to low and cook for 10-15 minutes, stirring occasionally. If gravy seems too thick, simply whisk in additional water, 1 tbs at a time until desired consistency is reached. Adjust salt and pepper to taste. Gravy will thicken as it cools.

Gravy keeps well in the refrigerator for several days. To serve at a later time, reheat slowly over a medium flame, making sure to stir well. Add 1-2 tbs of water, if necessary. Yields 2 cups.

Approximate nutritional analysis per serving w/o gravy:
Calories 281, Protein 5 g, Carbohydrates 53 g, Fat 6 g, Cholesterol 16 mg, Sodium 349 mg

Approximate nutritional analysis per serving w/ ¼ cup gravy:
Calories 344, Protein 6 g, Carbohydrates 60 g, Fat 10 g, Cholesterol 16 mg, Sodium 622 mg

BROCCOLI & MUSHROOM-STUFFED POTATOES

4 large russet potatoes
1 cup (240 ml) broccoli, trimmed
    and chopped
1 cup (240 ml) mushrooms, sliced
olive oil or vegetable spray
8-oz container (240 g) low-fat
    cottage cheese
3 tbs (45 ml) low-fat milk
salt, to taste
pepper, to taste
1 pkg GREEN HOUSE Fresh Chives,
    chopped, or to taste

Bake potatoes until soft. Cut tops off potatoes and let cool for 10 minutes. In medium frying pan, sauté broccoli and mushrooms in olive oil spray until soft. Scoop out potatoes, leaving shell. Mash potatoes with cottage cheese, milk (to desired consistency), salt and pepper. Add fresh chives, broccoli and mushrooms to potato mixture. Fill potato shells with mixture. The potatoes can be made ahead to this point. If so, cover and chill. Bring to room temperature before baking. Bake for 30 minutes at 350°F (180°C). Serves 4.

Approximate nutritional analysis per serving:
Calories 272, Protein 14 g, Carbohydrates 51 g, Fat 2 g, Cholesterol 6 mg, Sodium 257 mg

SCALLOPED POTATOES

6 cups (1.4 l) water
6 medium potatoes, pared and cut
    into ¼-inch slices
¾ cup (180 ml) chopped onion
½ cup (120 ml) diced green pepper
2 tbs (30 ml) margarine
4 tbs (60 ml) flour
2 cups (480 ml) Unsweetened
    WESTSOY
1½ cups (355 ml) shredded cheddar
    cheese alternative
¼ cup (60 ml) pimentos
¼ tsp (1 ml) garlic powder
salt, to taste
pepper, to taste

Bring water to boil, add potatoes, onion and green pepper. As soon as water resumes boiling, remove from heat and drain vegetables. Turn into a greased 7½x12-inch baking dish. Melt margarine in medium-size pan, stir in flour until well mixed. Gradually stir in soy milk and cook, stirring until mixture thickens and begins to boil. Remove from heat and stir in 1 cup shredded cheese alternative, pimentos, garlic powder, salt and pepper to taste. Pour over potatoes and stir gently to combine. Sprinkle remaining cheese alternative over top. Bake, uncovered, at 350°F (180°C) for 35-40 minutes until potatoes are tender and the sauce is bubbly around the edges. Serves 8.

Approximate nutritional analysis per serving:
Calories 230, Protein 10 g, Carbohydrates 36 g, Fat 6 g, Cholesterol 0 mg, Sodium 380 mg

INDIAN ROCK'S ROASTED SUNCHOKES, POTATOES & SHALLOTS

1 lb (455 g) sunchokes
2 lbs (910 g) yellow potatoes
½ lb (230 g) whole peeled shallots
½ cup (120 ml) olive oil
½ bunch fresh thyme leaves,
    chopped
sea salt, to taste
freshly ground black pepper,
    to taste

Pare sunchoke skin and cut into 1-inch cubes. Cut unpeeled potatoes into 1-inch cubes. Split any large shallot. Toss together with remaining ingredients. Place all in a single layer in a roasting pan. Roast in a hot 400°F (205°C) oven for 30 minutes, shaking every 10 minutes so vegetables roast and brown evenly. Mixture should be crusty and brown when cooked. Serve immediately. Serves 12.

Approximate nutritional analysis per serving:
Calories 151, Protein 2 g, Carbohydrates 17 g, Fat 9 g, Cholesterol 0 mg, Sodium 30 mg

LADYBUG PRODUCE KIMPIRA GOBO
Braised Burdock

1 tbs (15 ml) sesame oil
2 burdock (gobo) roots, scrubbed
    and cut into matchstick-size
    pieces
¼ cup (60 ml) water
1 tbs (15 ml) tamari, or to taste
1 tsp (5 ml) honey, or to taste
pinch of cayenne, or to taste

Heat oil, sauté burdock on medium heat approximately 5 minutes. Stir to prevent scorching. Add water, tamari, honey and pepper; stir and cover. Reduce heat to low. Braise until tender, approximately 20 minutes. Serve hot or cold. Serves 4.

Approximate nutritional analysis per serving:
Calories 94, Protein 2 g, Carbohydrates 15 g, Fat 4 g, Cholesterol 0 mg, Sodium 206 mg

INDIAN ROCK'S ROASTED SUNCHOKES, POTATOES & SHALLOTS

SPAGHETTI-STUFFED PEPPERS

¼ cup (60 ml) low-salt chicken broth
1 cup (240 ml) chopped zucchini, yellow crookneck, pattypan, scallopini or sunburst squash
½ cup (120 ml) FRIEDA'S Fresh Shiitake Mushrooms or brown mushrooms, chopped
¼ cup (60 ml) sliced green onion
1 tbs (15 ml) FRIEDA'S Fresh Basil, chopped
    or 1 tsp (5 ml) crushed dried basil
1 tbs (15 ml) FRIEDA'S Fresh Thyme, chopped
    or 1 tsp (5 ml) crushed dried thyme
1 clove garlic, minced
¼ tsp (1 ml) pepper
1½ cups (355 ml) FRIEDA'S Spaghetti Squash, cooked, seeded and fluffed into strands
4 sweet bell peppers, any color
¼ cup (60 ml) shredded nonfat or low-fat Swiss or cheddar cheese

In a skillet, heat broth to simmering. Add squash, mushrooms, onion, herbs, garlic and pepper. Simmer, uncovered, stirring occasionally, for 4 minutes, or until vegetables are tender. Remove from heat. Stir in cooked spaghetti squash. Slice tops off of bell peppers and discard seeds. Spoon filling into peppers; sprinkle on shredded cheese. Add tops. Place in a shallow baking dish sprayed with aerosol cooking spray. Cover and bake in a 375°F (190°C) oven for 30-35 minutes, or until heated through. Serves 4.

Approximate nutritional analysis per serving:
Calories 73, Protein 4 g, Carbohydrates 13 g, Fat 2 g, Cholesterol 2 mg, Sodium 17 mg

TABOULI-STUFFED PEPPERS

1 pkg FANTASTIC FOODS Tabouli
8-oz can (240 ml) tomato sauce
½ cup (120 ml) parsley, chopped
¼ cup (60 ml) black olives, chopped
4 large red or green bell peppers
olive rounds, for garnish

Prepare tabouli according to package directions, omitting tomatoes. After liquids have been absorbed, add tomato sauce, parsley and chopped olives. Cut peppers in half vertically, removing seeds but leaving stems intact. Steam, open side down, for 5 minutes. Stuff peppers with tabouli. Garnish with olive rounds. Place in a large baking dish and cover with aluminum foil. Bake at 375°F (190°C) for 20-25 minutes. Serves 8.

Approximate nutritional analysis per serving:
Calories 113, Protein 4 g, Carbohydrates 24 g, Fat 4 g, Cholesterol 0 mg, Sodium 547 mg

WALNUT ACRES' ZESTY STUFFED PEPPER POTS

4 large green bell peppers
1 tbs (15 ml) safflower oil
1 cup (240 ml) diced celery
½ cup (120 ml) diced onion
1 medium jalapeño pepper,
    seeded and minced
1 cup (240 ml) WALNUT ACRES
    Garbanzo Beans, cooked and
    mashed
1 cup (240 ml) canned crushed
    tomatoes
1 tbs (15 ml) basil leaves, minced
½ tsp (3 ml) garlic powder or
    2 cloves fresh garlic
¼ tsp (1 ml) black pepper
4 tbs (60 ml) plain low-fat yogurt

Cut tops from peppers and remove seeds. Remove stems, leaving a hole in the center of tops. Parboil peppers and tops for 3 minutes, drain and set aside. In a large skillet, heat oil and sauté celery and onions for 3 minutes. Remove from heat and add ½ of the minced jalapeño along with garbanzo beans, tomatoes, basil, garlic powder and pepper. Combine well and stuff peppers with the mixture. Combine remaining jalapeño with yogurt and spoon 1 tbs on top of each pepper. Cover with pepper tops and place peppers in a nonstick baking pan. Bake at 350°F (180°C) for 40-45 minutes. Serves 4.

Approximate nutritional analysis per serving:
Calories 152, Protein 6 g, Carbohydrates 23 g, Fat 5 g, Cholesterol .3 mg, Sodium 172 mg

MEDITERRANEAN STUFFED TOMATOES

MEDITERRANEAN STUFFED TOMATOES

1 cup (240 ml) parsley
2-3 tbs (30-45 ml) capers
1-2 cloves garlic
4 tbs (30 ml) oil
2 tbs (30 ml) lemon juice
½ cup (120 ml) walnuts,
    roughly chopped
2 6.1-oz pkgs (366 g) SOY DELI
    Garden Style Tofu Burgers,
    crumbled
salt, optional
4 large ripe tomatoes

Place parsley, capers and garlic in a blender with 2 tbs oil. Blend for 15 seconds, add 2 more tbs oil and blend for 5-10 seconds, leaving some texture to the ingredients. Scrape into a bowl and add 2 tbs lemon juice. Add chopped walnuts, crumbled tofu burgers and salt, if necessary. Cut the tops off tomatoes and trim bottoms slightly so they will stand; remove insides leaving a wall ⅓-inch thick. Fill with the tofu mixture and chill 3-4 hours before serving. Serves 4.

Approximate nutritional analysis per serving:
Calories 384, Protein 15 g, Carbohydrates 16 g, Fat 30 g, Cholesterol 0 mg, Sodium 662 mg

STUFFED SQUASH

4 buttercup or acorn squash
1 large apple, chopped
⅓ cup (80 ml) walnuts, chopped
¼ cup (60 ml) sugar
¼ cup (60 ml) raisins
2 tbs (30 ml) butter or margarine
¼ cup (60 ml) maple syrup

Preheat oven to 400°F (205°C). Wash squash. Cut tops off and scrape out seeds and strings. Place cut side down on baking sheet and bake until squash is tender when pricked with fork. Combine remaining ingredients in saucepan and heat gently until well blended and soft. When squash is done, remove from oven and fill cavities with filling. Pour a little maple syrup over each just to moisten tops, and return to oven to heat through. Serves 8.

Approximate nutritional analysis per serving:
Calories 248, Protein 4 g, Carbohydrates 50 g, Fat 6 g, Cholesterol 8 mg, Sodium 39 mg

Courtesy of Michigan Maple Syrup Association and Cooperative Extension Services Michigan State University.

COUSCOUS-STUFFED TOMATOES

1 box FANTASTIC FOODS
    Quick Couscous Pilaf
6 medium-size tomatoes
3 tbs (45 ml) water
pine nuts or walnuts, for garnish

Prepare couscous pilaf according to package directions. Cut large hollows in tomatoes and invert them to drain while couscous is cooking. Fill the tomatoes with prepared couscous and place them in a pan with the water. Bake at 350°F (180°C) for 12 minutes. Garnish with pine nuts or walnuts. Serves 6.

Approximate nutritional analysis per serving:
Calories 219, Protein 8 g, Carbohydrates 46 g, Fat 1 g, Cholesterol 0 mg, Sodium 354 mg

STUFFED SQUASH

BULGUR-STUFFED SQUASH

½ of a large squash, such as
    FRIEDA'S Hubbard, Butternut,
    Kabocha, Mediterranean,
    Spaghetti or Turban
1 tbs (15 ml) cooking oil
1 clove garlic, minced
½ cup (120 ml) chopped walnuts
    or pecans
2 cups (480 ml) cooked bulgur
    or rice
2 FRIEDA'S Shallots, chopped,
    optional
1 large tomato, chopped
¼ cup (60 ml) water or
    chicken broth
1½ tsp (8 ml) FRIEDA'S Fresh
    Rosemary, chopped
    or ½ tsp (3 ml) dried rosemary,
    crushed
1½ tsp (8 ml) FRIEDA'S Fresh
    Oregano, chopped
    or ½ tsp (3 ml) dried oregano,
    crushed
1½ tsp (8 ml) FRIEDA'S Fresh Basil,
    chopped
    or ½ tsp (3 ml) dried basil,
    crushed
salt, to taste
pepper, to taste
¾ cup (180 ml) shredded Swiss,
    Monterey Jack or mozzarella
    cheese

Parboil squash in a little water in a Dutch oven or large saucepan for about 20 minutes. Drain and scoop out seeds; discard. Scoop out the flesh, leaving a ½-inch shell. Chop squash or separate into strands if using spaghetti squash. Set aside.

In a large skillet heat oil; add garlic and walnuts. Sauté 2 minutes over medium heat. Add cooked bulgur, shallots, tomato and water. Stir until well blended; cook 3 minutes. Add herbs; blend well. Taste the mixture; season with salt and pepper, if desired. Add squash pieces; mix well.

Place squash shell, cut side up, in a baking pan with a small amount of water in bottom of pan. Spoon filling mixture into shell. Cover with foil. Bake in a 375°F (190°C) oven for 20 minutes. Uncover; sprinkle shredded cheese on top. Bake 10 minutes more or until hot and cheese is bubbly. Serve immediately. Serves 3.

Approximate nutritional analysis per serving:
Calories 556, Protein 26 g, Carbohydrates 67 g, Fat 26 g, Cholesterol 25 mg, Sodium 110 mg

BULGUR-STUFFED SQUASH

VEGETABLES, RICE AND CHEESE PLATTER

1 tbs (15 ml) cooking oil
1 medium onion, sliced
2 medium carrots, cut into
    julienne strips
2 medium yellow squash or
    zucchini, halved lengthwise
    and thinly sliced
1 ripe tomato, seeded and chopped
1 cup (240 ml) sliced fresh
    mushrooms
11-oz pkg (330 g) FRIEDA'S
    Black-Eyed Peas, cooked
2 cups (480 ml) FRIEDA'S Black
    Wild Rice or brown or white rice,
    cooked
½ cup (120 ml) low-sodium chicken
    or beef broth
1 tbs (15 ml) FRIEDA'S Fresh Savory
    or Basil, chopped
    or 1 tsp (5 ml) crushed dried
    herbs
½ tsp (3 ml) salt
¼ tsp (1 ml) pepper
½ cup (120 ml) shredded sharp
    cheddar cheese
½ cup (120 ml) shredded Monterey
    Jack or mozzarella cheese

In a large skillet, heat oil; sauté onion and carrots for 5-8 minutes or until tender. Add squash or zucchini, tomato and mushrooms; cover and cook 3 minutes more. Drain peas; stir into skillet with rice, broth, savory or basil, salt and pepper. Cook, covered, for a few minutes to heat. Sprinkle cheeses over the top; cover skillet until cheese melts. Serve at once. Serves 5 as a main dish.

Approximate nutritional analysis per serving:
Calories 448, Protein 23 g, Carbohydrates 66 g, Fat 11 g, Cholesterol 22 mg, Sodium 380 mg

VEGETABLES, RICE AND CHEESE PLATTER

SQUASH & MILLET CASSEROLE

2 medium zucchini squash
2 medium yellow crookneck squash
1½-2 tsp (8-10 ml) herb salt
pepper, to taste
1 bell pepper, chopped
1 large onion, chopped
½ lb (230 g) grated cheese, optional
1½ cups (355 ml) raw ARROWHEAD
    MILLS Millet
2 1-lb cans (910 g) stewed tomatoes
    and juice

Preheat oven to 350°F (180°C). Generously oil a 2-quart casserole dish. Chop all squash into ½-inch thick slices. Sprinkle with herb salt and pepper. Toss all remaining ingredients with squash until well mixed. Cover very tightly and bake 1 hour or until squash is tender and millet is puffed and tender. Serves 4.

Approximate nutritional analysis per serving:
Calories 283, Protein 11 g, Carbohydrates 66 g, Fat 2 g, Cholesterol 0 mg, Sodium 583 mg

SQUASH & MILLET CASSEROLE

SPANISH SQUASH CASSEROLE

1 box ARROWHEAD MILLS Spanish
    Quick Brown Rice, uncooked
3 medium squash, of choice
1 medium bell pepper, chopped
1 lb (455 g) stewed tomatoes
    or 4 fresh tomatoes

Mix all ingredients in an oiled 9x13-inch baking dish. Cover tightly with aluminum foil or tight fitting baking dish lid. Bake for 30 minutes at 350°F (180°C) or until squash is tender. Serves 4.

Approximate nutritional analysis per serving:
Calories 211, Protein 7 g, Carbohydrates 44 g, Fat 2 g, Cholesterol 0 mg, Sodium 269 mg

GREEN BEANS IN CI'BELLA MUSHROOM SAUCE

1½ lbs (683 g) green beans
3 tbs (45 ml) olive oil, divided
1 medium onion, chopped
1 tsp (5 ml) minced garlic
4½-oz jar (135 g) sliced mushrooms, drained
1 jar WESTBRAE'S Ci'Bella Mushroom Sauce
½ cup (120 ml) Italian-style bread crumbs

Trim ends from green beans and snap into bite-size pieces. Place beans in a medium saucepan with 3 cups of water and bring to boil over high heat. Cover, reduce heat to moderate and cook 20 minutes. Drain immediately.

Meanwhile heat 1 tbs olive oil in a large skillet over moderate heat. Add chopped onion and garlic and sauté until onions are softened. Combine drained beans, onion, garlic, mushrooms and sauce and turn into a lightly oiled 2-quart casserole. Combine remaining 2 tbs olive oil with the bread crumbs and sprinkle evenly over the top of the casserole. Bake, uncovered, in a 350°F (180°C) oven for 20 minutes or until hot. Serves 8 as a side dish.

Approximate nutritional analysis per serving:
Calories 154, Protein 5 g, Carbohydrates 23 g, Fat 6 g, Cholesterol .3 mg, Sodium 582 mg

GREEN BEANS IN CI'BELLA MUSHROOM SAUCE

LAYERED ROOT VEGETABLE STEW

1 piece wakame (sea vegetable),
   soaked and diced
1 cup (240 ml) spring water
1 onion, cut in segments
2 tbs (30 ml) tamari
1 turnip, cut in segments
1 small rutabaga, cut in
   small pieces
1 daikon radish, cut on a diagonal
1 scallion, thinly sliced
1 carrot, sliced
1 piece burdock, thinly sliced
1 lotus root, thinly sliced

In a pot, place water and wakame. Turn up flame until water boils, reduce to medium flame. Begin by layering onions over wakame. Sprinkle a little tamari on onions and then layer turnip. Sprinkle a little tamari on turnips and continue to sprinkle and layer rest of the roots in the order they are listed. Cover the pot and simmer for 50 minutes. Gently stir and serve over rice or as a side dish. Serves 4.

Approximate nutritional analysis per serving:
Calories 162, Protein 4 g, Carbohydrates 38 g, Fat .5 g, Cholesterol 0 mg, Sodium 671 mg

VEGETABLE & HERB CURRY

1 box ARROWHEAD MILLS
   Vegetable and Herb Quick
   Brown Rice
½ medium onion, thinly sliced
2 stalks celery, chopped
1 green bell pepper, chopped
2 tbs (30 ml) vegetable oil
1 fresh apple, chopped
   or ½ cup (120 ml) dried apples,
   chopped
¼ cup (60 ml) raisins
¼ cup (60 ml) water
2 tsp (10 ml) curry powder
salt or tamari soy sauce, to taste

Cook rice according to package directions. While rice is cooking, sauté vegetables in oil until barely tender, 3-5 minutes. Stir in the apples, raisins and water. Cover and steam for a few minutes until the raisins are softened. When the rice is done, add it and the curry powder to the vegetables. Stir gently until well mixed. Let sit a few minutes for the flavors to mingle. Add salt or tamari soy sauce to taste. Serves 6.

Approximate nutritional analysis per serving:
Calories 274, Protein 6 g, Carbohydrates 49 g, Fat 6 g, Cholesterol 0 mg, Sodium 214 mg

VEGETABLE & HERB CURRY

BEAN-VEGETABLE CASSEROLE WITH PESTO

½ cup (120 ml) diced onions
½ cup (120 ml) diced carrots
1 tbs (15 ml) chopped fresh garlic
½ cup (120 ml) diced celery
1 tbs (15 ml) olive oil
2 15-oz cans (900 g) low-sodium
    beans, pinto, kidney, black,
    garbanzos or great northern,
    drained
1 cup (240 ml) quartered tomatoes
1 cup (240 ml) diced yellow or
    green squash

PESTO:
1 large fresh red bell pepper
½ tbs (8 ml) chopped fresh garlic
¼ cup (60 ml) GREEN HOUSE Fresh
    Italian Parsley, plus sprigs for
    garnish
2 tbs (30 ml) GREEN HOUSE
    Fresh Rosemary, plus sprigs
    for garnish
2 tbs (30 ml) olive oil
¼ cup (60 ml) walnuts
¼ cup (60 ml) grated Parmesan
    cheese
fresh ground pepper

2 cups (480 ml) cooked rice

In a thick-bottomed saucepan sauté onion, carrot, garlic and celery in the olive oil for 5 minutes. Add the beans and tomatoes and simmer for 5 minutes more. Add the squash and cook an additional 5 minutes.

Pesto: Seed the pepper and remove the leaves from the rosemary. Place the peppers and garlic in a blender or food processor and purée. Add the herbs, pour in the oil and last add the nuts, cheese and black pepper. Yields approximately 1 cup pesto.

To serve, place ½ cup rice into soup or pasta bowls and ladle bean mixture over. Top each serving with 1 tbs of Pesto and garnish with sprig of rosemary or parsley. Serves 4.

Approximate nutritional analysis per serving:
Calories 369, Protein 16 g, Carbohydrates 61g, Fat 8 g, Cholesterol 1 mg, Sodium 71 mg

SESAME-VEGETABLE STIR FRY

SESAME-VEGETABLE STIR-FRY

3 tbs (45 ml) CALIFORNIA
    CLASSICS Sesame Oil or High
    Oleic Safflower Oil
4 cups (960 ml) broccoli florets,
    or choice of vegetables
½ cup (120 ml) chicken broth
2 tbs (30 ml) rice vinegar
1½ tbs (25 ml) OISHII Tamari
    Soy Sauce
2 tsp (10 ml) cornstarch
¼ cup (60 ml) sesame seeds

In a wok or large skillet, heat sesame oil until very hot. Add vegetables and cook, tossing, about 3 minutes. Add chicken broth and bring to boil. Cover and cook over medium heat until vegetables are tender, 5-7 minutes. In a mixing bowl, combine rice vinegar, tamari soy sauce and cornstarch; stir into vegetable mixture, tossing to coat. Sprinkle with sesame seeds and serve immediately. Serves 4.

Approximate nutritional analysis per serving:
Calories 180, Protein 5 g, Carbohydrates 9 g, Fat 15 g, Cholesterol 0 mg, Sodium 507 mg

WALNUT BROCCOLI STIR-FRY

2 carrots, thinly sliced
2 cups (480 ml) broccoli florets
2 onions, thinly sliced
1 tbs (15 ml) vegetable oil
1 cup (240 ml) mushrooms, sliced
½-1 cup (120-240 ml) walnut halves
1 tbs (15 ml) cornstarch
3 tbs (45 ml) soy sauce
½ tsp (3 ml) black pepper
1 cup (240 ml) vegetable stock
3 6.1-oz pkgs (549 g) **SOY DELI** Teriyaki Tofu Burgers, cut into 1-inch cubes

Steam carrots and broccoli until tender, reserving 1 cup liquid to use as stock. In a wok or large frying pan sauté onions in oil until soft, then add mushrooms and walnut halves. Increase heat to medium-high and add the carrots and broccoli. Stir. Add corn-starch, soy sauce and black pepper to vegetable stock. Pour over the vegetables and add tofu burger cubes. Stir and cook until bubbling. Serve over hot rice or Chinese noodles. Serves 6.

Approximate nutritional analysis per serving w/o rice:
Calories 363, Protein 19 g, Carbohydrates 28 g, Fat 17 g, Cholesterol 0 mg, Sodium 896 mg

WALNUT BROCCOLI STIR-FRY

HONEYED STIR-FRY RICE AND VEGETABLES

3 tbs (45 ml) peanut oil
1 bunch green onions, bulbs and tops chopped separately
1 medium sweet potato, pared and halved lengthwise and thinly sliced
1 small green bell pepper, cut into thin strips
2 carrots, thinly sliced
1 zucchini, thinly sliced
2 cups (480 l) cooked brown rice
1 cup (240 ml) bean sprouts
1 cup (240 ml) fresh mushrooms, sliced
¼ cup (60 ml) **DAWES HILL** Clover/Alfalfa Honey
¼ cup (60 ml) tamari soy sauce

Heat oil in wok or large heavy skillet over medium-high heat. Stir-fry onion bulbs, sweet potato, bell pepper, carrots and zucchini until barley tender. Add rice, sprouts, mushrooms and onion tops. Cook quickly; if necessary, add more oil. Combine honey and tamari soy sauce in cup. Pour over stir-fry mixture and stir. Serve immediately. Serves 7.

Approximate nutritional analysis per serving:
Calories 202, Protein 4 g, Carbohydrates 34 g, Fat 7 g, Cholesterol 0 mg, Sodium 604 mg

HONEYED STIR-FRY RICE AND VEGETABLES

STIR-FRY SUPREME

**14-oz pkg (420 g) firm tofu,
drained and cubed**
1 tbs (15 ml) sesame flavor oil
1 tsp (15 ml) chopped garlic
1 tbs (15 ml) chopped fresh ginger
**12-oz pkg (360 g) fresh oriental
vegetable mix or a combination
of Napa cabbage, bean sprouts,
celery and bok choy**
1 cup (240 ml) sliced mushrooms
**1½ cups (355 ml) stir-fry sauce of
choice: oyster, Szechwan, sweet
and sour or teriyaki**
**1 pkg GREEN HOUSE Oriental
Bouquet, cut into small pieces**
**1 red bell pepper, cut into small
strips**
4 cups (960 ml) cooked white rice

To warm tofu, microwave on high for 2 minutes, or place in 350°F (180°C) oven for 10 minutes.

Place a wok or fry pan on high heat and add oil, garlic and ginger, stirring constantly until it becomes light brown. Add vegetables and mushrooms and cook for 2-4 minutes depending on crispness desired. Add the sauce and bring to a boil. At the last moment add half the fresh herbs and pour the mixture over the warmed tofu. Garnish with red pepper strips and the rest of the herbs. Serve over rice. Serves 4.

Approximate nutritional analysis per serving:
Calories 500, Protein 15 g, Carbohydrates 90 g, Fat 9 g, Cholesterol 0 mg, Sodium 325 mg

STIR-FRY SUPREME

CONDIMENTS

CORN, JICAMA & PINEAPPLE SALSA

1½ cups (355 ml) FRIEDA'S Jicama, peeled and finely chopped
1 cup (240 ml) fresh pineapple, finely chopped
1 cup (240 ml) whole kernel corn
½ cup (120 ml) green or red bell pepper, diced
1 FRIEDA'S Dried Habañero Chile, rehydrated and very finely chopped
2 tbs (30 ml) FRIEDA'S Fresh Cilantro, chopped
1 clove garlic, minced

In a medium bowl combine jicama, pineapple, corn, bell pepper, habañero chile, cilantro and garlic. Process in 2 batches in food processor or blender, using a few stop-and-start motions, for a relishlike consistency. Cover and chill at least 1 hour to allow flavors to blend. Serve with fresh vegetable crudités or spoon over any steamed or cooked vegetable, barbecued meats, poultry or fish or over scrambled eggs. Yields 3½ cups.

Approximate nutritional analysis per 1 tbs serving:
Calories 6, Protein .2 g, Carbohydrates 1 g, Fat .1 g, Cholesterol 0 mg, Sodium 16 mg

CORN, JICAMA & PINEAPPLE SALSA

HABAÑERO PEPPER SAUCE

1 cup (240 ml) finely minced onion
2 tbs (30 ml) FRIEDA'S Fresh Cilantro, chopped
1 FRIEDA'S Fresh Habañero Chile, seeded and very finely chopped
1 clove garlic, minced
3 tbs (45 ml) olive oil
2 tbs (30 ml) orange juice
1 tbs (15 ml) lemon or lime juice
dash salt

Measure all ingredients into a food processor bowl or blender container. Cover and process 10 seconds or until it reaches a relishlike consistency. Let stand at least 1 hour to blend flavors. Store in refrigerator in a tightly covered container for up to 1 month. Use to season salsa, soups, stews or sandwiches. Yields 1 cup.

Approximate nutritional analysis per 1 tbs serving:
Calories 29, Protein .2 g, Carbohydrates 1 g, Fat 3 g, Cholesterol 0 mg, Sodium 62 mg

HABAÑERO PEPPER SAUCE

AVOCADO & JICAMA SALSA WITH CILANTRO & LIME

2 ripe avocados, diced
4 oz (120 g) jicama, peeled and
    finely diced
1 small red onion, peeled and
    finely diced
1 large ripe tomato, diced
juice of 2 limes
2 tbs (30 ml) SPECTRUM WORLD
    EATS Southwestern Oil
4 tbs (60 ml) cilantro, chopped
salt, to taste
fresh ground pepper, to taste

In a large bowl, combine the avocado, jicama, onion and tomato. Add lime juice and oil. Add the cilantro and season well with salt and pepper. Mix well and allow to sit for at least 10 minutes. Serve separately with chips or use as a salsa for chicken, fish or as a dip for raw vegetables. Yields 3½ cups.

Approximate nutritional analysis per 1 tbs serving:
Calories 19, Protein .4 g, Carbohydrates 2 g, Fat 3 g, Cholesterol 0 mg, Sodium 2 mg

**AVOCADO & JICAMA SALSA
WITH CILANTRO & LIME**

SALSA WITH FRESH CILANTRO

¼ cup (60 ml) GREEN HOUSE
    Fresh Cilantro Leaves, chopped
2 medium tomatoes, chopped
1 small green chile, serrano or
    jalapeño, peeled, seeded and
    minced
¼ cup (60 ml) onion, chopped
1 clove garlic, minced
½ tsp (3 ml) red wine vinegar

Mix all ingredients. Serve with tortilla chips or Mexican foods. Great in guacamole. Yields 1 cup.

Approximate nutritional analysis per 1 tbs serving:
Calories 6, Protein .2 g, Carbohydrates 1 g, Fat .1 g, Cholesterol 0 mg, Sodium 55 mg

SALSA WITH FRESH CILANTRO

LADYBUG PRODUCE SALSAS

SALSA BASE:
3 cups (720 ml) tomatoes,
    chopped or diced
2 cups (480 ml) white onions,
    chopped
¾ cup (180 ml) fresh cilantro,
    chopped

SALSA CARIBE:
2 cups (480 ml) ripe mangos, diced,
    or papaya/nectarine combo
3 yellow wax chiles, chopped
juice of 1 lime
red Italian or sweet Spanish onions,
    optional
any hot yellow or red chile, optional
salt, optional

SALSA FRESCA:
2-3 jalapeños, seeded, veined and
    chopped
juice of ½ lemon
green onions, optional
garlic, optional
serrano (hot) or Anaheim (mild)
    chiles, optional
salt, optional

BURNT SALSA:
2 roasted poblanos, seeded,
    veined and diced
4 roasted cloves garlic, chopped
salt, optional
juice of 1 lemon
1 tbs (15 ml) fresh oregano
roasted tomatoes and onions,
    optional
chipotle peppers added to poblanos,
    optional

SALSA VERDE:
3 cups (720 ml) tomatillos
2-3 jalapeños, chopped
serrano (hot) or Anaheim (mild)
    chiles, optional
salt, optional

Assemble Salsa Base and add ingredients for any of the variations. Improvise freely with optional ingredients. Chop by hand for a coarser texture. Flavors will blend after standing for an hour. Salsa is best served fresh but will keep, refrigerated, for up to 3 days.

Salsa Caribe: Add mango, chiles and lime juice to Salsa Base. Yields 7½ cups.

Salsa Fresca: Add jalapeños and lemon juice to Salsa Base. Yields 5½ cups.

Salsa Verde: Substitute tomatillos for tomatoes in Salsa Base. Purée tomatillos and onion. Add jalapeño. Yields 5½ cups.

Burnt Salsa: Add poblanos, garlic, salt, lemon juice and oregano to Salsa Base. Yields 5½ cups.

Salsa Verde: Substitute tomatillos for tomatoes in Salsa Base. Purée tomatillos and onion. Add jalapeño. Yields 5½ cups.

Approximate nutritional analysis per 1 tbs serving Salsa Caribe: Calories 3, Protein .1 g, Carbohydrates 1 g, Fat .03 g, Cholesterol 0 mg, Sodium 4 mg

Approximate nutritional analysis per 1 tbs serving Salsa Fresca: Calories 8, Protein .3 g, Carbohydrates .4 g, Fat .1 g, Cholesterol 0 mg, Sodium 10 mg

Approximate nutritional analysis per 1 tbs serving Salsa Verde: Calories 8, Protein .3 g, Carbohydrates 2 g, Fat .1 g, Cholesterol 0 mg, Sodium 7 mg

Approximate nutritional analysis per 1 tbs serving Burnt Salsa: Calories 8, Protein .3 g, Carbohydrates 2 g, Fat .1 g, Cholesterol 0 mg, Sodium 2 mg

LADYBUG PRODUCE SALSAS

FRIEDA'S HOMEMADE SALSA

6 FRIEDA'S Fresh Yellow Chiles
6 FRIEDA'S Fresh Serrano or
    Jalapeño Chiles
2 green or red bell peppers
2 large red tomatoes, chopped
1 cup (240 ml) minced onion
2 cloves garlic, minced
3 tbs (45 ml) lime juice
¼ tsp (1 ml) salt
½ tsp (3 ml) fresh ground black
    pepper

Preheat broiler. Pierce each chile and the green peppers near the stem with a sharp knife. Arrange chiles and peppers on a lightly greased baking sheet; roast, turning frequently with thongs, until all sides of peppers and chiles are blistered, but not black. Remove from oven; place chiles and peppers in a brown paper bag to soften skins. Let stand 15 minutes; slip skins off peppers. Wear plastic gloves, or cover fingers with plastic sandwich bags to prevent chile burn. Chop chiles and peppers. Discard the seeds and veins if you prefer a milder salsa. Stir together the chopped chiles and peppers with remaining ingredients. Taste for seasoning. Store in a tightly covered jar in refrigerator for up to 1 week, or in freezer for 2-3 months. Yields 2 cups.

Approximate nutritional analysis per 1 tbs serving:
Calories 13, Protein .5 g, Carbohydrates 3 g, Fat .1 g, Cholesterol 0 mg, Sodium 339 mg

CUCUMBER & TOMATO RAITA

1 medium cucumber, peeled
1 tbs (15 ml) finely chopped onion
2 tsp (10 ml) salt
1 small tomato, cut into
    1-inch cubes
1 tbs (15 ml) finely chopped
    fresh coriander
1 tsp (5 ml) ground cumin
1 cup (240 ml) STONYFIELD FARM
    Plain Nonfat Yogurt

Dice the cucumber into ½-inch cubes. Combine the cucumber with the onion and salt. Let stand for 5 minutes, then squeeze out as much liquid as possible. Place the cucumber mixture in a bowl and add tomato and coriander.

Toast the cumin in an ungreased skillet for 30 seconds over medium-low heat. Add the cumin and yogurt to the cucumber mixture; toss and serve. Yields 2 cups, serves 4.

Approximate nutritional analysis per ½ cup serving:
Calories 50, Protein 4 g, Carbohydrates 8 g, Fat .3 g, Cholesterol 1 mg, Sodium 1116 mg

CUCUMBER & TOMATO RAITA

Opposite: FRIEDA'S HOMEMADE SALSA

MASTO-KHIAR RAITA

1 large or 2 small cucumbers
1 cup (240 ml) **STONYFIELD FARMS**
    Plain Nonfat Yogurt
2 tbs (30 ml) honey
¼ cup (60 ml) raisins
½ cup (120 ml) chopped walnuts
1 small onion, grated, optional
1 tbs (15 ml) crushed dried
    mint leaves
salt, to taste
pepper, to taste

Peel and grate the cucumbers. Squeeze the cucumbers in a towel to remove excess liquid, then mix well with the yogurt and honey. Add raisins, walnuts, onion, mint, salt and pepper; mix well. Chill before serving. Yields 2½ cups, serves 5.

Note: Up to 1 additional cup of yogurt can be added, to taste.

Approximate nutritional analysis per ½ cup serving:
Calories 162, Protein 6 g, Carbohydrates 20 g, Fat 7 g, Cholesterol .8 mg, Sodium 40 mg

MASTO-KHIAR RAITA

QUICK MANGO CHUTNEY

2 tbs (30 ml) **SPECTRUM**
    NATURALS Super Canola Oil
1 medium yellow onion, minced
3 tbs (45 ml) garlic, minced
2 cups (480 ml) fresh mango,
    peeled and diced
⅔ cup (160 ml) organic apple juice
5 tbs (75 ml) **SPECTRUM**
    NATURALS Organic Mango
    Vinegar
½ cup (120 ml) raisins
1 apple, peeled and cut into
    small dice
1 tbs (15 ml) ginger, finely minced
½ tsp (3 ml) allspice

Heat the oil over medium heat in a 2-quart saucepan. Add the onions and sauté 5 minutes. Add the garlic, mango, apple juice and vinegar. Simmer for 10 minutes, stirring often. Add the raisins, apple, ginger and allspice. Continue to simmer until the moisture has evaporated, about 10 more minutes. Refrigerate. Serve as a delicious condiment as an accompaniment to spicy foods or like a jam. Yields 3½ cups.

Approximate nutritional analysis per 2 tbs serving:
Calories 45, Protein .3 g, Carbohydrates 9 g, Fat 1 g, Cholesterol 0 mg, Sodium 1 mg

QUICK MANGO CHUTNEY

TOMATO KETCHUP

3 lbs (1.4 kg) tomatoes
3 tbs (45 ml) sea salt
2 cups (480 ml) OMEGA Apple Cider Vinegar
3 tbs (45 ml) raw sugar
2 tsp (10 ml) mustard powder
1 tsp (5 ml) black pepper

Blanch tomatoes and chop. Sprinkle with the sea salt and let stand for at least 3 hours. Combine all ingredients in a saucepan and bring to boil. Let simmer for at least 30 minutes, or more for a denser ketchup. Stir frequently. When thick, fill clean bottles and let sit for a few days in the refrigerator before using. Yields 2 cups.

Note: For a smooth professional texture, remove skins after blanching tomatoes and put tomatoes through a food mill after simmering for 15 minutes; return to pot to thicken over low heat.

Approximate nutritional analysis per 1 tbs serving:
Calories 15, Protein .4 g, Carbohydrates 3 g, Fat .2 g, Cholesterol 0 mg, Sodium 603 mg

TOMATO KETCHUP

CHUNKY GINGERED CRANBERRY SAUCE

1 ¼ cups (295 ml) apple cider or juice
3-oz pkg (90 g) FRIEDA'S Dried Cranberries
1 cup (240 ml) chopped dried apples or pears
⅓ cup (80 ml) raisins
1 ½ tsp (8 ml) FRIEDA'S Fresh Ginger, minced

In saucepan combine all ingredients. Bring to a boil; simmer, covered, 10 minutes. Remove from heat; cool. Serve warm or chilled as a meat or poultry accompaniment, or on sandwiches as a condiment. Yields 2 cups.

Approximate nutritional analysis per ¼ cup serving:
Calories 59, Protein .4 g, Carbohydrates 15 g, Fat .1 g, Cholesterol 0 mg, Sodium 6 mg

CHUNKY GINGERED CRANBERRY SAUCE

INDIAN ROCK'S BEET-GARLIC RELISH

6-8 medium sized beets
10 peeled cloves garlic
1 cup (240 ml) champagne vinegar
½ cup (120 ml) water
½ cup (120 ml) sugar
4 whole peppercorns
½ medium bay leaf
1 tbs chopped fresh mint
3 tbs (45 ml) minced shallots
salt, to taste
pepper, to taste

Scrub the beets under cold running water until all dirt is removed. Simmer in lightly salted water until fork tender about 20-30 minutes. Remove from the water and allow to cool. Peel off the outer skin of beets by rubbing with paper towels. Poach the garlic cloves in vinegar, water, sugar, black peppercorns and bay leaf until tender. Remove from the heat and allow the garlic to cool in the poaching liquid. Slice the garlic thinly and dice the beets into ⅓-inch cubes. Toss the diced beets, poached garlic, chopped mint and minced shallots; season to taste with salt and black pepper. Adjust the acidity level with champagne vinegar or sugar if necessary. Serves 6.

Approximate nutritional analysis per serving:
Calories 98, Protein 1 g, Carbohydrates 24 g, Fat .1 g, Cholesterol 0 mg, Sodium 40 mg

INDIAN ROCK'S BEET-GARLIC RELISH

ROASTED RED PEPPERS ITALIA

9 large red Italian frying peppers
**   or 6 red bell peppers**
¼ cup (60 ml) olive oil, or less
¼ cup (60 ml) CHESHIRE GARDEN
**   Blenda d'Italia Vinegar**

Roast peppers over flame or in oven until charred. Place in a paper bag to cool; peel off skins. Whisk half of the oil into the vinegar, taste and slowly add more if needed. Slice peppers into strips and drizzle with marinade. Chill for several hours. Serve with mozzarella cheese. Serves 12.

Approximate nutritional analysis per serving w/o cheese:
Calories 50, Protein .3 g, Carbohydrates 2 g, Fat 5 g, Cholesterol 0 mg, Sodium .7 mg

ROASTED RED PEPPERS ITALIA

SAUTÉED MUSHROOMS WITH CARAMELIZED ONIONS & PEPPERS

1 pkg GREEN HOUSE Hamburger
    Bouquet, contains thyme,
    rosemary, basil
12 oz (360 g) crimini or regular
    white mushrooms
1 tbs (15 ml) extra-virgin olive oil
1 cup (240 ml) thin-sliced red onions
1 tbs (15 ml) chopped fresh garlic
1 cup (240 ml) green or red
    bell peppers
fresh ground pepper
salt, optional

Chop thyme and rosemary leaves finely. Reserve 6 whole basil leaves for garnish; chop the rest and combine with thyme and rosemary. Wash and quarter the mushrooms. Heat the oil in a nonstick skillet on high and sauté the onions until they are light brown. Add garlic and cook for 1 minute. Add the peppers and mushrooms; cook for 5 minutes then add chopped herbs. Season with ground pepper and salt, if desired. Serve over veggie, turkey or beef burgers. Also delicious over penne pasta. Serves 6.

Approximate nutritional analysis per serving:
Calories 49, Protein 2 g, Carbohydrates 6 g, Fat 3 g, Cholesterol 0 mg, Sodium 3 mg

**SAUTÉED MUSHROOMS
WITH CARAMELIZED
ONIONS & PEPPERS**

EGGLESS PROVENÇAL ROUILLE
Hot Red Pepper Sauce

2 tbs (30 ml) SPECTRUM
    NATURALS California Extra
    Virgin Olive Oil
10-oz container (300 g) SPECTRUM
    SPREAD
1 large red bell pepper, roasted,
    peeled, seeded and finely diced
2 tbs (30 ml) fresh garlic,
    very finely minced
1 pinch saffron, optional
1 tsp (5 ml) salt
fresh ground pepper, to taste

In a stainless steel or glass bowl, whisk the olive oil into the Spectrum Spread. Stir in the peppers and the garlic. Stir in the saffron. Season with salt and pepper. Cover and refrigerate until ready for use. This quick easy condiment is delicious in seafood soups, on steamed vegetables or as an appetizer spread thinly onto small toasts. Yields approximately 2 cups.

Approximate nutritional analysis per 2 tbs serving:
Calories 139, Protein .07 g, Carbohydrates .5 g, Fat 17 g, Cholesterol 0 mg, Sodium 257 mg

EGGLESS PROVENÇAL ROUILLE

CITRUS SALAD DRESSING

1 tbs (15 ml) natural rice vinegar
¼ tsp (1 ml) Dijon-style mustard
¼ tsp (1 ml) evaporated cane juice
2 tsp (10 ml) CALIFORNIA
   CLASSICS Lemon Oil
salt, to taste, optional
pepper, to taste, optional

In a small bowl, combine all ingredients. Season to taste. Whisk together for a citrus-tasting dressing. Serves 1.

Approximate nutritional analysis per serving:
Calories 85, Protein .1 g, Carbohydrates 1 g, Fat 9 g, Cholesterol 0 mg, Sodium 17 mg

CITRUS SALAD DRESSING

YOGURT DIJON SALAD DRESSING

3 tbs (45 ml) Dijon mustard
½ cup (120 ml) STONYFIELD FARM
   Plain Low Fat Yogurt
½ tsp (3 ml) salt
pinch of freshly ground pepper
3 tbs (45 ml) lemon juice
1 tsp (5 ml) sugar
1 clove garlic, finely chopped
1 tbs (15 ml) capers, drained

Combine the mustard, yogurt, salt, pepper, lemon juice, sugar and garlic in a small bowl; beat well. Stir in the capers and serve. Yields 1 cup.

Approximate nutritional analysis per 1 tbs serving:
Calories 20, Protein <1 g, Carbohydrates 5 g, Fat <1 g, Cholesterol <1 mg, Sodium 149 mg

LEAH'S BERRY-POPPY SEED DRESSING

⅓ cup (80 ml) plain nonfat yogurt
2 tbs (30 ml) CHESHIRE GARDEN
   Raspberry or Strawberry
   Vinegar
1 tbs (15 ml) maple syrup
½ tbs (8 ml) poppy seeds

Mix all ingredients and serve over salad of red and green lettuce, oranges, avocado and kiwi. Yields ½ cup.

Approximate nutritional analysis per 1 tbs serving:
Calories 26, Protein .7 g, Carbohydrates 3 g, Fat 1 g, Cholesterol .2 mg, Sodium 25 mg

LEAH'S BERRY-POPPY SEED DRESSING

SUPREMO SALAD DRESSING

¼ cup (60 ml) balsamic vinegar
1 tsp (5 ml) Dijon mustard
2-4 cloves garlic, crushed
1 tsp (5 ml) Worcestershire sauce
6 drops Tabasco sauce
1 tbs (15 ml) sweet basil
½ tsp (3 ml) tarragon
½ tsp (3 ml) oregano
¼ cup (60 ml) Parmesan cheese
½ tsp (3 ml) maple syrup
1 tbs (15 ml) sun-dried tomatoes, chopped
¾ cup (180 ml) OMEGA Flax Seed Oil

Blend all ingredients, except for oil, in blender for 20 seconds. Slowly pour in oil, with the blender on. The slower you pour, the thicker the dressing. Store leftover salad dressing in the refrigerator. The dressing will be good for several days. Yields 1¼ cups.

Approximate nutritional analysis per 1 tbs serving:
Calories 79, Protein .6 g, Carbohydrates .4 g, Fat 9 g, Cholesterol 1 mg, Sodium 33 mg

SUPREMO SALAD DRESSING

SESAME RASPBERRY DRESSING

1 oz (30 ml) raspberry vinegar
½-1 tsp (3-5 ml) fresh ginger, shredded
1 tsp (5 ml) chopped dried figs
½ cup (120 ml) OMEGA Sesame Oil
sea salt, to taste, optional
pepper, to taste, optional

Combine vinegar, ginger and figs in blender. Blend for 10 seconds. Add oil, in a slow stream, while blender is on. Serve chilled. Store leftover dressing in the refrigerator. This dressing will be good for several days. Yields ½ cup.

Approximate nutritional analysis per 1 tbs serving:
Calories 138, Protein .1 g, Carbohydrates 1 g, Fat 15 g, Cholesterol 0 mg, Sodium 24 mg

COUSIN RICHARD'S SIMPLY SALAD DRESSING

COUSIN RICHARD'S SIMPLY SALAD DRESSING

1 tbs (15 ml) UNCLE DAVE'S Kickin' Mustard
1 tbs (15 ml) UNCLE DAVE'S Honey
juice of 1 lime

Mix all quite vigorously and pour over your favorite greens, shredded carrot salad or coleslaw. Yields 2 tbs.

Approximate nutritional analysis per 1 tbs serving:
Calories 35, Protein 0 g, Carbohydrates 8 g, Fat 0 g, Cholesterol 0 mg, Sodium 20 mg

TOFU PEANUT SAUCE

16-oz pkg (480 g) SURATA
    SOYFOODS CO-OP Firm Tofu,
    drained
4 tbs (60 ml) peanut butter or
    crushed peanuts
1 large garlic clove
1 tbs (15 ml) ginger
1 tsp (5 ml) lemon or lime juice
½ tbs (3 ml) soy sauce
1 tsp (5 ml) red chile flakes
1 tsp (5 ml) mint leaves
½ cup (120 ml) coconut milk
1-2 scallions
1 tsp (5 ml) cilantro leaves

Put everything in the blender and blend until smooth. Toss with pasta, steamed veggies or rice. It is also a great spread for broiled tempeh. Yields 4 cups.

Approximate nutritional analysis per ½ cup serving:
Calories 165, Protein 12 g, Carbohydrates 6 g, Fat 13 g, Cholesterol 0 mg, Sodium 76 mg

TOFU PEANUT SAUCE

GADO-GADO

1 cup (240 ml) chopped onion
2 cloves garlic, minced
1 bay leaf
2 tsp (10 ml) ginger root, grated
2 tbs (30 ml) butter or margarine
    for frying
1 cup (240 ml) EAST WIND
    Peanut Butter
1 tbs (15 ml) honey
¼ tsp (1 ml) cayenne pepper
juice of 1 lemon
1 tbs (15 ml) cider vinegar
3 cups (720 ml) water
½-1 tsp (3-5 ml) salt
dash of tamari or other soy sauce

In a saucepan, cook the onions, garlic, bay leaf and ginger in butter. When onion becomes translucent, add the remaining ingredients. Mix thoroughly. Simmer on lowest possible heat for 30 minutes, stirring occasionally.

Cool for use as salad dressing or serve warm over fresh vegetables such as shredded cabbage, steamed or raw; carrot slices, celery slices, snow peas, steamed broccoli spears; fresh green beans and mung bean sprouts; cubes of tofu, marinated in soy and honey and lightly fried or baked in ⅛ tsp sesame oil; apple slices, raisins, toasted seeds and nuts. Yields approximately 5¼ cups.

Approximate nutritional analysis per ¼ cup serving:
Calories 252, Protein 5 g, Carbohydrates 14 g, Fat 19 g, Cholesterol 8 mg, Sodium 188 mg

KICKIN' SEAFOOD SAUCE

1 cup (240 ml) UNCLE DAVE'S
    Ketchup
2 tbs (30 ml) UNCLE DAVE'S
    Carrot/Horseradish
4 tbs (60 ml) diced fennel or celery

Mix everything together and serve with your favorite cooked cold seafood (scallops, leftover fish, shrimp, crab claws, etc.). Yields approximately 1 1/3 cups.

Approximate nutritional analysis per 1 tbs serving:
Calories 13, Protein .01 g, Carbohydrates 3 g, Fat .01 g, Cholesterol 0 mg, Sodium 73 mg

MADAME SHARON'S PUTANESCA SAUCE

1-oz can (30 g) anchovies, undrained
6-oz can (180 g) tuna fish, drained
1 jar UNCLE DAVE'S Excellent
    Marinara
2 oz (60 g) capers, drained
1/2 cup (120 ml) imported Greek
    olives, chopped

In a large pot mash anchovies into a paste and mix with flaked tuna fish. Add remaining ingredients and heat through. Serve over pasta. Yields 3 cups.

Approximate nutritional analysis per 1/2 cup serving:
Calories 123, Protein 11 g, Carbohydrates 10 g, Fat 4 g, Cholesterol 12 mg, Sodium 1002 mg

KICKIN' SEAFOOD SAUCE

HOMEMADE PASTA SAUCE

2 tbs (30 ml) olive oil
1 cup (240 ml) chopped onion
1/2 cup (120 ml) chopped green
    bell pepper
2 cloves garlic, minced
28-oz can (840 g) MUIR GLEN
    Organic Whole Peeled Tomatoes,
    undrained
2 tbs (30 ml) chopped fresh parsley
1/2 tsp (3 ml) basil leaves, crushed
1/4 tsp (1 ml) oregano leaves, crushed
1/4 tsp (1 ml) salt
pinch pepper

Heat oil in large saucepan over medium-low heat. Add onion, green bell pepper and garlic; cook until tender. Stir in tomatoes, parsley, basil, oregano, salt and pepper. Crush tomatoes with spoon. Cook, stirring often, uncovered, until thickened, about 20-30 minutes. Serve immediately over hot cooked pasta, or cool and freeze. Yields 2 cups.

Approximate nutritional analysis per 1/4 cup serving:
Calories 60, Protein 1 g, Carbohydrates 6 g, Fat 3 g, Cholesterol 0 mg, Sodium 216 mg

MADAME SHARON'S PUTANESCA SAUCE

TOMATO & OREGANO PASTA SAUCE

3 tbs (45 ml) olive oil
2 cloves garlic, minced
1 lb (455 g) sweet Italian sausage, casings removed
1 medium onion, chopped
2 lbs (910 g) Roma tomatoes, peeled and diced
½ cup (120 ml) red wine
6-oz can (180 ml) tomato paste
1 tsp (5 ml) sugar
3 tbs (45 ml) GREEN HOUSE Fresh Oregano, minced

Heat olive oil in a large saucepan over medium heat. Add garlic and stir 1 minute. Add sausage. Break up sausage with a spoon and cook until lightly browned. Add onions and tomatoes and cook for 4 minutes. Mix in wine, tomato paste and sugar. Reduce heat and simmer for about 20 minutes, stirring frequently. Stir in fresh oregano and remove from heat. Serve over hot cooked pasta. Serves 6.

Approximate nutritional analysis per serving:
Calories 405, Protein 14 g, Carbohydrates 17 g, Fat 31 g, Cholesterol 57 mg, Sodium 792 mg

QUICK TWO-TOMATO SAUCE WITH NIÇOISE OLIVES

2 tbs (30 ml) SPECTRUM NATURALS Super Canola Oil
1 medium yellow onion, minced
4 cups (960 ml) MUIR GLEN Organic Diced Tomatoes or ripe garden tomatoes, peeled, seeded and diced
⅓ cup (80 ml) dried tomatoes, chopped
4 cloves garlic, minced
½ cup (120 ml) Niçoise olives, pitted
3 tbs (45 ml) fresh parsley, chopped
3 tbs (45 ml) fresh basil, chopped
3 tbs (45 ml) SPECTRUM NATURALS California Extra Virgin Olive Oil
2 tbs (30 ml) SPECTRUM NATURALS Organic Red Wine Vinegar
salt, to taste
fresh ground pepper, to taste

QUICK TWO-TOMATO SAUCE WITH NIÇOISE OLIVES

Heat the canola oil in a 2- or 3-quart saucepan over medium heat. Add the onions and sauté for 5 minutes. Add the diced tomatoes, the dried tomatoes and garlic. Simmer for 15 minutes. Add the olives and continue to simmer until all of the juice from the tomatoes has evaporated. Stir in the parsley and basil. Simmer 5 more minutes. Stir in the olive oil and vinegar. Simmer for 5 more minutes, stirring often. Season with salt and fresh ground pepper. Yields 5½ cups.

This simple yet complex flavored tomato sauce is delicious with pasta, as an accompaniment to grilled or steamed fish or simply spread cold on toast rounds as an appetizer.

Approximate nutritional analysis per ½ cup serving:
Calories 91, Protein 1 g, Carbohydrates 6 g, Fat 7 g, Cholesterol 0 mg, Sodium 208 mg

TOMATO & OREGANO PASTA SAUCE

HAZELNUT PESTO

4 cloves garlic, crushed
2 cups (480 ml) fresh cilantro, chopped
¼ cup (60 ml) OMEGA Hazelnut Flour
⅓ cup (80 ml) Parmesan cheese
1 cup (240 ml) OMEGA Hazelnut Oil
sea salt, to taste

Blend all ingredients in food processor or blender for 20 seconds or until desired consistency is reached. This sauce is delicious on pasta. Yields approximately 1 cup.

Approximate nutritional analysis per 2 tbs serving:
Calories 278, Protein 4 g, Carbohydrates 2 g, Fat 29 g, Cholesterol 3 mg, Sodium 79 mg

TWO-COLOR PESTO

⅔ cup (160 ml) pine nuts or walnuts
⅔ cup (160 ml) olive oil
3 cloves garlic, minced
¼ cup (60 ml) hot water
1 cup (240 ml) Parmesan cheese, freshly grated
1 pkg GREEN HOUSE ROYAL Opal Basil
1 pkg GREEN HOUSE Fresh Basil Tops

Process pine nuts, olive oil, garlic and water in a food processor or blender until finely chopped. Blend in Parmesan cheese. Place ½ of the cheese mixture in a bowl. Add the Royal Opal Basil to the processor and mix until well blended; remove purple pesto to a new bowl. Place the remaining cheese mixture in the food processor and add the basil. Process until well blended. Toss green pesto with hot cooked pasta. Place pasta in serving bowls and top with a dollop of purple pesto. Yields approximately 2 cups.

Approximate nutritional analysis per 2 tbs serving:
Calories 141, Protein 4 g, Carbohydrates 1 g, Fat 14 g, Cholesterol 5 mg, Sodium 117 mg

HAZELNUT PESTO

OLIO SANTO DIPPING SAUCE

1 tbs (15 ml) garlic, very finely minced
2 tbs (30 ml) balsamic vinegar
1 tsp (5 ml) salt
1½ tsp (8 ml) crushed hot red chile flakes
4 tbs (60 ml) SPECTRUM WORLD EATS Mediterranean Oil
fresh ground black pepper, to taste

Combine the garlic, balsamic vinegar, salt and chile flakes in a small bowl. Let stand for at least 15 minutes. Stir in oil. Season with fresh ground black pepper to taste. Serve in place of butter with good crusty bread. Yields scant ½ cup.

Approximate nutritional analysis per 2 tbs serving:
Calories 121, Protein .05 g, Carbohydrates .2 g, Fat 14 g, Cholesterol 0 mg, Sodium 533 mg

SPICY JERK BARBECUE SAUCE

6 oz (180 ml) fresh orange juice
2 oz (60 g) dried apricots
   or mangoes
1 tbs (15 ml) SPECTRUM WORLD
   EATS Caribbean Oil
1 tbs (15 ml) molasses or honey
2 tbs (30 ml) raisins
½ medium white onion, diced
1 garlic clove
½ tsp (3 ml) anise seed
¼ tsp (1 ml) ground allspice
¼ tsp (1 ml) salt, or more to taste

Combine all ingredients in a blender or food processor and process until smooth. The sauce should be fairly thick and spreadable with a brush. Taste for salt and thin with water or orange juice, if necessary. Use sauce on your favorite grilled fish, chicken or tofu. Yields approximately 1¼ cups.

Approximate nutritional analysis per ¼ cup serving:
Calories 98, Protein 1 g, Carbohydrates 19 g, Fat 3 g, Cholesterol 0 mg, Sodium 110 mg

SPICY JERK BARBECUE SAUCE

HONEY-MUSTARD BBQ GLAZE FOR GRILLED HEALTH SEA SAUSAGES

½ cup (120 ml) honey
½ cup (120 ml) Dijon mustard
2 cloves garlic, minced
1 tbs (15 ml) Tabasco or
   other hot sauce
1 tbs (15 ml) lemon juice
1 tbs (15 ml) cider or other vinegar

Combine all ingredients. Score each sausage with 6 small cuts. Cook sausages on hot barbecue grill, basting generously every minute or so for 6-8 minutes, turning frequently. When hot and lightly browned serve at once. Yields 1¼ cups.

Approximate nutritional analysis per ¼ cup serving glaze only:
Calories 102, Protein 2 g, Carbohydrates 13 g, Fat 6 g, Cholesterol 0 mg, Sodium 477 mg

SOLAIT PARSLEY GRAVY

3 cups (720 ml) water
1½ tsp (8 ml) celery salt
3 celery sticks
¾ cup (180 ml) SOLAIT Instant
   Soy Beverage
3 tbs (45 ml) canola oil
3½ tbs (53 ml) arrowroot powder
   or cornstarch
1 cup (240 ml) fresh parsley,
   chopped

Blend all ingredients, except parsley, until smooth. Simmer in saucepan until thick, stirring constantly. When thick, add parsley. Yields approximately 3¼ cups.

Approximate nutritional analysis per ¼ cup serving:
Calories 90, Protein 2 g, Carbohydrates 10 g, Fat 5 g, Cholesterol 0 mg, Sodium 57 mg

LOUISIANA FIRE DIPPING GLAZE FOR HEALTH SEA SAUSAGES

3 oz (180 g) butter
1 tbs (15 ml) fresh garlic, minced
6 oz (180 g) Louisiana hot sauce
**2 tbs (30 ml) light or dark
corn syrup**
**1 tsp (5 ml) PAUL PRUDHOMME Veg
Magic, a seasoning blend,
optional**

Melt butter in saucepan and lightly cook garlic for 2 minutes. Add remaining ingredients and heat until hot. Grill salmon sausages brushing glaze on every minute or so for 6-8 minutes. Sausages should be lightly browned. Can also be used as Buffalo wing sauce. Yields approximately 1¼ cups.

Approximate nutritional analysis per ¼ cup serving:
Calories 153, Protein .5 g, Carbohydrates 8 g, Fat 14 g, Cholesterol 37 mg, Sodium 159 mg

**LOUISIANA FIRE DIPPING GLAZE
FOR HEALTH SEA SAUSAGES**

SHELTON'S SECRET SAUCE

**16-oz can (480 ml) SHELTON'S
Chicken Broth**
½ cup (120 ml) lemon juice
1 cup (240 ml) red wine vinegar
**½ cup (120 ml) honey or brown
sugar**
**½ cup (120 ml) barbecue sauce or
ketchup**

Combine all ingredients in saucepan and bring to boil. Use as a dipping sauce for cooked chicken. Yields 4½ cups.

Approximate nutritional analysis per ½ cup serving:
Calories 73, Protein .8 g, Carbohydrates 19 g, Fat .3 g, Cholesterol 0 mg, Sodium 127 mg

**SPICY SZECHWAN NOODLE
SAUCE**

SPICY SZECHWAN NOODLE SAUCE

**1 cup (240 ml) EAST WIND Smooth
Peanut Butter**
**¼ cup (60 ml) tamari or
other soy sauce**
2 tbs (30 ml) vinegar
2-4 cloves minced fresh garlic
1 tsp (5 ml) black pepper
¼-½ tsp (1-3 ml) cayenne
½ tsp (3 ml) cumin
½ tsp (3 ml) powdered ginger
½ cup (120 ml) water
**2 tbs (30 ml) olive oil or other
vegetable oil**

Combine all ingredients and mix very well. Yields 1½ cups.
You can toss this with cooked pasta and serve cold along with fresh bean sprouts and lettuce for a salad. Or you can warm the sauce in the microwave or on the stovetop and toss with hot noodles for a main dish. Try using half peanut butter and half tahini paste, too.

Approximate nutritional analysis per ¼ cup serving:
Calories 328, Protein 7 g, Carbohydrates 26 g, Fat .1 g, Cholesterol 26 mg, Sodium 719 mg

TAHINI SAUCE

⅓ cup (80 ml) olive or vegetable oil
3 large cloves garlic, minced
½ cup (120 ml) EAST WIND Tahini
¼ cup (60 ml) soy sauce

Heat oil in skillet. Add garlic and cook until tender. Add tahini and soy sauce. Stir over low heat until sauce thickens. Serve hot. Yields 1 generous cup.

Toss together cooked pasta, sauce, and your choice of steamed vegetables. Stir tahini sauce in with cooked rice, too; serve with steamed or stir-fried vegetables on top.

Approximate nutritional analysis per ¼ cup serving:
Calories 354, Protein 6 g, Carbohydrates 8 g, Fat 35 g, Cholesterol 0 mg, Sodium 1029 mg

HERBED HONEY-LIME SAUCE

½ cup (120 ml) minced onion
1 tbs (15 ml) olive oil
1 cup (240 ml) dry white wine
 or chicken broth
¼ cup (60 ml) honey
¼ cup (60 ml) lime juice
2 tsp (10 ml) dry mustard
1 tsp (5 ml) minced fresh rosemary
½ tsp (3 ml) salt
dash pepper
1 tsp (5 ml) cornstarch
1 tsp (5 ml) water

Sauté onion in olive oil in medium saucepan over medium heat until onions is softened. Stir in wine, honey, lime juice, mustard, rosemary, salt and pepper; mix well and bring to a boil. Combine cornstarch and water in small bowl or cup, mixing well. Add to sauce. Cook over low heat, stirring until sauce comes to a boil and thickens. Serve over cooked turkey, chicken, fish or pork. Yields 2 cups.

Approximate nutritional analysis per ¼ cup serving:
Calories 78, Protein .4 g, Carbohydrates 11 g, Fat 2 g, Cholesterol 0 mg, Sodium 135 mg

Courtesy of The National Honey Board.

WHITE SAUCE

2 tbs (30 ml) margarine
3 tbs (45 ml) flour
1 cup (240 ml) Unsweetened
 WESTSOY
¼ tsp (1 ml) salt
dash cayenne pepper, optional

Melt margarine; add flour and blend. Add soy milk slowly, stirring to blend. Cook over medium heat, stirring constantly, until mixture comes to a boil and thickens. Add salt and cayenne. Yields 1 cup.

Approximate nutritional analysis per ¼ cup serving:
Calories 56, Protein 1 g, Carbohydrates 4 g, Fat 4 g, Cholesterol 0 mg, Sodium 138 mg

LOW-FAT HOLLANDAISE SAUCE

10½-oz pkg (315 g) MORI-NU
    Silken Soft Tofu, drained
4 tbs (60 ml) plain nonfat yogurt
2 tbs (30 ml) yellow mustard
1 tbs plus 1 tsp (20 ml) white wine
    Worcestershire sauce
2 dashes white pepper
dash cayenne pepper
1 tbs (15 ml) lemon juice
1 tbs (15 ml) honey

In a blender or a food processor, whip all ingredients until smooth and creamy. Heat sauce thoroughly and spoon immediately over fresh cooked asparagus or any other fresh vegetables.
Yields 1⅓ cup.

Approximate nutritional analysis per ⅓ cup serving:
Calories 74, Protein 5 g, Carbohydrates 8 g, Fat 2 g, Cholesterol 0 mg, Sodium 160 mg

LOW-FAT HOLLANDAISE SAUCE

RED WINE MARINADE

1 pkg GREEN HOUSE
    Bouquet Garni
1 cup (240 ml) full-bodied
    dry red wine
1 cup (240 ml) fruity extra-virgin
    olive oil
3 cloves minced or pressed garlic
½ tsp (3 ml) fresh ground
    black pepper

Remove herb leaves from stems and cut into small pieces; do not chop. Combine all ingredients and mix well. Store in a sealable container until needed. Pour the marinade over chicken or meat 1 hour before needed, turning every 15 minutes. Drain well and cook as desired, basting occasionally. Yields 2 cups.

Approximate nutritional analysis per ⅛ cup serving:
Calories 131, Protein .07 g, Carbohydrates .4 g, Fat 14 g, Cholesterol 0 mg, Sodium .8 mg

RED WINE MARINADE

ORGANIC YOGURT MARINADE

⅔ cup (160 ml) HORIZON
    Organic Yogurt
juice and grated rind of ½ lemon
1 tsp (5 ml) mixed herbs
1 clove crushed garlic
salt, to taste
pepper, to taste

Mix together all ingredients. Spread the mixture over 2-2½ lbs meat, fish or tempeh. Marinate for at least 1 hour before cooking as usual. Yields ¾ cup.

Approximate nutritional analysis per ¼ cup serving:
Calories 35, Protein 3 g, Carbohydrates 5 g, Fat .1 g, Cholesterol .9 mg, Sodium 43 mg

THAI LEMON HERB & HONEY GLAZE FOR HEALTH SEA SAUSAGES

¼ cup (60 ml) lime juice
¼ cup (60 ml) Thai fish sauce
2 tbs (30 ml) clover honey
2 tbs (30 ml) rice vinegar
2 tsp (10 ml) green peppers, minced
3 cloves fresh garlic, minced
2 tbs (30 ml) water
2 scallions, minced
1 tsp (5 ml) fresh cleaned thyme

Combine all liquid ingredients and blend well. Stir in remaining ingredients. Adjust all amounts and ingredients to taste. Best when used immediately. Yields approximately 1 cup.

Approximate nutritional analysis per ¼ cup serving:
Calories 56, Protein 4 g, Carbohydrates 10 g, Fat .2 g, Cholesterol 10 mg, Sodium 156 mg

THAI LEMON HERB & HONEY GLAZE FOR HEALTH SEA SAUSAGES

PEARS ELEGANZA

5 large pears, peeled, with stems on
2 cups (480 ml) water
½ cup (120 ml) sugar
1 cinnamon stick
1 inch fresh ginger, peeled
¾ cup (180 ml) plus 1 tbs (15 ml)
    Grand Marnier
¾ cup (180 ml) heavy cream
1 tbs (15 ml) confectioners sugar
1 cup (240 ml) STONYFIELD FARM
    Plain Nonfat Yogurt, divided
½ lb (230 g) carob chips

Core the pears from the bottom, keeping the stems in place and leaving walls about ½-inch thick. Reserve the cores. Place the pears upright in a large saucepan with the water, sugar, cinnamon stick, ginger and ½ cup Grand Marnier. Cook the pears until they are tender but not mushy – anywhere from 3-15 minutes, depending on the variety and ripeness. Cool, then add another ¼ cup Grand Marnier to the poaching liquid. Let stand in refrigerator overnight.

Just before serving, whip together ½ cup heavy cream, the confectioners sugar and 1 tbs Grand Marnier in an electric mixer until stiff. On slow speed, beat in ½ cup yogurt. Remove pears from liquid; fill the cavities of the pears with this semistiff mixture. Trim a ½-inch thick piece from each reserved pear core and plug the pear cavities to keep the filling in place. To make the pears easy to eat, slice them horizontally at the point where the base narrows into the neck.

Melt the carob chips in a double boiler. Slowly add ¼ cup heavy cream and ½ cup yogurt, beating until smooth. Heat just until warmed through; do not allow to simmer. Pour the sauce over the pears and serve. Any additional whipped cream mixture may be served separately on the side. Serves 5.

Note: The poaching liquid can be stored in the refrigerator and used to make this special dessert again.

Approximate nutritional analysis per serving:
Calories 756, Protein 7 g, Carbohydrates 92 g, Fat 29 g, Cholesterol 51 mg, Sodium 90 mg

INDIAN ROCK'S FRUIT PARFAIT

24 strawberries
2 mangos
¼ cup (60 ml) fresh squeezed
    orange juice
4 kiwis, peeled and sliced
12 raspberries

Put strawberries in the blender. When puréed, pour into bottom of 6 parfait glasses or wide bowl red wine glasses. Combine mangos and orange juice in blender. Purée until smooth. Pour into parfait glasses on top of strawberries. Decorate with kiwi slices and raspberries. Place in refrigerator until ready to serve. Serves 6.

Approximate nutritional analysis per serving:
Calories 124, Protein 2 g, Carbohydrates 31 g, Fat 1 g, Cholesterol 0 mg, Sodium 5 mg

INDIAN ROCK'S FRUIT PARFAIT

YOGURT CHEESE PARFAIT

1½ qts (1.4 l) STONYFIELD FARM
Plain Nonfat Yogurt, generously
measured
1 cup (240 ml) sugar
1 tbs (15 ml) finely grated
lemon rind
2 cups (480 ml) fresh raspberries,
blueberries or hulled and sliced
strawberries

Four hours or the day before serving, stir the yogurt and sugar together. To make yogurt cheese, line a colander with several layers of cheesecloth and place it over a bowl. Measure yogurt mixture into cheesecloth, cover and refrigerate. Let this mixture drain for 4 hours or overnight. The next day, add the grated lemon rind to the yogurt cheese and mix well. If the yogurt cheese is too thick, it can be thinned slightly with additional yogurt. Spoon the yogurt cheese into parfait glasses, alternating with layers of fresh berries. Serves 4.

Approximate nutritional analysis per serving:
Calories 429, Protein 22 g, Carbohydrates 85 g, Fat 1 g, Cholesterol 7 mg, Sodium 281 mg

FRUIT COBBLER

1½ tbs (25 ml) butter
1½ cups (355 ml) ARROWHEAD
MILLS Multi Blend or
Whole Wheat Flour
1 tsp (5 ml) non-alum
baking powder
½ cup (120 ml) honey
1 egg, beaten
1 cup (240 ml) skim milk, soy milk
or water
2 cups (480 ml) fresh fruit or
canned in natural juices

Melt butter in a 9x9-inch pan or other baking dish of similar size. Mix the flour, baking powder, honey, egg and milk. Pour mixture into butter. Add the fruit on top of batter. Bake 30 minutes at 400°F (205°C). Serves 9.

Approximate nutritional analysis per serving:
Calories 170, Protein 4 g, Carbohydrates 37 g, Fat 2 g, Cholesterol 23 mg, Sodium 83 mg

Opposite: FRUIT COBBLER

YOGURT CHEESE PARFAIT

PEAR CRISP

4 cups (960 ml) pears, sliced
    (peeled or unpeeled)
¼ cup (60 ml) water
¼ cup (60 ml) powdered skim milk
¼ cup (60 ml) rolled oats
6 tbs (90 g) flour
2 tbs (30 ml) ZUMBRO Jerusalem
    Artichoke Flour
½ cup (120 ml) brown sugar
1 tsp (5 ml) cinnamon
½ cup (120 ml) butter
¼ tsp (1 ml) salt

Place sliced pears and water in a deep buttered baking dish. Mix remaining ingredients with a fork and spread over the pears. Bake at 350°F (180°C) until pears are tender and the crust is brown, about 30 minutes. Serve with cream or whipped cream. Serves 4.

Variation: Apples may be used instead of pears, however increase water to ½ cup, depending upon the juiciness of the apples.

Approximate nutritional analysis per serving:
Calories 462, Protein 4 g, Carbohydrates 62 g, Fat 24 g, Cholesterol 62 mg, Sodium 384 mg

PEAR CRISP

STRAWBERRY COMPOTE CRÊPES

1 cup (240 ml) sliced strawberries
2 kiwi fruit, peeled and sliced
1 navel orange, halved, peeled
    and sectioned
1 FRIEDA'S Cherimoya, peeled,
    seeded and chunked
    or 1 cup (240 ml) pineapple
    chunks
½ cup (120 ml) red or green
    seedless grapes, halved
3 tbs (45 ml) Grand Marnier or
    Triple Sec (orange) liqueur
4 FRIEDA'S Table de France Crêpes,
    at room temperature
4 tbs (60 ml) light frozen nondairy
    whipped topping, thawed
fresh star fruit slices or mint,
    for garnish

In bowl, toss together fruit with Grand Marnier. Chill for up to several hours. To serve, divide fruit among 4 crêpes: fold crêpes over fruit. Top each crêpe with 1 tbs whipped topping and garnish of choice. Serves 4.

Approximate nutritional analysis per serving:
Calories 301, Protein 5 g, Carbohydrates 62 g, Fat 3 g, Cholesterol 41 mg, Sodium 120 mg

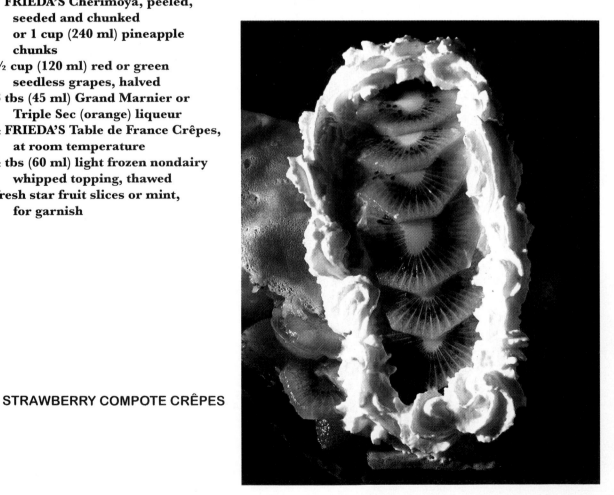

STRAWBERRY COMPOTE CRÊPES

APPLE-LEMON TART

CRUST:
1 cup (240 ml) VITA-SPELT Flour
¼ cup (60 ml) almond paste
2 tbs (30 ml) brown sugar
1 egg, beaten
5 tbs (75 ml) butter, softened

FILLING:
2 eggs, separated
¾ cup (180 ml) sugar
⅓ cup (80 ml) lemon juice
⅓ cup (80 ml) skim milk
2 tbs (30 ml) VITA-SPELT Flour
1 tbs (15 ml) poppy seeds
1 tbs (15 ml) butter, softened
1 tsp (5 ml) lemon peel,
    finely grated
1 cup (240 ml) apples,
    finely chopped
2 tbs (30 ml) sliced almonds
powdered sugar, for dusting

APPLE-LEMON TART

Crust: Combine first four ingredients in medium bowl. Stir in butter until mixture resembles coarse crumbs. Gather and press over bottom and up sides of ungreased 9-inch tart pan with removable bottom. Bake at 350°F (180°C) for approximately 20 minutes. Cool on rack.

Filling: Whisk together egg yolks, sugar, lemon juice, milk, flour, poppy seeds, butter and lemon peel until blended. Beat egg whites until stiff; fold into lemon juice mixture. Sprinkle apples over crust. Pour lemon juice mixture evenly over apples. Sprinkle with almonds. Bake at 350°F (180°C) for approximately 30-35 minutes or until golden brown and set. Cool on rack. Sprinkle lightly with powdered sugar before serving. Serves 8.

Approximate nutritional analysis per serving:
Calories 259, Protein 5 g, Carbohydrates 31 g, Fat 14 g, Cholesterol 94 mg, Sodium 116 mg

EASY BUT EXOTIC FRUIT TART

9-inch pie crust

FILLING:
3 eggs
1½ cups (355 ml) milk
¼ cup (60 ml) brown sugar
¼ tsp (1 ml) salt
1 tbs (15 ml) rum
    or 1 tsp (5 ml) vanilla

FRUIT TOPPING:
1 FRIEDA'S Persimmon, sliced
1 small fresh FRIEDA'S Asian Pear
    or regular pear, cored and sliced
1 FRIEDA'S Kiwifruit, peeled and
    thinly sliced
½ cup (120 ml) toasted sliced
    almonds
whipped cream or yogurt, optional

Roll out pie crust dough to fit a 9-inch tart pan, pie pan or quiche dish. Place crust in pan; flute edges. Bake in a 425°F (220°C) oven for 8-10 minutes until golden. Cool.

Filling: Beat together eggs, milk, sugar, salt and rum until blended. Place in a saucepan; cook and stir over medium heat until custard thickens and coats a metal spoon. Place pan in a bowl of ice water, stirring custard to chill quickly, for about 5 minutes. Pour custard into cooled crust.

Fruit Topping: Cut out the leaf bases of the persimmon and halve fruit lengthwise. Carefully peel fruit; slice. Arrange persimmon, pear and kiwi slices decoratively over custard. Sprinkle almonds over top. Cover tart and refrigerate until serving time. Serve with whipped cream or yogurt, if desired. Serves 10.

Approximate nutritional analysis per serving:
Calories 213, Protein 6 g, Carbohydrates 22 g, Fat 12 g, Cholesterol 57 mg, Sodium 189 mg

EASY BUT EXOTIC FRUIT TART

FROZEN LEMON OR LIME PIE

¾ **cup (180 ml) fresh lemon or lime juice**
1½ **tsp (8 ml) POMONA'S Universal Pectin Powder**
¾ **cup (180 ml) honey**
1½ **cups (355 ml) plain nonfat yogurt, warmed**
1 **cup (240 ml) whipping cream**
¾ **tsp (4 ml) vanilla extract**
1 **graham cracker crumb crust or prebaked dough crust**

Bring juice to boil in saucepan. Add pectin along with 2 tbs honey. Boil 1 minute, stirring vigorously. Stir in remaining honey and remove from heat. Combine with warmed yogurt (90-100°F [38°C]). Chill in shallow pan until semifirm, ½ hour. Whip cream and vanilla and fold into chilled yogurt mixture. Pour into crust; freeze until firm or frozen. Serves 10.

Approximate nutritional analysis per serving:
Calories 346, Protein 3 g, Carbohydrates 49 g, Fat 17 g, Cholesterol 33 mg,

FROZEN LEMON OR LIME PIE

CREAMY TOFU-PUMPKIN PIE

16-oz **can (480 g) low sodium pumpkin**
1 **cup (240 ml) DEVANSWEET granulated sweetener**
½ **tsp (3 ml) salt**
1 **tsp (5 ml) ground cinnamon**
¼ **tsp (1 ml) nutmeg**
½ **tsp (3 ml) ground ginger**
¼ **tsp (1 ml) ground cloves**
10 oz **(300 g) silken or soft tofu, blended until smooth**
9-inch **unbaked pie crust**

Preheat oven to 425°F (220°C).

In a large bowl or blender, combine the pumpkin, Devansweet, salt, cinnamon, nutmeg, ginger, cloves and tofu in the order given; mix until creamy. Pour the filling into the pie crust. Bake the pie for 15 minutes, then lower the heat to 350°F (180°C) and bake the pie for an additional 40 minutes. Cool before serving. Serves 10.

Approximate nutritional analysis per serving:
Calories 267, Protein 5 g, Carbohydrates 37 g, Fat 11 g, Cholesterol 0 mg,
Sodium 265 mg Sodium 219 mg

CREAMY TOFU-PUMPKIN PIE

CAJETA TART

TART DOUGH:

1½ cups (355 ml) unbleached white flour
¼ cup (60 ml) DEVANSWEET, granulated sweetener
¼ cup (60 ml) arrowroot powder
1 tsp (5 ml) sea salt
1 tsp (5 ml) unrefined corn oil
1 tsp (5 ml) pure vanilla extract
6 tbs (90 g) butternut squash, peeled, cubed, steamed and puréed

CUSTARD FILLING:

2 cups (480 ml) DEVANSWEET, granulated sweetener
2 tbs (30 ml) lemon juice
⅓ cup (80 ml) almond butter
1 cup (240 ml) SOLAIT Milk Powder
4 cups (960 ml) SOLAIT Soy Milk, reconstituted
½ tsp (3 ml) baking soda
2 tbs (30 ml) agar flakes mixed into:
2 tbs (30 ml) water
3 tbs (45 ml) arrowroot powder or cornstarch dissolved in:
2 tbs (30 ml) water
1 tsp (5 ml) pure vanilla extract

Preheat oven to 350°F (180°C).

Tart Dough: Into a mixing bowl, add the flour, Devansweet, arrowroot and salt, then mix together well. Add the oil, vanilla and squash purée, then mix well into a dough. Place flour on the work surface and the dough, then roll ⅛-inch thick into a rectangle 14x10-inches. Lay the dough into a lightly oiled 14x10-inch baking pan. Set aside while preparing the custard filling.

Filling: Caramelize Devansweet by placing into a large saucepan, at least 3-4 quarts, and cook on medium heat for 3 minutes. Add the lemon juice and continue to cook until it becomes a smooth syrup. Add the almond butter, mix until smooth, then cover and set aside.

In a separate bowl, whip the soy beverage powder into the soy milk. Place the caramel on low heat, then slowly add the soy mixture to the warm caramel in 1-cup increments, stirring constantly after each addition until the caramel is well dissolved. Add the baking soda, which will cause the mixture to foam up (thus the large saucepan). Next add the agar/water mixture and continue to simmer for 10 minutes. Add the arrowroot/water mixture and the vanilla; continue to stir constantly and simmer for several more minutes until the mixture begins to thicken. Pour the filling into the dough-lined baking pan and bake for 30 minutes.
Yields 35 squares.

Approximate nutritional analysis per serving 2 inch square:
Calories 110, Protein 2 g, Carbohydrates 21 g, Fat 2 g, Cholesterol 0 mg, Sodium 94 mg

LORI'S EASY PUMPKIN PIE

1 cup (240 ml) Original or Vanilla RICE DREAM
2 large eggs, lightly beaten
16-oz can (480 ml) unsweetened canned pumpkin
½ cup (120 ml) maple syrup
1 tsp (5 ml) cinnamon
¼ tsp (1 ml) ginger powder
½ tsp (3 ml) nutmeg
½ tsp (3 ml) allspice
½ tsp (3 ml) sea salt
1 unbaked 9-inch pie crust

Preheat oven to 425°F (220°C).

Mix all ingredients and pour into unbaked pie crust. Bake for 15 minutes, reduce heat to 350°F (180°C) and bake for 40-50 minutes, or until inserted knife comes out clean. Remove from oven and set on a wire rack to cool. Serves 10.

Approximate nutritional analysis per serving:
Calories 179, Protein 3 g, Carbohydrates 26 g, Fat 7 g, Cholesterol 37 mg, Sodium 228 mg

CRANBERRY-HONEY-PECAN CRUNCH PIE

2 cups (480 ml) cranberries,
    fresh or frozen
1 cup (240 ml) fresh orange juice
½ cup (120 ml) honey
2 tbs (30 ml) cornstarch
2 tbs (30 ml) cold water
½ tsp (3 ml) orange extract
9-inch baked pie crust with
    fluted rim

TOPPING:
⅓ cup (80 ml) packed light
    brown sugar
3 tbs (45 ml) honey
3 tbs (45 ml) butter or margarine
1¾ cups (415 ml) pecan halves

In medium saucepan, combine cranberries, juice and honey. Cook, uncovered, over low heat for 15 minutes if using fresh cranberries or 20 minutes if using frozen berries. Cool. Purée cranberry mixture in blender; return to saucepan. Combine cornstarch and water in small bowl. Stir into cranberry mixture. Bring to boil and cook until thickened. Stir in orange extract. Cool; then pour into pie shell. Spoon prepared Topping evenly over cranberry mixture. Bake at 350°F (180°C) for 20 minutes or until top is bubbly. Cool on wire rack. Serve at room temperature or chilled. Serves 10.

    Topping: In medium saucepan, combine brown sugar, honey and butter; cook and stir 2 minutes or until mixture is smooth. Stir in pecan halves until well coated.

Approximate nutritional analysis per serving w/o topping:
Calories 173, Protein 1 g, Carbohydrates 29 g, Fat 6 g, Cholesterol 0 mg, Sodium 99 mg

Approximate nutritional analysis per serving w/ topping:
Calories 380, Protein 3 g, Carbohydrates 43 g, Fat 24 g, Cholesterol 9 mg, Sodium 136 mg

Courtesy of The National Honey Board.

CRANBERRY-HONEY-PECAN CRUNCH PIE

PERFECT APPLE PIE

6-7 sweet baking apples
½ cup (120 ml) sugar
2 tbs (30 ml) all-purpose flour
2 tbs (30 ml) ZUMBRO Jerusalem
    Artichoke Flour
½-1 tsp (3-5 ml) cinnamon
dash nutmeg
dash salt
2 tbs (30 ml) butter
2 9-inch pie crusts

PERFECT APPLE PIE

Pare apples and slice thin. Combine sugar, flours, spices and salt; mix with apples. Line a 9-inch pie plate with pastry, fill with apple mixture, dot with butter. Adjust top crust and sprinkle with granulated sugar for sparkle, if desired. Bake in hot 400°F (205°C) oven for 50-60 minutes. Serves 10.

Approximate nutritional analysis per serving:
Calories 326, Protein 3 g, Carbohydrates 47 g, Fat 15 g, Cholesterol 6 mg, Sodium 232 mg

CHOCOLATE-YOGURT CHEESECAKE

CRUST:
16 chocolate wafers, crumbled
¼ cup (60 ml) butter, melted

FILLING:
2 8-oz pkgs (480 g) cream cheese, softened at room temperature
1 cup (240 ml) sugar
3 eggs, at room temperature
1½ tsp (8 ml) vanilla
6 squares semisweet chocolate, melted and cooled
1 cup (240 ml) STONYFIELD FARM Plain Nonfat Yogurt

GLAZE (optional):
2 squares semisweet chocolate, melted
2 tbs (30 ml) butter, melted
1 tbs (15 ml) corn syrup
½ tsp (3 ml) vanilla
2 oz (60 g) white chocolate

Crust: Mix the chocolate wafer crumbs and butter together. Press the mixture onto the bottom and against the sides of an 8-9-inch spring-form pan. Chill.

Preheat oven to 300°F (150°C).

Filling: Cream together the cream cheese and sugar. Stir in the eggs, then add the vanilla, melted chocolate and yogurt, and stir until all the ingredients are combined. Spoon the mixture into the crust.

Place the cheesecake on the middle rack of the oven and place a pan of water on the bottom rack. Bake 50-60 minutes. Do not open the oven door while the cheesecake is baking. Turn off oven; allow the cake to cool in the oven with the door ajar.

Glaze: Mix the chocolate, butter, corn syrup and vanilla together while the chocolate and butter are still warm. Allow the glaze to cool, then spread on top of the slightly cooled cheesecake. For a decorative feathered effect, melt the white chocolate. Using a pastry tube, pipe lines of white chocolate across the still-warm glaze, and then drag a knife across the lines to create a pattern. Serves 12.

Approximate nutritional analysis per serving w/ glaze:
Calories 438, Protein 8 g, Carbohydrates 35 g, Fat 33 g, Cholesterol 105 mg, Sodium 256 mg

Approximate nutritional analysis per serving w/o glaze:
Calories 367, Protein 7 g, Carbohydrates 29 g, Fat 27 g, Cholesterol 99 mg, Sodium 229 mg

GALAXY GRAHAMS PIE CRUST

4 cups (960 ml) EREWHON Galaxy Grahams Cereal
½ cup (120 ml) melted butter
1 tsp (5 ml) ground ginger, optional

Crush cereal with a rolling pin or in a food processor. Mix in melted butter and ginger, if desired. Press into pie plate. Fill with your favorite pie filling. Yields 1 crust, serves 10.

Approximate nutritional analysis per serving:
Calories 94, Protein 2 g, Carbohydrates 12 g, Fat 5 g, Cholesterol 12 mg, Sodium 47 mg

GRAHAM CRACKERLESS CRUST

1 cup (240 ml) AMBERWAVES BRAND Organic Whole Wheat Flour
½ tsp (3 ml) salt
1 tsp (5 ml) baking powder
½ cup (120 ml) sugar
1 tbs (15 ml) dry milk
6 tbs (90 ml) margarine, melted
½ tsp (3 ml) vanilla

Mix together dry ingredients. Add margarine and vanilla. Mix well. Press into a 9-inch pie plate. Bake at 400°F (205°C) for 5 minutes. Yields 1 crust, serves 10.

Approximate nutritional analysis per serving:
Calories 141, Protein 2 g, Carbohydrates 19 g, Fat 7 g, Cholesterol .03 mg, Sodium 237 mg

"BETTER THAN CHEESECAKE"

1 lb (455 g) TOFUTTI "Better Than
    Cream Cheese"
¾ cup (180 ml) sugar
4 oz (120 g) TOFUTTI Egg Watchers
1 tbs (15 ml) vanilla extract
1 tbs (15 ml) lemon juice
1 tbs (15 ml) flour
1 9-inch pie crust

Preheat oven to 350°F (180°C).
    Combine all ingredients and pour into pie crust. Bake for 10 minutes. Lower oven to 300°F (150°C) and bake an additional 30 minutes. Serve plain or with your favorite topping. Serves 10.

Approximate nutritional analysis per serving:
Calories 291, Protein 4 g, Carbohydrates 26 g, Fat 19 g, Cholesterol 0 mg, Sodium 333 mg

MY-KINDA-PIE-CRUST!

¼ cup (60 ml) shortening
¼ tsp (1 ml) salt
¾ cup (180 ml) AMBERWAVES
    BRAND Organic Whole Wheat
    Flour
¼ cup (60 ml) ice cold water

Mix together shortening, salt and flour until crumbly. Stir in ice water. Roll out, adding flour as needed. Yields 1 crust, serves 10.

Approximate nutritional analysis per serving:
Calories 76, Protein 1 g, Carbohydrates 7 g, Fat 5 g, Cholesterol 0 mg, Sodium 54 mg

MOM'S PIE CRUST

4 cups (960 ml) unbleached
    white flour
1 tsp (5 ml) sea salt
1½ cups (355 ml) OMEGA
    NUTRITION Coconut Butter
2 tsp (10 ml) OMEGA NUTRITION
    Apple Cider Vinegar
1 cup (240 ml) ice water

Mix flour and salt in large bowl. Cut in coconut butter with pastry knife until crumbly. Add vinegar to ice water. Stir in ⅔ water/vinegar to flour mixture. Add in rest of water/vinegar until you have desired consistency. Refrigerate for 1 hour before rolling into pie crust. Keeps up to 1 week in refrigerator or several months in freezer. Yields 4 crusts, serves 40.

Approximate nutritional analysis per serving:
Calories 121, Protein 1 g, Carbohydrates 10 g, Fat 9 g, Cholesterol 0 mg, Sodium 54 mg

OAT-COCONUT PIE CRUST

½ cup (120 ml) crushed
    ARROWHEAD MILLS Oat Bran
    Flakes
½ cup (120 ml) shredded
    unsweetened coconut
2 tsp (10 ml) ARROWHEAD MILLS
    Fresh! Oil
¼ tsp (1 ml) vanilla extract
½ tsp (3 ml) cinnamon, optional

Mix all ingredients together thoroughly and press into pie pan. If crust is to be used for no-bake pie filling, prebake pastry crust at 325°F (155°C) for 5 minutes. Yields 1 crust, serves 10.

Approximate nutritional analysis per serving:
Calories 38, Protein .8 g, Carbohydrates 3 g, Fat 3 g, Cholesterol 0 mg, Sodium 1 mg

NONFAT YOGURT PEACH & VANILLA SAUCE

2 cups (480 ml) plain nonfat yogurt
4 tsp (20 ml) pure vanilla extract
6 tbs (90 g) pure maple syrup
4 tbs (60 ml) SPECTRUM
    NATURALS Organic Peach
    Vinegar

In a stainless steel or glass bowl, whisk together all ingredients. Toss with chilled fresh fruit. Yields approximately 2½ cups, serves 4.

Approximate nutritional analysis per ½ cup serving:
Calories 118, Protein 6 g, Carbohydrates 24 g, Fat .2 g, Cholesterol 2 mg, Sodium 77 mg

DELICIOUS CHOCOLATE SAUCE

3½-oz bar (105 g) RAPUNZEL
    Organic Bittersweet Chocolate
3½-oz bar (105 g) RAPUNZEL
    Organic Milk Chocolate
½ cup (120 ml) light corn syrup
1 tbs (15 ml) unsalted butter
¼ cup (60 ml) half-and-half
    or cream
½ tsp (3 ml) vanilla

Coarsely chop or grate chocolate and melt in double boiler with corn syrup. Mix well and add cream. Blend well and stir in butter. Remove from heat and add vanilla. Mix well. Serve warm or may be cooled and refrigerated. Yields approximately 1 cup, serves 8.

Serve over fresh fruit, with frozen yogurt or fresh fruit sorbet as a chocolate accent.

Approximate nutritional analysis per 2 tbs serving:
Calories 203, Protein 2 g, Carbohydrates 29 g, Fat 11 g, Cholesterol 9 mg, Sodium 39 mg

FRESH FRUIT WITH CHOCOLATE-MINT SAUCE

1½ cup (355 ml) nonfat milk
2 tbs (15 ml) low-fat margarine
½ cup (120 ml) unsweetened
    cocoa powder
½ cup (120 ml) sugar
1 pkg GREEN HOUSE Fresh Mint
    Leaves, finely chopped
1 tsp (5 ml) vanilla extract
4 cups (960 ml) fresh raspberries
    or bananas

Scald milk in small saucepan. In separate saucepan, melt margarine and add cocoa; stir well. Stir milk into cocoa mixture. Stirring with wire whisk, add sugar and fresh mint; stir until sauce thickens, about 5 minutes. Add vanilla and remove from heat. Cool. Serve over ½ cup fresh raspberries per serving. Also delicious over frozen yogurt. Serves 8.

Approximate nutritional analysis per serving:
Calories 117, Protein 3 g, Carbohydrates 24 g, Fat 3 g, Cholesterol .8 mg, Sodium 59 mg

YOGURT CREAM MOLD WITH RASPBERRY SAUCE

YOGURT CREAM MOLD:
4 tsp (20 ml) unflavored gelatin
¼ cup (60 ml) cold water
1½ cups (355 ml) heavy cream
½ cup (120 ml) sugar
2¼ cups (540 ml) STONYFIELD
    FARM Nonfat Plain Yogurt
1 tsp (5 ml) vanilla

RASPBERRY SAUCE:
2 10-oz pkgs (600 g) frozen
    raspberries in syrup, thawed
2 tbs (30 ml) sugar
1 tbs (15 ml) lemon juice
kiwi or orange slices, for garnish,
    optional

Yogurt Cream Mold: In a small bowl, soften the gelatin in the cold water for about 10 minutes. In a saucepan, combine the cream and sugar, then cook over medium heat, stirring constantly, for 5 minutes or until the sugar is dissolved. Remove from heat. Add the gelatin mixture and stir until the gelatin is dissolved. Transfer to a bowl. Let the mixture cool for about 5 minutes, then whisk in the yogurt and vanilla. Mix well.

Rinse a pretty 1-quart mold or individual molds with cold water; shake the mold(s) but don't dry. Pour in the yogurt mixture; chill for 2 hours.

Dip a knife in warm water and run the blade around the edge of the mold. Invert the mold and rap on it to loosen the yogurt cream.

Raspberry Sauce: Just before serving, top with a sauce of combined raspberries, sugar and lemon juice. Garnish with kiwi slices if desired. Serves 6.

Approximate nutritional analysis per serving:
Calories 446, Protein 10 g, Carbohydrates 54 g, Fat 22 g, Cholesterol 83 mg, Sodium 100 mg

BAKED RICE PUDDING

2 cups (480 ml) brown rice, cooked
2 cups (480 ml) Original or Vanilla
    RICE DREAM
1½ tsp (8 ml) cinnamon
3 tbs (45 ml) whole wheat
    pastry flour
¼ cup (60 ml) maple syrup or
    rice syrup
1 tsp (5 ml) vanilla extract
2 tbs (30 ml) almond butter
⅓ cup (80 ml) raisins or dates
roasted almonds, slivered,
    for topping

Preheat oven to 400°F (205°C). Place rice in a mixing bowl. Using a wooden spoon, break up any clumps of rice. In a blender or food processor, blend together Rice Dream, cinnamon, flour, syrup, vanilla and almond butter. Pour mixture into rice, add raisins and mix well. Transfer to a baking dish; cover and bake for 45 minutes. Remove from oven and allow to cool for a few minutes. Serve topped with almonds. Serves 6.

Approximate nutritional analysis per serving:
Calories 221, Protein 4 g, Carbohydrates 43 g, Fat 5 g, Cholesterol 0 mg, Sodium 36 mg

**Opposite: YOGURT CREAM MOLD
WITH RASPBERRY SAUCE**

MRS. PAVICH'S ORGANIC RAISIN RICE PUDDING

⅓ cup (80 ml) raw sugar (turbinado)
2 tbs (30 ml) cornstarch
pinch salt
2 cups (480 ml) skim milk
2 egg yolks
2 tbs (30 ml) soft butter
    or 1 tbs (15 ml) canola oil
2 tsp (10 ml) vanilla
2 cups (480 ml) cooked rice
1 tsp (5 ml) cinnamon
½ tsp (3 ml) nutmeg
1 cup (240 ml) PAVICH Organic
    Thompson Seedless Raisins

In a saucepan, combine sugar, cornstarch and salt. In a separate bowl, combine milk, egg yolks, then slowly stir into sugar mixture. Bring to a boil over medium heat, stirring constantly. When boiling point is reached, stir 1 minute more or until mixture thickens. Remove from heat and add butter or oil, vanilla, rice, spices and raisins. Mix well, cover, cool and chill. Serves 9.

Approximate nutritional analysis per serving:
Calories 191, Protein 4 g, Carbohydrates 39 g, Fat 3 g, Cholesterol 8 mg, Sodium 87 mg

TAPIOCA PUDDING

1 cup (240 ml) Vanilla Bean SOLAIT
    Soy Beverage Powder
3 cups (720 ml) water
¾ cup (180 ml) tapioca
½ cup (120 ml) DEVANSWEET,
    granulated sweetener
3 tbs (45 ml) pure maple syrup

Blend soy beverage powder and water in double boiler. Mix with wire whisk. Add tapioca and cook the mixture in the double boiler until thickened. Add Devansweet and maple syrup. Mix well. Transfer the pudding to a covered container and refrigerate until chilled. The pudding will thicken slightly as it chills. Serve with fruit, fruit syrup, cinnamon sprinkle or whipped topping. Serves 8.

Approximate nutritional analysis per ½ cup serving:
Calories 204, Protein 6 g, Carbohydrates 37 g, Fat 4 g, Cholesterol 13 mg, Sodium 135 mg

BREAD PUDDING

3 eggs, beaten
    or 5 egg whites
10 oz (300 g) soft tofu, mashed
1 tsp (5 ml) vanilla
½ tsp (3 ml) cinnamon
½ tsp (3 ml) nutmeg
1 cup (240 ml) DEVANSWEET,
    granulated sweetener
4 cups (960 ml) stale bread, grain,
    raisin or whole wheat, cubed
1 cup (240 ml) SOLAIT Instant Soy
    Beverage, reconstituted
½ cup (120 ml) nuts and/or raisins,
    optional

Mix eggs and tofu in an 8x8-inch baking pan. Add vanilla, cinnamon, nutmeg and Devanswet. Add cubed bread to tofu mix, then soy beverage. If desired, add nuts and/or raisins. Mix well.

Bake at 350°F (180°C) for 50 minutes or until center is set. This recipe is good for breakfast. Make it the day before and reheat or serve cold. Serves 8.

Approximate nutritional analysis per serving w/ eggs:
Calories 308, Protein 12 g, Carbohydrates 49 g, Fat 7 g, Cholesterol 71 mg, Sodium 204 mg

Approximate nutritional analysis per serving w/ egg whites:
Calories 294, Protein 12 g, Carbohydrates 49 g, Fat 5 g, Cholesterol .4 mg, Sodium 218 mg

ALBERT'S ORGANICS FLAN CUSTARD

2 qts (1.9 l) soy milk
½ cup (120 ml) agar flakes
2 tsp (10 ml) pure vanilla extract
½ cup (120 ml) maple syrup
1 tsp (5 ml) cinnamon

Combine all ingredients in a large saucepan. Stirring constantly, bring mixture to a boil, cover, reduce flame and simmer for 20 minutes. Stir gently, then pour into 8 custard cups. Chill for 2 hours before serving. Serves 8.

Approximate nutritional analysis per 1 cup serving:
Calories 149, Protein 8 g, Carbohydrates 19 g, Fat 5 g, Cholesterol 0 mg, Sodium 37 mg

ALBERT'S ORGANICS KABOCHA PUMPKIN CUSTARD

1 medium to large kabocha squash
½ tsp (3 ml) sea salt
1 tsp (5 ml) pumpkin pie spice
   (cinnamon, nutmeg)
¼ cup (60 ml) kanten flakes
¾ cup (180 ml) spring water
½ cup (120 ml) maple syrup or
   brown rice syrup
2 tbs (30 ml) kudzu
2 tbs water
mint leaves, for garnish

Wash kabocha, cut away top and bottom stems. Steam cut pieces with sea salt and ½ tsp pumpkin pie spice until soft. Meanwhile, in saucepan dissolve kanten in ¾ cup water, cover and simmer for 5 minutes. Add syrup, remaining pumpkin pie spice and simmer an additional 5 minutes. Remove kabocha from steamer, scoop from skin and purée in Foley food mill or blender. Add to kanten liquid and stir. Dissolve kudzu in 2 tbs cold water and add to pumpkin, stirring constantly for 3-5 minutes on a very low flame. Place in custard cups to set 1-2 hours. Garnish with mint leaves. Serves 4.

Approximate nutritional analysis per serving:
Calories 160, Protein 10 g, Carbohydrates 31 g, Fat .3 g, Cholesterol 0 mg, Sodium 293 mg

TAHINI CUSTARD

3 cups (720 ml) apple juice
¼ cup (60 ml) honey
¼ cup (60 ml) water
¼ cup (60 ml) arrowroot
½ cup (120 ml) EAST WIND Tahini
1 tsp (5 ml) salt

In a large saucepan, boil apple juice and honey. In a separate bowl, mix water and arrowroot, then stir into juice mixture. Add tahini and salt and cook and stir until smooth. Chill 1-2 hours before serving. Serves 8.

Approximate nutritional analysis per ½ cup serving:
Calories 182, Protein 3 g, Carbohydrates 26 g, Fat 9 g, Cholesterol 0 mg, Sodium 270 mg

ALBERT'S ORGANICS KABOCHA PUMPKIN CUSTARD

PURPLE PUDDING

2½ cups (590 ml) grape juice or any
    other dark fruit juice
¾ cup (180 ml) ARROWHEAD
    MILLS Blue Cornmeal
1 cup (240 ml) plain nonfat yogurt
natural sweetener to taste

APPLE-RAISIN
PUDDING

1 egg, beaten
½ cup (120 ml) WOLFF'S Kasha,
    fine or medium granulation
¾ tsp (4 ml) salt
2 tbs (30 ml) butter or margarine
1 cup (240 ml) water
2 eggs
¼ cup (60 ml) brown sugar,
    firmly packed
1 cup (240 ml) tart apple, peeled
    and chopped
½ cup (120 ml) raisins
1 tsp (5 ml) grated lemon rind
1 tbs (15 ml) lemon juice

PURPLE PUDDING

Combine juice and blue cornmeal in a saucepan, and stir over low
heat with a wire whisk until very thick. Combine mixture with
yogurt and sweetener and beat with an electric mixer or in a
blender, until creamy and smooth. Pour into small bowls and chill.
Serves 8.

Approximate nutritional analysis per ½ cup serving:
Calories 114, Protein 3 g, Carbohydrates 24 g, Fat .7 g, Cholesterol .6 mg,
Sodium 26 mg

Combine beaten egg, kasha and salt. In medium-size frying pan,
cook mixture in butter 3 minutes, or until lightly toasted, stirring
often. Stir in water; bring to boil. Cook, tightly covered, over low
heat for 10 minutes. Remove from heat; cool, uncovered, about
15 minutes.

In medium bowl, beat eggs with sugar. Stir in apples, raisins,
lemon rind, juice and kasha mixture. Pour into well-oiled 1½-quart
casserole. Bake at 350°F (180°C) for 45 minutes or until center
appears firm. Serve warm with whipped topping or your favorite
lemon, orange or custard sauce. Serves 5.

Approximate nutritional analysis per serving:
Calories 247, Protein 6 g, Carbohydrates 40 g, Fat 8 g, Cholesterol 125 mg,
Sodium 409 mg

Opposite: APPLE-RAISIN PUDDING

FROZEN RASPBERRY-YOGURT CREAM

12-oz pkg (360 g) frozen raspberries
    without sugar, thawed
¾ cup (180 ml) sugar, or more
    to taste
squeeze of fresh lemon juice
2 cups (480 ml) STONYFIELD FARM
    Plain Nonfat Yogurt
¾ cup (180 ml) heavy cream
2-3 tbs (30-45 ml) raspberry liqueur,
    optional

Purée the thawed raspberries in a food processor, using the steel blade. Transfer to a sieve and press the mixture through the sieve into a bowl. Discard the seeds. Mix the sugar, lemon juice, yogurt, cream and optional raspberry liqueur into the raspberry juice. Place in the container of an ice cream maker, and freeze according to manufacturer's instructions. Serves 6.

This dessert can be eaten right away or transferred to a freezer container and stored in the freezer.

Approximate nutritional analysis per serving:
Calories 304, Protein 6 g, Carbohydrates 47 g, Fat 11 g, Cholesterol 42 mg, Sodium 74 mg

CREAMY RASPBERRY SHERBET

1 cup (240 ml) SOLAIT Instant Soy
    Beverage, premixed
1 cup (240 ml) raspberries, fresh
    and chilled or frozen
4-6 tbs (60-90 ml) DEVANSWEET

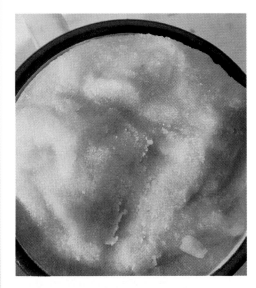

Pour premixed Solait in a divided ice cube tray, freeze until solid, about 3 hours. Refrigerate berries until very cold, or freeze them.

Shortly before serving, remove frozen Solait and berries, if frozen, from freezer. Let stand about 5 minutes at room temperature. Remove Solait cubes from tray. If cubes are large, cut them into small chunks in food processor or blender, whip Solait chunks a portion at a time, use on-off pulse at first to break up chunks. Then whip continuously until velvety. Drop in berries, about ⅓ at a time, and sweetener. Blend until smooth, then serve.
Yields 3 cups, serves 3.

Store any leftover sherbet in an airtight container in the freezer. Let hard frozen sherbet stand at room temperature until softened, 15-30 minutes, before scooping.

Variations: Substitute blueberries, peaches, strawberries or a fruit of your choice for raspberries.

Approximate nutritional analysis per 1 cup serving:
Calories 395, Protein 14 g, Carbohydrates 66 g, Fat 2 g, Cholesterol 0 mg, Sodium 280 mg

CREAMY RASPBERRY SHERBET

MANGO-CITRUS SORBET

MANGO-CITRUS SORBET

2 cups (480 ml) mango, puréed
juice of 1 lemon
juice of 1 lime
1 egg white, lightly beaten

SIMPLE SYRUP:
1 cup (240 ml) sugar
2 cups (480 ml) water

Simple Syrup: Cook sugar and water in saucepan over medium heat for 5-7 minutes to dissolve sugar. Chill syrup.

Put puréed mango into a bowl. Add citrus juices and chilled syrup. Freeze in ice cream machine, according to manufacturer's directions. Add beaten egg white halfway through the freezing process. Yields 4 cups.

Approximate nutritional analysis per 1 cup serving:
Calories 265, Protein 1 g, Carbohydrates 68 g, Fat .3 g, Cholesterol 0 mg, Sodium 16 mg

INDIAN ROCK'S CRANBERRY SORBET

1½ cups (355 ml) water
1½ cups (355 ml) sugar
1 lb (455 g) fresh cranberries
½ cup (120 ml) fresh orange juice
¼ cup (60 ml) fresh lemon juice
1 tbs (15 ml) raspberry liqueur
1 egg white

Make a syrup by combining the water and sugar in a nonreactive saucepan and bringing it to a boil. Add the cranberries and orange juice and simmer until the berries burst from their skin, 25-30 minutes. Remove from the heat, purée in a food processor, and strain through a fine sieve to remove the skins. Let cool. Then combine the cranberries, lemon juice and raspberry liqueur. Beat egg white until stiff, blend into the purée and freeze. Serves 6.

Approximate nutritional analysis per serving:
Calories 126, Protein 1 g, Carbohydrates 31 g, Fat .2 g, Cholesterol 0 mg, Sodium 11 mg

MINT SORBET

1 cup (240 ml) water
3 oz (90 g) sugar
6 large sprigs of flavored mint
juice of large lemon
1 egg white
sprigs of mint to decorate

Boil water and sugar together to dissolve sugar. Remove from heat and let stand 20 minutes with mint sprigs. Strain into rigid container, add lemon juice and leave to cool. Freeze until half frozen; chop to loosen ice granules and fold in stiffly beaten egg white. Refreeze, rechop again in ½ hour if sorbet is too solid (versus granular). Decorate with mint sprigs. Serves 4.

Approximate nutritional analysis per serving:
Calories 90, Protein .9 g, Carbohydrates 23 g, Fat .02 g, Cholesterol 0 mg, Sodium 14 mg

MINT SORBET

HONEY-OAT BISCOTTI

HONEY-OAT BISCOTTI

½ cup (120 ml) butter or margarine
¾ cup (180 ml) honey
2 eggs
1 tsp (5 ml) vanilla
2 cups (480 ml) flour
3 tsp (15 ml) ground cinnamon
1 tsp (5 ml) baking powder
½ tsp (3 ml) baking soda
½ tsp (3 ml) salt
2 cups (480 ml) rolled oats
½ cup (120 ml) chopped nuts

Cream butter; beat in honey, eggs and vanilla. Combine flour, cinnamon, baking powder, baking soda and salt; mix well. Stir into butter mixture. Stir in oats and nuts. On greased baking sheet shape dough into 2 - 10x3x1-inch logs. Bake at 375°F (190°C) for 12-15 minutes or until lightly browned. Cool 5 minutes; remove to cutting board. Cut each log into ½-inch strips; place on cookie sheet. Bake at 300°F (150°C) for 25-30 minutes or until crisp throughout. Cool thoroughly. Yields 3 dozen.

Approximate nutritional analysis per biscotti:
Calories 101, Protein 2 g, Carbohydrates 14 g, Fat 4 g, Cholesterol 17 mg, Sodium 90 mg

Courtesy of The National Honey Board.

KAMUT GRAHAM CRACKERS

⅓ cup (80 ml) dry milk
½ cup (120 ml) water
2 tbs (30 ml) vinegar
1 cup (240 ml) brown sugar
½ cup (120 ml) honey
1 cup (240 ml) canola oil
2 tsp (10 ml) vanilla
2 eggs, beaten slightly
6 cups (1.4 l) KAMUT BRAND
   Whole Wheat Flour
½-1 tsp (3-5 ml) salt
1 tsp (5 ml) soda

Mix together dry milk, water, vinegar. In a separate bowl, mix the next 5 ingredients together in the order listed. Blend well to keep the oil in emulsion. Combine the 2 mixtures. Add the flour, salt and soda.

Divide dough into 4 equal parts. Place each part on a greased and floured cookie sheet. Roll from center until ⅛-inch thick. Prick with a fork. Bake at 375°F (190°C) for 15 minutes or until light brown. Remove from oven and cut in squares immediately. Yields 5 dozen.

Approximate nutritional analysis per cracker:
Calories 93, Protein 2 g, Carbohydrates 14 g, Fat 4 g, Cholesterol 6 mg, Sodium 43 mg

KAMUT GRAHAM CRACKERS

APPLESAUCE-KASHA COOKIES

1¾ cups (180 ml) all-purpose flour
1 tsp (5 ml) baking soda
½ tsp (3 ml) baking powder
½ tsp (3 ml) salt
1 tsp (5 ml) cinnamon
¼ tsp (1 ml) cloves
pinch nutmeg
½ cup (120 ml) butter or margarine
¾ cup (180 ml) brown sugar
1 egg
1 cup (240 ml) unsweetened
   applesauce
½ cup (120 ml) regular rolled oats
½ cup (120 ml) raisins or currants
½ cup (120 ml) WOLFF'S Kasha,
   medium granulation, cooked

Sift together flour, soda, baking powder, salt and spices; set aside. In large mixing bowl, cream butter and brown sugar until light and fluffy, then beat in egg and applesauce. Slowly stir in flour mixture; mix well. Add oats, raisins and kasha. Drop mixture by teaspoonful onto greased baking sheets. Bake at 375°F (190°C) for 10 minutes or until golden brown. Yields 4 dozen.

Approximate nutritional analysis per cookie:
Calories 61, Protein 1 g, Carbohydrates 10 g, Fat 2 g, Cholesterol 9 mg, Sodium 76 mg

APPLESAUCE-KASHA COOKIES

MRS. PAVICH'S ORGANIC RAISIN-OATMEAL COOKIES

2 cups (480 ml) unbleached flour
1 cup (204 ml) turbinado (raw) sugar
1 tsp (5 ml) salt
1 tsp (5 ml) baking soda
1 tsp (5 ml) nutmeg
1 tsp (5 ml) cinnamon
2 cups (480 ml) rolled oats
1 cup (240 ml) PAVICH
   Organic Raisins
6 oz (180 g) carob or chocolate chips,
   optional
2 eggs
¾ cup (180 ml) canola oil
½ cup (120 ml) skim milk
1 tsp (5 ml) vanilla

In a large bowl, sift together flour, sugar, salt, soda, nutmeg and cinnamon. Stir in oats, raisins and carob or chips, if desired. In a separate bowl, beat eggs and stir in oil, milk and vanilla. Add to dry ingredients and mix well. Drop from tbs 2 inches apart on a lightly greased cookie sheet. Bake at 350°F (180°C) for 13-15 minutes. Yields 4 dozen.

Approximate nutritional analysis per cookie:
Calories 92, Protein 2 g, Carbohydrates 13 g, Fat 4 g, Cholesterol 8 mg, Sodium 75 mg

DANNY'S NUT BUTTER COOKIES

¾ cup (180 ml) EAST WIND
   Nut Butter, peanut, almond
   or cashew
½ cup (120 ml) margarine
1 egg
1 tsp (5 ml) vanilla
½ cup (120 ml) white sugar
½ cup (120 ml) brown sugar, packed
1¼ cups (295 ml) flour
½ tsp (3 ml) salt
½ tsp (3 ml) baking powder

VARIATION:
¼ cup (60 ml) honey

Beat together nut butter, margarine, egg and vanilla. In a separate bowl combine dry ingredients. Gradually add dry ingredients to nut butter mixture until well combined. Roll into balls. Place on oiled sheet, and flatten with fork. Bake at 375°F (190°C) for 10 minutes. Yields 3 dozen.

Variation: Substitute honey for brown sugar, adding the honey to the liquid ingredients.

Approximate nutritional analysis per cookie:
Calories 94, Protein 1 g, Carbohydrates 10 g, Fat 5 g, Cholesterol 5 mg, Sodium 73 mg

Approximate nutritional analysis per cookie variation:
Calories 93, Protein 1 g, Carbohydrates 10 g, Fat 5 g, Cholesterol 5 mg, Sodium 72 mg

DANNY'S NUT BUTTER COOKIES

GINGERBREAD PEOPLE COOKIES

3 cups (720 ml) ARROWHEAD
MILLS Whole Wheat Flour
1 tsp (5 ml) non-alum
baking soda
2 tsp (10 ml) ground ginger
½ tsp (3 ml) allspice
½ cup (120 ml) butter
½ cup (120 ml) honey
¼ cup (60 ml) black strap molasses
1 egg or egg substitute

Mix flour, baking soda and spices in medium-size bowl. In large bowl, blend butter, honey and molasses together. Beat in egg. Gently mix into dry ingredients thoroughly. Wrap dough in plastic wrap or waxed paper and refrigerate until firm, approximately 1 hour.

Preheat oven to 350°F (180 °C).

Divide dough into pieces. Roll each piece out on lightly floured surface. Cut into desired shapes and place carefully on oiled or buttered cookie sheet. Bake in middle of oven for 6-10 minutes, depending on size of cookies. Remove from sheet carefully. Yields 2 dozen.

Approximate nutritional analysis per cookie:
Calories 117, Protein 2 g, Carbohydrates 19 g, Fat 2 g, Cholesterol 18 mg, Sodium 97 mg

ALMOND COOKIES

2 tbs (30 ml) ARROWHEAD MILLS
Unrefined Vegetable Oil
2 tbs (30 ml) honey
½ tsp (3 ml) almond extract
1 tsp (5 ml) vanilla
1 egg, beaten, optional for
lighter cookies
½ cup (120 ml) ARROWHEAD
MILLS Rice Flour
2 tbs (30 ml) ARROWHEAD MILLS
Low Fat Soy Flour
½ tsp (3 ml) non-alum
baking powder

Mix oil, honey, flavoring and egg, if desired, thoroughly. Combine dry ingredients. Stir dry and liquid ingredients together. Roll dough into ¾-inch diameter balls. Place on oiled cookie sheet, flatten slightly. Bake at 350°F (180°C) for 8-10 minutes or until cookies begin to brown around the edges. Cool before removing. Yields 2 dozen.

Approximate nutritional analysis per cookies:
Calories 32, Protein .7 g, Carbohydrates 4 g, Fat 1 g, Cholesterol 8 mg, Sodium 13 mg

ALMOND COOKIES

586

Opposite: GINGERBREAD PEOPLE COOKIES

SPELTIES

½ cup (120 ml) margarine
1 cup (240 ml) sugar
3 eggs
½ cup (120 ml) chunky peanut
    butter
1½ tsp (8 ml) vanilla
1 cup (240 ml) VITA-SPELT Flour
2½ tsp (13 ml) baking powder
½ tsp (3 ml) salt
1 cup (240 ml) chocolate chips or
    carob chips

Preheat oven to 350°F (180°C).

Cream margarine and sugar well. Add eggs, one at a time, and cream after each egg. Add peanut butter and vanilla, beating well. In a separate bowl mix together flour, baking powder and salt. Add blended dry ingredients to wet ingredients and mix until smooth. Stir in chocolate chips. Spread in greased 9x12-inch pan. Bake for approximately 30-35 minutes or until done. Place on wire rack to cool in the pan. Cut into bars while warm. Yields 3 dozen.

Approximate nutritional analysis per spelty:
Calories 96, Protein 2 g, Carbohydrates 10 g, Fat 6 g, Cholesterol 16 mg,
Sodium 99 mg

SPELTIES

KAMUT CAROB BROWNIES

½ cup (120 ml) margarine
½ cup (120 ml) honey
12 oz (360 g) carob drops sweetened
    with date sugar (nondairy type)
1 tsp (5 ml) vanilla
4 eggs, separated
¼ tsp (1 ml) salt
1 cup (240 ml) KAMUT BRAND
    Flour

Preheat oven to 350°F (180°C).

Melt together margarine, honey and carob drops. Allow to cool a bit. Add vanilla, beaten egg yolks, salt and flour. Whip egg whites until stiff. Fold into mixture. Pour into 10x7x1¾-inch baking dish. Bake for 30 minutes. Yields 16.

Approximate nutritional analysis per brownie:
Calories 240, Protein 5 g, Carbohydrates 26 g, Fat 14 g, Cholesterol 48 mg,
Sodium 147 mg

KAMUT CAROB BROWNIES

DESSERTS

ONCE AGAIN TAHINI BARS

1 cup (240 ml) ONCE AGAIN NUT
    BUTTER Tahini or Organic
    Tahini*
1 cup (240 ml) light brown sugar
1 tbs (15 ml) vanilla
2 cups (480 ml) unbleached
    all-purpose flour
2 tsp (10 ml) ground cinnamon
1½ tsp (8 ml) baking powder
¼ tsp (1 ml) salt
1 cup (240 ml) orange juice
1 cup (240 ml) chopped walnuts
½ cup (120 ml) raisins
½ cup (120 ml) chopped glacé
    cherries and pineapple or raisins

* If Tahini has separated, stir to blend before measuring.

Combine tahini, brown sugar and vanilla on medium speed in a large mixer bowl; mix until crumbly. Combine flour, cinnamon, baking powder and salt in a small bowl. On medium speed, alternately add flour mixture and orange juice to brown sugar mixture. Beat until smooth. Stir in walnuts, raisins and fruit. Spread batter evenly in a well-greased and floured 9x13-inch baking pan. Bake at 350°F (180°C) for 40-45 minutes or until golden brown, cool. Cut into bars. Yields 2 dozen.

Approximate nutritional analysis per bar:
Calories 138, Protein 3 g, Carbohydrates 14 g, Fat 9 g, Cholesterol 0 mg, Sodium 56 mg

ONCE AGAIN TAHINI BARS

CAROB-NUT FUDGE

⅔ cup (160 ml) peanut butter
⅔ cup (160 ml) honey
⅔ cup (160 ml) roasted
    carob powder
⅓ cup (80 ml) walnuts, chopped
    and lightly toasted
⅔ cup (160 ml) sunflower seeds,
    lightly toasted
⅓ cup (80 ml) sesame seeds,
    lightly toasted
⅓ cup (80 ml) raisins, soaked
    and drained
2 tbs (30 ml) ZUMBRO Jerusalem
    Artichoke Flour

Heat peanut butter and honey in saucepan until smooth. Remove from heat. Stir in carob powder; add remaining ingredients. Press into an 8x8-inch pan that has been sprayed with a nonstick coating. Chill. Yields 16 squares.

Approximate nutritional analysis per square:
Calories 201, Protein 6 g, Carbohydrates 22 g, Fat 12 g, Cholesterol 0 mg, Sodium 7 mg

CAROB-NUT FUDGE

590

DOUBLE-CHOCOLATE HONEY RING

½ cup (120 ml) butter or margarine
1 cup (240 ml) honey
3 eggs
1 tsp (5 ml) vanilla
1 cup (240 ml) all-purpose flour
½ cup (120 ml) unsweetened
    cocoa powder
2 tsp (10 ml) baking powder
1 tsp (5 ml) salt
1 tsp (5 ml) baking soda
½ cup (120 ml) low-calorie
    sour cream
1 cup (240 ml) semisweet
    chocolate chips
½ cup (120 ml) chopped nuts
White Chocolate Glaze, optional
    (recipe below)
additional unsweetened cocoa
    powder, optional

WHITE CHOCOLATE GLAZE:
2 oz (60 g) white chocolate
2 tsp (10 ml) skim milk

Preheat oven to 325°F (165°C).

Cream butter in large bowl with electric mixer. Gradually add honey, beating until light and fluffy. Add eggs, one at a time, beating thoroughly after each addition. Mixture may appear slightly curdled. Beat in vanilla. Combine flour, cocoa, baking powder, salt and baking soda in small bowl. Add dry ingredients alternately with sour cream to butter mixture. Fold in chocolate chips and nuts.

Pour batter into greased 12-cup fluted tube pan. Bake in oven 50-55 minutes or until wooden toothpick inserted near center comes out clean. Cool in pan on wire rack 10 minutes. Remove from pan and cool completely on wire rack. Glaze with White Chocolate Glaze and sprinkle with additional cocoa, if desired. Serves 12.

White Chocolate Glaze: Melt white chocolate in top of double boiler. Stir in milk. Drizzle glaze over cake with spoon.

Approximate nutritional analysis per serving w/o glaze:
Calories 329, Protein 5 g, Carbohydrates 44 g, Fat 18 g, Cholesterol 71 mg, Sodium 464 mg

Approximate nutritional analysis per serving w/ glaze:
Calories 355, Protein 6 g, Carbohydrates 47 g, Fat 19 g, Cholesterol 73 mg, Sodium 468 mg

Courtesy of the National Honey Board.

ALMOND TORTE

¼ cup (60 ml) honey
    or ½ cup (120 ml) sugar
1 tsp (5 ml) lemon juice
⅓ cup (80 ml) EAST WIND
    Almond Butter
2 egg yolks
2 egg whites
¼ tsp (1 ml) salt

Preheat oven to 350°F (180°C).

Beat honey, lemon juice, almond butter and egg yolks together. In another bowl, beat egg whites and salt until stiff. Fold egg whites into almond butter mixture. Place in an 8x8-inch oiled pie pan and bake for 20 minutes. Serve warm. Serves 8.

Approximate nutritional analysis per serving:
Calories 116, Protein 3 g, Carbohydrates 11 g, Fat 7 g, Cholesterol 47 mg, Sodium 82 mg

DOUBLE-CHOCOLATE HONEY RING

WHOLE WHEAT CARROT CAKE

2 cups (480 ml) shredded carrots
1 cup (240 ml) coconut
1 cup (240 ml) chopped nuts
8¼-oz can (248 g) crushed
    pineapple, undrained
1 cup (240 ml) oil
½ cup (120 ml) raisins
3 eggs, beaten
2 cups (480 ml) sugar
2 tsp (10 ml) vanilla
2 cups (480 ml) AMBERWAVES
    BRAND Organic Whole Wheat
    Flour
2 tsp (10 ml) soda
1 tsp (5 ml) salt
2 tsp (10 ml) cinnamon

CREAM CHEESE FROSTING:
3 tbs (45 ml) skim milk
3-oz pkg (60 g) cream cheese,
    softened
¼ cup (60 ml) softened butter
4 cups (960 ml) powdered sugar
¼ cup (60 ml) finely chopped nuts

Preheat oven to 350°F (180°C).

Mix carrots, coconut, nuts, pineapple, oil and raisins. Mix together eggs, sugar and vanilla. Add to first mixture. In separate bowl, mix flour, soda, salt and cinnamon. Add to first mixture and beat well. Bake in greased and floured 9x13-inch pan for 1 hour. Frost with Cream Cheese Frosting or leave unfrosted. Serves 16.

Frosting: Cream together all ingredients except nuts. Spread on cooled cake. Sprinkle nuts on top.

Approximate nutritional analysis per serving w/o frosting:
Calories 392, Protein 6 g, Carbohydrates 46 g, Fat 22 g, Cholesterol 35 mg, Sodium 310 mg

Approximate nutritional analysis per serving w/ frosting:
Calories 566, Protein 7 g, Carbohydrates 77 g, Fat 28 g, Cholesterol 49 mg, Sodium 356 mg

MRS. PAVICH'S ORGANIC RAISIN CAKE

4 eggs
2 cups (480 ml) raw sugar
    (turbinado)
1½ cups (355 ml) canola oil
2 cups (480 ml) wheat flour
1 tsp (5 ml) baking soda
2 tsp (10 ml) salt
2 tsp (10 ml) cinnamon
1 cup (240 ml) PAVICH Organic
    Select Thompson Seedless
    Raisins
½ cup (120 ml) chopped pecans
    or walnut
powdered sugar, optional

Preheat oven to 350°F (180°C).

Beat eggs until fluffy. Add sugar and oil gradually. Sift flour, baking soda, salt and cinnamon together, and add raisins and chopped nuts. Combine thoroughly with eggs, sugar and oil. Oil and lightly flour a 9x13-inch cake pan. Pour in batter, and bake in oven for 30-35 minutes. Serve plain or dusted with powdered sugar. Serves 8.

Approximate nutritional analysis per serving:
Calories 797, Protein 8 g, Carbohydrates 90 g, Fat 48 g, Cholesterol 94 mg, Sodium 565 mg

MRS. PAVICH'S ORGANIC RAISIN CAKE

MAPLE-COFFEE CAKE

FILLING:
6 tbs (90 ml) canola oil
½ cup (120 ml) maple granules
2 tsp (10 ml) cinnamon
1 cup (240 ml) chopped nuts
½ cup (120 ml) diced apples,
   optional

BATTER:
1¾ cups (415 ml) VITA-SPELT Flour
¼ cup (60 ml) oat flour
1 tsp (5 ml) baking powder
1 tsp (5 ml) baking soda
½ cup (120 ml) canola oil
⅓ cup (80 ml) maple syrup
1 tsp (5 ml) vanilla
3 eggs
1 cup (240 ml) plain nonfat yogurt

Preheat oven to 350°F (180°C).
   Filling: Mix together filling ingredients, except apples, if using.
   Batter: Sift flours, baking powder and baking soda. Warm oil and maple syrup just until warm to touch. Add vanilla and 1 egg at a time, mixing after each egg. Add flour mixture and yogurt alternately to the maple syrup mixture and blend after each addition. Spread half of mixture into a greased and lined loaf pan. Add ½ of the Filling mixture. All diced apples should be added at this time, if using. Add remaining Batter and finally remaining Filling on top. Bake for approximately 50-60 minutes or until done. Serves 8.

Approximate nutritional analysis per serving:
Calories 450, Protein 9 g, Carbohydrates 30 g, Fat 35 g, Cholesterol 71 mg, Sodium 265 mg

APPLE-SPICE CAKE

½ cup (120 ml) margarine
1 cup (240 ml) brown sugar, packed
3 eggs
2 cups (480 ml) VITA-SPELT Flour
1½ tsp (8 ml) baking soda
½ tsp (3 ml) salt
3½ tsp (18 ml) baking powder
½ tsp (3 ml) allspice
1½ tsp (8 ml) cinnamon
½ tsp (3 ml) nutmeg
1½ cups (355 ml) applesauce
1 cup (240 ml) raisins
½ cup (120 ml) walnuts
whipped topping, optional

Preheat oven to 350°F (180°C).
   Cream margarine and brown sugar until smooth. Add eggs one at a time, creaming after each egg. Mix flour, soda, salt, baking powder and spices together. Add to creamed mixture alternating with applesauce. Stir in raisins and nuts. Pour into greased 9x13-inch pan. Bake approximately 40 minutes or until done. Cool in the pan placed on a rack. Serve plain or with a dab of whipped topping, if desired. Serves 8.

Approximate nutritional analysis per serving:
Calories 350, Protein 6 g, Carbohydrates 46 g, Fat 18 g, Cholesterol 70 mg, Sodium 748 mg

MAPLE-COFFEE CAKE

ROMAN MEAL CINNAMON STREUSEL CAKE

TOPPING:
½ cup (120 ml) flour
½ cup (120 ml) packed brown sugar
2 tsp (10 ml) cinnamon
2 tbs (30 ml) melted butter or
    margarine

1 cup (240 ml) all-purpose flour
2 tsp (10 ml) baking powder
½ tsp (3 ml) salt
1 cup (240 ml) ROMAN MEAL
    Cereal
¼ cup (60 ml) granulated sugar
¼ cup (60 ml) skim milk
1 cup (240 ml) plain nonfat yogurt
2 tbs (30 ml) molasses
2 egg whites
    or 1 whole egg

Preheat oven to 375°F (190°C).

Topping: Blend flour, brown sugar and cinnamon; stir in melted butter and set aside.

Grease and flour 9x9x2-inch baking pan. Set aside. In medium bowl, stir together flour, baking powder, salt, cereal and sugar. Beat milk, yogurt and molasses with egg whites; add all at once to dry ingredients. Stir until just blended. Spread half into prepared baking pan and sprinkle with half of Topping. Cover with remaining batter and sprinkle with rest of Topping. Bake for about 35 minutes or until toothpick inserted in center comes out clean. Serve warm. Serves 16.

Approximate nutritional analysis per serving:
Calories 122, Protein 4 g, Carbohydrates 24 g, Fat 2 g, Cholesterol 4 mg, Sodium 167 mg

NUT BUTTER COFFEE CAKE

TOPPING:
½ cup (120 ml) brown sugar, packed
½ cup (120 ml) whole wheat flour
¼ cup (60 ml) EAST WIND Almond,
    Cashew or Peanut Butter
3 tbs (45 ml) margarine or butter

CAKE:
2 cups (480 ml) whole wheat flour
1 cup (240 ml) brown sugar, packed
2 tsp (10 ml) baking powder
½ tsp (3 ml) baking soda
1 cup (240 ml) skim milk
½ cup (120 ml) EAST WIND
    Almond, Cashew or
    Peanut Butter
2 eggs
¼ cup (60 ml) margarine or butter

Preheat oven to 375°F (190°C).

Topping: Stir together the brown sugar and flour. Cut in the nut butter and margarine or butter until crumbly

Cake: In a mixing bowl, stir together flour, brown sugar, baking powder and baking soda. Add milk, nut butter, eggs and margarine or butter. Beat together thoroughly, by hand or with an electric mixer. Pour the batter into a greased 13x9x2-inch pan, spreading evenly. Sprinkle with Topping. Bake for about 30 minutes or until toothpick inserted in center comes out clean. Serve warm. Serves 12.

Approximate nutritional analysis per serving:
Calories 341, Protein 9 g, Carbohydrates 40 g, Fat 3 g, Cholesterol 32 mg, Sodium 240 mg

ROMAN MEAL CINNAMON STREUSEL CAKE

Overleaf: WHOLE WHEAT CARROT CAKE

amaranth: A broad leafed plant that produces seeds that can be consumed like grains, as flour, whole grain, or in dry cereal and crackers. Amaranth is higher than most grains in protein and rich in amino acids, lysine and methionine which are deficient in beans.

Anaheim chile pepper: A mild green or red chile named after the California city. Anaheim peppers are long and thin; they can be purchased fresh, canned or dried.

arame: A fibrous sea vegetable. Soak before using.

Arborio rice: A short, fat-grained Italian rice. Its high-starch kernels are perfect for risotto.

arrowroot: A highly digestible thickening agent for sauces and puddings made from the dried powdered root of the arrowroot tuber. It requires less cooking than cornstarch so it is an ideal thickener for sauces that use yogurt. Mix it with a small amount of cold liquid before adding it to sauces or stews.

bulgur: Wheat kernels that have been steamed, dried and crushed. Available in coarse, medium and fine grinds, it is commonly used in stuffing, for salads such as tabouli, and pilafs.

baba ganouj: A Middle Eastern puree of roasted eggplant, tahini, olive oil, lemon juice and garlic; served with pita bread.

basmati rice: A fragrant rice associated with Indian cuisine; both brown and white varieties cook more quickly than other rice.

broccoli rabe: A bitter green that is related to the cabbage and turnip families. It can be braised, sauteed, or steamed. Also known as rape (rayp), its seeds produce rapeseed oil, marketed under the name canola oil, a near equal to olive oil in its proportion of monounsaturated fat.

buckwheat: The triangular buckwheat seeds can be ground finely into a flour, as for blini, or eaten as whole hulled kernels, as in kasha. It is high in protein with well-balanced amino acid, rich in calcium and riboflavin.

bulgur: Wheat grains that have been steamed, dried and crushed. In the Middle East it is the basis for tabouli, a salad of tomato, olive oil, lemon juice, parsley and mint.

carob: Also known as St. John's bread and locust bean, the carob pod contains a sweet pulp that is dried and roasted, then ground into a powder. It is often used as a chocolate substitute.

chipotle chile: smoked jalapenos

cilantro: Also known as Chinese parsley, cilantro is distinctively flavored herb characteristic of Mexican and some Asian cuisines. The seeds of the plant, coriander, are ground and used in curries.

couscous: Couscous refers both to the finely cracked wheat or semolina that, steamed, is the basis of the North African dish often containing lamb or chicken with vegetables, chick peas and raisins.

Enoki: Cultivated mushrooms that grow in clumps of long thin stems with tiny white caps. They are very delicately flavored and crunchy, best served raw or added at the last minute to cooked dishes.

falafel: Middle Eastern deep-fried patties or balls made from ground chick peas. They are often served with tahini sauce.

garam masala: A northern Indian spice mixture consisting of roasted then ground cinnamon, cardamom, cloves, cumin seeds, coriander, black peppercorns, nutmeg and mace.

galanga : Also known as galangal, galanga is a ginger-like underground stem, which flavors Indonesian and Thai cuisine. With its orange or whitish pulp and reddish skin, galanga is slightly reminiscent, in color and flavor, of saffron.

jackfruit: Grown in parts of Africa, Brazil and Southeast Asia, the jackfruit is an oversized relative of the fig. Used in curries when green and in desserts when sweet and ripe.

Japanese eggplant: Looking a bit like a purple zucchini, the Japanese eggplant is a tender, sweet-fleshed version of its large relative. Also known as oriental eggplant/

Jerusalem artichoke: A native American tuber that is a member of the sunflower genus, the Jerusalem artichoke is now marketed in the U.S. as a sunchoke. They can be eaten raw as a sweet and nutty additions to salads or cooked. A source of calcium, magnesium, and iron, Jerusalem artichokes are dried and ground into a flour which can be added as a supplement to breads or cakes and cookies.

jicima: The jicima is an underground tuber. It can be used raw as a sweet crunchy addition to salads. Cooked it will remain crunchy, much like a water chestnut. Low in sodium and calories, jicima is a fair source of potassium and vitamin C.

kabocha: A winter squash with a lovely green skin and a pale orange flesh. Typically, about 2 to 3 pounds, they must be halved and seeded before cooking, then they can be baked or steamed.

kalamata olive: A soft textured purple-black olive, the kalamata is soaked in a wine-vinegar marinade to give it its distinctive wine-like taste.

kamut: Kamut is a variety of high-protein wheat grown in Montana from a mere thirty-six kernels brought to that state during the 1940s. The name comes from the ancient Egyptian word for wheat, and the grain is thought to be an ancestor of grains. Kamut flour ground from the grain can be used to bake bread, although its gluten content is lower than conventional wheat.

kanten: A setting agent that is stronger properties than gelatin, kanten is derived from dried seaweed. Also known as agar or agar-agar, it is tasteless, thickens at room temperature, and comes in flakes, granules or bars. It is almost calorie free.
kombu - A member of the kelp family, kombu is a greyish-black algae. It is sold sundried and folded in sheets. It is an especially valuable addition to soup stock.

kasha: see buckwheat

kudzu - Made from the root of the kuzu vine, (and sometimes called kuzo), kudzo powder is used to thicken sauces and glaze fruits. Like arrowroot or cornstarch dilute in cold water before adding to a recipe.

lemon grass: One of the characteristic seasonings of Thai cooking, lemon grass grows in stalks which are often sold dried. Its sour lemon flavor comes from an essential oil, citral, which is also found in lemon peel.

lumpia: The Philippine version of the egg roll is made with a lumpia wrapper or lettuce leaves enclosing a filling of raw or cooked vegetables or meat in various combinations. The wrapper is made from flour or cornstarch eggs and water.

millet: Millet's popularity among Western Europeans peaked during the Middle Ages but it remains a staple in India, and is still grown in China, Egypt, tropical Africa and South America and the Soviet Union. It has more protein than rice, corn or oats. It can be ground into a flour for puddings or added to wheat flour for breads and cakes. You know it as birdseed.

mirin: A sweet wine made from glutinous rice used as a sweetener in Japanese cooking.

miso: Miso is a fermented soybean paste made, like yogurt, when a cultured mold is injected into a soybean base. It can be brown, golden or reddish, depending on the other grains added, as well as the amount of salt or culture added. Aging also influences color, flavor and texture.

plantain: These are referred to as cooking bananas; they are cooked at different stages of ripening as the skin goes from green to black. They are treated like a starch and have a squash-like flavor.

quinoa: A rediscovered ancient grain, quinoa was a staple of the ancient Incas. It contains more protein than any other grain and an excellent balance of essential amino acids. To top it off its higher in unsaturated fats and lower in carbohydrates than most other grains. It can be cooked like rice but only takes 15 minutes.

shiitake: On the average a 3- to 6-inch mushroom with a brown cap; shiitakes were originally grown exclusively in Japan but are now grown in the United States. Most plentiful in spring and autumn.

shoyu: A naturally-fermented soy sauce made from soybeans, wheat and salt.

soy flour: Made from defatted ground soybeans, soy flour is an excellent protein supplement when substituted in small amounts for wheat flour in recipes for breads, cakes or other baked goods. It contains from 40 to 60 percent protein. The proteins in soy and wheat complement each other to form a complete vegetable protein.

tabouli: see bulgur

tahini: A thick paste made of ground sesame seeds commonly used in Middle Eastern dishes like hummus and baba ganouj.

tamari: Originally a by product of miso production, this soy-based sauce is more commonly a commercial variation on soy sauce.

tempeh: Made from cultured soybeans, tempeh is a low fat, low sodium source of protein originally developed in Indonesia.

tofu: Soy milk is curdled and when the curds are separated from the whey, and pressed, the result is tofu. Depending upon how much water remains, the tofu will be firm or soft. Firmer tofu has a higher proportion of protein, but all tofu is an excellent source of low fat, low sodium protein.

tomatillo: Also known as the Mexican green tomato, tomatillos resemble small tomatoes with a thin papery covering over their shiny green skin. As the basis for salsa they can be used raw or cooked; cooking sweetens their flavor which can be quite acidic.

wasabi: A Japanese horseradish that can be quite fiery. Ground into a paste it is served with sushi and sashimi. It can be purchase dry and mixed into a paste much like dry mustard.

CHESHIRE GARDEN
(603) 239-4173
Products available: Organic specialty foods; fruit and herbal vinegars, preserves, dessert sauces and berry hot sauces.

COMMUNITY MILL & BEAN
(800) 755-0554
Products available: Certified organic flours and baking mixes under OLD SAVANNAH brand name, such as Buckwheat Pancake Mix, Buttermilk Biscuit Mix, Whole Cornmeal, Whole Wheat Pastry Flour, Brown Rice Flour; organic grains including hulled millet, quinoa; organic seeds and heirloom beans, such as purple appaloosa beans, French (DuPuy) lentils and mung beans. Also offers a variety of cookbooks.

DELFTREE FARM
(800) 243-3742
Products available: Fresh Shiitake Mushrooms, Exotic Dried Mushrooms (mixed wild mushrooms, oyster mushrooms, boletes, shiitake, morels, chanterelles, matsutake), gourmet Wild Mushroom Soup, Gourmet Hunter Sauce and Shiitake and Sesame Vinaigrette.

FISH BROTHERS
(800) 244-0583
Products available: All Natural Smoked Salmon (original pepper and garlic) and Smoked Albacore Tuna.

FRIEDA'S
(800) 241-1771
Products available: Unusual exotic fruits and vegetables, including a full assortment of lettuces, legumes, squashes, potatoes, herbs and mushrooms; *Foods of the Orient,* such as Chinese long beans, water chestnuts, kumquats; *Lost Crops,* such as quinoa, Jackson wonderbeans. Also available, dried fruits, mushrooms and tomatoes.

INTERNATIONAL RESOURCES
(800) 669-7742
Products available: Curry Mix, Salt-Free Curry Mix, Tandoori Chicken Marinade Mix, Vegetable Spice, Salt-Free Vegetable Spice, Garam Masala Indian Spice, Cumin-Coriander Powder, Turmeric Powder, Cumin Seeds, Stainless Steel Spice Box with or without Spices, Stainless Steel Mini Wok Set with or without Spices, Decorated Wooden Platform and Roller and Imported Cheesecloth.

MAPLE ACRES
(616) 264-9265
Products available: Pure Northern Michigan Maple Syrup.

MONTANA FLOUR & GRAINS
(406) 622-5436
Products available: AMBERWAVES BRAND Organic Whole Wheat Flour and KAMUT BRAND Flour and Grain.

PAVICH FAMILY FARMS
Organically Grown
(209) 782-8700
Products available: Flame Seedless Raisins and New Thompson Seedless Raisins.

POMONA'S
Workstead Industries
(413) 772-6816
Products available: Universal Pectin.

ROMAN MEAL
(206) 474-3277
Products available: Original Wheat, Rye, Bran, Flax Cereal, Oats, Wheat, Rye, Bran, Flax Cereal, Apple Cinnamon Multi-Bran Cereal, Oats, Wheat, Dates, Raisins, Almonds Cereal, Oats, Wheat, Honey, Coconut, Almonds Cereal and Cream of Rye Organic Cereal.

SPECTRUM NATURALS
(800) 995-2705
Products available: Super Canola Oil, Organic Brown Rice Vinegar, Organic All-Purpose White Vinegar, Organic Apple Cider Vinegar and Organic Wine Vinegars (red, white, garlic, Italian herb, raspberry).

UNCLE DAVE'S
(800) 327-7537 or (802) 244-8771 (Mail Order available through Cold Hollow Cider Mill Catalog)
Products available: Excellent Marinara, Excellent Marinara with Mushrooms, Original Ketchup, Kickin' Ketchup, Kickin' Mustard, Tex-Mex with Pine Nuts, Spicy Peanut Sauce, Sun Dried Tomato Basil Sauce, ABSOLUT Best Bloody Mary Fixin's, Kickin' Grill Sauce and Kickin' Carrot Horseradish.

WALNUT ACRES
(800) 433-3998
Products available: More than 300 certified organic and natural foods including vegetables, fruits, grains, juices, hot and cold cereals, soups, nut butters and all-natural personal care and household products.

INDEX